The International Relations of Northeast Asia

Asia in World Politics
Series Editor: Samuel S. Kim

Cooperation or Conflict in the Taiwan Strait?
by Ralph N. Clough

Pacific Asia? Prospects for Security and Cooperation in East Asia
by Mel Gurtov

East Asia and Globalization
edited by Samuel S. Kim

The International Relations of Northeast Asia
edited by Samuel S. Kim

In the Eyes of the Dragon: China Views the World
edited by Yong Deng and Fei-Ling Wang

North Korea and Northeast Asia
edited by Samuel S. Kim and Tai Hwan Lee

The International Relations of Northeast Asia

Edited by Samuel S. Kim

ROWMAN & LITTLEFIELD PUBLISHERS, INC.
Lanham • Boulder • New York • Toronto • Oxford

ROWMAN & LITTLEFIELD PUBLISHERS, INC.

Published in the United States of America
by Rowman & Littlefield Publishers, Inc.
A wholly owned subsidiary of The Rowman & Littlefield Publishing Group, Inc.
4501 Forbes Boulevard, Suite 200, Lanham, Maryland 20706
www.rowmanlittlefield.com

P.O. Box 317, Oxford OX2 9RU, United Kingdom

British Library Cataloguing in Publication Information Available

Library of Congress Cataloging-in-Publication Data

The international relations of northeast asia / edited by Samuel S. Kim.
p. cm. — (Asia in world politics)
Includes bibliographical references and index.
ISBN 0-7425-1694-6 (Cloth : alk. paper) — ISBN 0-7425-1695-4 (Paper: alk. paper)
1. East Asia—Relations—Foreign countries. I. Title. II. Series
DS518.1 .K49 2004
327'.095—dc21 2003008106

Printed in the United States of America

∞ ™ The paper used in this publication meets the minimum requirements of American National Standard for Information Sciences—Permanence of Paper for Printed Library Materials, ANSI/NISO Z39.48-1992.

Contents

List of Tables vii

List of Figures ix

List of Acronyms and Abbreviations xi

Preface xiii

Part I: Theory and Practice

1 Northeast Asia in the Local–Regional–Global Nexus: Multiple Challenges and Contending Explanations 3
Samuel S. Kim

Part II: Major Power Interaction

2 China's International Relations: The Political and Security Dimensions 65
Alastair Iain Johnston

3 China's International Relations: The Economic Dimension 101
Thomas G. Moore

4 Japan's International Relations: The Political and Security Dimensions 135
Thomas Berger

5 Japan's International Relations: The Economic Dimension 171
William W. Grimes

6 Russian Foreign Policy in Northeast Asia 201
Gilbert Rozman

7 U.S. Foreign Policy in Northeast Asia 225
Kent E. Calder

Part III: Flashpoints in the Divided Nations

8 South Korea's International Relations: Challenges to Developmental Realism? 251
Chung-in Moon and Taehwan Kim

9 North Korea's International Relations: The Successful Failure? 281
C. S. Eliot Kang

10 Taiwan's External Relations: Identity versus Security 301
Lynn T. White III

Part IV: Region Building

11 The Emerging Northeast Asian Regional Order 331
Lowell Dittmer

Index 363

About the Contributors 367

Tables

1.1.	Northeast Asia in Regional "Minilateral" Institutions, 2002	14
1.2.	NEA's Participation in International Organizations, 1960–2002	16
1.3.	Changing Major-Power Shares of Global GNP and Industrial Production, 1980–1997	20
1.4.	Amounts, Ranks, and Shares of Material Power Resources, 2001	21
1.5.	Military Expenditures of Northeast Asian Countries, 2001	22
1.6.	NEA Countries' Voting Coincidence with the United States in the UN General Assembly in Comparative Perspective, 1991–2001	25
1.7.	NEA in "Democratic/Freedom Ranking"	31
1.8.	NEA's GDP Growth Rate in Comparative Perspective, 1990–2001	32
1.9.	Changing Distribution of NEA-5's Intraregional and Interregional Trade with the United States, 1985–2000	34
1.10.	NEA and Foreign Direct Investment, 2000	35
1.11.	The Tumen River Area Development Programme (TRADP) Characteristics and Indicators, 2000	37
1.12.	Multinational Citizens' Perceptions of Other Northeast Asian Countries, Late 2000	46

1.13. Multinational Citizens' Perceptions of Threat in Northeast Asia, Late 2000 47
1.14. Multinational Citizens' Perceptions of the Most Influential Power in Asia, Late 2000 48
1.15. NEA-5 in the Pew Global Attitudes Surveys, Late 2002 49
8.1. Balance Sheet for FTAs involving Korea, Japan, and China: GDP Growth and Economic Gains 269

Figures

2.1. Mean Similarity Index with Select Countries per Foreign Policy Period 73

2.2. Similarity Index with Northeast Asian States, 1991–1996 73

2.3. Annual Frequency of the Terms "Multipolarity" *(duojihua)* and "Globalization" *(quanqiuhua)* in the *People's Daily*, 1990–2000 78

5.1. Japan's Trade, 1976–1999 173

Acronyms and Abbreviations

ADB	Asian Development Bank
AFC	Asian financial crisis
AMF	Asian Monetary Fund
AMS	Academy of Military Science
APEC	Asia Pacific Economic Cooperation
APT	ASEAN Plus Three
ARATS	Association for Relations across the Taiwan Strait
ARF	ASEAN Regional Forum
ASEAN	Association of Southeast Asian Nations
ASEM	Asia–Europe Meeting
BIT	bilateral investment treaty
BSA	bilateral swap agreements
CASS	Chinese Academy of Social Sciences
CCP	Chinese Communist Party
CICIR	Chinese Institute of Contemporary International Affairs
CMI	Chiang Mai Initiative
CNP	comprehensive national power
CSCA	Conference on Security and Cooperation in Asia
CSCAP	Council for Security Cooperation in the Asia Pacific
CTBT	Comprehensive Test Ban Treaty
DMZ	demilitarized zone
DPP	Democratic Progressive Party (Taiwan)
DPRK	Democratic People's Republic of Korea
EAEG	East Asian Economic Group
EU	European Union
FDI	foreign direct investment

FIE	foreign-invested enterprises
FTA	free-trade agreement, free-trade area
GATT	General Agreement on Tariffs and Trade
GDP	gross domestic product
G-7	Group of Seven
IAEA	International Atomic Energy Agency
IMF	International Monetary Fund
IR	international relations
JASA	Japanese–American Security Alliance
JDA	Japan Defense Agency
JFDI	Japanese outward FDI
KEDO	Korean Peninsula Energy Development Organization
KMT	Kuomintang (Taiwan)
LDP	Liberal Democratic Party
MNC	multinational corporations
MOFAT	(South Korean) Ministry of Foreign Affairs and Trade
NAFTA	North American Free Trade Agreement
NEA	Northeast Asia
NEASED	North-East Asian Security Dialogue
NGO	nongovernment organizations
NIC	newly industrializing country
NMD	National Missile Defense
NPT	Non-Proliferation Treaty
ODA	Official Development Assistance
OECD	Organization for Economic Cooperation and Development
OEM	original equipment manufacturing
PLA	People's Liberation Army
PPP	purchasing power parity
PRC	People's Republic of China
QDR	Quadrennial Defense Review
ROC	Republic of China (Taiwan)
SARS	severe acute respiratory syndrome
SCO	Shanghai Cooperation Organization
SDF	Self Defense Force (Japan)
SEF	Straits Exchange Foundation
TCOG	Trilateral Coordination and Oversight Group
TMD	Theater Missile Defense
TRADP	Tumen River Area Development Programme
UNCLOS	United Nations Convention on the Law of the Sea
UNCTAD	United Nations Conference on Trade and Development
WMD	weapons of mass destruction
WTO	World Trade Organization

Preface

Despite or perhaps because of Northeast Asia's unparalleled geopolitical and geoeconomic significance and the omnipresence of the United States as the de facto superpower, the literature on the international relations of Northeast Asia is relatively underdeveloped and undertheorized, in contrast with studies on country-specific foreign policy. This volume seeks to fill this lacuna by offering a multidimensional and multidisciplinary analysis of the international relations of Northeast Asia. Combining a variety of theoretical perspectives with interaction-specific and issue-specific studies, the contributors explore the local, regional, and global pressures that influence the choice of options and strategies of the Northeast Asian states, as well as the complex and evolving interplay of national, regional, and global forces shaping the region's security, economy, and identity. Historically and culturally informed narratives along with contending theoretical perspectives are employed to track and explain the changes and continuities of relations among the Northeast Asian states bilaterally, regionally, and globally.

In pursuit of these lines of inquiry, the book is organized in four parts. Part I sets forth some of the key puzzles and questions for the study of Northeast Asia's international relations, discusses the so-called new regionalism as a way of defining and depicting *sui generis* regional characteristics of Northeast Asia as an international region and as a way of highlighting the possibilities and limitations of creating Northeast Asia's regional multilateralism, and evaluates contending theoretical perspectives and explanations for a contextual analysis of the region's international relations in the post–Cold War era. Part II focuses on the place of Northeast Asia in the international relations of the Big Four—China, Russia, Japan, and the United States—and the impact of major power interaction bilaterally, regionally, and globally. Part III deals with the regional flashpoints in the divided nations of South and North Korea and of Taiwan and China. Part IV explores in retrospect and in terms of prospects the emerging regional order in Northeast Asia.

This undertaking has involved the work and love of many. There was no huge grant to dole out, nor was this a product of a funded research conference. This book would not have seen the light of day without the intellectual and entrepreneurial initiative and sustained support and prodding of Susan McEachern, social science editor at Rowman & Littlefield Publishers. From the inception of our collegial effort, it was the intention, in keeping with Susan's own serious engagement, to produce a primer for undergraduate- and graduate-level courses in East Asia or Asia–Pacific international relations. I want to thank the chapter authors for their acuity, hard work, and patience, often beyond the call of duty, in meeting our many demands for revisions and updates as we raced against the rapidly changing headlines. I also want to thank the Weatherhead East Asian Institute of Columbia University for continuing encouragement and support, and especially my graduate research assistants, Emma Avery-Chanlett and Ji In Lee, for their characteristically skillful, efficient, and multitasking work in library and online research and for stage managing the preparation of the book manuscript.

Finally, it was my pleasure to work with Rowman & Littlefield Publishers in the production of this book. I am particularly grateful to Susan McEachern for her unflagging support and encouragement and for her role as an invisible collaborator and invaluable navigator. Special thanks are also due to April Leo and Dave Compton for their efficient steering of the manuscript through the various stages of production. The usual disclaimer still applies: the editor and chapter authors alone are responsible for any remaining errors in fact or interpretation.

Samuel Kim
New York City
May 2003

I

THEORY AND PRACTICE

1

Northeast Asia in the Local–Regional–Global Nexus: Multiple Challenges and Contending Explanations

Samuel S. Kim

This volume offers a multidimensional and multidisciplinary analysis of international relations in Northeast Asia (hereafter NEA). The primary focus is on the complex and evolving interplay of national, regional, and global forces shaping the region's security, economy, and identity. Historically and culturally informed narratives along with contending theoretical perspectives are employed to track and explain the changes and continuities in relations among the NEA states bilaterally, regionally, and globally. The accelerating and intensifying interactions between regional and global politics amid turbulent domestic politics raise many empirical, theoretical, and policy-relevant questions that are pertinent to scholars and policy makers alike who are concerned about the shape of the emerging Northeast Asian order. Combining a broad analytical framework with interaction-specific and issue-specific studies, the contributors explore the following related questions:

- What are the key determinants of the regional patterns of interaction? How are they affected by historical legacies, changes in balances of power (global and local), and changes in patterns of economic, social, and cultural relations? Which theoretical model best explains NEA's international relations?

- How are the forces of regionalization and globalization conceived of and addressed by the key decision makers in the NEA countries? What are the similarities and differences in the regionalization/globalization promises (policy pronouncements) and actual performance in each of these countries? What are the implications of the Asian financial crisis of 1997–1998 for the future of Northeast Asian regional and global orders?
- How well do the NEA countries cope with wrenching national identity difficulties in the post–Cold War world? Does the nation–state remain a pivotal pillar of global as well as territorial constructions of collective identity? Has the amount of force used by states in the pursuit of their policy objectives increased or decreased? Is there such thing as a set of "Asian values" at work in NEA? What role, if any, do such values play in coping with the twin challenges of globalization and localization?
- What are the trends in levels of conflict and cooperation in the region? How is security conceived and practiced in Northeast Asian countries? What are the similarities and differences in their security policies? What are the possibilities and limitations of establishing a regional multilateral security regime? To what extent and in what specific ways can the Big Four—China, Japan, Russia, and the United States—meet the post–Cold War challenge of preventing, controlling, restraining, or encapsulating regional conflicts?

In pursuit of these lines of inquiry, this introductory chapter is organized into four main sections. The first section focuses on the regional environment at a high level of generalization, as a background for more interaction-specific and issue-specific analyses. The second section explores the second wave of regionalism—and the so-called new regionalism—in order to define and depict in broad strokes *sui generis* regional characteristics of Northeast Asia as an international region and to highlight the possibilities and limitations of creating NEA's regional multilateralism. The third section deals with contending theoretical perspectives for a contextual analysis of NEA's international relations in the post–Cold War era by examining how the local, regional, and global forces have influenced the changing patterns of interaction in NEA's response to geopolitical, geoeconomic, and national-identity challenges. The fourth section assesses future prospects of establishing a more peaceful and prosperous regional order in the uncertain years ahead.

THE OLD/NEW NORTHEAST ASIAN ENVIRONMENT

To examine NEA's international relations in the post–Cold War era is to be confronted with multiple and contradictory forces. There is something very old and very new (and very uncertain and unsettling) in the Northeast Asian environment. At one level of generalization, *plus ça change, plus c'est la même chose*—the more things change, the more they stay the same." A glance at the map and the geopolitical implications of the latest U.S.–North Korea nuclear standoff suggests why NEA is among the world's most important yet volatile and sensitive regions. With the Korean peninsula as its strategic pivot, it is the one and only international region or subregion where the world's four major powers—China, Japan, Russia, and the United States—uneasily meet and interact and where their respective interests coalesce, compete, or clash in a situation-specific way.

What remains unchanged and unchangeable is the geographical location of the Korean peninsula, tightly enveloped by the three big neighboring powers. Geography matters in the shaping of any state's foreign policy, to be sure, but this is especially true for the foreign policies of the two Koreas and the three neighboring powers. The Korean peninsula, divided or united, shares land and maritime borders with China, Russia, and Japan, uniquely situating it within the geopolitics of NEA. The Korean peninsula has long been a highly contested strategic crossroads, the site of great power rivalry and sanguinary wars that have involved, to varying degrees, czarist Russia, the Soviet Union, Qing China, the Republic of China, the People's Republic of China, imperial Japan, and the United States.

Nonetheless, Northeast Asia is more than a geographical referent. As a region, it encompasses China, the two Koreas, and Japan as the core states and the Russian Far East, while it also involves the United States as the extraterritorial, lone superpower. The region claims vital importance in America's security and economic interests, and the U.S. role remains a crucial component (perhaps the most crucial) of the regional geostrategic and geoeconomic equation. The United States, by dint of its deep interest and involvement in Northeast Asian geopolitics and geoeconomics, provides more than 80 percent of the 100,000 troops, concentrated mostly in Japan and South Korea, deployed in the Asia–Pacific region.[1] Accordingly, the world's heaviest concentration of military and economic capabilities is in this region: the world's three largest nuclear weapons states (the United States, Russia, and China), one seminuclear state (North Korea), three threshold nuclear weapons states (Japan, South Korea, and Taiwan), the world's three largest economies on a purchasing power parity basis (the United States, China, and Japan),[2] three of the world's five largest trading countries (the United States, Germany, Japan, France, and China), and Asia's three largest economies (Japan, China, and South Korea). Japan's projected launching of a spy satellite in early 2003 buttresses Kent Calder's argument in chapter 7 that with every country in the region becoming both a consumer and a producer of missiles, the dangerous and unsettling reality is missile proliferation.

It was in NEA where the Cold War turned into a hot war. Indeed, the restructuring impact of the Korean War (1950–1953) upon the national, regional, and global systemic levels cannot be overemphasized. More than any other postwar international event, the Korean War had great catalytic effect in enacting the rules of the Cold War game, deeply congealing patterns of East–West conflict across Northeast Asia and beyond.[3] The region was more involved in Cold War politics than any other region or subregion without nonaligned states. Even with the end of the Cold War and superpower rivalry, the region is still distinguished by continuing, if somewhat anachronistic, Cold War alliance systems linking the two Koreas, Japan, China, and the United States in a bilateralized regional security complex.

Following the reunification of both Vietnam and Germany, NEA now contains the world's largest concentration of divided polities: divided China and divided Korea, the two most prominent potential flashpoints. And yet, whereas the ninety-mile-wide Taiwan Strait provides a significant geostrategic barrier—the cooling power of water, so to speak—the same cannot be said for the so-called demilitarized zone (DMZ) of the divided Korean peninsula. Even today, almost half a century after the Korean War "ended" with an armistice accord, the DMZ remains the most heavily fortified and sensitive conflict zone in the post–Cold War world, where more than 1.8 million military personnel, including thirty-seven thousand U.S. military personnel, confront each other, armed to the teeth with the latest weapons systems. Furthermore, in the latter half of the 1990s the volcano of potential implosion or explosion in the North seemed to have become more active than ever before. An unstable or collapsing North Korea with proximity to Seoul (in rocket sights within three minutes), inordinate asymmetrical military capabilities, and the highest possible resolve for survival have extraordinary refractory ramifications for great power politics in Northeast Asia and beyond. Coping with North Korean security or insecurity behavior in multiple and mutating forms, aided and abetted by America's rogue-state demonization strategy, has become an integral part of both the NEA security problem and the NEA security solution.

Northeast Asia is not without its share of territorial and maritime disputes in varying degrees of intensity: the China–Russia border (low), the China–North Korea border (low), the China–Tajikistan border (low), the China–Japan maritime (the Diaoyu/Senkaku Islands; moderate), the Japan–Russia maritime (the Northern Territories; moderate), the Japan–South Korea maritime (Tokdo/Takeshima Islands; moderate), the North Korea/South Korea maritime (the Northern Limit Line on the Yellow/West Sea; low), and the Spratley Islands, involving China versus six other East Asian states (low).[4] With the entry into force of the United Nations Convention on the Law of the Sea (UNCLOS) in 1994, the enlarged exclusive economic zones pose a clear and present danger of a new pattern of maritime conflict in the region. Stripped of the overlay imposed by superpower rivalry, the region's old geopolitical and national-identity fault lines seem to have become more exposed and sensitive. In addition, despite some cultural similarities derived from ancient times, NEA is burdened if not paralyzed by vast disparities in levels of economic and political development and by divergent preferences on the formation of a regional security regime.

For several reasons, the divide in Northeast Asia between regional and global politics is substantially overlapping, if not completely erased. First, the region is "strategic home" to three of the five permanent members of the UN Security Council and also three of the five "original" nuclear-weapons states that are shielded by the two-tiered discriminatory Non-Proliferation Treaty (NPT) regime. Second, Japan remains the world's second-largest financial contributor to the United Nations and its associated specialized agencies. Finally, a rising China with the world's fastest economic growth in the post–Cold War era and the world's fifth largest trading country has sired many debates in the West in general and the United States in particular.

At another level of generalization, the Northeast Asian environment looks far more peaceful now than it has at any time in the past. Despite periodic escalations of tension on the Korean peninsula, there has not been a single intrastate or interstate war during the post–Cold War era. Although the region faces some serious security challenges, it has somehow managed to enjoy relative peace and prosperity. Particularly notable has been the bi-multilateral processes leading to the resolution of disputes along China's border of some seven thousand kilometers with Russia and the members of the Commonwealth of Independent States, including several places where sharp border clashes erupted in the spring of 1969. These clashes resulted in heavy mutual fortifications, making this longest land border in the world also the most explosive one. As Lowell Dittmer argues in chapter 11, the Sino–Russian post–Cold War "partnership," as sealed in a new Friendship Treaty signed by Jiang Zemin and Vladimir Putin in the Kremlin in July 2001, represents, to all appearances, the best relationship between these two territorially imposing neighbors in nearly fifty years.

Geoeconomically, three core NEA countries (Japan, China, and Korea) accounted for only 4 percent of world GNP in 1960 (compared to 37% for North America). By 1992, however, the combined economies of Japan, China, the four East Asian tigers (South Korea, Taiwan, Hong Kong, and Singapore), and the Association of Southeast Asian Nations (ASEAN) states nearly matched that of either North America or Western Europe, each of which accounted for about 30 percent of world GDP.[5] By 2000, Japan,

Greater China (China, Hong Kong, and Taiwan), and South Korea together accounted for about 25 percent of world GDP.[6] As of September 2002, NEA was home to the world's five largest holders of foreign-exchange reserves: Japan ($443.09 billion, or 19.3% of the global total), China ($259.43 billion, or 11.3% of the global total), Taiwan ($156.12 billion, or 6.8% of the global total), South Korea ($117.09 billion, or 5.1% of the global total), and Hong Kong ($108.20 billion, or 4.8% of the global total).[7]

The underpublicized peace in NEA defies not only the region's own bloody Cold War history but also the growing salience of intrastate armed conflicts in the post–Cold War world. East Asia, especially Northeast Asia, stood out as the world's most prominent regional killing field during the post–World War II period, with greater numbers of fatalities occurring here than in any other international region—3 million in the Korean War, 2 million in the Vietnam War, 1 million in the Chinese civil war, and 1.2 million in the Pol Pot genocide.[8]

Part of the answer to the question of recent, relative peace in NEA lies in the rise of China as a responsible regional power that has transformed not only its foreign policy but also in the process the geopolitical and geoeconomic landscape of Asia, including Northeast Asia. Within the wheel of emerging Asian regionalism, China serves as the hub power and has managed to radiate a series of cooperative bilateral and bi-minilateral (mini-multilateral) spokes. Viewed in this light, geopolitics is no longer the only game in town in post–Cold War NEA international relations; it coexists and even competes with geoeconomics and geogovernance.

At still another level of generalization, as a result of the uneasy juxtaposition of continuity and discontinuity, there is emerging in place of the clarity, simplicity, and apparent discipline of bipolarity a new Northeast Asian regional order with multiple complexities and uncertainties that is of indeterminate shape and content. The structural impact of power transition and globalization seems to have accentuated the uncertainties and complexities of great power politics in the region. With a rising China, a declining post–Soviet Russia, a rising South Korea, and a declining North Korea, the world's greatest shifts in power in the past two decades—defined and measured in economic terms—have taken place in this region (see below).[9] All the same, the forces of globalization of the 1990s transformed both the context and the conditions under which Northeast Asian regional geopolitics and geoeconomics can be played out. Contrary to the claims of Thomas Friedman, globalization has not yet become the new international system to replace the Cold War system, at least not in Northeast Asia.[10] Instead, globalization as a worldwide, multidimensional revolutionary process has greatly accelerated interconnectedness in all aspects of human relations and transactions, while simultaneously entailing a reduction in control at the national level. As a consequence, Northeast Asian states must now worry not only about their military power but also, more importantly, about the economic power, cultural power, and knowledge power needed to survive and prosper in a world that is becoming increasingly globalized and competitive.[11]

It is a unique, combustible cocktail of *sui generis* regional characteristics—high capability, abiding animus, deep albeit differentiated entanglement of the Big Four in Korean affairs, North Korea's recent emergence as a loose nuclear cannon, the absence of multilateral security institutions, and the resulting uncertainties and unpredictability in the international politics of Northeast Asia—that challenges scholars and policy makers alike to divine the shape of things to come in the emerging regional order. In short, the parameters of post–Cold War NEA international relations are still in a state of flux. Northeast Asia conflates in one place all the challenges of the new world order that pivot around two central concerns: the source of possible threats to the region's stability and the feasible and desirable conflict-management models needed to establish peace and prosperity in the region.

IN SEARCH OF A REGIONAL IDENTITY

Despite or perhaps because of Northeast Asia's unparalleled geopolitical and geoeconomic significance and the omnipresence of the United States as the de facto superpower, NEA has had enormous difficulty finding a comfortable regional identity in the global community. In the burgeoning literature on regionalism, the absence of any reference to NEA as a distinct region is striking, and in Asia "only Southeast Asia receives recognition as a 'region'—courtesy of the establishment of ASEAN in 1967."[12] Lacking cooperative oxygen or breathing space in this tough neighborhood, the three core states of the region—Japan, China, and South Korea (hereafter NEA-3)—often think and act out of the box in their attempts to capitalize on Southeast Asian or Asia–Pacific "open regionalism." Canadians (not surprisingly) and others have suggested that NEA's regional cooperation can move forward only if the region is reconfigured as the North Pacific.

The first wave of regionalism (and regional studies) began in Western Europe in the 1950s and gradually fizzled out in the 1960s and early 1970s, especially in the wake of the 1965 European Community crisis and the challenge to supranationalism posed by de Gaulle's high politics. Many grandiose projects for European regional integration had limited impact.[13] In 1975, Ernst Haas, a pioneer of regional integration studies, pronounced that the neofunctional theory of regional integration had become obsolete because its core assumptions had become less and less relevant to the key state actors in regional organizations.[14] In sync with this pronouncement, international organization research has shifted from regional multilateralism to global multilateralism, from regional integration to the issues of "complex global interdependence" and their management via "international regimes," defined as a set of norms, rules, and governing procedures around which actors' expectations converge in a given issue area.[15]

The second wave of regionalism came about as a result of a series of momentous developments in the late 1980s and early 1990s, all of which are said to have greatly increased the significance of the intrinsic dynamics of regional and subregional forces at the expense of global factors. Once again the rejuvenation of European integration, as epitomized by the Single European Act of 1986, served as the initial catalyst, accompanied by a number of other factors: removal of the superpower overlay, recurring fears over the stability of the GATT-based global trade regime associated with the Uruguay Round, the formation of the Asia Pacific Economic Cooperation (APEC) in 1989, the successful negotiation of the North American Free Trade Agreement in 1994, and increased cooperation within ASEAN over its expansion in the form of the ASEAN Regional Forum (ARF) in 1994.[16] The second wave gave rise to the so-called new regionalism that is associated with or caused by a multitude of recent developments, such as the Asian financial crisis of 1997–1998; the stagnation of global trade liberalization, epitomized by the collapse of the 1999 World Trade Organization (WTO) talks in Seattle; and the launching of a common currency by eleven European Union (EU) member states in 1999. Despite its seemingly remarkable comeback, regionalism today is far from monolithic, since regions define and redefine themselves as they evolve out of shared interests and perceived threats among constituent member states. The post–Cold War world order increasingly reflects and affects different forms and patterns of regionalization taking place simultaneously.

The new regionalism is more concerned, however, with geoeconomics than geopolitics. Although evaluating the capabilities and effectiveness of regional organizations to manage armed conflicts in the post–Cold War world is not an easy task, it is apparent that regional organizations have been less effective than the United Nations in conflict management. More often than not, regional organizations allow regional conflicts to escalate beyond the point at which the institutions can manage them, and then they export them to the UN as extraregional conflicts that threaten international peace and security. Rather than in tackling the difficult regional conflicts, the effectiveness of regional political organizations has generally been limited to (1) conflicts of low intensity involving minimal fighting, (2) conflicts in which there is a threat to the organization's consensual norms, (3) conflict abatement and isolation rather than conflict settlement, (4) interstate conflicts threatening the consensual norm of state sovereignty with virtually no impact on intrastate conflicts, and (5) conflicts of limited subregional geographical scope involving smaller and weaker member states. With regional organizations under tight resource and personnel constraints, it is unlikely that the actions of most such organizations will expand in the near future beyond a role subordinate to UN leadership.[17]

The new regionalism reflects and affects a complex interplay of local, regional, and global forces, simultaneously involving state as well as nonstate, market, and societal actors. Regionalism/regionalization and globalization should be seen in symbiotic rather than dichotomizing terms, as they are sometimes mutually reinforcing and at other times contradictory. Regionalization can take place at the same time as globalization, given the lower transport costs associated with geographic proximity. Even in Europe, where regionalism has gone further and deeper than in other parts of the world, the European Union has been a spur, not a barrier, to globalization.[18] While regionalism/regionalization is a component and reflection of globalization, it can also act as a modifying response to globalization pressures.[19] In short, regional and globalizing forces are mutually constitutive, reinforcing, and competing more than ever before, as on the one hand both de facto and de jure regionalization are occurring and on the other regionalization is fostering globalization by stimulating cooperation and competition within the broader context of global transformations.

What then is the place of NEA in the new regionalism? Presenting a satisfactory definition of "regionalism" is a necessary first step to any meaningful discussion of NEA's regional identity. In definitional terms, the literature stresses two or three key linkage factors as necessary conditions under which regionalism or regional integration takes place among a group of states, including linkage by geographical proximity and contiguity and by various forms of shared political, economic, social, cultural, or institutional affinities. Regions are also defined as combinations of geographical, psychological, and behavioral characteristics.[20]

While geographical proximity and contiguity is important, defining NEA in these terms alone is more problematic than apparent at first glance, because of the inclusion or exclusion of Russia and the United States in the NEA regional grouping. While the NEA region involves and conflates the Big Four in its international relations, only Japan and the two Koreas are entirely ensconced within its geographical perimeter—the northeastern part of the Asian continent. As a continental power, China provides geographical links with all other subregions of Asia, especially Southeast Asia, while

Russia's geographical and demographic position in NEA is on the margins. Not only is Moscow some 9,288 kilometers away from Vladivostok via the Trans-Siberian Railway, but also the "Asian" population in the Russian Far East is less than a third that of the smallest Northeast Asian polity (North Korea, with a population of 22 million). The Mongolians intruded into the region in the distant past, but their core population and territory have long remained in Central Asia.[21] More importantly, the United States as the extraterritorial lone superpower has to be excluded from such a geographical referent.[22] By any reckoning, however, the United States is of central importance to all the NEA states. Hence, any strictly "geographical" approach would hide rather than reveal the critical role of the United States in NEA's international relations and, especially, its geopolitics.

To define NEA in terms of shared characteristics such as regional consciousness, identity, or cohesiveness is no less problematic, for few if any of these attributes are present within the region. Since there is no such thing as a "natural region," all regions are socially constructed and politically contested, and all definitions are keyed to the particular problems or questions under investigation. To explore the patterns of distinctive regional interaction is to define the NEA region in terms of the patterned interactions among its constituent member states. The quality of interactions may be cooperative or conflictual, but to count as a region, as Barry Buzan suggests, "it needs to display an intensity of interaction sufficient to mark it out as a distinctive subsystem in some significant way."[23]

In this volume, using for analytical convenience the two linkage factors of geographical adjacency and patterned interaction and interdependence, we define NEA as referring to the three traditional core states of Japan, Korea, and China now expanded to the five states (Japan, North and South Korea, China, and Taiwan) plus Russia and the United States, as a way of more fully capturing the dynamics of regional geopolitics in a rapidly globalizing and fragmenting post–Cold War world. In terms of regional geoeconomics, however, our definition can be further relaxed by expanding and delimiting it to the core economies—Japan, South Korea, China, Taiwan, and Hong Kong (hereafter NEA-5)—so as to better compare and contrast intraregional and interregional economic relations—that is, intraregional trade among NEA-5 nations as against interregional trade between NEA-5 nations and the United States or North America. Thus, our geoeconomic definition excludes North Korea, Russia, and the United States.

Since "regionalism" and "regionalization" have been applied in various ways to Northeast Asia, East Asia, or even Asia, often interchangeably and without any conceptual consistency or clarity, it seems useful to distinguish regionalism from regionalization. Just as globalization is not the same as "globalism" or "universalism," regionalization is not the same as regionalism.[24] Like globalism, regionalism is a normative concept referring to shared values, norms, identity, and aspirations. In contrast, regionalization refers to a series of complex, interrelated processes of stretching and accelerating regionwide interconnectedness in political, economic, and social relations. Some scholars distinguish regionalism from regionalization in terms of intergovernmental collaboration, with regionalism used as a shorthand for regional intergovernmental agreements to manage various regional problems and regionalization referring to an ongoing process of creating greater economic interdependence within the region.[25]

It is worth noting in this connection that three major books present sharply contrasting analyses and conclusions about NEA as a region. Peter Katzenstein, the foremost analyst of Asia's new regionalism, boldly claims that "Asian regionalism is coming of age, and weak institutionalization makes it distinctive."[26] And yet this so-called Asian regionalism is said to be not a psychological construct but rather something occurring in the material forces of production and commercial networks focusing on Japanese *kereitsu* structures and Chinese family firms bringing about "economic integration without explicit institutional links."[27] Thus, Katzenstein conflates regionalism and regionalization—and Asia and Northeast Asia—into a single sweeping category to arrive at an upbeat assessment of "Asian regionalism."

In contrast, Tsuneo Akaha's argument is anything but upbeat, because it proceeds from the dubious premise that Northeast Asia is largely a geographical referent. Consequently, the NEA grouping envelops Mongolia and Russia along with the three core states and excludes the United States, Taiwan, and Hong Kong. Moreover, Akaha defines NEA in terms of what it lacks (e.g., regional consciousness, regional institutions, deep economic integration, political community, effective leadership, and vibrant transnational actors) as well as what it has in inexhaustible supply (e.g., national rivalries, unresolved historical animosities, negative mutual images, political and ideological conflicts, divided states, incompatible economic systems, crumbling economies, and a cultural and civilizational divide).[28] Yoshinobu Yamamoto stakes out an alternative conception of regionalism, arguing that the distinctive feature in Asia is regionalization without regionalism, if regionalism is defined in terms of identity and shared consciousness. Yamamoto's argument is that if a regional identity is to emerge it will coalesce around nascent institutions rather than being the foundation for creating them.[29]

When regionalism and regionalization are defined and differentiated following Yamamoto, post–Cold War East Asia in general and NEA in particular can be said to be experiencing some economic regionalization with little political or security regionalism to speak of. Northeast Asia has spawned all kinds of strategic triangles over the years, but there has been no virtuous cooperative triangulation of Beijing, Moscow, and Tokyo on most regional or global issues. As shown in table 1.1, there emerged in post–Cold War Northeast Asia a handful of regional or subregional "bi-multilateral" or "mini-multilateral" forums and arrangements—it is a stretch to call them "institutions"—to deal with regional security and economic issues in an ad hoc and situation-specific manner. None of these regional forums has all eight NEA countries as participating member states. APEC is the most inclusive regionalism, containing all but North Korea as participating countries or economies. With the exception of the ARF and APEC, which remain more Southeast Asian and Asia–Pacific than Northeast Asian in structure and orientation, none of the five forums has all three Northeast Asian powers in membership. Japan and Russia are excluded from the currently stalled Four-Party Peace Talks. China and Russia are excluded from the Trilateral Coordination and Oversight Group (TCOG) and the Korean Peninsula Energy Development Organization (KEDO; which has been rapidly unraveling since late 2002). Japan and the United States are not members of the Tumen River Area Development Programme, and Russia is not a member of ASEAN Plus Three (China, Korea, and Japan, hereafter APT).

Table 1.1. Northeast Asia in Regional "Minilateral" Institutions, 2002 (member countries)

	ARF (23) 1994	*Four-Party Talks (4) 1997*	*TCOG (3) 1999*	*KEDO (3 + 10) 1995*	*APEC (21) 1989*	*TRADP (5) 1992*	*TEMM (3) 1999*	*APT (13) 1997*
DPRK	x	x				x		
ROK	x	x	x	x	x	x	x	x
U.S.	x	x	x	x	x			
Japan	x		x	x	x		x	x
China	x	x			x	x	x	x
Russia	x				x	x		
Taiwan					x			
Hong Kong					x			

x = Participating member country or economy.

ARF = ASEAN Regional Forum
TCOG = Trilateral Coordination and Oversight Group
KEDO = Korean Peninsula Energy Development Organization
APEC = Asia Pacific Economic Cooperation
TRADP = Tumen River Area Development Programme
TEMM = Tripartite Environment Ministers Meeting
APT = Association of Southeast Asian Nations plus Japan, China, and Korea

This is not to say that NEA countries are isolated from the global community as symbolized and structured by the United Nations and its specialized agencies. As shown in table 1.2, the three core NEA states—China, Japan, and South Korea—are fully integrated into the world of (global) international organizations. Viewed in this light, both nationalism and globalization trump NEA regionalism.

There are many reasons for stunted regionalism, especially security regionalism, in NEA. Where there is a high level of great power conflict and rivalry, there will also be a low level of regional security cooperation. It is hardly surprising that Northeast Asia has been more resistant than Southeast Asia to new forms of regional multilateral security dialogue and forums. Unlike in Europe, the primary threat in NEA after the post–World War II era remained intraregional, not extraregional. The comfort level that exists in security dialogue in Southeast Asia does not exist in Northeast Asia. This explains as well why the Big Four of NEA had to move southward to gain breathing space for more open East Asian regional cooperation.

Japan as an economic superpower obviously looms large in NEA's regional international politics. However, the difficulty of Japan's role as a regional hegemon is vastly compounded by the long shadows of the Greater East Asian Co-Prosperity Sphere—an ever present reminder of pernicious regionalism during the heyday of Japanese imperialism—coupled with Japan's seeming inability and unwillingness to come clean on its imperial atrocities. The "Greater China" model is potentially more promising, but it depends on a host of unpredictable variables including, most importantly, the sustainability of China's relentless economic growth and it's international conduct as a responsible great power in the uncertain years ahead. America's role too is controversial, as bilateralism consisting of Cold War alliances with Taiwan (lapsed or in a state of limbo since 1979), Japan, and South Korea consistently trumps any regional multilateralism in America's East Asia security strategy. Of the Big Four, then, only Moscow as a Eurasian continental power with long-standing regional ambitions but limited access to the Pacific has worked steadily toward NEA regionalism, promoting the concept of multilateral security arrangements in Asia for more than two decades, beginning with Brezhnev's "Asian Collective Security System" in 1969. Also, as part of his "new thinking," Mikhail Gorbachev proposed in 1986 and 1988 a Conference on Security and Cooperation in Asia modeled on the Conference on Security and Cooperation in Europe, only to be spurned by Beijing and Washington. In the post–Cold War era, Moscow almost alone has shown continued interest in collective or cooperative schemes for the region as ways of enhancing its economic and status interests in the region.

However, the first initiative calling for multilateral security arrangements

Table 1.2. NEA's Participation in International Organizations, 1960–2002

Country	*1960*	*1977*	*1986*	*1987*	*1989*	*1994*	*1995*	*1996*	*1997*	*1998*	*1999*	*2000*	*2001*	*2002*
North	**2**	**12**	**16**	**22**	**20**	**20**	**18**	**18**	**18**	**18**	**18**	**17**	**18**	**19**
Korea	22	63	137	155	141	175	179	186	185	187	184	172	181	183
South	**19**	**39**	**36**	**39**	**41**	**47**	**48**	**50**	**51**	**52**	**51**	**52**	**51**	**49**
Korea	102	371	686	761	820	1034	1072	1138	1200	1250	1301	1315	1387	1431
China	**2**	**21**	**32**	**35**	**37**	**50**	**49**	**51**	**52**	**52**	**51**	**50**	**49**	**46**
	30	7	403	504	677	955	1013	1079	1136	1191	1258	1275	1366	1406
Taiwan	**22**	**10**	**6**	**6**	**6**	**7**	**8**	**10**	**11**	**10**	**9**	**11**	**11**	**11**
	108	239	419	464	554	775	809	865	908	932	982	1008	1081	1196
Japan	**42**	**71**	**58**	**60**	**58**	**62**	**61**	**63**	**63**	**63**	**63**	**63**	**61**	**59**
	412	878	1222	1420	1583	1863	1889	1970	2019	2059	2124	2122	2246	2279
U.S.	**59**	**78**	**33**	**59**	**64**	**62**	**64**	**64**	**65**	**64**	**63**	**63**	**62**	**61**
	612	1106	804	1579	1933	2273	2327	2418	2490	2560	2648	2685	2858	2891
USSR/	**29**	**43**	**69**	**69**	**61**	**48**	**58**	**62**	**61**	**63**	**66**	**60**	**63**	**62**
Russia	179	433	646	714	806	822	1093	1300	1492	1582	1673	1752	1901	1928
Global	**154**	**252**	**369**	**311**	**300**	**263**	**266**	**260**	**258**	**254**	**251**	**241**	**243**	**232**
Total	1255	2502	4649	4235	4621	4928	5121	5472	5585	6020	6076	6177	6357	6398

Sources: Adapted from Union of International Associations, *Yearbook of International Organizations 1985/86,* 3d ed., vol. 2 (Munich: Saur, 1985), 1479, 1481–83; *1986/87,* 4th ed., vol. 2 (1986): tabs. 2 and 3; *1988/89,* 6th ed., vol. 2 (1988), tabs. 2 and 3; *1989/90,* 7th ed. vol. 2 (1989), tabs. 2 and 3; *1994/95,* 12th ed., vol. 2 (1994), 1681, 1683–85; *1995/96,* 13th ed., vol. 2 (1995), 1682–87; *1999/2000,* 36th ed., vol. 2 (1999), 1482–84; *2000/2001,* 37th ed., vol. 2 (2000), 1466, 1471–78; *2001/2002,* 38th ed., vol. 2 (2001), 1519–28; *2002/2003,* 39th ed, vol. 2 (2001), 1607–15.

Note: Intergovernmental organization figures are in bold type throughout the table; international nongovernmental organization figures are in lightface type.

at the Northeast Asian level was made not by Moscow but by South Korean president Roh Tae Woo, who in his October 1988 address to the UN General Assembly proposed a Consultative Conference for Northeast Asia, to include the two Koreas and the Big Four, which would form a type of subregional security regime. President Kim Dae Jung also proposed a six-nation North-East Asian Security Dialogue (NEASED) involving the two Koreas and the Big Four, but this time as an extension of the Four-Party Talks. While Japan and Russia (excluded from the Four-Party Talks) have naturally supported the six-party NEASED forum, this and similar proposals for collective or cooperative security have fallen by the wayside because they have failed to gain the support of China and the United States.

Nonetheless, with the changing realities on the ground the regional discourse and praxis have undergone an important transformation over the past decade, the study of international regions is adjusting, as it must. Within a decade, the Asia–Pacific region along with NEA has moved from a complete multilateral institutional void to a point where proposals for new collaborative arrangements have mushroomed across the region.[30] Indeed, the rise of China more than any other factor seems to have served as a kind of force multiplier in catalyzing three East Asian regional arrangements: the Council for Security Cooperation in the Asia Pacific (CSCAP), the ARF, and APT.

The CSCAP as an unofficial "Track II" organization (involving nongovernmental organizations, or NGOs, and government officials acting in their private capacity) and the ARF as a "Track I" organization (i.e., an intergovernmental organization) were established in 1993 and 1994, respectively. To date they represent the most significant efforts to create inclusive regional multilateral regimes for two-track dialogue, confidence building, and norm diffusion (socialization). Both regimes as offspring of the "ASEAN Way" stand out as rare examples in which the leadership role was played by the middle powers of Southeast Asia, thus raising the comfort level for China's participation. As Johnston and Evans argue, both were created with China in mind, "either as *a* principal or *the* principal reason for their existence . . . against the backdrop of uncertainty about the post–Cold War security order in Eastern Asia, and particularly the rise of China and the regional debate about the appropriate response."[31]

Although the Asian financial crisis of 1997–1998 (AFC) served as the proximate catalyst for the rapid rise of APT, the broader strategic motive was to integrate an increasingly powerful China into a regional finance regime—similar to Japan's 1997 proposal for an Asian Monetary Fund (AMF)—parallel to China's integration into the global multilateral trading system through its then-pending accession to the WTO. This has been identified in

Japan as a critical function of APT. In Southeast Asia, too, APT is seen as a soft East Asian–style regime for coping with the rise of China as a "great power," in sync with the more explicitly security-oriented ARF.[32] With the AFC fully exposing the many institutional problems and pitfalls of ASEAN and APEC while simultaneously illustrating the rise of China and economic interdependence as the two main driving forces behind East Asian political economy, we have been witnessing the emergence of a new yet embryonic regime, APT, as a way of creating closer integration between Southeast Asia and Northeast Asia. APT is another example of how ASEAN countries coaxed the three core states of Northeast Asia—and Asia's three largest economies—into Southeast Asia's open regionalism to play a collective leadership role in the making of East Asian economic integration.

Nonetheless, the proponents of regional multilateralism rarely present it as an immediate substitute for the existing security order, which depends heavily on bilateral diplomacy and a U.S. strategic presence. For Washington, Tokyo, and Seoul, the ARF is seen as complementary to bilateral defense cooperation.[33] Another significant trend is the use of regional regimes such as the ARF to supplement rather than substitute for global norms and practices developed in global multilateral institutions like the UN.

THE MANY FACES OF NORTHEAST ASIA'S INTERNATIONAL RELATIONS

Northeast Asia encompasses in one place all the new world order challenges pivoting around two central issues: the source of possible threats to the region's stability and the feasible and desirable conflict-management models needed to establish peace and stability in the region. There are at least three major contending theoretical perspectives of real-world significance for NEA international relations: realism, liberalism, and social constructivism. Applying the available empirical indicators and the three theoretical perspectives, this section considers briefly the geopolitical, geoeconomic, and ideational dimensions of NEA's international relations, with primary attention to recent developments.

Realism: Geopolitical Challenges

The debate about Northeast Asian security has been dominated by realists, who argue that states, as undifferentiated and unitary rational actors in international anarchy, are compelled to maximize power, security, or influence.

The assumption is that continuity in the basic nature of world politics is shaped by the structure of the international system (i.e., the distribution of material power at the systemic level) and by the perennial struggle for power and plenty. The concern for relative power gains at the unit level led many realists in the early 1990s to make dire predictions that Asia was primed for the revival of a classical great power rivalry. The end of the Cold War was understood as a return to multipolar systems, or at least to the uneasy juxtaposition of global unipolarity and regional multipolarity that was said to be more prone to instability and conflict than bipolar systems.[34]

The most influential trend that many realists fear will shape the future of Northeast Asia, however, is the political dynamics associated with power transitions. In an argument that draws insights from Thucydides' explanation of the Peloponnesian War, fast-rising powers are believed almost invariably to be revisionist challengers seeking to change the existing international order and supplant the dominant power. Realists have argued that signs of a power transition process in post–Cold War Northeast Asia during the early 1990s—that is, a rising China, a declining Russia, a stagnant Japan, and a retreating hegemon (the United States)—indicate that it will be as difficult to achieve a stable, lasting peace in this region as it was in Europe over the previous several centuries. These dynamics will make the political environment ripe for Sino–American and Sino–Japanese rivalry.

Applying the thesis of the clash of civilizations—a kind of "cultural realism"—to the debate on the rise of China, Huntington argues that Asian countries will be more likely to bandwagon with China than to balance against it, and that Asia's Sino-centric past, not Europe's multipolar past, "will be Asia's future," even as "China is resuming its place as regional hegemon."[35] Through the prism of "offensive realism," John Mearsheimer pessimistically predicts China's emergence as a regional hegemon in Northeast Asia as the most dangerous scenario the United States might face in the early twenty-first century, warning and prodding Washington to do what it can to reverse or slow the rise of China.[36] Writing in 1996 or 1997, Richard Bernstein and Ross Munro predicted with confidence that "within a few years, China will be the largest economy in the world."[37] The rise-of-China thesis is often conflated with the "China threat theory," that Europe's half-millennium history of rivalries and major wars is to be Asia's future.

By the logic of realist power transition theory, belligerent, preemptive, or preventive actions are motivated less by aggressive intentions than by fear and a fundamental dissatisfaction with the status quo, largely as a result of closing windows of opportunity and increasing vulnerability brought on by relative power shifts.[38] It is in this region that the rises and falls of China, post–Soviet Russia, South Korea, and North Korea have brought about the greatest swings in power in the past half century. As shown in table 1.3, U.S. and Japanese shares of global GNP and industrial production from 1980 to 1997 declined only slightly. The most dramatic changes are seen in the rapid rise and decline of China's and Russia's shares of global GNP. For most realists, the "back to the future" correlation between rapid internal growth and external expansionism has troubling implications for the future of Northeast Asian regional order. Tables 1.4 and 1.5 show the ranking of the NEA countries in realist/material terms as of the end of 2001.

Some optimistic realists reject the ascendant-China thesis. For example, William Wohlforth argues that the post–Cold War international system is unprecedentedly and unambiguously unipolar. The United States, he contends, enjoys such a "larger margin of superiority over the next most powerful states or, indeed, all other great powers combined than any leading states in the last two centuries," in all the underlying economic, military, technological, and geopolitical components of power that the unipolar moment can finally become a unipolar era. He argues further that the current unipolarity is not only peaceful and stable but durable as well. It minimizes strategic peer competition among the other great powers, and the second-tier powers have an incentive to bandwagon with the unipolar superpower rather than to balance against it.[39] Thus Wohlforth rejects the "unipolar moment" thesis of the neoconservative journalist Charles Krauthammer as profoundly mistaken and pessimistic and the ascendant-China thesis as profoundly mistaken and optimistic.[40] Krauthammer now joins the chorus of a unilateral/unipolar era thesis, arguing that "after a decade of Prometheus playing pygmy, the first

Table 1.3. Changing Major-Power Shares of Global GNP and Industrial Production, 1980–1997

	1980	*1990*	*1995*	*1997*
Shares of Global GNP (%)				
USSR/Russia	7.0	5.6	1.9	1.7
USA	22.3	22.5	20.8	20.6
China	3.3	6.6	10.7	10.7
Japan	8.1	9.0	7.7	7.7
Shares of Global Industrial Production (%)				
USSR/Russia	9.0	7.0	2.0	1.8
USA	18.7	17.4	16.9	16.6
China	3.0	8.0	14.1	15.3
Japan	7.3	8.7	7.1	6.9

Source: Adapted from Viktor N. Paviatenko, "Russian Security in the Pacific Asian Region: The Dangers of Isolation," in *Russia and East Asia: The 21st Century Security Environment,* ed. Gilbert Rozman, Mikhail G. Nosov, and Koji Watanabe (Armonk, N.Y.: Sharpe, 1999), 20–21.

Table 1.4. Amounts, Ranks, and Shares of Material Power Resources, 2001

	China	*Russia*	*Japan*	*United States*
Basic Resources				
Population in mn (rank)	1,271.9 (1)	144.8 (6)	127.1 (9)	284.0 (3)
% of global total	20.7	2.4	2.1	4.7
Territory, 1994 (rank)	2	1	59	4
% of global total	7.3	13.2	0.3	7.1
Economy				
GDP in $bn (rank)	1,159 (6)	309.9 (18)	4,245 (2)	10,171 (1)
% of global total	3.7	1.0	13.6	32.5
GDP at PPP in $bn	5,415 (2)	1,255 (10)	3,487 (3)	9,902 (1)
$ of global total	11.7	2.7	7.5	21.3
Trade as % of GDP	44	51	18	19
Military				
Nuclear Warheads	3	1	—	2
% of global total	2.1	48.1		45.5
Military Expenditure $bn (IISS)	46.0 (3)	63.7 (2)	39.5 (4)	322.4 (1)
Military Expenditure $bn (SIPRI)	27.0 (7)	43.9 (2)	38.5 (4)	281.4 (1)
Military Expenditure as % of GDP (IISS)	4.0	4.3	1.0	3.2
Military Expenditure as % of GDP (SIPRI)	2.1	3.6	1.0	3.1
Military Personnel (rank)	2,310,000 (1)	977,100 (5)	239,800 (21)	1,367,700 (2)

Sources: Adapted from Robert A. Pastor, "The Great Powers in the Twentieth Century: From Dawn to Dusk," in *A Century's Journey: How the Great Powers Shape the World,* ed. Robert A. Pastor (New York: Basic, 1999), 19; World Bank, *World Development Report 2003* (New York: Oxford University Press, 2002), 234–42; International Institute of Strategic Studies, *The Military Balance 2002–2003* (London: IISS, 2002), tab. 26, 332–37; Stockholm International Peace Research Institute, *SIPRI Yearbook 2002: Armaments, Disarmament, and International Security* (New York: Oxford University Press, 2002), 235, 284–87.

task of the new administration is to reassert American freedom of action. . . . [T]he new unilateralism recognizes the uniqueness of the unipolar world we now inhabit and thus marks the real beginning of American post–Cold War foreign policy."[41]

There are several problems with most realist visions of post–Cold War Northeast Asian international relations. First, the historically derived correlation between system transition and war causation may no longer apply. There are many differences between ascendant China and the rise of Wilhelmine Germany, and furthermore world history may well be in a different normative (anti-imperial) cycle.[42] Indeed, what distinguishes the post-1945

Table 1.5. Military Expenditures of Northeast Asian Countries, 2001*

Country	*Defense Expenditure (U.S.$bn)*	*Defense Expenditure as % of GDP*	*Military Manpower (1,000 persons)*	*Defense Expenditure per capita (U.S.$)*
U.S. (IISS)	322.4	3.2	1,368	1,128
U.S. (SIPRI)	281.4	3.1		
Japan (IISS)	39.5	1.0	240	310
Japan (SIPRI)	38.5	1.0		
Russia (IISS)	63.7	4.3	977	440
Russia (SIPRI)	43.9	3.6		
China (IISS)	46.0	4.0	2,398	36
China (SIPRI)	27.0	2.1		
Taiwan (IISS)	10.4	3.7	370	472
Taiwan (SIPRI)	7.2	2.5		
ROK (IISS)	11.2	2.7	683	237
ROK (SIPRI)	10.2	2.8		
DPRK (IISS)	2.0	11.6	1,082	91
DPRK (SIPRI)	1.4	—		
Regional Total (IISS)	495.2	4.36 (average)	7,118	387.7 (average)
Regional Total (SIPRI)	409.6	2.52 (average)		
% of Global Total (IISS)	59.3%	3.5 (global average)	34.9%	226 (global average)
% of Global Total (SIPRI)	48.8%	2.6 (global average)		

* Based on 2001 constant prices.
Sources: Adapted from International Institute of Strategic Studies (IISS), *The Military Balance 2002–2003* (London: IISS, 2002), tab. 26, 332–37. Stockholm International Peace Research Institute, *SIPRI Yearbook 2002: Armaments, Disarmament, and International Security* (New York: Oxford University Press, 2002), 235, 284–87.

international system is the extent to which international organizations have become prominent and permanent parts of a complex, increasingly interdependent global system. In the post–Cold War era, thanks to globalization dynamics, the games that nation-states play have lost much of the realist simplicity of the struggle for power and plenty. Moreover, with the third wave of democratization, "democracies seem able to influence international norms and institutions, thereby affecting the probability that force will be used even by states that are not themselves particularly democratic."[43] The most significant and troubling geopolitical trend since the end of the Cold War is the predominance of intrastate armed conflict, not traditional interstate war or great power rivalry, and NEA has yet to experience a single interstate or intrastate war in the post–Cold War era.

If anything, the past quarter century has seen a double failure in prediction. While no pundit or international relations theorist predicted such momentous events as the end of the Cold War, German reunification, or the collapse of the Soviet Union, many predictions on the rise of Soviet primacy in strategic rivalry, the rise of Japan as a superpower, and the hegemonic decline of America have all fallen by the wayside. The lesson is that we should shy away from committing the fallacy of premature extrapolation conflating China's actual power with its potential power. Overestimations of Chinese power could easily play into the hands of Cold War hard-liners in the United States, if they have not already done so, lending support to reckless self-fulfilling prophecies of the inevitable conflict with China.[44]

There is a double paradox at work in the heated rise-of-China debate. While China today is more integrated into the "global community" and exhibits greater levels of cooperative (status quo) behavior within that community than ever before by most available indicators, the core premise of the contending approaches of containment, engagement, and constrainment (congagement)—as Johnston demonstrates in chapter 2—is that China as a dissatisfied revisionist (non–status quo) power is operating outside the global community on a range of international norms, thus posing the most difficult questions and challenges for the future of regional and global orders.

Although the People's Liberation Army has been involved in nine wars and armed conflicts—fought for ideological reasons and for the protection of national sovereignty and territorial integrity—most of the actions were taken in the 1950s and 1960s, and no war involving China took place in the 1990s, reflecting the peaceful settlement of territorial disputes with Russia, Mongolia, Central Asian countries, Burma, Pakistan, and Vietnam and the demise of the ideological basis for war.[45] To focus on "war" is perhaps to miss the larger picture of Chinese conflict behavior and crisis management. Yet Johnston's empirical analysis of China's militarized interstate dispute behavior for the period 1949–1992 concludes that "China will be more likely to resort to force—and relatively high levels of force—when disputes involve territory and occur in periods where the perceived gap between desired and ascribed status is growing or larger," that therefore the growth in Chinese power is not likely to translate into a more aggressive use of that power, and that, in fact, China may be less involved in conflicts, so long as its territorial integrity and international status is afforded proper respect.[46] The combined interactive effects of (1) the globalization pressures that sharply increase the costs of the use of force; (2) China's successful settlements of territorial disputes with most of its neighbors, with the corresponding sense of enhanced state sovereignty; (3) the demise of ideological conflict; and (4) the substantial accomplishment of China's drive for status as a great power augur well for the peace and stability of the East Asian region and beyond.

The irony here is that it is the United States, not China, who is more often than not outside the global community. In a 1999 article for *Foreign Affairs*, even a mainstream realist such as Samuel Huntington had to concede America's creeping unilateralism: "On issue after issue, the United States has found itself increasingly alone, with one or a few partners, opposing most of the rest of the world's states and peoples. . . . On these and other issues, much of the international community is on one side and the United States is on the other."[47] In its first two years, the Bush administration seems to have accomplished a diplomatic mission impossible by turning creeping unilateralism into runaway unilateralism, trashing multilateral treaties or treaties in the making, one after another (the ABM treaty, the Biological Weapons Convention, the Comprehensive Test Ban Treaty, the Kyoto Protocol, the International Criminal Court, a draft treaty on international small arms sales, etc.). On May 6, 2002, the Bush administration took an unprecedented step in "unsigning" the Rome Statute of the International Criminal Court by informing the UN secretary-general of its decision not to become a party to the treaty and that the United States had no legal obligation arising from President Clinton's signature on December 31, 2000.[48] The message seems loud and clear: the United Nations is relevant only to the extent that the world organization marches on the military drumbeat of America's unilateral triumphalism. As shown in table 1.6, China's voting coincidence with the United States in the UN General Assembly has never exceeded 29.7 percent (peak year of 1996). What is even more revealing is that the global/UN average rose from 27.8 percent in 1991 to 50.6% in 1995, before dropping down to 31.7 in 2001. An even more depressing picture emerges from the forty-four-country global attitudes survey of the Pew Research Center for the People & the Press conducted in July–October 2002 (see table 1.15).[49]

Equally paradoxically, China's own assessments of trends in what the Chinese call "comprehensive national power" (*zonghe guoli*, or CNP) in comparative terms are increasingly pessimistic about China's ability to catch up to the United States at a time when the rise of China as a great power has become nearly conventional wisdom among most scholars, pundits, and policy makers in the West. Indeed, since 1996, especially after the successful projection of U.S. power in Kosovo in the face of the growing military capability gap between the United States and any and all potential competitors, Chinese assessments of the future security environment have become increasingly pessimistic, concluding that multipolarization trends are not

Table 1.6. NEA Countries' Voting Coincidence with the United States in the UN General Assembly in Comparative Perspective, 1991–2001

UNGA Session, Year	*46th, 1991*	*47th, 1992*	*48th, 1993*	*49th, 1994*	*50th, 1995*	*51st, 1996*	*52d, 1997*	*53d, 1998*	*54th, 1999*	*55th, 2000*	*56th, 2001*
China	16.4	16.4	10.6	22.8	21.5	29.7	27.6	27.3	21.1	25.0	17.2
Japan	61.7	53.7	65.8	78.4	75.4	72.4	67.3	60.4	63.3	58.8	48.3
Russia*	41.9	59.5	68.6	66.6	73.1	59.3	58.6	55.1	46.0	44.4	34.5
ROK	35.3	36.2	44.2	55.9	64.3	60.0	62.5	60.0	61.4	52.2	45.3
DPRK	15.5	12.9	7.8	9.1	8.7	13.0	4.3	5.0	4.1	4.7	2.1
France	70.5	63.8	71.0	75.8	76.9	77.8	78.3	73.6	73.4	64.6	59.6
UK	79.6	73.5	80.0	84.0	85.1	79.1	79.4	74.5	75.8	71.7	63.2
Global Average	27.8	31.0	36.8	48.6	50.6	49.4	46.7	44.2	41.8	43.0	31.7

*1991 figure is for the former Soviet Union.

Sources: Adapted from the U.S. Department of State, *Voting Practices in the United Nations 1998,* Department of State Publication 10245 (1999), 33–37; *Voting Practices in the United Nations 1996,* Department of State Publication 10327 (March 1996), 31–55; *Voting Practices in the United Nations 2001,* Department of State Publication 10955 (June 2002), 33–37.

moving in the direction the Chinese leadership would prefer. While the assessments by Senior Colonel Huang Shoufeng of the Academy of Military Science (AMS) and a group of scholars at the civilian Chinese Academy of Social Sciences (CASS) agree that China will become one pole among five or more equals in spite of its much faster economic growth rate, they differ sharply in how to assess the rate of China's rise and America's decline. The orthodox AMS study suggests that China might catch up to the United States (achieving 97% of America's CNP) by 2020, while the reformist CASS study sees China's CNP reaching only 61 percent of America's and achieving a rank of seventh in the world, even below that of South Korea, at 65 percent of America's CNP.[50] As Johnston argues in chapter 2, the most recent calculations by the China Institute of Contemporary International Relations suggest that under the most optimistic growth scenarios China will reach only around 50 percent of America's CNP by 2020. An even more pessimistic growth scenario reduces this to 40 percent. Hence, the struggle for a multipolar world order would now last far longer—some twenty to thirty years longer—than previously estimated.

Moreover, diplomatic and military history does not fully support the core assumption of the realist peer competitor argument that power parity (bipolarity) and the preponderance of power buy peace and stability because weaker powers will not challenge the security interests of the stronger states. The literature on asymmetric conflicts shows that, more often than not, wars involve weaker powers engaging against stronger adversaries, and that big powers frequently lose wars in asymmetric conflicts (e.g., the Vietnam War).[51] According to a recent study, weak states were victorious in nearly 30 percent of all asymmetric wars in the approximately two-hundred-year period covered in the Correlates of War data set. More tellingly, weak states have won with increasing frequency over time.[52]

In reviewing fifty years of Chinese diplomacy, Beijing still calls the Korean War a war of aggression that the imperialists launched to strangle the new People's Republic; the Chinese performance in Korea is still publicly exalted as "a world miracle in which the weak vanquished the strong," even as "the signing of the Korean armistice rewrote the history of Chinese diplomatic negotiations which [prior to the coming of the PRC] had always ended with sacrifice of China's national interests."[53] Weaker states have also initiated many brinkmanship crises that fell short of war.[54]

Drawing theoretical insights from asymmetric conflict and negotiation theory, we may also explain the logic of North Korea's nuclear brinkmanship strategy as structured by four key variables: the weak state's proximity to the strategic field of play, the availability to the stronger state of viable alternatives, the level of stakes for both states in conflict and the degree of resolve for each, and the degree of control for all involved parties.[55] As a weaker state in conflict with the world's lone superpower and its allies (South Korea and Japan), North Korea has exercised and relied upon issue-specific and situation-specific power, the effectiveness and credibility of which has required resources and skills other than those of aggregate structural power. Pyongyang's proximity to the strategic field of play, its compensating brinkmanship strategy, and its high stakes, resolve, and control have all reinforced one another to make a strong actor's aggregate structural power somewhat irrelevant. North Korea has adopted a wide range of tactics in and out of the asymmetric conflict and negotiation processes in order to reduce the opponent's viable alternatives and weaken the opponent's resolve and control.

North Korea's geographical location is also of considerable strategic concern and importance to the Northeast Asian powers. Located at the pivot point of Northeast Asian security and at the most important strategic nexus of the Asia–Pacific region, Pyongyang is capable, by instigating hostility or instability, of entrapping any or all four great powers in a spiral of conflict escalation these governments would rather avoid. If Pyongyang's brinkmanship or Washington's coercive sanctions diplomacy escalates to war, the cost to all involved parties would be exorbitant[56]

North Korean nuclear and missile brinkmanship also illustrates with particular clarity that when the enactment of a national identity is blocked in one domain, it seeks to compensate in another. From Pyongyang's military-first perspective, developing asymmetrical capabilities such as ballistic missiles, special operations forces, and weapons of mass destruction (WMD—nuclear, chemical, and biological) serves as strategic *sine qua non* in its survival strategy. It remains one of a few areas in which the DPRK (Democratic People's Republic of Korea) commands comparative advantage in the military balance of power and status competition with the South. North Korea's humiliating defeat by its southern counterpart in the first-ever naval clash in June 1999 further emphasizes its WMD and ballistic missiles as a strategic equalizer. In sum, Pyongyang's proximity to the strategic field of play, its high stakes, resolve, and control, its relative asymmetrical military capabilities, and its coercive leverage strategy have all combined to enable the DPRK to exercise bargaining power disproportionate to its aggregate structural power in the U.S.–DPRK asymmetric conflict and negotiations.[57]

In a real-world situation, it is not so much the overall aggregate military power across Northeast Asia that will shape the emerging Northeast Asian order as it is the complex and dynamic interplay of domestic politics, elite perceptions, and diplomatic and security strategies in the capitals of the Big Four, involving specific military capabilities in specific geographic and political contexts. Foreign policy decision makers are not preprogrammed to be constrained by the structure of the international system as they choose strategies from a set of feasible and desirable alternatives. Indeed, differences in internal constructions and resulting domestic politics have a greater impact on how states or their decision makers define threats and vulnerabilities, and therefore on the whole security problematic, than does the structure of the international system.[58] As the realist ship of state encounters the turbulence of domestic politics in the post–Cold War era, more and more scholars have been shifting their attention away from conventional concerns about great power wars and superpower rivalry and toward domestic and societal sources of international conflict. The current position of domestic societal-level explanatory variables at the center of the study of international conflict is a belated acknowledgment of and response to their long neglect in the literature, as well as a response to the growing empirical anomalies of structural realism and the increasing salience of the "black-hole syndrome" reflecting and effecting many weak or failing states.[59]

Indeed, the obsession with the structure of the international system explains why most realists failed to see that North Korea, not China, would be the vortex of NEA's geopolitical and geoeconomic turbulence, or to predict the radical transformation of American foreign policy with the coming of the hard-line Bush administration. Contrary to the new conventional wisdom, the second U.S.–DPRK nuclear standoff did not begin in October 2002, when Pyongyang reportedly admitted the existence of a secret highly enriched uranium (HEU) nuclear program. In June 2000, the State Department announced its decision to expunge the term "rogue state" from the U.S. foreign policy lexicon in favor of the more diplomatic-sounding "states of concern," explaining that the "rogue state" category had already outlived its usefulness. Yet candidate Bush continued to use the term "rogue state" to refer to North Korea, Iran, and Iraq. Then came the "axis of evil" state of the union speech in January 2002, which upgraded the rogue-state strategy to the evil-state strategy. It became increasingly evident that this was more than rhetorical posturing, as shown by a series of radical shifts in America's military doctrine (e.g., the Quadrennial Defense Review that called for a paradigm shift from threat-based to capability-based models, the Nuclear Posture Review lowering the threshold of use of tactical nukes, and the Bush doctrine of preemption).

More seriously, the evil-state strategy generates many unintended consequences for American foreign policy. Although domestically appealing (to satisfy the right-wing fundamentalists) and necessary (to mobilize public support), in order to take whatever action, the term "rogue state" has no standing in international law, hence it is a tough sell in the international community. Moreover, a strategy built around the notion of rogue states prematurely constrains America's strategic and negotiating flexibility.[60] After all, "evil" is something to be destroyed, not something to negotiate with. Indeed, any deviation from the hard-line rollback or containment strategy would arouse accusations of appeasement (as it already has at the time of this writing). The Bush administration has boxed itself—and North Korea—into a corner. Faced with the harsh realities on the ground, where Pyongyang commands what Gen. John H. Tilelli Jr., former commander in chief of United States Forces in Korea (USFK), called "tyranny of proximity"[61] and asymmetrical military capabilities, President Bush shifted gears in early 2003 to conducting non sequitur diplomacy—he is willing to talk but never negotiate!

The Nuclear Posture Review, leaked in March 2002, less than two months after the "axis of evil" speech, proposes lowering the overall number of U.S. nuclear warheads, but widens the circumstances thought to justify a possible nuclear response and expands the list of seven "target countries," which includes China. It envisions, for example, the threat of nuclear retaliation in case of an Iraqi attack on Israel, a North Korean attack on South Korea, or a military confrontation over Taiwan. Allies and nuclear strategists have begun asking a question not heard in Washington for decades: would the president ever consider a preemptive nuclear strike?[62] Making such a threat as President Bush has done to a country as volatile as the DPRK will do nothing if not push the latter into a corner, and it is possible that North Korea will lash out. The term "axis of evil" is reminiscent of President Reagan's "evil empire" description of the Soviet Union, although Reagan never threatened the Soviets with a preemptive strike.

In a world where numerous countries are developing nuclear, biological, and chemical weapons, the United States must retain a credible nuclear deterrent. However, lowering the threshold for using nuclear weapons and undermining the effectiveness of the Non-Proliferation Treaty is ultimately not in anyone's interest. The treaty, long the main tool for the United States to discourage nonnuclear countries from developing nuclear weapons, is backed by promises that as long as signatories stay nonnuclear and avoid combat alongside a nuclear ally, they will not be attacked with nuclear weapons. If the Pentagon proposals become U.S. policy, that promise would be withdrawn and countries could conclude that they have no incentive to stay nonnuclear. The review also calls for the United States to develop a new nuclear warhead designed to blow up deep, underground bunkers. Adding a new weapon to America's nuclear arsenal would normally require a resumption of nuclear testing, ending the voluntary moratorium on such tests that is supposed to restrain the nuclear weapons programs of countries like North Korea. Is it not reasonable to expect that while the United States considers acquiring such capabilities that other countries should be able to do the same?

This is not to say that balance-of-power realism has lost much of its salience in NEA geopolitics, especially in Sino–American relations. On the contrary, the Republican victory in the 1994 congressional elections and the Republican "victory" in the 2000 presidential election have combined to bring about some radical unilateralist shifts in U.S. foreign policy, including China policy. In several respects, Mearshemeir's warning against a rising China has already become part of the U.S.'s Northeast Asia strategy. As stated in the latest *Quadrennial Defense Review* (QDR) *Report*, "The possibility exists that a military competitor with a formidable resource base will emerge in the region" (East Asia and the East Asian littoral).[63] Dividing East Asia into Northeast Asia and the littoral states in the southeast, the QDR report refers to these as "critical areas" where no "hostile domination" can be permitted to rise.[64] The strategic logic seems simple enough—that the time for upgrading America's military preparedness is now, while China is still too weak to respond, which would thereby prevent or slow China's ascendancy. Moreover, the Bush administration has taken a more supportive stance toward the defense of Taiwan, moving from expanded weapons sales to growing military-to-military cooperation.[65]

Liberalism: Geoeconomic Challenges

While acknowledging both conflict and cooperation as basic features of international life, liberalism in its many variants represents a more positive collective response to the perennial question of whether peace is possible through economic interdependence, international organizations, and democratic regimes in the absence of a world government. Mainstream institutional liberals accept some of the core assumptions of structural realism (neorealism) but reject the realist claims that cooperative security via multilateral institutions is a mirage and that international law is nothing more than a reflection of the interests of world powers.

The core assumption of liberalism is that international organizations help states to cope with uncertainty and to pursue their interests cost-effectively. Through international organizations, regulative norms, rules, and governing procedures are established to provide member states with convergent expectations, transparency of actions, and improved communication. Multilateral institutions, including security institutions, represent a response to the problems of international cooperation created by large numbers of actors, and such institutions can affect the "national interest" cost-benefit calculations of states through their functions of generating and disseminating information, thus increasing the likelihood of international cooperation in N-person games.[66]

Some liberals, however, argue that international politics are best explained by domestic sources: a state's foreign-policy behavior in general, and its war-prone behavior in particular, depends more on its specific type of national government or social system than on the structure of the international system. Proceeding from sharply divergent premises, Wilson and Lenin both identified the cause of war and the conditions for peace in the nature of the social and political systems of the state. More recently, the second-image theory of democratic peace—that liberal democracies rarely fight against each other—has gained wide if not paradigmatic acceptance in international relations theory.[67] Kantian liberals argue that a stable peace can be achieved through the triangulation of the expansion of economic interdependence, the enlargement of democracy, and the enhancement of international organizations and law. Bruce Russett and John Oneal advance the empirically grounded argument that Immanuel Kant's perpetual peace is no longer utopia but a living reality.[68] Some liberals view Northeast Asia, absent widespread liberal democracies, extensive economic interdependence, and multilateral institutions—the three liberal/Kantian conditions for international peace—as primed more for international conflict than for international cooperation.

Each of the conditions of the Kantian triad in the NEA region requires a brief analysis. As table 1.7 shows, NEA cannot be said to constitute a democratic zone. According to Freedom House's *Freedom in the World 2002* survey, which divides all 192 countries into three broad categories, the region is split into three zones: a "free"/democratic zone (the United States, Japan, South Korea, and Taiwan), a "partly free"/democratic zone (Russia), and a "not free"/no democratic zone (China and North Korea). When measured in terms of six major human rights conventions and eight basic labor rights conventions, however, the normative picture of the region is quite different, with the United States scoring lower than any other regional power. One of the most important arguments by Kantian liberals is that the benefits of peace can be and indeed are extended to countries that are not democratic, economically open, or participating extensively in international organizations.

Of the three elements of the Kantian peace, economic interdependence that stems from growing trade seems to be the most important contribution to fostering regional peace. Although the Cold War never ended completely or neatly in NEA, the region has experienced a profound geoeconomic transformation in the post–Cold War era. China, at the center of this transformation, is rapidly becoming a major source of a wider East Asian economic integration. By late 2002, China had begun to rival Japan as the pivotal player in the political economy of East Asia. It has become the largest export

Table 1.7. NEA in "Democratic/Freedom Ranking"

	China	*Japan*	*DPRK*	*ROK*	*Russia*	*Taiwan*	*U.S.*
Political Rights Score	7	1	7	2	5	2	1
Civil Liberties Score	6	2	7	2	5	2	1
Freedom Ranking	not free	free	not free	free	partly free	free	free
# of 6 major international human rights conventions signed or ratified	5	6	4	6	6	n/a	3
# of 8 major labor rights conventions signed or ratified	2	6	n/a	4	7	n/a	2

Source: Adapted from Freedom House, *Freedom in the World 2002,* at freedomhouse.org/ (accessed January 5, 2003); United Nations Development Program, *Human Development Report 2002* (New York: Oxford University Press, 2002).

market for both South Korea and Taiwan and has elbowed out Japan to become Asia's largest exporter to the United States. Almost overnight, China has become South Korea's largest economic partner and a major economic threat. South Korea's industrial hollowing is expected to spread by 2007 to such technology-intensive industries as electronics and automobiles, as production lines may start moving to China.[69]

How has this come about? As early as 1991, the World Bank had singled out post-Mao China as having garnered an all-time global record by doubling per capita output in the shortest period (1977–1987).[70] China's GDP growth rate in the post–Cold War period of 1990 to 2001 is even more impressive, nearly four times the world average, as shown in table 1.8. China easily won the global sweepstakes in economic growth rate and ranking, with the nearest peer competitor being the tiny city-state of Singapore—one of the fastest runners in the globalization race.

China's trade has exploded, from only several million dollars in the 1950s to $20 billion in the late 1970s and $510 billion in 2001, as trade as a percentage of GDP (a widely used measure of a country's integration into the global economy) has more than doubled once every decade, from 5.2 percent in 1970 to 12.9 percent in 1980, 26.8 percent in 1990, and 44 percent in 2001, compared to 11 percent for North Korea, 18 percent for Japan, 19 percent for the United States, and 20 percent for India in 2001. Contrary to popular misconceptions shared by proponents of both engagement and containment, China's economy is now two times more integrated into the global

Table 1.8. NEA's GDP Growth Rate in Comparative Perspective, 1990–2001

Country	*Average Annual Growth Percentage, 1990–2001*
China	10.0
Singapore	7.8
India	5.9
South Korea	5.7
Hong Kong	3.9
United States	3.5
France	1.8
Germany	1.5
Japan	1.3
North Korea	−2.0
Russia	−3.7
World Average	2.7

Sources: Adapted from World Bank, *World Development Report 2003* (New York: Oxford University Press, 2003), tab. 3, 238–39; North Korea's GDP is based on the Bank of Korea (Seoul).

capitalist economy than that of Japan or the United States![71] By 2001, China, with $510 billion for the year, had already emerged as the world's sixth largest trading country, after the United States ($1.911 trillion), Germany ($1.063 trillion), Japan ($755 billion), France ($642 billion), and the United Kingdom ($606 billion), but ahead of Canada ($490 billion).[72] In 2002, China's trade reached $620.8 billion, registering a 22 percent increase over 2001, as China overtook the United Kingdom as the world's fifth largest trading country.[73] Thus Nicholas Lardy's recent prediction that China "seems almost certain in the next few years to overtake Canada, France, and the United Kingdom to become the fourth largest trading country in the world" and that "within a decade China's trade is likely to surpass that of Japan and Germany, making China the world's second largest trader,"[74] has nearly come true.

As another sign of its growing importance to the world economy, China has attracted record foreign direct investment (FDI), especially in the 1990s, which has gone into bolstering China's position as the world assembly line. China now produces more steel than Japan and the United States combined, and it is also a leader in almost every category of manufactured goods, from shoes to semiconductors.[75] While the accumulated total of utilized FDI for the first decade of the reform era (1979–1989) was only $17.2 billion, China's FDI exploded in the wake of Deng's famous southern trip in the spring of 1992. Over most of the 1990s, China became the world's second largest recipient of FDI—with its cumulative total for 1979–2000 at $348.3 billion—behind only to the United States. China's FDI more than doubled from $11 billion in 1992 to $27.5 billion in 1993 (thus exceeding the accumulated total of $17.2 billion for the decade of 1979 to 1989) and increased to $37.5 billion in 1995, $41.7 billion in 1996, $45.3 billion in 1997, $45.5 billion in 1998, $40.3 billion in 1999, and $40.7 billion in 2000.[76] For 2002, China's FDI amounted to $52.7 billion, surpassing the United States for the first time as the world's largest recipient.[77] As well, for the first time a developing country has become the world's largest recipient of FDI.

Table 1.9 shows changing patterns of intraregional and interregional trade (NEA with the United States) in recent years. Russia is excluded from the NEA-5 category (the core economies of Japan, South Korea, China, Taiwan, and Hong Kong) since Moscow's trade is heavily skewed in favor of Europe (71%); its trade with NEA-5 amounts to no more than about 8 percent of its total trade volume. The process of growing economic regionalism among NEA-5 is evident in the declining importance of the United States both as a market and as a source of investment for NEA-5's economies, as intraregional trade and FDI flows have increased. For the period 1985–2000, the United States declined as a market for all NEA-5 economies except China,

Table 1.9. Changing Distribution of NEA-5's Intraregional and Interregional Trade with the United States, 1985–2000 (% of Total)

	Japan			*South Korea*			*Taiwan*			*Hong Kong*			*China*		
	1985	*1997*	*2000*	*1985*	*1997*	*2000*	*1985*	*1997*	*2000*	*1985*	*1997*	*2000*	*1985*	*1977*	*2000*
Exports to NEA	17.7	24.4	26.6	20.8	32.7	34.2	21.0	38.8	37.8	34.4	44.9	43.0	48.0	48.2	34.8
Exports to United States	37.6	28.1	30.1	35.6	15.8	22.0	57.9	27.6	23.5	30.8	21.8	23.3	8.5	17.9	20.8
Imports from NEA	11.4	21.0	24.9	26.8	28.4	31.0	29.7	35.2	40.0	61.1	63.6	74.6	46.5	47.3	34.8
Imports from United States	20.0	22.4	19.2	21.0	20.7	18.2	23.4	17.8	17.9	9.5	7.8	6.8	12.1	11.5	9.9

Sources: Calculated from International Monetary Fund (IMF), *Direction of Trade Statistics Yearbook 1988* (Washington, D.C.: International Monetary Fund, 1989), 136–38, 217–19, 243–45, 250–52; IMF, *Direction of Trade Statistics Yearbook 1995* (Washington, D.C.: International Monetary Fund, 1996), 153–55, 234–36, 261–63, 269–71; IMF, *Direction of Trade Statistics Yearbook 2001* (Washington, D.C.: International Monetary Fund, 2002), 166–69, 276–78, 285–87.

whose exports to the United States increased sharply in the same period. On the import side, however, the relative decline of the United States is less sharply registered. Still, intraregional trade among NEA-5 has increased, but not dramatically so, from 12.1 percent in 1990 to 19.1 percent in 2000. The result of redirection of both exports and imports in NEA economies as a whole is the marked growth of intraregional trade combined with the concurrent decline of interregional trade. With the exception of Japan, NEA is now the largest market for the exports of the other four NEA economies. As table 1.10 shows, the United States as the origin of NEA-5's FDI inflows is even less impressive.

Despite the growing intraregional economic interdependence and the proliferation of bilateral free-trade agreements (FTAs), NEA-5 economies have shown no interest or willingness to form a discriminatory trading bloc because the emerging NEA economic system is already highly integrated into the larger global economic system. A recent comparative analysis of different combinations of FTAs concludes that the most desirable trading arrangement is WTO-based global liberalization. Regardless of types and sizes of trading arrangements, the aggregate gains from liberalization are estimated to be 50 percent higher than under the most favorable agreement for both the world as a whole and for the combined APEC membership. The second-best option proves to be APEC membership or the creation of a larger regional grouping comprising the whole of East Asia and the Western Pacific.[78]

From the perspective of mainstream neoliberal institutionalism, NEA's institutional deficit may not augur well for forming a pluralistic security community. Yet such a perspective does not fully take into account the "Asian way"—or the ASEAN way—to international cooperation, an informal con-

Table 1.10. NEA and Foreign Direct Investment, 2000

	FDI Inflows 2000		
	$bn	*%GDP*	*Origins of FDI (leading partners with %)*
China	38.4	3.6	Hong Kong (41); EU (11); U.S. (10)
Japan	8.2	0.2	U.S. (32); Germany (9); Switz. (7)
South Korea	9.3	2.9	EU (29); U.S. (19); Japan (16)
Russia	2.7	1.1	U.S. (28); Neth. (14); Germany (8)
United States	287.7	2.9	

Source: Richard J. Ellings and Aaeron L. Friedberg, eds., *Strategic Asia 2002–03: Asian Aftershocks* (Seattle: National Bureau of Asian Research, 2002), 399.

sultative and networking model that emphasizes multilateral dialogue and consensus building rather than formal regimes with a high degree of institutionalization. Indeed, the prevalence of informal "bi-multilateral" or "minilateral" institutions is one of the defining features of East Asia in general and Northeast Asia in particular. Despite the myriad interconnections on a wide range of issue areas in the past decade, Northeast Asia spawned only a handful of such "mini-multilateral" forums. This only underscores the ineluctable truth that NEA countries, with the exception of North Korea, are fully integrated into the global multilateral institutions, as shown in table 1.2.

Of the eight "minilateral institutions," the Tumen River Area Development Programme (TRADP) and APT are perhaps best for testing neoliberal institutionalism in the Northeast Asian setting. Nearly a decade old, the TRADP, in which China, North and South Korea, Russia, and Mongolia have all been involved, seems tailor made for exploring the possibilities and limitations of a multilateral Northeast Asian economic regime. The TRADP presents a unique case of regime formation involving multiple sets of actors—provincial, national, and international—all engaged in bargaining over the nature, scope, and direction of Northeast Asian economic development. As originally conceived, the TRADP was an ambitious project to turn the sleepy backwaters of Rajin in North Korea, Hunchun in China, and Posyet in Russia's Far East into a Northeast Asian Hong Kong, with estimated costs of $30 billion over a fifteen- to twenty-year period. The six participating member states—the earlier five plus Japan—were meant to complement one another. Japan and South Korea would provide investment capital, modern technologies, and management and marketing skills; North Korea and China would provide cheap labor; and China and Russia would supply the coal, timber, minerals, and other raw materials. China needed a port outlet to the Sea of Japan. Russia wanted to integrate the political economy of its Far Eastern region into the dynamics of the Northeast Asian economy. Mongolia, as a landlocked country, obviously wanted access to an international port. North Korea apparently wanted to turn the Tumen River into a Chinese-style special economic zone, and South Korea saw another gateway to North Korea.

By the end of 2000, the original grandiose multilateral infrastructure project had not collapsed so much as downsized into smaller bilateral or trilateral projects. As shown in table 1.11, cumulative FDI for 1991 through 2000 was only $1.6 billion, less than one-eighteenth of the $30 billion originally envisioned, and showed a highly skewed distribution.

What went wrong? The economic feasibility of the TRADP as originally conceived was closely keyed to the economic and political context of the Soviet Union, Mongolia, and North Korea in the late 1980s, along with the

Table 1.11. The Tumen River Area Development Programme (TRADP) Characteristics and Indicators, 2000

	Yanbian Korean Autonomous Prefecture, China	*Rajin–Sonbong Economic and Trade Zone, DPRK*	*Eastern Mongolia*	*Prmorsky Territory, Russian Federation*
Area	42,700 sq km	746 sq km	287,500 sq km	165,900 sq km
Population	2,185,000	150,000	222,000	2,200,000
Major City (Population)	Yanji (340,000)	Rajin (67,000)	Choibalsan (46,000)	Vladivostok (650,000)
International Arrivals	57,000	81,175	7,600	120,000
Main Industries	Light industry; forest products; tourism; agriculture; food processing; pharmaceuticals	Light industry; aquaculture; wood & seafood processing; tourism; transport services	Mining; agriculture; agro-processing; tourism	Aquaculture; food processing; forest products; engineering; mining; tourism
Labor costs per month	$60	$80	$60	$70–100
GDP per capita	$619	$491	$417	$1,398
GDP growth	4.4%	N/A	−4.6%	3.5%
Cumulative FDI (1991 through 2000)	$519 million	$88 million	$392 million	$576 million

Source: Adapted from TRADP at www.tumenprogramme.org (accessed on December 15, 2002).

assumed willingness of Japan and South Korea to provide the lion's share of the capital needed to launch the project. With the collapse of the Soviet economy, and consequently North Korea's as well, the initial conditions and context dramatically changed. Tokyo's interest in the Tumen project had been limited; from the outset, Japan refused to become a participating member state. Beijing's somewhat unusual activism suggests that China stood to gain the most from the project. China saw the project's potential to expand subregional economic cooperation between the two Koreas and to provide access to the Sea of Japan.

The TRADP, which involved both central and local decision makers from its five participating states (plus the United Nations Development Program), shows that international cooperation becomes more difficult as the number of actors increases and historical, civilizational, and national-identity fault lines remain intact. This is because international cooperation requires both recognition of opportunities for the advancement of mutual interests and policy coordination once such opportunities have been identified. As the number of actors with conflicting identities and interests increases, however, the likelihood of defection also increases, while the feasibility of sanctioning defectors diminishes. Likewise, transaction costs rise with the multiplicity and complexity of each player's payoff structure and mutual interests, thus militating against any easy identification and realization of common interests.[79]

The APT process, which has emerged in recent years, now has the potential to become the dominant push toward regionalization of East Asia as a whole, organically linking the three core NEA states with ASEAN. It is hardly surprising that the informal summit meeting of APT in late 1997 coincided with the Asian financial crisis (AFC). In several respects, the AFC served as the main catalyst in the APT process. The AFC has put to rest claims that all the frenzy about globalization amounted to nothing more than "globaloney," while it simultaneously demonstrated the ineffectiveness of APEC and ASEAN in meeting globalization challenges and the need for an alternative regionalist response. The APT process is not so much antiglobalization or a closed regionalist movement as it is a search for new and better ways of managing the forces of globalization to the region's advantage by combining the resources of Northeast Asia and Southeast Asia.[80]

The most important accomplishment of the APT process to date has been the so-called Chiang Mai Initiative. Meeting in May 2000 on the sidelines of the annual Asian Development Bank meeting in Chiang Mai, Thailand, the finance ministers of the APT endorsed an expanded currency swap arrangement among the member states' central banks that was designed to avert AFC-II. The Chiang Mai Initiative is now claimed as constituting the first step of East Asian monetary integration, which would eventually lead to a monetary union. As home to the world's five largest holders of foreign exchange reserves, NEA is well positioned to play a leadership role in the making of East Asian monetary regionalism.

Relying upon the networks and connections developed through the APT process, East Asian states have also negotiated bilateral agreements on a range of subjects. China has signed long-term, security-oriented "cooperation agreements" with Thailand, Indonesia, Malaysia, and Vietnam, among others. The majority of these agreements call for frequent consultations among foreign ministries, cooperation on certain defense issues, naval port calls, and promises of humanitarian assistance in the event of natural disaster. This has occurred just as Japan has inked a bilateral agreement on free trade with Singapore and has opened discussions on a bilateral agreement with South Korea. Thanks to China's incremental multilateralism, APT has launched a series of meetings in which the NEA powers and ASEAN's member states have discussed regional security issues, such as shipping, refugees, and narcotics. As a consequence, there have been no major exchanges of fire in the vicinity of the Spratly Islands since the middle of 2000.[81] Once again we see China and Japan break out of the tough NEA neighborhood to carry out their cooperation or competition within the parameter of Southeast Asian open regionalism.

The AFC seems to have generated far-reaching consequences for the restructuring of the political economy of the NEA region. For years "Asian values" have been touted as the reigning force behind the East Asian miracle. But the AFC has not only put to rest neorealist mercantilist antiglobalization claims but has also seriously punctured cultural-relativist claims about "Asian values" or any single Asian developmental model. The fact that some East Asian countries were severely hit while others escaped the crisis relatively unscathed, with nations showing differing prospects and paces of recovery, is better explained by country-specific circumstances and the pressures of globalization than by Asian values or an Asian "situational uniqueness."[82]

The fact that China emerged relatively unscathed from the crisis despite its deep integration into the global economic system can be explained by a combination of factors, such as the nonconvertibility of its currency, substantial foreign exchange reserves to defend against speculative attacks on the yuan, and the large inflow of FDI, only a small percentage of which is portfolio investment that is more vulnerable to quick withdrawal in a panic. In any event, China's response to the AFC shows how a variety of considerations are at work in the shaping of China's policy and behavior. Of the many factors, however, China's integration into the global community as a responsible great power seems primary. China's policy elites seldom fail to cite Beijing's refusal to devaluate the *renminbi* and the fact that China provided $1 billion each to Thailand and Indonesia and pledged $4 billion overall as proof positive of its status as a responsible great power. Beijing's decision not to devalue the *renminbi* is explained in terms of "grabbing with two hands." On the one hand, the nondevaluation of the *renminbi* is said to have demonstrated to the world community China's formidable economic muscle. On the other hand, China has also impressed its neighbors as a country that does not take advantage of others' misfortune, showing its sense of responsibility for the stability of the world economic system. As Moore puts it in chapter

3, "China's current enthusiasm for regional economic multilateralism is unprecedented."

China and Japan have begun to compete for regional economic leadership in East Asia, particularly within the APT process and in the wake of the AFC (see chapters 3 and 5). Although regionalization and globalization are seen in NEA as complementary rather than contradictory forces, since the AFC the center of gravity for economic regionalization has been shifting away from APEC toward APT. Increasingly moving away from economic relations centered on the United States, Japan too has turned more toward China, South Korea, and Taiwan. The fact that Japan no longer resists supporting or joining any East Asian regional organization that excludes the United States, such as APT, underscores this reorientation. The single greatest fear among Japanese policy makers and the public at large, as Grimes argues in chapter 5, has to do with the rise of China as the world's manufacturing center and the role of China in contributing to the "hollowing out" of Japan's industrialized economy in an era of globalization.

No Asian country was hit by the AFC as severely as South Korea; in President Kim Dae Jung's words, the country was confronted with "the greatest crisis since the Korean War" (1950–1953). Indeed, Seoul was forced to apply to the International Monetary Fund (IMF) for help in order to avert the imminent financial meltdown. The IMF responded with a $58 billion rescue package, the largest bailout program in IMF history.[83] As Moon and Kim argue in chapter 7, however, there occurred a subtle and significant shift in South Korea's foreign economic policy, as its economic arrangements moved away from an emphasis on multilateral megaregionalism toward bilateralism and subregionalism. Seoul's current preoccupation with the formation of the Northeast Asia Free Trade Agreement, comprising China, Japan, and Korea, exemplify this trend.

There is consensus among the contributors to this volume that NEA's geopolitics is more divisive than its geoeconomics and that growing economic regionalization and interdependence have often served as a bulwark against persistent or periodic political tensions in Sino–American, Sino–Japanese, Sino–Taiwanese, and even Sino–South Korean relations. Thus the pacifying effects of economic interdependence find some empirical and behavioral support—after all, the region has managed to avoid armed conflict in the post–Cold War era. The related proposition of neoliberal institutionalism that international institutions shape state preferences, even in powerful states, through the subtle and slow processes of learning and socialization seems to stand on somewhat weaker empirical ground. While most NEA countries are fully participating in global multilateral institutions, the same cannot be said about regional multilateral institutions. As shown in the APT process, NEA-

3 would have to think and act out of the box (the tough and unforgiving neighborhood) to capitalize on an East Asian open regionalism and to cope with the twin pressures of regionalization and globalization. This southward movement for a wider East Asian economic regionalization may be too new to provide sufficient "data points" for accurate assessment of the pacifying effects of the slow process of learning and socialization.

Constructivism: National-Identity Challenges

Mainstream structural realists and the vast majority of neoliberals and rational choice theorists have slighted the impact of ideational variables (norms, culture, and identity) in international relations. They have assumed that state identities and interests are either permanently fixed or merely derivative of their perennial struggle for power and plenty. The end of the Cold War and the collapse of the Soviet Union opened up considerable space for cultural and sociological perspectives in international relations scholarship; it is no coincidence that almost all major studies of national identity have been published in the post–Cold War era.[84] This is further testimony to the empirical anomalies in state behavior and in the dominant structural realist paradigm.

Social constructivists shift their primary attention away from power and security to show not only that ideational variables are important but also why and how identity politics matter in post–Cold War global politics. Unlike primordialists, most constructivists argue that national identity is formed and changed through repeated interactions with significant international reference groups. The identity of a state (national identity), more than anything else, provides a cognitive framework for shaping its interests, preferences, worldview, and consequent foreign policy actions. An understanding of this identity will therefore contribute to more accurate accounts of state behavior. A state actor in the international system understands other states based on the identity it ascribes to them, and it often responds accordingly. International structures are shaped and reshaped by what state actors actually do in the course of enacting their identities. In a state-centric world, the substantive content of national identity is the state, which defines itself by what it is as well as what it does.[85] Hence, the distribution of identities of relevant states, rather than the international power structure (structural realism) or international regimes (neoliberal institutionalism), best explains and predicts whether international cooperation is possible. Collective memory of the past is central to the constructivist thesis.[86]

The shifting roles of the Big Four in the region have much to do with the difficulties of adjusting national identities in a new post–Cold War era. With the Cold War overlay of stark bipolarity lifted, Northeast Asia reemerged as the site of civilizational divides (between Russia and China and between Russia and Japan) and of historical- and national-identity animus (between North and South Korea, China and Taiwan, China and Vietnam, Korea and Japan, China and Japan, Russia and Japan, and so on). Indeed, at no time has the challenge of redefining new national identities seemed more urgent and open-ended than in recent post–Cold War years, particularly in the Northeast Asian region. Unlike in post–World War II Europe, history has always cast a long shadow in Northeast Asian international relations, often serving as a major source of national-identity animus.

Since the collapse of the traditional Sino-centric world order in the late nineteenth century, China, the proud and frustrated "Sick Man of Asia," has had enormous difficulty overcoming the tyrannies and grievances of the past. This frustration, combined with the belief that China—by dint of its demographic weight and civilizational greatness—has a natural and inalienable right to great power status, at least partly explains the wild swings in national-identity projection over the years. The world has witnessed this projection mutating through a series of roles: self-sacrificing junior partner in the Soviet-led socialist world, self-reliant hermit completely divorced from and fighting both superpowers, revolutionary vanguard of an alternative United Nations, self-styled third world champion of a New International Economic Order, and favored recipient of largesse at the World Bank. None of these identities has much to do with Asian regional identity. Paradoxically, Beijing has made tremendous strides in projecting its revamped national identity as a responsible great power, rather than as a lone socialist global power in a post–Cold War and postcommunist world. To understand China's regional identity and role, it is important to recognize that there is an uneasy, shifting balance of competing forces and identities—both conflictive and cooperative—in Beijing's foreign policy. The most dangerous "security" threat China faces in the post–Cold War era is internal, not external, and a threat of this kind is not easily analyzed or managed through classical balance of power.

China's ambivalent Asian identity largely mirrors that of Japan, which is no less awkward and problematic. Across the ideological spectrum, as Masaru Tamamoto notes, there is an abiding Japanese doubt about Tokyo's capacity for self-restraint should it assume East Asian leadership.[87] At the same time, there is a widely shared perception in East Asia, although more in Northeast Asia than in Southeast Asia, that Japan is *in* but not *of* Asia and thus unfit to be a successor-leader. This perception has a lot to do with pendulum swings in Japan's Asian identity between seeking to escape and seeking to conquer Asia. On the Chinese side, there is also the tension between positive and negative images and perceptions. The paradox of China's Japan policy, which moves between hostile imagery and pragmatic self-interest, is never fully or satisfactorily resolved and seems to wane or wax according to the circumstances.[88]

Situated at the junction of Chinese, Korean, and Russian historical enmities but protected by American hegemony in East Asia during the Cold War, Japan sought comfort and safety in a relatively low-profile, quiescent role in international affairs, and this has given rise to its postwar identity as a pacifist and reactive state. As Berger argues in chapter 4, the Japanese have very strong historical memories, but these have focused more on the suffering that the Japanese people themselves have endured than on the suffering that they have inflicted on other East Asians.

In the past several years, however, Japan's assertive rising-sun nationalism has been growing apace, reviving its problematic "Asian identity." In a move that spoke of strong nationalist sentiment among Japan's politicians, in August 1999 the upper house of the Diet voted resoundingly—166 to 71—to officially designate the rising-sun flag and longtime unofficial anthem as legal symbols of the nation.[89] Far from a simple matter of symbols, the debate turned into a contest among politicians and intellectuals over Japan's national identity and its international role a half century after its defeat in World War II. This cause has long been dear to right-wing nationalists but has been at odds with the country's postwar efforts to project a pacifist identity.

This is a lightening-rod issue for Northeast Asian countries, especially for Korea and China, because it is organically linked with Japan's imperial aggression and atrocities. Note for comparison that Germany discarded its "Deutschland über Alles" anthem and the swastika flag after World War II. Of course such right-wing nationalism in Japan can only beget right-wing and left-wing nationalism in Seoul, Beijing, and Moscow, let alone in Pyongyang. Its official acceptance signals a shift toward a more hawkish stance that is emerging across a broad range of political opinions and is likely to rattle regional rivals in Northeast Asia. More than 60 percent of the public now support some constitutional change to "remake" Japan as a "normal state" and a whopping 90 percent of Diet members under fifty years of age want the constitutional revision.[90]

Upon assuming office as president of Russia in May 2000, Vladimir Putin reaffirmed his pledge to restore Russia as a great power. His state visit to Pyongyang in July 2000 coincided with the completion and ratification of three national security and foreign policy blueprint documents that year: a new national security concept (January), a new military doctrine (April), and a new foreign policy concept (July). Together, these blueprints put inordinate stress on safeguarding Russia's "national" interests, defined in terms of Russian exceptionalism, great power prerogatives, and economic interests.[91]

Russian exceptionalism is said to stem from the ineluctable geographical fact that even post–Soviet Russia has the largest territory in the world, and it also stems from Russia's status as the only truly Eurasian continental power. That is, even in an era of globalization, size matters in the mobilization and projection of Russia's identity as a great power. It also expresses Moscow's inability and unwillingness to define its identity as anything but a great power, and "great powers seldom operate under the same rules and constraints as lesser powers."[92] As Gilbert Rozman argues in chapter 6, Russia's NEA policy is shaped and conditioned by the logic of great power relations, with Moscow retaining a superpower appetite despite a stomach reduced to the size of a second-level European state. For its sense of national purpose and great power identity and for the satisfaction of powerful interest groups at home, Rozman concludes, Russia is unlikely to abandon the preoccupation with boosting its great power status.

Although China, Russia, and Japan, as the three Northeast Asian powers, share common interests in maintaining the peace and stability of the region, a high degree of distrust born of historical and contemporary concerns and competing great power identities stands in the way of restructuring this trilateral relationship on a stable footing. With the end of the shared Soviet threat, long-standing differences regarding questions of past aggression, territorial and commercial disputes, human rights, and competing foreign-policy goals have often been exposed and exacerbated by the rise of unstable domestic politics in Moscow, Tokyo, and Beijing. Indeed, there is little that binds the Chinese, Japanese, and Russian states and societies together, but much that divides them. "Of China, Russia, and Japan's six images of each other," according to Rozman, "not one could properly be called positive."[93]

A major international conference held at Yonsei University (Seoul) in 1996 to explore the interplay of history, cognition, and peace in East Asia concluded with a rather pessimistic assessment that historical, national-identity, and citizen perceptions in the region are more negative than initially expected and that growing political, economic, social, and cultural ties have not remedied perceptions of mutual hostility deeply rooted in history. Studies and surveys of "current" (late 1996) citizen perceptions—and perception ordering—among Japanese, (South) Koreans, and Chinese reveal two important findings:

> For Japan, Korea is the least favored, and China is more favored than Korea. For both China and Korea, Japan is the least favored. We can infer from this finding that China and South Korea could easily form an alliance against Japan. The other

> finding is that the United States is the most favored country by Japan, China, and South Korea. This suggests that even in the post–Cold War era, the United States could still make constructive engagements in the region as an honest broker and a productive stabilizer.[94]

A significant multinational citizens' opinion survey, jointly sponsored by *Tong-a Ilbo* (Seoul) and *Asahi Shimbun* (Tokyo), was conducted in October and November 2000 in the full glow of the inter-Korean summit. This survey, involving national samples of 2,000 in South Korea, 3,000 in Japan, 1,024 in the United States, and 1,000 in China, shows with disturbing clarity why NEA has little if any social and psychological foundation upon which to forge truly cooperative regional multilateral institutions. The lack of regional identity is perhaps the most formidable barrier to the formation of NEA regionalism (see tables 1.12 to 1.14).

As shown in table 1.12, of the six NEA countries and peoples involved in the survey—the United States, Russia, China, Japan, South Korea, and North Korea—none elicited a majority positive ("like") perception. The United States received the highest average positive perception (31%), while North Korea received the lowest positive perception (1.9%, from Japanese respondents). North Korea elicited the highest negative ("dislike") perception (56.7% from Japanese respondents), followed by Japan, which was perceived negatively by 43.2 percent of Chinese respondents and by 42.2 percent of South Korean respondents.

People's threat perceptions, in answer to the question "By which country do you feel most militarily threatened?" show a sharp bifurcation (see table 1.13). While North Korea elicits a high threat perception from South Koreans (53.7%) and Japanese (44.2%), the United States receives the highest threat perception, from 62.8 percent of Chinese respondents. When the question is rephrased and focused on North Korea—"Do you feel threatened by North Korea?"—Pyongyang "wins" with huge majorities: 86.8 percent in South Korea, 71.5 percent in Japan, and 94 percent in the United States (combining the "strongly" and "to a certain extent" categories of responses). As shown in table 1.13, then, the China-threat theory is almost exclusively an American elite perception, especially strong among right-wing Republicans. Only 38.1 percent of the American respondents in the survey singled out China as most militarily threatening, compared to only 7.7 percent of South Koreans. What is most surprising is that only 9.4 percent of Japanese singled out China as most militarily threatening.

It is in the question of "national influence" perception that we begin to see the popularity of the ascendant-China perspective. As shown in table 1.14, China is expected to be the most influential country in Asia in ten

Table 1.12. Multinational Citizens' Perceptions of Other Northeast Asian Countries, Late 2000 (%)

		ROK	*Japan*	*U.S.*	*China*
Q-1: (ROK, Japan, China) Do you like or dislike, or neither like nor dislike, the **United States**?	1. Like	30.7	29.4		33.0
	2. Dislike	18.7	7.6		31.0
	3. Neither like nor dislike	50.6	60.9		33.4
	4. Do not know/No response	—	2.1		2.6
Q-2: Then, do you like or dislike, or neither like nor dislike, **Russia**?	1. Like	11.0	3.7	17.2	38.3
	2. Dislike	26.4	40.4	21.4	15.4
	3. Neither like nor dislike	62.6	52.8	58.4	42.4
	4. Do not know/No response	—	3.1	3.0	3.9
Q-3: (ROK, Japan, U.S.) Then, do you like or dislike, or neither like nor dislike, **China**?	1. Like	22.6	17.1	12.6	
	2. Dislike	20.6	20.1	39.6	
	3. Neither like nor dislike	56.8	59.4	45.5	
	4. Do not know/No response	—	3.4	2.3	
Q-4: (ROK, U.S., China) Then, do you like or dislike, or neither like nor dislike, **Japan**?	1. Like	17.1		47.0	18.8
	2. Dislike	42.2		10.6	43.2
	3. Neither like nor dislike	40.7		40.3	33.6
	4. Do not know/No response	—		2.1	4.4
Q-5: (Japan, U.S., China) Then, do you like or dislike, or neither like nor dislike, **South Korea**?	1. Like		20.4	22.7	34.5
	2. Dislike		16.8	14.5	15.8
	3. Neither like nor dislike		60.0	59.7	44.8
	4. Do not know/No response		2.8	3.1	4.9
Q-6: Then, do you like or dislike, or neither like nor dislike, **North Korea**?	1. Like	29.5	1.9	7.1	37.4
	2. Dislike	21.9	56.7	32.7	16.7
	3. Neither like nor dislike	48.6	36.9	57.2	41.2
	4. Do not know/No response	—	4.5	3.0	4.7

Source: "Multi-National Citizens' Poll on Current States Surrounding Korean Peninsula," *Tong-a Ilbo* (Seoul), December 4, 2000.

Note: South Korea: N = 2,000, survey conducted October 25–November 18, 2000. Japan: N = 3,000, survey conducted November 11–19, 2000. U.S.: N = 1,024, survey conducted November 13–18, 2000. China: N = 1,000, survey conducted November 1–10, 2000.

years (2010) by 52.6 percent of South Koreans, 47.2 percent of Japanese, and 73.2 percent of Chinese, but only 18.9 percent of Americans. In contrast, Russia was chosen by a paltry 1.1 percent of Japanese, 1.4 percent of Chinese, 2.1 percent of South Koreans, and 4.7 percent of Americans, and Japan was chosen by a surprisingly low 8.4 percent of Japanese, 3.8 percent of Americans, 7.7 percent of Chinese, and 23.3 percent of South Koreans. This shows

Table 1.13. Multinational Citizens' Perceptions of Threat in Northeast Asia, Late 2000 (%)

		ROK	*Japan*	*U.S.*	*China*
Q-1: By which country do you feel most militarily threatened? Please select one country	1. United States	12.4	13.2	—	62.8
	2. Russia	4.0	9.5	20.9	1.2
	3. China	7.7	9.4	38.1	—
	4. Japan	20.7	—	2.5	12.4
	5. ROK	—	1.1	0.1	0.4
	6. North Korea	53.7	44.2	6.0	0.2
	7. No not know/No response	0.3	8.0	10.0	13.7
Q-2: Do you think the U.S.–Japan security agreement is helpful or is not helpful in maintaining peace and security in the Asia–Pacific region?	1. Helpful	54.5	66.4	53.6	4.1
	2. Not helpful	43.5	15.0	19.8	54.8
	3. Neither way	—	—	—	—
	4. No not know/No response	2.0	18.6	26.6	41.1
Q-3: (ROK, Japan, U.S.) Do you feel threatened by North Korea? How strongly do you feel threatened?	1. Strongly	11.1	11.7	38.2	
	2. To a certain extent	75.7	59.8	55.8	
	3. Not threatened	13.2	22.0	6.0	
	4. Do not know/No response	—	6.5	—	

Source: "Multi-National Citizens' Poll on Current States Surrounding Korean Peninsula," *Tong-a Ilbo* (Seoul), December 4, 2000.

Note: South Korea: N = 2,000, survey conducted October 25–November 18, 2000. Japan: N = 3,000, survey conducted November 19–20, 2000. U.S.: N = 1,024, survey conducted November 13–18, 2000. China: N = 1,000, survey conducted November 1–10, 2000.

the extent to which the familiar "Japan as Number One" chorus of the 1980s has completely vanished from NEA's collective memory.

The Pew Global Attitudes Project's worldwide public-opinion survey of more than thirty-eight thousand people in forty-four countries including Russia, China (limited or censored), Japan, and South Korea shows that, despite an initial outpouring of public sympathy for America following the September 11, 2001, terrorist attacks, discontent with the United States, especially with its runaway unilateralism, has grown apace around the world over the past two years under President Bush's watch. As table 1.15 shows, there are some major gaps and discrepancies between different kinds of public perceptions on different issues; perceptions of the United States in general terms garner higher marks than perceptions of U.S. foreign policy. While perceptions of the United States as a country elicited a high positive rating of 53 percent among South Korean respondents, 72 percent among Japanese respondents, and 61 percent among Russian respondents, an even higher percentage responded negatively to U.S. foreign policy—especially on such unilateralism versus multilateralism questions as whether the United

Table 1.14. Multinational Citizens' Perceptions of the Most Influential Power in Asia, Late 2000 (%)

		ROK	*Japan*	*U.S.*	*China*
Q1: Which country do you think will become the most influential in Asia in 10 years? Please select one country, whether it is an Asian country or not.	1. United States	8.1	13.7	54.9	9.6
	2. Russia	2.1	1.1	4.7	1.4
	3. China	52.6	47.2	18.9	73.2
	4. Japan	23.3	8.4	3.8	7.7
	5. ROK	10.7	4.3	0.9	1.1
	6. North Korea	1.0	2.3	2.1	0.1
	7. India	0.1	0.9	1.8	0.4
	8. Vietnam	–	0.3	1.3	–
	9. Others	1.2	0.6	2.0	1.9
	10. None	0.1	7.3	–	–
	11. Do not know/No response	0.8	13.9	9.6	4.6
Q2: (ROK, Japan, China) In the global economy, do you think the importance of Asia will grow in the future, remain the same, or diminish?	1. Grow	65.3	57.6		75.5
	2. Remain the same	29.3	26.8		18.3
	3. Diminish	5.4	4.1		4.4
	4. Do not know/No response	–	11.5		1.8

Source: "Multi-National Citizens' Poll on Current States Surrounding Korean Peninsula," *Tong-a Ilbo* (Seoul), December 4, 2000.

Note: South Korea: N = 2,000, survey conducted October 25–November 18, 2000. Japan: N = 3,000, survey conducted November 19–20, 2000. U.S.: N = 1,024, survey conducted November 13–18, 2000. China: N = 1,000, survey conducted November 1–10, 2000.

States "takes into account the interests of countries like yours?" On this question, negative answers accounted for those from 73 percent of South Korean respondents, 59 percent of Japanese respondents, and 70 percent of Russian respondents. One global issue that more or less united the three core countries of NEA was environmental pollution, not nuclear weapons or terrorism, as posing the greatest danger to the world: 70 percent of Chinese respondents; 55 percent of Japanese respondents; and 73 percent of South Korean respondents. One would have expected that at least a majority of South Korean respondents would have positively responded to the question, "Do you favor or oppose the U.S.-led war on terrorism?" especially given the fact that North Korea still remains on the U.S. list of terrorism-sponsoring rogue states. And yet a whopping 72 percent expressed their resounding "no." The findings of a *Time* magazine (European edition) Internet poll are even more revealing. The question, "Which country poses the greatest danger to world peace in 2003?" elicited the responses of some 318,000 votes with the following breakdown: North Korea, 7 percent; Iraq, 8 percent; and the United States, 84 percent.[95]

Such responses as described above can easily be used or misused to gener-

Table 1.15. NEA-5 in the Pew Global Attitudes Surveys, Late 2002 (%)

	U.S.	*China*	*Japan*	*ROK*	*Russia*
Q-1: How do you view the U.S.?					
a. Favorably			72	53	61
b. Unfavorably			26	44	33
c. Do not know/no response			2	3	6
Q-2: What is the greatest danger to the world?					
a. AIDs & infectious diseases	32	39	19	24	45
b. Religious & ethnic hatred	52	n/a	38	28	41
c. Nuclear weapons	59	26	68	30	38
d. Rich/poor gap	30	58	19	43	34
e. Pollution/environment	23	70	55	73	40
Q-3: In making international policy decisions, to what extent do you think the U.S. takes into account the interests of countries like (survey country)?					
a. Great deal/fair amount	75		36	23	21
b. Not much/not at all	20		59	73	70
c. Don't know	5		5	4	9
Q-4: Do you believe that the U.S. doesn't solve problems and increases the rich/poor gap?					
a. U.S. does too much/too little			60	65	54
b. U.S. increases gap			69	67	53
Q-5: Do you favor or oppose the U.S.-led war on terrorism?					
a. Favor			61	24	73
b. Oppose			52	72	16
Q-6: Do you think the world would be a safer place or a more dangerous place if there was another country equal in military power to the United States?					
a. Safer place	19		6	36	25
b. More dangerous	69		88	56	53
c. Don't know	12		6	8	22

Source: Adapted from *What the World Thinks in 2002* (Washington, D.C.: Pew Research Center for the People & the Press, 2002).

Note: United States: N=1,501; South Korea: N=719; Japan: N=702; Russia: N=1,002; China: N=3,000.

ate unwarranted generalizations or even destructive self-fulfilling prophecies that Northeast Asia is now culturally and cognitively primed for inevitable conflict or war. There is no denying that modern Chinese and Korean nationalism defined itself largely in opposition to Japan (as Berger argues in chapter 4) or that there remains a high degree of historical and national-identity animus and mutual distrust between Japanese and Koreans and between Chinese and Russians. Indeed, what seems unique to Northeast Asia is the immense distrust of Japan shared in varying degrees by Koreans, Chinese, and Russians.

Yet such a psychocultural approach seems to assume an absence of variation in state behavior that leaves nothing much to be explained. As cultural analyses of religion and ideology show, coherent, integrated, and consistent sets of normative assumptions, ideas, and axioms may have only tenuous linkages to observable behavioral choices.[96] Likewise, perception theory is plagued by the attitude/behavior problem. It is true that human behavior, including state behavior, tends to be patterned on a few core values and dominant perceptions. But it is equally true that a word/deed or perception/policy dichotomy exists in all state behavior—an inevitable corollary of the differential capabilities of human thought and rhetoric (which can easily transcend temporal and spatial bounds) and human behavior (which cannot). One of the most important findings to emerge from a collaborative project on learning in Soviet and American foreign policy is that a change in beliefs and perceptions does not necessarily result in a change of foreign policy; rather, policy change often takes place in the absence of a prior change in beliefs and perceptions, when political leaders pragmatically redefine their national interest with little or no reassessment of basic beliefs and goals.[97] State behavior—including national-identity projection—is often time- and situation-specific. (Astronaut Frank Borman, looking at planet Earth from 240,000 miles away, could confidently and fleetingly project a global human identity, "From out there it really is 'one world.'")

What all of this suggests is that it is generally easier to specify when policies changed than it is to establish a direct causal link with changes in beliefs. It is difficult to operationalize and measure the precise effects, if any exist, of changing public opinions on the making of foreign policy. Constructivist identity arguments, too, are not easy to define and operationalize in falsifiable terms. In the end, one is left with the puzzle or suspicion that a great many contingency and leadership factors are hiding behind any seemingly parsimonious explanation for the differences across NEA states in their foreign policy strategies. That is, political leadership combined with dominant or reprioritized geostrategic concerns ultimately matters more than changing public opinions and perceptions. The puzzle of Japan–South Korea alignment despite historical enmity is explained by Victor Cha with the concept of quasi-alliances in which the United States plays a critical, triangulating role in security bridge building. While historical animus may color interaction between Japan and Korea, "it is the larger geostrategic concerns that ultimately determine outcomes."[98] The unexpected and somewhat paradoxical blossoming of the Sino–Russian partnership in the post–Cold War era, which Lowell Dittmer in chapter 11 argues is "a real and lasting one, comparable in historical significance, perhaps, to the Franco–German reconciliation at the end of World War II," has little to do with shared identity. Rather, as Dittmer argues, it was contrived from the top down, through the diplomacy of careful, incremental bridge building.

Toward Synthetic Interactive Explanations

The three theoretical/analytical perspectives reviewed above command varying degrees of explanatory power. The findings of the volume's contributors cannot be explained adequately without reference to the material, institutional, and historical/ideational factors. That is to say, all three analytical paradigms offer some insights into the various dimensions and their interactive effects in various issue areas of NEA foreign policies, but none provides a completely satisfactory explanation of NEA's international politics as a whole. Regional and country-specific variations suggest that no one theory may be adequate. To fully capture the dynamic interplay of local, regional, and global forces at work in various issue areas requires more synthetic interactive explanations. In considering the question of Pyongyang's uncanny resilience and "the power of the weak" in the context of Northeast Asian geopolitics, there is no single monocausal explanation, but a consideration of multiple and mutually interactive influences can help us solve the puzzle.

Indeed, there has been such a move away from monocausal or single-level explanations toward a multifaceted and multidimensional approach to international conflict analysis in the post–Cold War era. We may do well to proceed from the premise that NEA's geopolitics and geoeconomics also have multiple issues and challenges underlying them. The progressive decay of the Westphalian sovereignty-bound world order, combined with the twin pressures of globalization from above and without and localization from below and within makes it all the more important that we take a synthetic, multidimensional approach to the study of Northeast Asian international politics. The synthetic interaction approach directly tackles the important yet understudied gaps between the different cultures of academe and government and between theory and practice in international relations.[99] As Peter Katzenstein and Muthia Alagappa, among others, have argued, "analytical eclecticism," not theoretical parsimony, is a more promising yet underexplored way of more fully capturing and explaining the complex links and interactions between power, interests, and norms underlying Asian international relations. Such synthetic interactive analyses of the many empirical puzzles and behavioral anomalies underlying the foreign policies of NEA states can be constructed through combining realist, liberal, and constructivist modes of explanation.[100]

WHITHER NORTHEAST ASIA?

Predicting the future of world politics, always hazardous, has never been more so than today, when the international system itself is undergoing profound and long-term transformation. One lesson of the sudden and unexpected demise of the Cold War and the Soviet Union is, as Robert Jervis and others have observed, that if past generalizations are no longer valid, they cannot provide a sure guide for the future. To a significant degree, the flow of world politics has become contingent or path-dependent, since certain unexpected events—such as the terrorist attacks on America of September 11, 2001—can easily force world politics along quite unexpected trajectories.[101] The difficulties of predicting the future shape of world politics are directly connected to the challenge of prognosticating on the future of NEA international politics, especially in the wake of the September 11 attacks.

That being said, however, we have little choice but to project a spectrum of plausible scenarios, if only to learn from egregious errors and then return to the drawing board to ascertain where and why they were made. As a result of the uneasy juxtaposition of continuities and changes, a new Northeast Asian regional order is emerging, with multiple pathways, complexities, and uncertainties and of indeterminate shape and content. The end of global bipolarity and the U.S.–China–USSR strategic triangle has not brought a new global and regional order. Although great power conflict and rivalries in traditional form have dissipated, uncertainties abound over the shape of the Northeast Asian regional order to come. Although the war on terrorism provided an opportunity for improving Russo–American and Sino–American relations, this improvement has not significantly altered the looming tensions and mistrust between the United States and China over the Taiwan Strait conflict or other substantive strategic issues of contention between them. Nor has the war on terrorism improved America's allied relations with Japan and South Korea.

As elucidated by Lowell Dittmer in chapter 11, what is most striking about post–Cold War Northeast Asia is not the emergence of a coherent "new order" but rather the extent to which political and economic developments have contravened to bring about at least four competing pathways and paradigms in the emerging regional order: the blossoming of Sino-Russian partnership, the collapse of any coherent strategic structure among the Big Four, the failure of any political or economic community to take shape, and the intractability of the region's explosive "hot spots" (the Korean peninsula and the Taiwan Strait).

There are also a variety of "futurible" scenarios for the creation of a new regional order: a hegemonic model (whether Sino-centric or America-centric), an intraregional balance-of-power model, a "concert of powers" condominial model, a collective security model, and an Asia–Pacific or East Asian economic community model.[102] The most fundamental question seems simple and clear enough: What kind of regional order do the countries of Northeast Asia themselves wish to conceive and create?

The principal finding emerging from this volume is that the state is still the primary agent driving NEA's international politics. Successfully coping with today's multiple challenges requires an effective strategy for choosing among various competing and constantly evolving options, in the correct sequence, even as the state, precariously balanced between domestic and international politics, is constrained simultaneously by what external globalization agents and pressures will accept and what domestic constituencies will ratify. The role of state adaptability is crucial in this respect. More than ever before in human history, the rise or fall of an effective state, even a "great power," seems closely keyed to and determined by the speed with which the state can establish a fruitful congruence between domestic and foreign policies amid the changing trends and requirements of regionalization cum globalization.

The challenge for the uncertain years ahead is therefore neither making a false choice between regionalization and globalization nor seeking an alternative supranational regional or global organization, but finding a greater synergy among the many types of state and nonstate actors in order to collaborate for more effective prevention, regulation, and resolution of simmering conflict in the two regional flashpoints, while simultaneously expanding multilateral dialogues and economic integration as vehicles for order-building and problem solving.

NOTES

1. In the latest *Quadrennial Defense Review* (QDR) *Report*, "Northeast Asia" along with "the East Asian littoral" are defined as "critical areas" for precluding hostile domina-

tion by any other power. See Department of Defense, *Quadrennial Defense Review Report*, September 30, 2001, 2 (hereafter cited as *QDRR2001*) at www.defenselink.mil/pubs/gdr2001.pdf (accessed on January 15, 2002).

2. According to the purchasing power parity (PPP) estimates of the World Bank (which are problematic), China, with a 1994 gross domestic product (GDP) of just under $3 trillion, has become the second-largest economy in the world, after the United States. See *Economist*, January 27, 1996, 102; World Bank, *World Development Report, 1996* (New York: Oxford University Press, 1996), 188.

3. See Robert Jervis, "The Impact of the Korean War on the Cold War," *Journal of Conflict Resolution*, 24, no. 4 (December 1980): 563–92.

4. See Jianwei Wang, "Territorial Disputes and Asian Security: Sources, Management, and Prospects," in *Asian Security Order: Instrumental and Normative Features*, ed. Muthiah Alagappa (Stanford, Calif.: Stanford University Press, 2003), 385.

5. Peter J. Katzenstein, "Introduction: Asian Regionalism in Comparative Perspective," in *Network Power: Japan and Asia*, ed. Peter J. Katzenstein and Takashi Shiraishi (Ithaca, N.Y.: Cornell University Press, 1997), 12.

6. See Richard J. Ellings and Aaron L. Friedberg, eds., *Strategic Asia 2002–03: Asian Aftershocks* (Seattle: National Bureau of Asian Research, 2002), 396.

7. "A Survey of Asian Finance," *Economist*, February 8, 2003, 15.

8. See "Armed Conflicts and Fatalities 1945–1994," in *Military Balance 1997/98* (London: International Institute for Strategic Studies, 1997).

9. Viktor N. Pavliatenko, "Russian Security in the Pacific Asian Region: The Dangers of Isolation," in *Russia and East Asia: The 21st Century Security Environment*, ed. Gilbert Rozman, Mikhail G. Nosov, and Koji Watanabe (Armonk, N.Y.: Sharpe, 1999), 20–21.

10. Thomas Friedman, *The Lexus and the Olive Tree* (New York: Farrar Straus Giroux, 1999), 7–8.

11. For further discussion in the context of South Korea and East Asia, see Samuel S. Kim, ed., *Korea's Globalization* (New York: Cambridge University Press, 2000) and *East Asia and Globalization* (Lanham, Md.: Rowman & Littlefield, 2000).

12. John Ravenhill, *APEC and the Construction of Pacific Rim Regionalism* (New York: Cambridge University Press, 2001), 43.

13. Ernst Haas, *The Obsolescence of Regional Integration Theory* (Berkeley: Institute of International Studies, University of California, 1975); Samuel S. Kim, "Regional Associations: Political," in *Encyclopedia of Government and Politics*, vol. 2, ed. M. Hawkesworth and M. Kogan (London: Routledge, 1992), 982–1001; and Michael Schultz, Fredrik Soderbaum, and Joakim Ojendal eds., *Regionalization in a Globalizing World: A Comparative Perspective on Forms, Actors and Process* (London: Zed, 2001).

14. Haas, *The Obsolescence*, 6.

15. Stephen D. Krasner, ed., *International Regimes* (Ithaca, N.Y.: Cornell University Press, 1983).

16. Louise Fawcett and Andrew Hurrell, eds., *Regionalism in World Politics: Regional Organization and International Order* (Oxford: Oxford University Press, 1995); Peter J. Katzenstein, Natasha Hamilton-Hart, Kozo Kato, and Ming Yue, eds., *Asian Regionalism* (Ithaca, N.Y.: East Asia Program, Cornell University, 2000).

17. See Samuel S. Kim and Abraham Kim, "Conflict Management," in *Encyclopaedia of Government and Politics*, 2d ed., ed. Mary Hawkesworth and Maurice Kogan (London: Routledge, forthcoming).

18. David Held, Anthony McGrew, David Goldblatt, and Jonathan Perraton, *Global Transformations: Politics, Economics and Culture* (Stanford, Calif.: Stanford University Press, 1999), 74–77; Charles Oman, *Globalisation and Regionalisation: The Challenge for Developing Countries* (Paris: Organization for Economic Cooperation and Development, 1994).

19. Michael Schultz, Fredrik Soderbaum, and Joakim Ojendal, "Introduction: A Framework for Understanding Regionalization," in *Regionalization in a Globalizing World*, 4–5; and James Mittleman and Richard Falk, "Global Hegemony and Regionalism," in *Regionalism in the Post–Cold War World*, ed. Stephen C. Calleya (Burlington, Mass.: Ashgate 2000), 19–20.

20. Bruce Russett, *International Regions and the International System* (Chicago: Rand McNally, 1967); Andrew Hurrell, "Regionalism in Theoretical Perspective," in *Regionalism in World Politics Regional Organization and International Order*, ed. Louise Fawcett and Andrew Hurrell (Oxford: Oxford University Press, 1995), 38.

21. Michael Ng-Quinn, "The Internationalization of the Region: The Case of Northeast Asian International Relations," *Review of International Studies* 12 (1986): 107–125.

22. The exclusion of the United States is one of the major shortcomings of the otherwise excellent book, Tsuneo Akaha, ed., *Politics and Economics in Northeast Asia: Nationalism and Regionalism in Contention* (New York: St. Martin's, 1999).

23. Barry Buzan, "The Asia–Pacific: What Sort of Region in What Sort of World?" in *Asia–Pacific in the New World Order*, ed. Anthony McGrew and Christopher Brook (London: Routledge 1998), 70.

24. For a succinct definition and differentiation of "globalism" and "globalization," see James N. Rosenau, "The Dynamics of Globalization: Toward an Operational Formulation," *Security Dialogue* 27, no. 3 (1996): 247–62.

25. John Ravenhill, "The Growth of Intergovernmental Collaboration in the Asia–Pacific Region," in *Asia–Pacific in the New World Order*, ed. Anthony McGrew and Christopher Brook (London: Routledge 1998), 250–51.

26. Peter J. Katzenstein, "Varieties of Asian Regionalisms," in *Asian Regionalism*, ed. Peter J. Katzenstein, Natasha Hamilton-Hart, Kozo Kato, and Ming Yue (Ithaca, N.Y.: East Asia Program, Cornell University 2000), 1.

27. Katzenstein, "Varieties of Asian Regionalism," 17–18.

28. Akaha, *Politics and Economics*, xxiii.

29. Yoshinobu Yamamoto, *Globalism, Regionalism & Nationalism: Asia in Search of Its Role in the 21st Century* (Malden, Mass.: Blackwell, 1999).

30. Ravenhill, "Growth of Intergovernmental Collaboration," 260–61.

31. Alastair Iain Johnston and Paul Evans, "China's Engagement with Multilateral Security Institutions," in *Engaging China: The Management of an Emerging Power*, ed. Alastair Iain Johnston and Robert S. Ross (London: Routledge 1999), 257 (emphasis in original).

32. Douglas Webber, "Two Funerals and a Wedding? The Ups and Downs of Regionalism in East Asia and Asia–Pacific after the Asian Crisis," *Pacific Review* 14, no. 3 (2001): 359.

33. Paul Evans, "Reinventing East Asia: Multilateral Cooperation and Regional Order," *Harvard International Review* 18, no. 2 (Spring 1996): 17.

34. For realist analyses along this line, with some variations, see Richard K. Betts,

"Wealth, Power, and Instability: East Asia and the United States after the Cold War," *International Security* 18, no. 3 (Winter 1993–1994): 34–77; Aaron L. Friedberg, "Ripe for Rivalry: Prospects for Peace in a Multipolar Asia," *International Security* 18, no. 3 (Winter 1993–1994): 5–33; Friedberg, "Will Europe's Past Be Asia's Future?" *Survival* 42, no. 3 (Autumn 2000): 147–59; and Barry Buzan and Gerald Segal, "Rethinking East Asian Security," *Survival* 36, no. 2 (Summer 1994): 3–21.

35. Samuel P. Huntington, *The Clash of Civilizations and the Remaking of World Order* (New York: Simon and Schuster, 1996), 238.

36. This is the conclusion of his latest book, *The Tragedy of Great Power Politics* (New York: Norton, 2001), 401–2.

37. Richard Bernstein and Ross H. Monro, *The Coming Conflict with China* (New York: Knopf, 1997), 4.

38. On power transitions, see Robert Gilpin, *War and Change in World Politics* (Cambridge: Cambridge University Press, 1981); A. F. K. Organski, *World Politics* (New York: Knopf, 1968), chapter 14; Joshua Goldstein, *Long Cycles: Prosperity and War in the Modern Age* (New Haven: Yale University Press, 1988); George Modelski, "The Long Cycle of Global Politics and the Nation-State," *Comparative Studies in Society and History* 20 (April 1978), 214–35; William Thompson, *On Global War: Historical–Structural Approaches to World Politics* (Columbia: University of South Carolina, 1988); Paul Kennedy, *The Rise and Fall of the Great Powers: Economic Change and Military Conflict from 1500 to 2000* (New York: Random House, 1987); Jacek Kugler and A. F. K. Organski, "The Power Transition: A Retrospective and Prospective Evaluation," in *Handbook of War Studies*, ed. Manus I. Midlarsky (Boston: Unwin Hyman, 1989), 171–94; and Charles Kupchan, *The Vulnerability of Empire* (Ithaca, N.Y.: Cornell, 1994).

39. William C. Wohlforth, "The Stability of a Unipolar World," *International Security* 24, no. 1 (Summer 1999): 5–41.

40. For the unipolar moment thesis, see Charles Krauthammer, "The Unipolar Moment," *Foreign Affairs* 70, no. 1 (1991). For the alarmist and sensational account of the rise-of-China argument, see Richard Bernstein and Ross H. Monroe, *The Coming Conflict with China* (New York: Knopf, 1997).

41. Charles Krauthammer, "The New Unilateralism," *Washington Post*, June 8, 2001.

42. The German case illustrates how national roles can change over time. German nationalism quickly withered away after World War II, whereas previous defeats (1806 and 1918) had only fueled more radical nationalism. Harold James finds an explanation in the changing international milieu—the changing international normative cycle—that molded national role expectations. See Harold James, *A German Identity, 1770–1990* (New York: Routledge, 1989).

43. Bruce Russett and John Oneal, *Triangulating Peace: Democracy, Interdependence, and International Organizations* (New York: Norton, 2001), 275.

44. Avery Goldstein, "Great Expectations: Interpreting China's Arrival," *International Security* 22, no. 3 (Winter 1997–1998): 73.

45. You Ji, "The PLA, the CCP and the Formulation of Chinese Defense and Foreign Policy," in *Power and Responsibility in Chinese Foreign Policy*, ed. Yongjin Zhang and Greg Austin (Canberra: Asia Pacific, 2001), 119–20.

46. Alastair Iain Johnston, "China's Militarized Interstate Dispute Behaviour 1949–1992: A First Cut at the Data," *China Quarterly* 153 (March 1998): 1–30; quote at p. 29.

47. Samuel Huntington, "The Lonely Superpower," *Foreign Affairs* 78, no. 2 (March–April 1999), 41.

48. See "Status of Multilateral Treaties Deposited with the Secretary-General" at untreaty.un.org/English/access.asp (accessed January 15, 2003).

49. *What the World Thinks in 2002* (Washington, D.C.: Pew Research Center for the People & the Press, 2002).

50. For a detailed analysis, see Michael Pillsbury, *China Debates the Future Security Environment* (Washington, D.C.: National Defense University Press, 2000), chapter 5 (203–253).

51. See Andrew Mack, "Why Big Nations Lose Small Wars: The Politics of Asymmetric Conflict," *World Politics* 27, no. 2 (January 1975): 175–200; John Anquilla, *Dubious Battles: Aggression, Defeat, and the International System* (Washington, D.C.: Crane and Russak, 1992); T. V. Paul, *Asymmetric Conflicts: War Initiation by Weaker Powers* (New York: Cambridge University Press, 1994); Thomas Christensen, "Posing Problems without Catching Up: China's Rise and Challenges for U.S. Security Policy," *International Security* 25, no. 4 (Spring 2001): 5–40.

52. Ivan Arreguin-Toft, "How the Weak Win Wars: A Theory of Asymmetric Conflict," *International Security* 26, no. 1 (Summer 2001): 96.

53. *Renmin ribao* (People's Daily), September 3, 1999, 1.

54. Richard Ned Lebow, *Between Peace and War: The Nature of International Crisis* (Baltimore: Johns Hopkins University Press, 1981), 57–97.

55. Habeeb argues that "issue-specific structural power is the most critical component of power in asymmetrical negotiation." William Habeeb, *Power and Tactics in International Negotiation: How Weak Nations Bargain with Strong Nations* (Baltimore: Johns Hopkins University Press, 1988), 21, 130.

56. According to Gen. Gary Luck, former commander of U.S. Forces Korea, another Korean war would cost $1 trillion in economic damage and one million human casualties, including 52,000 U.S. military casualties. Cited in Victor D. Cha and David C. Kang, "The Korea Crisis," *Foreign Policy*, no. 136 (May–June 2003): 24.

57. For an analysis along this line, see Samuel S. Kim, "North Korea and Northeast Asia in World Politics," in *North Korea and Northeast Asia*, ed. Samuel S. Kim and Tai Hwan Lee, 3–58 (Lanham, Md.: Rowman & Littlefield, 2002), especially 47–51.

58. Barry Buzan, "Security, the State, the 'New World Order,' and Beyond," in *On Security*, ed. Ronnie D. Lipschutz (New York: Columbia University Press, 1998), chapter 7.

59. Jack Levy, "Theories of Interstate and Intrastate War: A Levels-of-Analysis Approach," in *Turbulent Peace: The Challenges of Managing International Conflict*, ed. Chester A. Crocker, Fen Osler Hampson, and Pamela Aall (Washington, D.C.: United States Institute of Peace, 2001), 3–27; K. J. Holsti, *The State, War, and the State of War* (New York: Cambridge University Press, 1996).

60. See Robert Litwak, "What's in a Name? The Changing Foreign Policy Lexicon," *Journal of International Affairs* 54, no. 2 (Spring 2001): 375–92, and Robert Litwak, *Rogue States and U.S. Foreign Policy* (Baltimore: Johns Hopkins University Press, 2000).

61. Cited in Vernon Leob and Peter Slevin, "Overcoming North Korea's 'Tyranny of Proximity,'" *Washington Post*, January 20, 2003, A16.

62. David Sanger, "Bush Finds That Ambiguity Is Part of Nuclear Deterrence," *New*

York Times, March 18, 2002; see also Nicholas D. Kristof, "Flirting with Disaster," *New York Times*, February 14, 2003, A31.

63. *QDRR2001*, 4.

64. *QDRR2001*, 2.

65. Lowell Dittmer, "East Asia in the 'New Era' in World Politics," *World Politics* 55, no. 1 (October 2002): 48–49.

66. For details, see Robert Keohane, *International Institutions and State Power: Essays in International Relations Theory* (Boulder, Colo.: Westview, 1989); Krasner, *International Regimes*.

67. See Jack S. Levy, "The Causes of War: A Review of Theories and Evidence," in *Behavior, Society, and Nuclear War* vol. I, ed. Philip E. Tetlock et al. (New York: Oxford University Press, 1989), 270. See also Michael Doyle, "Liberalism and World Politics," *American Political Science Review* 80, no. 4 (December 1986): 1151–69; Bruce Russett, *Grasping the Democratic Peace: Principles for a Post–Cold War World* (Princeton: Princeton University Press, 1993); David A. Lake, "Powerful Pacifists: Democratic States and War," *American Political Science Review* 86, no. 1 (1992): 24–37; and James Lee Ray, "The Democratic Path to Peace," *Journal of Democracy* 8, no. 2 (April 1997): 49–64.

68. For the most well-tested and well-documented study of Kantian liberalism, see Bruce Russett and John Oneal, *Triangulating Peace: Democracy, Interdependence and International Organizations* (New York: Norton, 2001).

69. James Brooke, "Korea Feeling Pressure as China Grows," *New York Times*, January 8, 2003, W1, W7.

70. World Bank, *World Development Report 1991: The Challenge of Development* (New York: Oxford University Press, 1991), 12 (fig. 1.1).

71. Johnston was the first to bring this much-ignored fact to our attention. See Alastair Iain Johnston, "Engaging Myths: Misconceptions about China and Its Global Role," *Harvard Asia Pacific Review* (Winter 1997–1998): 9–12.

72. World Bank, *World Development Report 2003* (New York: Oxford University Press, 2003), 240–41 (tab. 4).

73. WTO Press Release, April 23, 2003, "World Trade Figures 2002: Trade Recovered in 2002, but Uncertainty Continues," World Trade Organization website, at www.wto.org/english/res_e/statis_statis_e.htm (accessed April 28, 2003).

74. Nicholas Lardy, *Integrating China into the Global Economy* (Washington, D.C.: Brookings Institution, 2002), 176.

75. Joseph Kahn, "China's Hot, at Least for Now," *New York Times*, December 16, 2002.

76. Economist Intelligence Unit (EIU), *Country Profile 2001: China* (London: EIU, 2001), 57.

77. *Renmin ribao* (People's Daily), January 15, 2003.

78. Robert Scollay and John P. Gilbert, *New Regional Trading Arrangements in the Asia Pacific?* (Washington, D.C.: Institute for International Economics, May 2001).

79. For an elaboration of the theoretical and policy implications, see Kenneth A. Oye, "Explaining Cooperation under Anarchy: Hypotheses and Strategies," *World Politics* 38, no. 1 (October 1985): 1–24.

80. Richard Stubbs, "ASEAN Plus Three: Emerging East Asian Regionalism?" *Asian Survey* 42, no. 3 (May–June 2002): 440–55.

81. Joshua Kurlantzick, "Is East Asia Integrating?" *Washington Quarterly* 24, no. 4 (Autumn 2001): 23.

82. For fuller discussion and elaboration, see Samuel S. Kim, ed., *East Asia and Globalization* (Lanham, Md.: Rowman & Littlefield, 2000).

83. For a detailed analysis see Samuel S. Kim, ed., *Korea's Globalization* (New York: Cambridge University Press, 2000).

84. William Bloom, *Personal Identity, National Identity and International Relations* (New York: Cambridge University Press, 1990); Lowell Dittmer and Samuel Kim, eds., *China's Quest for National Identity* (Ithaca, N.Y.: Cornell University Press, 1993); Peter Katzenstein, ed., *The Culture of National Security: Norms and Identity in World Politics* (New York: Columbia University Press, 1996); Jill Krause and Neil Renwick, eds. *Identities in International Relations* (New York: St. Martin's, 1996); Yosef Lapid and Friedrich Kratochwil, eds., *The Return of Culture and Identity in IR Theory* (Boulder, Colo.: Rienner, 1996); Ilya Prizel, *National Identity and Foreign Policy: Nationalism and Leadership in Poland, Russia and Ukraine* (New York: Cambridge University Press, 1998); Rodney Bruce Hall, *National Collective Identity: Social Constructs and International Systems* (New York: Columbia University Press, 1999); Alexander Wendt, *Social Theory of International Politics* (New York: Cambridge University Press, 1999); and Samuel Huntington, *The Clash of Civilizations and the Remaking of World Order* (New York: Simon & Schuster, 1996).

85. For a full elaboration of such synthetic theory of national identity, see Lowell Dittmer and Samuel S. Kim, "In Search of a Theory of National Identity," in *China's Quest for National Identity*, ed. Lowell Ditmer and Samuel Kim (Ithaca, N.Y.: Cornell University Press, 1993), 1–31.

86. According to Consuelo Cruz, "Collective memory, by its very nature, impels actors to define themselves intersubjectively. Shaped by past struggles and shared historical accidents, collective memory is both a common discriminating experience and a 'factual' recollection of the group's past 'as it really was.'" Consuelo Cruz, "Identity and Persuasion: How Nations Remember Their Pasts and Make Their Futures," *World Politics* 52 (April 2000): 276.

87. See Masaru Tamamoto, "Japan's Uncertain Role," *World Policy Journal* 8 (Fall 1991): 584–85.

88. Allen S. Whiting, *China Eyes Japan* (Berkeley: University of California Press, 1989).

89. Howard W. French, "Japan Now Officially Hails the Emperor and a Rising Sun," *New York Times*, August 10, 1999, A3.

90. Michael Green, "Why Tokyo Will Be a Larger Player in Asia," Nautilus's Northeast Asia Peace and Security Network: Special Report, July 31, 2000.

91. Celeste Wallander, "Wary of the West: Russian Security Policy at the Millennium," *Arms Control Today* 30, no. 2 (March 2000): 7–12; "Russia's New Security Concept," *Arms Control Today* 30, no. 1 (January/February 2000): 15–20; Philipp C. Bleak, "Putin Signs New Military Doctrine, Fleshing Out New Security Concept," *Arms Control Today* 30, no. 4 (May 2000): 42.

92. Ronald Grigor, "Provisional Stabilities: The Politics of Identities in Post-Soviet Eurasia," *International Security* 24, no. 3 (Winter 1999–2000): 149.

93. Gilbert Rozman, "Mutual Perceptions among the Great Powers in Northeast Asia," in *Politics and Economics in Northeast Asia: Nationalism and Regionalism in Contention*, ed. Tsuneo Akaha (New York: St. Martin's, 1999), 47.

94. Chung-in Moon and Judy E. Chung, "Conclusion: Reconstructing New Identity and Peace in East Asia," in *History, Cognition and Peace in East Asia*, ed. Dalchoong Kim and Chung-in Moon (Seoul: Yonsei University Press, 1997), 269.

95. Cited in Nicholas Kristof, "Flogging the French," *New York Times*, January 31, 2003, A29.

96. See Edmund S. Glenn et al., "A Cognitive Interaction Model to Analyze Culture Conflict in International Relations," *Journal of Conflict Resolution* 14, no. 1 (1970): 35–50 and David Laitin, "Political Culture and Political Preferences," *American Political Science Review* 82, no. 2 (1988): 589–93.

97. George Breslauer and Philip Tetlocks, eds., *Learning in U.S. and Soviet Foreign Policy* (Boulder, Colo.: Westview, 1991).

98. Victor D. Cha, *Alignment Despite Antagonism: The United States–Korea–Japan Security Triangle* (Stanford, Calif.: Stanford University Press, 1999), 231.

99. Alexander George, *Bridging the Gap* (Washington, D.C.: United States Institute of Peace, 1993).

100. Peter J. Katzenstein and Nobuo Okawara, "Japan, Asia–Pacific Security, and the Case of Analytical Eclecticism," *International Security* 26, no. 3 (Winter 2001–2002): 153–85; and Muthia Alagappa, "Rethinking Security: A Critical Review and Appraisal of the Debate," in Muthia Alagappa, ed., *Asian Security Practice: Material and Ideational Influences* (Stanford, Calif.: Stanford University Press, 1998), 61–62.

101. Robert Jervis, "The Future of World Politics: Will It Resemble the Past?" *International Security* 16, no. 3 (Winter 1991–1992): 42–45.

102. Alagappa, ed., *Asian Security Order*.

FURTHER READING

Akaha, Tsuneo, ed. *Politics and Economics in Northeast Asia: Nationalism and Regionalism in Contention*. New York: St. Martin's, 1999.

Alagappa, Muthia, ed. *Asian Security Practice: Material and Ideational Influences*. Stanford, Calif.: Stanford University Press, 1998.

———, ed. *Asian Security Order: Instrumental and Normative Features*. Stanford, Calif.: Stanford University Press, 2003.

Calleya, Stephen C., ed. *Regionalism in the Post–Cold War World*. Burlington, Mass.: Ashgate, 2000.

Cha, Victor D. *Alignment Despite Antagonism: The United States–Korea–Japan Security Triangle*. Stanford, Calif.: Stanford University Press, 1999.

Dent, Christopher, and David W. F. Huang, eds. *Northeast Asian Regionalism: Learning from the European Experience*. London: Routledge, 2002.

Dittmer, Lowell. "East Asia in the 'New Era' in World Politics." *World Politics* 55, no. 1 (October 2002): 38–65.

Ellings, Richard J., and Aaron L. Friedberg, eds. *Strategic Asia 2002–03: Asian Aftershocks*. Seattle: National Bureau of Asian Research, 2002.

Evans, Paul. "Reinventing East Asia: Multilateral Cooperation and Regional Order." *Harvard International Review* 18, no. 2 (Spring 1996): 16–19, 68–69.

Fawcett, Louise, and Andrew Hurrell, eds. *Regionalism in World Politics: Regional Organization and International Order*. New York: Oxford University Press, 1995.

Gurtov, Mel. *Pacific Asia? Prospects for Security and Cooperation in East Asia*. Lanham, Md.: Rowman & Littlefield, 2002.

Hettne, Bjorn, Andras Inotai, and Osvaldo Sunkel, eds. *Globalism and the New Regionalism*. New York: St. Martin's, 1999.

Johnston, Alastair Iain, and Robert S. Ross, eds. *Engaging China: The Management of an Emerging Power*. London: Routledge, 1999.

Katzenstein, Peter J., and Takashi Shiraishi, eds. *Network Power: Japan and Asia*. Ithaca, N.Y.: Cornell University Press, 1997.

Katzenstein, Peter J., Natasha Hamilton-Hart, Kozo Kato, and Ming Yue, eds. *Asian Regionalism*. Ithaca, N.Y.: East Asia Program, Cornell University, 2000.

Kim, Dalchoong, and Chung-in Moon, eds. *History, Cognition and Peace in East Asia*. Seoul: Yonsei University Press, 1997.

Kim, Samuel S., ed. *North Korean Foreign Relations in the Post–Cold War Era*. New York: Oxford University Press, 1998.

———, ed. *East Asia and Globalization*. Lanham, Md.: Rowman & Littlefield, 2000.

———, ed. *Korea's Globalization*. New York: Cambridge University Press, 2000.

Kurlantzick, Joshua. "Is East Asia Integrating?" *Washington Quarterly* 24, no. 4 (Autumn 2001): 19–28.

Kwon, Youngmin. *Regional Community-Building in East Asia*. Seoul: Yonsei University Press, 2002.

McGrew, Anthony, and Christopher Brook, eds. *Asia–Pacific in the New World Order*. London: Routledge, 1998.

Ng-Quinn, Michael. "The Internationalization of the Region: The Case of Northeast Asian International Relations," *Review of International Studies* 12 (1986): 107–25.

Ravenhill, John. *APEC and the Construction of Pacific Rim Regionalism*. New York: Cambridge University Press, 2001.

Rozman, Gilbert. "Flawed Regionalism: Reconceptualizing Northeast Asia in the 1990s," *Pacific Review* 11, no. 1 (1998): 1–27.

Rozman, Gilbert, Mikhail G. Nosov, and Koji Watanabe, eds. *Russia and East Asia: The 21st Century Security Environment*. Armonk, N.Y.: M. E. Sharpe, 1999.

Scollay, Robert, and John P. Gilbert. *New Regional Trading Arrangements in the Asia Pacific?* Washington, D.C.: Institute for International Economics, May 2001.

Stubbs, Richard. "ASEAN Plus Three: Emerging East Asian Regionalism?" *Asian Survey* 42, no. 3 (May–June 2002): 440–55.

What the World Thinks in 2002. Washington, D.C.: Pew Research Center for the People & the Press, 2002.

Yamamoto, Yoshinobu. *Globalism, Regionalism & Nationalism: Asia in Search of Its Role in the 21st Century*. Malden, Mass.: Blackwell, 1999.

Zhang, Yongjin, and Greg Austin. eds. *Power and Responsibility in Chinese Foreign Policy*. Canberra: Asia Pacific, 2001.

II

MAJOR POWER INTERACTION

2

China's International Relations: The Political and Security Dimensions

Alastair Iain Johnston

In most aspects of its diplomacy, the People's Republic of China is more integrated into, and more cooperative inside, regional and global political and economic systems than ever before. Yet there is growing uneasiness among key decision makers in various Northeast Asian governments, specifically in the United States, Japan, and Taiwan, about the implications of "rising" Chinese power. Since the 1990s, in particular, the dominant discourse has been that China is outside the "international community" and that it needs to be pulled inside, or that it hasn't yet demonstrated sufficiently that it will "play by the rules." Many of the sharpest policy debates in the United States and, increasingly, in Japan and elsewhere have been over whether it is even possible to socialize a dictatorial, nationalistic, and dissatisfied China within this putative international community. To simplify, engagers argue it is already happening, though mainly in the sphere of economic norms (free trade, domestic marketization). Skeptics conclude either that it isn't happening, due to the nature of the regime, or that it could not possibly happen because China is a rising power that by definition is dissatisfied with the U.S.-dominated global and regional orders.

This chapter explores whether the indicators of the Chinese leadership's satisfaction (or indicators of no major dissatisfaction) with various global orders are replicated in fundamental attitudes toward Northeast Asian political and security affairs. The chapter first develops some concrete indicators for determining the degree to which a state challenges extant "rules of the game" in world politics. It then applies these to Chinese diplomacy and argues that globally and locally in most respects the PRC today exhibits greater levels of "status quo-ness" than ever before. It then examines two general hypotheses about why, given China's level of status quo-ness, there is a growing perception that in fact it is an increasingly revisionist state in Northeast Asia (and indeed globally). One hypothesis focuses on the Chinese leadership's interests, the other on domestically determined changes in perceptions of Chinese interests among actors in Northeast Asia. The chapter concludes that a third (hybrid) hypothesis—one in which China's limited revisionism, primarily on the Taiwan issue, interacts with changes in regional perceptions—makes the most sense. The effect of this interaction may be an emerging security dilemma in which China's level of satisfaction is in flux and may decline as or if the dilemma intensifies.

THE QUESTION OF CHINA'S "STATUS QUO-NESS"[1]

A common characterization of China in the past decade or so in the United States and elsewhere is that it is operating outside of, or only partly inside, the "international community" on a range of international norms. This assessment assumes, of course, that there *is* a well-defined extant international community and that this community shares common norms and values. But what does it mean to be a status quo or non–status quo power in international relations in the early twenty-first century?[2] Despite the centrality of the terms in international relations theorizing, and often in policy discourses, they tend to be undertheorized and vaguely defined. For Morgenthau, the father of modern realism, a status quo policy is opposed to any "reversal of the power relations among two or more nations, reducing, for instance, A from a first rate to a second rate power and raising B to the eminent position A formerly held." Any rising state is by definition a revisionist one as much as it wants to increase its power and change the global distribution.

Power transition theorists Organski and Kugler define status quo states as those that have participated in designing the "rules of the game" and stand to benefit from these rules. "Challengers" (e.g., revisionist states) want a "new place for themselves in international society" that is commensurate with their power, and they have a "desire to redraft the rules by which relations among nations work."[3]

Gilpin is more precise than other realists. He breaks down the "rules of the game" into somewhat more discrete components: the distribution of power, the hierarchy of prestige (which for realists, however, tends to be coterminus with the distribution of power), and "rights and rules that govern or at least influence the interactions among states."[4] Revisionist states push for *systemic* change; that is they demand fundamental changes in these components. Anything less and it becomes problematic calling the state revisionist or non–status quo.

It is unclear how one would operationalize these realist theorists' components to determine across the totality of a state's foreign policy preferences and actions whether the state is status quo or revisionist.[5] But as a first cut there are at least three indicators by which one can assess whether any particular actor is outside a "status quo" community.[6]

The first indicator might be, at its simplest, that a non–status quo actor is one that could be but simply isn't involved in the many international institutions that help constitute and mediate the relationships of the international community. On this score, China's membership in international institutions and organizations has increased steadily and quite dramatically in the post-Maoist period. From the mid-1960s to 2000, China moved from virtual isolation from international organizations to membership numbers approaching about 80 percent of those of the major industrialized states, and around 160 percent of the world average.[7] In addition, the percentage of treaties that China has joined relative to the number of multilateral treaties it has been eligible to join in any particular year has increased over time. This captures the *willingness* of China's leaders to participate in institutions. For example, for most of the 1970s China had signed on to fewer than 30 percent of the arms control regimes it was eligible to join. But by the mid-1990s, this figure had climbed to about 80 percent.

In Northeast Asia, there is really only one major intergovernmental security institution—the ASEAN Regional Forum (ARF). While its name indicates the geographical center of gravity of its substantive concerns, some of the ARF's confidence-building activities do spill over into Northeast Asian relationships. By most accounts China has, in relative terms, become an active and constructive member of the ARF since its founding in 1994. The only other institution that might constitute a multilateral security institution, by dint of its informal purpose of cementing a deal to restrain North Korean nuclear weapons development, is the Korean Peninsula Energy Development Organization (KEDO). China is not a member, but supports KEDO's operations. In any event, the institution's day-to-day function is not security, but energy development.

A second indicator of "non–status quo-ness" might be that although the actor participates in international institutions, it breaks the rules and norms of the community once inside these institutions (willfully, as opposed to doing so simply due to the lack of capacity to comply). The problem is that if one looks carefully at some of the major international regimes, or commonly identified clusters of international norms, the question of compliance becomes very complicated very quickly.

With regard to human rights, there are two questions: the first is, How should the "international community's" views on human rights be defined? If one uses a simple majority criterion—what the majority of states do about China's human rights practices—it should be noted that in the one major UN human rights forum where states can criticize other states, the United Nations Commission on Human Rights (UNCHR) in Geneva, the PRC can usually put together a majority coalition of states to support a "no decision resolution" that essentially kills any resolution critical of Chinese practices. Thus this criterion would place China on the inside of the international community and its human rights regime. While three of the five major Northeast Asian states are democracies, there is no consensus among them on how to respond to Chinese human rights conditions. In the UNCHR South Korea abstained on every no-decision vote on resolutions critical of the PRC; Russia opposed the no-decision resolutions through 1996, abstained in 1996 and 1997, and voted for the resolution (with the PRC) from 1999 to 2001. Only Japan and the United States have consistently opposed the no-decision vote. In 2003, even the United States did not propose a critical resolution, due to China's support for the U.S. war on terrorism.

If one uses the constitutional practices of the majority of states in the international system as a criterion, however, China would be outside the international community, but barely. A small majority of states in the international system function as constitutional democracies, but a large minority function as dictatorships or autocracies.[8] If one uses the practices of the states that constitute Northeast Asia as a criterion, then China is more obviously in the minority, since five of seven governments are democratically elected. Despite this, however, the PRC regime does not appear particularly threatened by democratic or democratizing regimes in the region. It is certainly not trying to reverse this distribution.[9]

A second question is: What defines the content of the international human rights regime? Technically, based on perhaps the most comprehensive, authoritative consensus statement of the content of the international human rights regime—the Vienna Conference Declaration of 1993—the "international community" recognizes the equal status of individual political civil liberties and collective social and economic rights (e.g., the right to development). There is no doubt that Chinese authorities, whether central or local governments, routinely violate both political and legal rights guaranteed by the Chinese constitution and by the human rights agreements that China has signed. The question is whether its performance on the other half of the international regime—social and economic rights—is equally egregious. This becomes a very tricky ideological question, since it requires judging whether socioeconomic advances, mainly in urban China, should be counted as gains in social and economic rights, or whether growing income inequality and environmental degradation, and the absence of equitable education, welfare, and health systems, mainly in rural China, violate social and economic rights. Interestingly enough, the United States is the only Northeast Asian actor that pushes the political definition in its diplomacy. For the most part, human rights has not been a major feature of Japanese or South Korean diplomacy globally or regionally.

Concerning free trade, in the reform period China has moved generally to support norms of global free trade outright. In concrete terms, China's average tariff rate has declined from more than 40 percent in 1992 to just under 20 percent in 1999. This figure will decline further with World Trade Organization (WTO) membership (to an average of 9.4% for industrial products and 14.5% for agricultural products by 2004–2005). China's entry into the WTO is the clearest statement that officially China embraces the extant free-trade regime. No doubt China will likely use many of the loopholes in WTO rules to protect politically important economic constituencies when necessary. But this is no different in kind from the arbitrary use of antidumping rules by the United States to protect important economic constituencies. Many experts also argue that China's primary compliance problem will not be a willful disregard of WTO commitments by the central government, but rather noncompliance by hard-to-control provincial and local economic interests.

China's embrace of global capitalist institutions, and increasingly their norms of free trade, and of open capital flows has been largely a function, apparently, of the Chinese Communist Party's (CCP's) to enhance its legitimacy through economic development. Arguably, then, there are strong political interests at the elite level in maintaining this fundamental orientation. There are also strong regional interests in preserving and expanding economic ties with Northeast Asian economies: Southeast coastal China benefits from trade and investment from Taiwan and Japan; Northeast China benefits from economic relationships with South Korea. While the WTO is now likely to be the main force pushing the further marketization of the Chinese economy, the Asia Pacific Economic Cooperation forum played a critical role in socializing key bureaucratic actors in the ideology of marketization—transparency, non–tariff barrier reduction, standardization, and the reduction of transaction costs, among others elements.

In terms of arms control and proliferation, China's performance has generally been no worse than that of other major powers in the past decade, though this is not a high standard to meet. The most dangerous exception is the transfer to Pakistan of nuclear weapons–related technology in the 1980s and M-11 ballistic missile components in 1992. Since agreeing to abide by the first version of the Missile Technology Control Regime, and the Comprehensive Test Ban Treaty (CTBT), the U.S. government officially adjudicates Chinese performance as improved, though problematic in some cases. As most recently put by a senior State Department official, the Chinese are "less active traders and proliferators than they used to be."[10] The continuing concerns are either in dual-use technologies that China has the legal right to transfer, or in the case of missile components to Pakistan, transfers that may violate unilateral statements made to the United States rather than formal multilateral agreements. More generally China has signed onto a number of potentially constraining arms-control agreements. The CTBT is the most notable, as it limits China's ability to modernize its nuclear weapons warhead designs. As yet, there is no credible evidence that China has violated this commitment.

In terms of conventional arms transfers to other states, there are few intrusive regimes that China could be accused of violating. Those that have emerged are not especially strong. The one regime that has a direct bearing on Northeast Asia is the Ottawa Treaty, which bans the use and transfer of antipersonnel land mines (APL). China opposes the treaty, largely for military reasons—it has long land borders and none of its neighbors in the region are signatories. But the United States also opposes the treaty, in part because the U.S. military claims APLs are needed for the defense of South Korea. So the absence of the regime in Northeast Asia is not solely the responsibility of the PRC.

Finally, with regard to perhaps the most deeply internalized fundamental norm in interstate diplomacy—sovereignty—China is one of the staunchest defenders of a more traditional, absolutist definition of the norm. Precisely because the meaning of sovereignty is historically contingent, and currently in flux, China is fighting a conservative action to reaffirm sovereignty and internal autonomy against challenges from concepts of human rights, domestic governance, and humanitarian intervention promoted by more progressive liberal democracies and nongovernmental organizations.[11]

In summary, on those norms for which criteria for determining the breadth and depth of China's involvement in the "international community" are relatively clear (proliferation, free trade), Chinese performance is generally improving. On those norms for which the criteria are unclear, or for which there is little consensus internationally (e.g., on the centrality of political rights in the human rights regime), it is harder to assess the degree to which China is upholding or challenging international norms at the global or regional levels, since these norms themselves are often contradictory. What constitutes a coherent body of international norms endorsed by a single international community when the sovereignty norm grates with the free-trade norm or the evolving humanitarian intervention norm?

A final indicator of non–status quo-ness might be that, although the actor may participate in international institutions, and may abide by their rules and norms temporarily, if given a chance it will try to change these rules and norms in ways that defeat the original purposes of the institution and the community. That is, it tries proactively to undermine the established "rules of the game."

China's performance in this regard is also hard to gauge because the term "rules of the game," as it is used both in realist theorizing and in public debates on foreign policy, is so vague. Let me suggest, however, that there are a couple of indicators one might logically look at to give more analytical substance to the phrase "rules of the game":

- Does a state try to change the formal and informal rules by which major international institutions operate once it is inside?
- Does a state routinely oppose the interests of unambiguously "status quo states" in major international institutions?

As for the first indicator, what has China proposed as rules for institutions versus what it has accepted? The gap may say something about what the rules would have looked like had Chinese leaders designed them predominantly by themselves.

In international economic institutions, at least, most academic observers are generally sanguine about China's conformity to extant rules. The best studies on China's involvement in the World Bank and the International Monetary Fund all suggest generally sound performance. The Chinese government has tended to meet its reporting requirements, for instance, and there have been no dramatic efforts to change the way decisions are made to favor China.[12]

Moreover, even if China desires to change these rules, it is not easy. Common usage in the punditry literature suggests that "changing the rules" means changing the norms or ideology of an institution. But most institutions have rules about rules; there are often procedures that govern how these norms, ideologies, and institutional purposes themselves can be changed. Not surprisingly, these procedures tend to be highly conservative. They are designed to prevent actors whose preferences might change, or new actors with different preferences, from easily altering the purposes of the institution. Institutions that require supermajorities or consensus, for example, are exceedingly hard to change. The dissatisfied actor has to put together a supercoalition *or* somehow overcome the veto of a single player in a consensus/unanimity system.[13] For instance, the only way that the major norms and values and targets embodied in the WTO can be changed is by dominating the various global negotiation rounds. Since decisions in these rounds are taken by consensus, a state has to dominate a round utterly, mobilize large coalitions, and somehow persuade the minority to go along. So it will not be easy to dilute the WTO's ideology of free trade and low barriers to the movement of capital even if the Chinese leadership wants to do so.[14]

As for the second indicator, does China increasingly oppose the interests of other states that one could uncontroversially call status quo states? Ideally, answering this requires inventorying a long list of economic, political, and social interests, expressed in a wide range of international forums. But one quick way of getting at this is to look at the congruence of voting in the United Nations General Assembly. Using an index of similarity in voting, basically a spatial model measuring the distances between country A and country B on one or more policy dimensions, over the 1980s and 1990s China and nonrevisionist developing states such as Indonesia and Mexico had relatively high degrees of congruence (see figure 2.1).[15] The index average is lower between China and status-quo-developed states such as Japan, Canada, and Britain, but has increased over the 1990s in the case of the latter two countries. It is lowest, by far, with the United States, with whom it has decreased over the 1990s. Thus, whatever growing friction there is between U.S. and Chinese interests—manifested in UN voting—this is not an across-the-board phenomenon in China's relations with a range of other status quo states. Figure 2.1 suggests, therefore, that the "problem" is not China's status quo or non–status quo behavior, but conflicts of interests with the United States. These two issues should be kept analytically separate.

As for China and other Northeast Asian states, from 1991, when the Koreas entered the UN, to 1996, with the exception of the United States the trend lines in the similarity index again suggest that China did not present an increasing challenge to the interests of most other states (figure 2.2).

In sum, using these specific definitional criteria, in relative terms the PRC is more status quo–oriented now than at any other time in its history. At the same time, however, there is a growing unease with Chinese power. There has been "containment" talk in the air. The not-so-subtle subtext of the most recent Department of Defense *Quadrennial Defense Review Report* is that U.S. military power and U.S. allies in Northeast Asia and elsewhere need to think about how to develop capabilities to deal with rising Chinese power.[16]

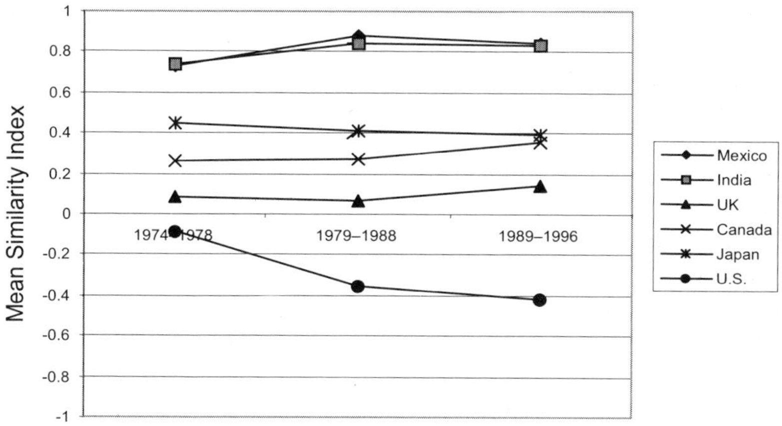

Figure 2.1. Mean Similarity Index with Select Countries per Foreign Policy Period

More recently, a report by the congressionally mandated U.S.–China Economic and Security Commission provides political arguments to go along with these military operational ones: China and the United States have fundamentally conflicting views of global order (multipolarity versus unipolarity), and PRC military power and economic development is ultimately aimed at shutting the United States out of Northeast Asia.[17] What explains, then, the apparent disconnection between evolving assessments of Chinese intentions and the apparent macrohistorical trends in the PRC approach to global and regional order?

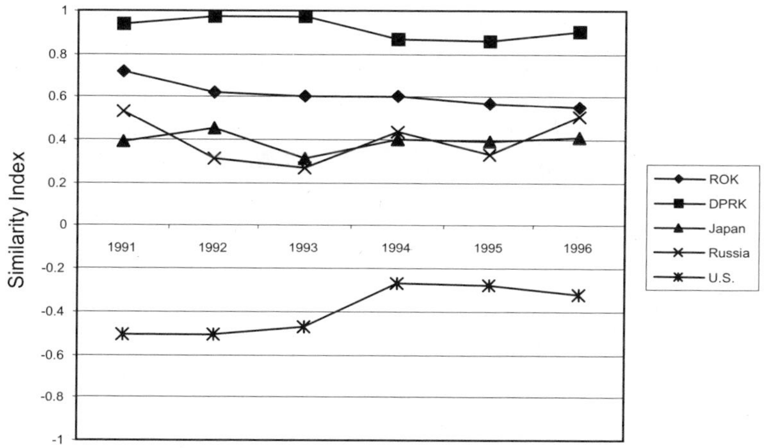

Figure 2.2. Similarity Index with Northeast Asian States, 1991–1996

Three Hypotheses

It's China

The first hypothesis is that in the 1990s the Chinese government has in fact become more revisionist in its diplomacy compared, say, to China of the 1970s and 1980s, when it collaborated with the United States against the Soviet Union. At one end are those who claim that China has a clear goal of establishing regional hegemony. This may now be the predominant argument in policy and punditry circles in Washington, though it has been temporarily dampened by Chinese cooperation with the United States in the war on terrorism.[18] These arguments variously invoke images of Middle Kingdom impulses, where Chinese leaders are alleged to be interested in restoring a tribute system, or more general historical analogies whereby China, like a rising Germany and a rising Japan in the past, would naturally want to change the power hierarchy in its region.

More narrowly construed are arguments that on specific issues—Taiwan and territorial disputes (such as the Diaoyu/Senkaku Islands dispute with Japan)—we can see revisionist elements in Chinese diplomacy. The corollaries to these revisionist aims are subgoals related to countering the main obstacle to changing the status quo, including inter alia U.S. military power in the region, U.S. plans for national missile defenses, and U.S. bilateral alliances, in particular the U.S.–Japan alliance and the evolving U.S.–ROC military relationship.

There are a number of issues raised by this general hypothesis about Chinese revisionism. The most fundamental is the question: Can China's leaders be said to have and share a well-thought-out intention to establish hegemony in the region, to push U.S. military power out of the region, and to establish some tribute system redux, or in Western IR parlance, a sphere of influence similar in essence to the Soviet sphere in Eastern Europe or the U.S. sphere in Latin America during the Cold War? This is a hard question to answer. If one were to list the range of "revisionist" goals that observers believe Chinese leaders have in the Northeast Asian region, it would include establishing Chinese hegemony in the region at the expense of U.S. power; establishing sovereign control over territory explicitly claimed by China (e.g., Diaoyu Islands); and reunification of Taiwan with the mainland under the one-China rubric.

Unfortunately, the evidence for these politicomilitary goals in the region is inconsistent. We have the best evidence for the desire eventually to revise the status quo on Taiwan. There are plenty of government documents and statements, think-tank studies, and interview data about the intent to at least prevent any further drift of Taiwan toward permanent separation. There is good evidence as well that military modernization programs, training exercises, and doctrinal innovation in the People's Liberation Army (PLA), particularly since 1996, are aimed primarily at dealing with the Taiwan issue.[19]

The evidence about the Diaoyu Islands, as it is with other ocean island claims (e.g., the Spratleys in the South China Sea), is somewhat more speculative. If the calculations about the Diaoyu Islands are anything like those behind Chinese diplomacy on the South China Sea, the long-term intention is probably still to establish sovereign control over the islands. For some in China, this should probably occur once China has the military capacity to make it happen. For others it should occur through diplomatic negotiations, joint development, and the use of international legal instruments because the costs of military action are too high.[20] At the moment, however, there doesn't appear to be any active efforts to physically control the Diaoyu (perhaps due to Japanese caution in this regard).

The evidence is most problematic when it comes to the goal of establishing Chinese hegemony in the region. Most who routinely make this claim infer it from particular parts of Chinese history. Some will invoke the more ancient "Middle Kingdom" or the more recent Qing dynasty tribute-system narratives as though the existence of these historical analogies is incontrovertible evidence for the current leadership's thinking. Others will make this inference on the basis of historical analogies from Europe (most commonly, the rise of Wilhelmine Germany).[21] However, the documentary paper trail for this claim as a long-term goal of the CCP's current or future leadership is sparse relative to the other two revisionist goals.

There are two pieces of evidence—one in the realm of discourse, the other in the realm of behavior—that would provide a reasonably sound basis for inferences about Chinese revisionism. One is the multipolarization *(duojihua)* discourse in China's diplomacy. Statements that multipolarity is an objective trend and a normative good explicitly challenge any continued U.S. unipolar status.[22] The other is the concrete evidence of power balancing against the United States in the region with the intention of eventually replacing U.S. power. I will look at both in turn.

Multipolarity. The multipolarity discourse is a long-standing one. Indeed it could be traced at least as far back as Mao Zedong's three-world thesis, in which he argued that in addition to two superpowers there was a second world (capitalist developed states) and a third or revolutionary world (mostly developing countries): the more powerful the second and third worlds were, the more constrained the superpowers would be. In the 1980s and 1990s, Chinese foreign policy discourse claimed the world was heading toward multipolarity, a more stable world of balanced power among five or so major centers (the United States, Russia, Europe, Japan, and China).[23] This was both a descriptive and normative claim. Three of these poles are Northeast Asian states, hence its potential relevance to understanding how Beijing thinks power should be redistributed in the region.

It is unclear, however, what precisely one can infer about Chinese strategic goals from this claim. First, the multipolarity discourse plays an ambiguous role in the policy process. It is unclear whether the multipolarity discourse *informs* leadership decisions, *reflects* leadership preferences, or is the manifestation of a deeply ingrained victimization view of China's relationship to the world. Thus, for instance, multipolarity has in very general terms been long favored by Chinese leaders because in principle it reflects a diminution of the power of superpowers and a relative rise in the international influence of developing states and China. But, as Christensen has pointed out, if one asks Chinese strategists if support for multipolarity means support for the rise in the relative power and strategic independence of Japan, for instance, the response is often a negative or ambivalent one.[24]

Second, it is clear that there has been much debate over precisely what multipolarity means for China. Typically, from the early 1990s on, the dominant claim was that international trends showed a movement toward multipolarity and away from the bipolarity of the Cold War. What was left ambiguous, however, was whether or not the current transition period was objectively one of U.S. unipolarity. For instance, some conservative nationalists argue that the world was indeed unipolar and that the official line was laughable. China therefore had to be cautious in the short run in challenging U.S. power, but in the long run needed to develop the strategic and diplomatic alliances to do so, since China was in the gun sights of U.S. hegemonism.[25] Some moderate, "pro-American" voices also argue that the era was essentially one of U.S. unipolarity, but that this is not entirely to China's disadvantage.[26] While the United States is the sole superpower, China can benefit from economic relations with the United States and from the relative global stability that U.S. hegemony has afforded and the public goods this stability has provided.[27] One analyst concludes that although it has supported a more just and reasonable international order, "China is by no means a challenger to the current international order. Under the current international system and norms, China can ensure its own national interests."[28] If there is policy advice from this group of moderates it is that China should use international institutions—multilateralism rather than military power—to constrain U.S. behavior.[29] Other moderates continue to claim that multipolarity is the main trend. But they do this to head off hard-liners who believe that the unipolar moment requires more vigorous balancing against the United States. Thus, for these moderates, multipolarity means that China does not need to confront and challenge U.S. interests so actively. For more centrist realpolitik voices, multipolarity means, essentially, an international system based on the five principles of peaceful coexistence—hardly revolutionary or revisionist values—whereby other states will have to take China's vital interests into account.[30]

Overall, then, during the 1990s it was simply not clear that there was a consensus among analysts on precisely what the trend lines were in the evolution of polarity.

Third, from the mid-1990s on, after the successful projection of U.S. power in Kosovo, and in the face of the growing military capabilities gap between the United States and any and all potential contenders, many Chinese analysts have, in fact, expressed increasing pessimism that multipolarity trends are going the way the Chinese leadership would prefer. Chinese assessments of comprehensive national power (CNP)—a composite index that weighs hard-power indicators (GNP, military power, levels of education, and so forth) and soft-power indicators (foreign policy influence, cultural dynamism, and so forth) to determine relative strength of major powers over the next ten to twenty years—are increasingly pessimistic about China's ability to close the gap with the United States. The earliest such study, done in the late 1980s by PLA analysts, suggested China might catch up to the United States by 2020. The most recent calculations, done by the Chinese Institute of Contemporary International Affairs (CICIR), China's Central Intelligence Agency, suggest that under the most optimistic growth scenarios, China will only reach around 50 percent of U.S. CNP by 2020. A more pessimistic growth scenario reduces this to 40 percent.[31]

Finally, the notion that multipolarity best describes the changing structure of world politics appears to be on the wane relative to new concepts such as globalization (see figure 2.3).[32] The globalization discourse recognizes that the factors that may constrain states in the future—their domestic economic choices, domestic cultural choices, foreign policies, and even domestic political choices—have less to do with material power distributions and more to do with one's openness to global capital, information, and technology flows. For some Chinese analysts, globalization does not so much replace the centrality of states in world politics as it creates a new structure of capital penetration within which states compete for the (often finite) benefits of the information and technology that capital brings with it.[33]

For others, the globalization trope dilutes somewhat the long-dominant vision of international politics as a struggle among states to enhance relative power in the international power structure (polarity). The metric for determining the vitality and longevity of the state and its political structures is

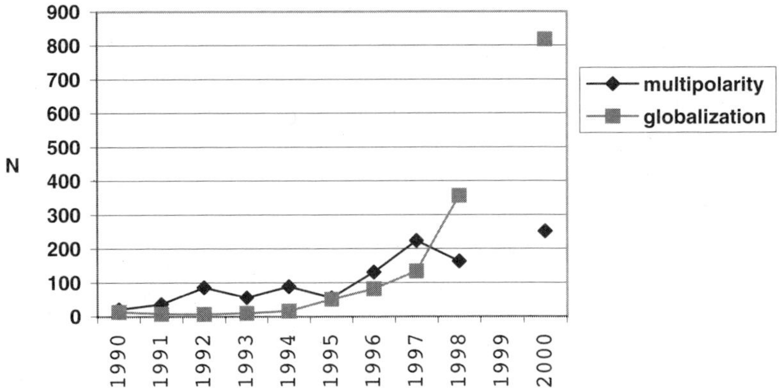

Figure 2.3. Annual Frequency of the Terms "Multipolarity" (*duojihua*) and "Globalization" (*quanqiuhua*) in the *People's Daily,* 1990–2000

not so much how much relative power the state controls, but how it has configured its economic and foreign policies to tap into the transnational production of new sources of wealth, status, and economic security. Some analysts push this further and argue that in a globalization framework for analysis, the nation-state is no longer the primary unit of analysis, and that within this framework one can talk about common global norms of behavior that transcend state interests. Moreover, globalization transforms political relations among major powers into more complex combinations of cooperative interactions (e.g., those dealing with transnational security problems such as drugs, crime, terrorism, and ecological damage) and conflictual interactions (e.g., those concerning markets and investment), the relative balance of which is not so clearly determined by polarity.[34]

In short, the multipolarity discourse is not such an unproblematic indicator of Chinese intentions these days.

Balancing against U.S. power in Northeast Asia. Is Chinese diplomacy in Northeast Asia consistent with a strategic goal of establishing regional hegemony or more limited revisionist goals of defending territorial claims? An active effort to reduce U.S. relative power and influence in the region would be called "balancing" in IR jargon. Is China balancing against the United States in the region?

Typically, states can balance internally (mobilizing economic, technological, and human resources to translate into military/strategic power) or externally (finding allies that share a common interest in opposing a stronger hegemon or dominant state). There seems to be little doubt that China's military modernization program over the 1990s has been aimed in large measure at developing capabilities to deter or slow the application of U.S. military power in the region. But it is also clear that the immediate and medium-term issue at stake for Chinese leaders has been Taiwan, not the U.S. strategic presence in the region per se, nor necessarily other military contingencies, such as a war in Korea. That is, the PLA has been tasked with minimizing the U.S. ability to defend Taiwan against Chinese military coercion in the event it is employed. PLA modernization, at the moment, is not primarily designed to seize, for instance, the Senkaku/Diaoyu Islands.

The rate of real increase in Chinese military expenditures grew substantially in the late 1990s (18% in 2000 and 2001). Nonetheless, it is unclear whether one should term this "balancing" in the sense of challenging the distribution of power. For one thing, balance-of-power literature is vague as to what kinds or levels of increases in military expenditures constitute balancing. Military expenditures are not simply functions of external threats/opportunities, but are also determined by technological innovation cycles, organizational interests, domestic ideologies, and so forth. For another thing, as a percentage of GDP, Chinese military expenditures do not appear to have reached a level where one could conclude the Chinese economy is being militarized and mobilized in order to balance against U.S. power.

As for external alliances, China is not trying very hard to construct anti-U.S. alliances or undermine U.S. alliances globally or regionally. For one thing, many Chinese analysts recognize that this kind of diplomacy would be unwelcome in many countries in Northeast Asia. They note that many countries in North and Southeast Asia basically support the U.S. role as a "balancer" in the region, particularly to prevent Chinese and Japanese competition for regional leadership.[35] While it recently signed a treaty of friendship with Russia, a treaty that embodied some of the Chinese normative vision of world politics (support for multipolarity, opposition to hegemony), it would be a stretch to call this an anti-U.S. alliance. Putin's fundamental impulse is to rely on closer ties with Europe and the United States to develop the Russian economy and, in the post-9/11 period, to combat Bin Ladenism on the Russian periphery. Strategically, Russia's most useful role for China is as a source of weapons, not as a partner for confronting and counterbalancing U.S. power and interests in every forum. For its part, the Russian motivation appears to be an economic one—keeping weapons industries and workers afloat. Moreover, even those shared Sino–Russian positions that are or were in some sense anti-American are often positions that would *strengthen* or *uphold* the international institutional status quo (e.g., strengthening the role of the UN or preserving existing arms control agreements, such as the Anti-Ballistic Missile Treaty).[36]

China does not appear to be all that active in trying to pry the United States and Japan or the United States and the Republic of Korea (ROK) apart. Beijing's official position has long been that foreign forces (e.g., the United States and, before that, the Soviets) should withdraw from the region. The current discourse stresses the obsolescence of "Cold War" bilateral alliances. Minor diplomatic offenses in places such as the ARF have been aimed at chipping away at the legitimacy of U.S. bilateral alliances. But the Chinese are not unequivocally against these alliances.

The U.S.–ROK alliance, for instance, serves Beijing's interest in stabilizing the peninsula's division.[37] Beijing appears to believe that the ROK shares an interest in a soft landing for the DPRK whereby some version of economic reform combined with engagement by outside powers ensures the peaceful evolution of the DPRK regime and its denuclearization. Thus the ROK's interests also act as a brake on any U.S. attempts to engineer a hard landing via a crippling economic embargo or military force that quickly topples the DPRK. The Chinese leadership appears to prefer the geopolitical status quo—the continuing existence of an independent ROK and an independent DPRK—even though they have become increasingly alarmed by and impatient with the DPRK's nuclear brinkmanship since the fall of 2002. Chinese analysts and policy makers believe that the main source of instability on the peninsula comes largely from the DPRK, whereby a political coup, an economic collapse, a ballistic missile test, or the development of nuclear weapons would be followed by a harsh economic, political, or military response by the United States.[38] Thus Beijing appears to believe that stability on the peninsula can best be realized by restraint on DPRK weapons of mass destruction (WMD) programs and delivery systems, by economic development and limited marketization roughly along the Chinese model, and by stable political relations among the key players—the DPRK, the ROK, China, the United States, and Japan.[39] This, evidently, has been China's message to the DPRK over the past decade.[40] By most accounts China has been relatively constructive in urging restraint in the DPRK's development of WMD capabilities and in supporting the institutions designed to ensure this restraint—the Framework Agreement of 1994, KEDO, and the Four-Party Peace Talks.[41] On relations with the ROK, Beijing doesn't have to worry much about public opinion in China. The Chinese public holds strongly positive views of the ROK, even though the latter is in a formal military alliance with the United States.[42]

For the most part, the ROK shares Beijing's interests when it comes to the DPRK, having calculated that the costs of rapid unification are excessively high (in 1998, estimates of the cost of unification after hard landing in 2000 were anywhere from $200 billion to $1.2 trillion more in government spending over an indefinite period).[43] But the ROK's stake in this status quo is directly related to its sense of security from the DPRK, and the alliance with the United States serves this purpose.[44]

Beijing's one major worry over the long term is the role the alliance will play in any post-DPRK scenario. Chinese strategists are concerned that the United States intends to stay and, worse, may want to deploy forces above the thirty-eighth parallel. Chinese military exchanges with the ROK no doubt are designed to press home Chinese concerns, particularly if U.S. policy shifts more obviously to forcing a hard landing for the DPRK regime. The PRC hopes to keep the DPRK alive because of the buffer it creates between U.S. military power and Chinese territory. It may also be the case that as long as the DPRK remains alive, in the context of conservative U.S. political leaders pushing for harder containment or roll-back policies toward the DPRK, the issue will be a source of friction between the United States and the ROK, something that is not altogether contrary to China's leaders' interests.[45]

As for the U.S.–Japan alliance, Chinese attitudes are exceedingly complex. Since the announcement of guidelines for revising the security treaty in 1996, Chinese strategists have been increasingly worried by the possibility that this alliance will become a tool for defending an independent or permanently separated Taiwan.[46] Many Chinese analysts and leaders believe, however, that a Japan within a bilateral alliance with the United States is still better than a Japan outside of such constraints *as long as* this alliance is not used to provide military cover for an independent Taiwan. Some of the more sophisticated analyses argue that in the post–Cold War era, one of the purposes of the alliance has shifted from being a "bottle cap" *(pinggai)* over Japanese power to being both a bottle cap on the Japanese *and* a constraint on Chinese and Russian power in the region. In other words, the bottle-cap role still exists; thus, implicitly, so does the Chinese interest in this aspect of the alliance.[47] It is the other purpose—tying China down in a U.S.-dominated security order, particularly as it relates to the Taiwan issue—to which China objects. Thus China's diplomacy toward the U.S.–Japan alliance, particularly from the mid-1990s on, has been largely aimed at extracting some kind of credible commitment—so far unsuccessful—that the alliance not be used to defend Taiwan in a conflict with the PRC.[48] More generally, it has been aimed at suggesting ways in which a weakened alliance might exist alongside, and subordinate to, multilateral institutions in the region, though this vision remains rather underdeveloped and is still rather self-servingly presented in places such as the ASEAN Regional Forum.

In short, the most accurate way of describing the Chinese leadership's preferences about the U.S.–Japan alliance *at this moment* is that it return to its pre-1996 form and function, not that it disappear entirely.[49] Chinese analysts usually are careful to state that they oppose the *strengthening* or *reinforcement* of the U.S.–Japan alliance, not the alliance's existence per se.[50]

Some Chinese strategists have also implied that China's diplomacy toward Japan in the past has been counterproductive, in part due to emotionalism about the history question and in part due to an incorrect devaluation of the economic benefits of a relationship with Japan. At base, the first argument, at least, implies a recognition of security dilemma dynamics in the dyadic relationship.[51] Some have also argued that Japanese militarism is generally in check because of everything from the U.S. alliance to political change, the inculcation of more pacific norms in the population, the persistent economic problems Japan has experienced over the past decade, the realism of Japanese politicians that having China as an enemy in such close proximity is contrary to Japan's interests, and the deepening economic interdependence between China and Japan.[52] Given these arguments, these strategists contend, China should use less emotional diplomacy (that is, invoke the history card less frequently and vociferously) to help prevent the emergence of more nationalist and revivalist voices in Japan.[53] In addition, good relations with the United States and Japan will help reduce the China element behind a strengthening U.S.–Japan alliance[54]—an interesting admission, by reverse logic, that a hard-line policy toward these two countries will have a counterproductive effect. These are hotly and publicly debated arguments,[55] so there is by no means a solid consensus behind them. But they appear to be the dominant arguments for the moment. This may help explain why the Chinese government shifted to what has been referred to as "smile diplomacy" toward Japan in 1999–2000. One manifestation of this was the PRC's relative quiet when Japan offered to send naval forces to assist U.S. operations against the Taliban and Al Qaeda in the fall of 2001.

Some among the Chinese public appear to agree with this more cautious understanding of Japanese power. While Chinese citizens do not like Japan and believe that the Japanese people and state are even more warlike than the Americans and the U.S. state,[56] they appear not to be too worried about the revival of Japanese militarism. According to the Beijing Area Study's random sample of Beijing residents in 2001, only 8 percent chose the revival of Japanese militarism as the main threat to China. Most considered domestic social unrest, Taiwan independence, or U.S. military power to be the major security threat.[57] It is likely, however, that were Japan to participate in U.S. military operations in defense of Taiwan, the lines between Taiwan independence, U.S. military power, and revived Japanese militarism would blur, and the ethnic/racialist emotions behind many Chinese views of Japan would come more obviously to the fore.

Finally, somewhat puzzling for a balancing argument is the fact that China has become more dependent rather than less dependent on the United States economically, even as U.S. relative power has increased after the Cold War. The percentage of Chinese exports to the United States as a percent of all of its exports has increased over time. U.S. foreign direct investment is also critical in certain sectors of the Chinese economy. Some argue that as the weaker state, running a large trade surplus with the United States, China's relative power benefits more from this relationship than if it did not exist. There is some merit to this argument, assuming that it is obvious how much of this net flow of economic resources to the PRC can be or has been translated into military power that can deter the United States from operating in the Western Pacific.

At the same time, the economic relationship also creates a dependence on U.S. markets and capital for economic growth. Economic growth is, in turn, directly related to the legitimacy and longevity of the CCP rule. The CCP's economic development strategy creates economic, social, and technological interdependencies that—given the relative size and primitiveness of the Chinese economy compared to the U.S. economy—means that an end to them is far more costly to the Chinese regime than to the United States.

Moreover, these interdependencies create constituencies inside the PRC that are not self-evidently hostile to the United States or supportive of all of China's external diplomacy. Economic interests groups along the coastline would be adversely affected by the militarization of East China in the event of a major conflict over Taiwan. An emerging middle class in urban China may be somewhat less supportive of strongly anti-American diplomacy than are other groups in China, including the military.[58]

In other words, under conditions of growing economic interdependence, mobilizing the economy and militarizing society to balance seriously against American power and influence in the region—with the goal of establishing a Chinese sphere of influence in the face of U.S. resistance—will create economic and social costs that, at this point, the regime appears unwilling to bear. This constrains China's ability to balance against U.S. power.[59] At best, one could describe China's balancing against American unipolarity as (in the words of one astute observer) "hesitant, low-key, and inconsistent."[60]

The exception that proves the rule about Chinese balancing behavior may be China's response to U.S. military power on the more limited issue of Taiwan. So-called asymmetric strategies, combined with relatively modest improvements in China's long-range cruise missile, ballistic missile, and submarine capability could slow down the U.S. response to a rapid military-political fait accompli presented to the Taiwanese government. The dangers of military conflict between China and the United States over Taiwan should not be underestimated. The interaction of China's symbolic commitment to sovereignty over Taiwan and the U.S. concern over preserving the credibility of its military commitments to friends and allies is upping the political-military stakes for both sides. The PLA appears to be relatively confident that a combination of counterforce conventional missile strikes, air superiority, and some option of either blockading Taiwanese ports or seizing some piece of territory (e.g., Penghu Island) will lead the ROC to negotiate a political solution that advantages the PRC, *if* this can be done before large-scale U.S. intervention.[61] The spillover effects from preparations for a war with the United States and its Asian allies are, of course, not limited to the immediate vicinity of Taiwan. Thus the fallout of a war would be regionwide, even though the Chinese goal would be the geographically and politically limited one of preventing Taiwanese independence or compelling Taiwan's reunification. Nonetheless, China's preparations for dealing with U.S. military power in a Taiwan conflict are not really the same thing as balancing against U.S. power writ large in the region or beyond.

Of course, the absence of clear evidence of a proactive effort to fundamentally alter the distribution of power regionally or globally does not mean such a desire does not exist. But the analytical problem that the regionwide or global scope of China's revisionism is not obvious should be recognized. More obvious are China's limited revisionist aims when it comes to Taiwan. Here, the evidence does seem to suggest that the regime is preparing the option of using force to change the political and military "facts on the ground." Not to make excuses for China's obtuse gunboat diplomacy in the 1990s, but it is hard to generalize from Taiwan to attitudes toward long-term regional distributions of power, let alone to global institutions or "rules of the game." The Taiwan issue could lead to the strengthening and expanding of more grandiose "revisionist" interests in China and the appearance of more authoritative evidence of such long-term goals (the defense of territorial integrity in an era of long-range, high-tech precision strikes means that the military operational perimeter has to expand outward and includes preemption).[62] But at present, the character of China's revisionism on the Taiwan issue doesn't appear to be reflective of China's broader diplomacy toward region or globe. It is a dangerous exception/outlier, but an exception nonetheless.

It's Others

If it is hard to find concrete evidence—apart from the Taiwan issue and its spillover effects on regional security—that China is a fundamentally revisionist state in Northeast Asia, there is a second explanation for the growing concern about Chinese power. That is, the primary changes have been in regional perceptions of Chinese goals, influenced by China's growing power relative to other states in the region, rather than Chinese diplomacy per se. It is regional leaders who are paying attention to power shifts and a few key watershed events (the Tiananmen massacre in 1989, the PLA exercises in the Taiwan Strait in 1995 and 1996, the collision of the Chinese fighter and the U.S. EP3 surveillance plane in April 2001, China's naval activities in the South China and East China Seas) and who are extrapolating to Chinese strategic goals. Decision makers often infer intentions from changing relative power. Mao certainly did. There are these kinds of voices close to the Bush administration. For instance, Friedberg and others who essentially if not so explicitly endorse power transition arguments about China, use historical analogies that underscore the virtual inevitability of a clash of Chinese and U.S. power (while holding out some limited possibility for avoiding collision). This contrasts, for instance, with the "liberal" engagement-constraint arguments during the Clinton administration.

This explanation compels us to look at political and ideological changes in countries around China's periphery to explain changing perceptions of China's threat to regional stability. This would be, in many respects, a domestic political story. Political change in some countries have reduced or narrowed definitions of shared interests with China.

Political and generational change in Japan has diluted the influence of older, pro-Beijing factions in the Liberal Democratic Party and brought a younger generation into positions of political and bureaucratic power that is alienated by China's use of the history card to bash Japan, by China's apparent ingratitude for Japanese assistance for its development, and by China's not-so-secret naval intelligence gathering inside Japan's exclusive economic zone, among other grievances.[63] With a growing role for nongovernmental organizations in Japan's civil society and foreign relations, there are now more voices inside Japan critiquing China from a liberal perspective on governance and human rights. In general, as Gilbert Rozman puts it, the contradictions between those advocating a "predominantly engagement" strategy and those supporting a "predominantly containment" approach sharpened over the 1990s. This has undermined a long-time "naïve romanticism" in popular and elite opinion, based on optimism about China's economic reform and integration and about Japan's own economic prospects.[64]

In the United States, politics has had a large impact on perceptions of shared or competing interests in Sino–U.S. relations. After the 1994 congressional election brought a range of new conservative voices into Congress, the congressional right wing became the locus for sharp critiques of rising Chinese power, for growing political support for Taiwan's permanent separation from the PRC, and for redefinitions of U.S. interest that eliminated areas of shared interest with the PRC. Congress mandated studies of Chinese military power, of the cross-strait military balance, and of allegations of Chinese espionage in the nuclear and missile technology fields. The mandate was driven by a view of the PRC that saw it as revisionist state, a potential competitor to the United States. Moreover, for ideological reasons the conservative, Republican-controlled Congress rejected a range of policy positions that the Clinton executive branch believed created shared Sino–U.S. interests. Congress opposed the 1996 CTBT treaty, whose final form was in large measure a function of hard U.S.–PRC bargaining. Congress also rejected the Kyoto treaty, and the conservatives in Congress brought the rejection of the notion that the United States and China had any shared interest in dealing with global warming as a global problem to begin with. The Bush administration, particularly the Department of Defense and the vice president's national security team, shared some of these congressional definitions of U.S. interest and interpretations of Chinese intentions. Moreover, whether one speaks of the Kissingerian/Scowcroft international realists or the neoimperial wing of the Bush administration, compared to the Clinton administration's understandings of the nature of international politics, both groups are more skeptical of the likelihood that rising, revisionist powers can be "socialized" inside international institutions. Thus the scope of issues on which the executive branch believed China and the United States had some overlap of interests has narrowed under the Bush administration.

Most recently, the scope appears to be narrowing further. One leg of the Sino–U.S. relationship—economics and trade—that the Clinton administration and centrist Republicans agreed was a source of stability in the overall relationship has come under some question by conservative voices close to the Bush administration. Until recently it was only the primacist right in the Republican Party that essentially saw the economic relationship as a potential threat to U.S. power. However, the recently released, congressionally mandated U.S.–China Security Commission Report also adopts a somewhat skeptical and conditional view of the value of economic integration. China's trade surplus, its access to dual-use technology, the massive inflows of foreign direct investment, and its overall commercial opacity and institutionalized corruption all mean that China's relative power may benefit from the relationship more than U.S. relative power. It is not surprising, then, that the report also concludes there are fundamental conflicts of interest between the United States and China in the region, starting with the Chinese intention of pushing U.S. power out of the region. This, then, would explain a change in the inferences drawn about Chinese intentions in the region and globally.[65] It remains to be seen how or whether the Bush administration responds to congressional legislation designed to "national securitize" the economic relationship, as the report recommends.

Internal changes in Taiwanese politics have clearly altered perceptions of Chinese intentions, inside Taiwan as well as Japan and the United States. Democratization and the rise of identity politics in Taiwan—in part functions of deliberate political strategy by Lee Teng-hui and his successor, Chen Shui-bian—have contributed to the Chinese leadership's worrying about the permanent separation of Taiwan and even a formal declaration of independence from an entity called the Republic of China.[66] This has led, in turn, to stepped-up military pressure on the ROC, beginning most dramatically with the military and missile exercises in 1995 and 1996, so as to deter independence. As Chinese military planners have thought through the options they have in a military crisis, this has led the PLA to develop doctrinal arguments and capabilities designed both to coerce Taiwan and to deter the United States and U.S. allies from interfering. These capabilities, in turn, have fed arguments in the United States, Taiwan, and elsewhere in the region that rising Chinese power is indeed a threat to regional stability.

In short, this explanation would focus primarily on domestic political changes that have redefined perceptions of China's interests and the purposes of its economic and military power. As attribution theory might suggest, such perceptions tend to lead to inferences about dispositions from observed behavior. That is, ideological shifts in these countries have tended to produce views of China that exaggerate the degree of unanimity inside China about what its preferences are, that discount the domestic and international situational variables to which Chinese behavior might be responding, and that tend toward worst-case inferences about intentions from extant capabilities.

It's Interactive

A final explanation is basically that it's an interaction of the policies and actions of China and other states. China's limited revisionist goals and behavior (primarily on the Taiwan issue) interact with domestic political changes/perceptions in other states. The result is growing ambivalence in China about the structures of power and influence in the region and growing doubts outside China about the benignness of rising Chinese power. The process began, for the most part, with China's military response to Taiwan's efforts to establish a more independent identity and stature in international politics via a high-profile visit by then-president Lee Teng-hui to the United States in the summer of 1995. The large-scale military exercises and missile tests in late 1995 and 1996 increased regional ambivalence about the long-term intentions of a rising and possibly revisionist China. While China-threat arguments existed before the Taiwan crisis of 1996, Chinese actions crystalized and mobilized a range of opinion within the United States and Japan in particular, alerting even those who supported engagement to the possibility that U.S. commitments to Taiwan would require the United States to eventually fight Chinese forces. During the latter half of the Clinton administration, the U.S. Department of Defense, in particular, initially pressed for closer military coordination with the ROC—including more transfers of hardware (arms sales) and software (doctrinal and planning exchanges)—because it believed it better to understand and control Taiwanese military responses to PRC military pressure.[67] Under the Bush administration, coordination with Taiwan has been pushed not only by this calculation, but also by an ideological affinity with the ROC, by astute Taiwanese lobbying among the right wing in Congress, and by concerns about the Chinese challenge to American primacy in the region.

This ambivalence, and in some cases outright certainty, about the malevolence of China's intentions in the region, translated into concrete military-political steps to hedge against Chinese power. While the U.S.–Japan treaty revision guidelines were initially conceived in the early 1990s as steps to prevent Japanese defection in a Korean crisis, after the Taiwan crisis there is little doubt that China is one of the foci of the revisions. The military relationship with Taiwan under the Bush administration has evolved into a quasi-alliance (the Taiwanese like to use the "A" word), far surpassing the level of coordination reached under the Clinton administration. As a result, the credibility of U.S. alliance commitments elsewhere in Northeast Asia, in Washington's eyes, rests increasingly on its commitment to Taiwanese security.

The Chinese leadership, in turn, picked up these hedging signals after the Taiwan crisis and interpreted them as malignant (discounting the carrots while focusing on the sticks). The Clinton administration's engagement strategy, for instance, was sometimes termed a "soft-containment" strategy. An influential voice in the Bush administration has explicitly called for a mixed engagement/containment strategy, but is basically at a loss as to how to reassure Beijing that engagement is not subterfuge or strategic deception.[68] So it is not surprising that a hedging strategy is viewed in Beijing as more sinister and less driven by uncertainty than its proponents claim. Even benign U.S. proposals for regional confidence building are now viewed through the "United States-wants-to-contain-China" lens.[69]

Chinese responses to U.S. hedging and the deepening military commitment to Taiwan have, in turn, contributed to "closing-windows-of-opportunity" thinking in Beijing.[70] The logic is as follows: if the United States intends to keep Taiwan permanently separated from the PRC, and if the

U.S.–Japan alliance is designed to prevent China from coercing Taiwan away from permanent separation or compelling unification,[71] then "fighting later is not as good as fighting earlier" *(zaoda bu ru wanda)*. It is unclear how widespread this logic is. But it is clear that the PLA has been directed to prepare a range of coercive options as soon as possible to give the political leadership the choice of coercing Taiwan before the U.S.–ROC military relationship becomes too close and sophisticated, before U.S. National Missile Defense poses problems for China's nuclear signaling and deterrence capacity, before regional Theater Missile Defense poses problems for the coercive capacity of China's conventional missiles, and before U.S.–Japanese treaty revisions lead to substantial improvements in their capacity to coordinate against Chinese military power, but after the PLA develops the capacity to deter or slow the use of U.S. long-range naval and air power (some of which is based in Japan) against the PLA. "Windows" logic has a corollary: the advantages of U.S. military power in the region (the bottle cap on Japanese power, the security of the ROK, and the containment of conflict on the Korean peninsula) are diminishing relative to their disadvantages (the defense of Taiwan and the threat to Chinese territorial claims and coastal sea lines of communication, among them).

We know this phenomenon well—it is called a security dilemma, a cycle of growing distrust and malevolent interpretations of behaviors among status quo–oriented (or mildly opportunistic) states that then lead to reactions that encourage these interpretations of intentions and capabilities. Thus it may well be that China's behavior is in some objective sense more "assertive" and decreasingly confident that the current distribution of power and influence in Northeast Asia serves Chinese interests as defined in Beijing. But a powerful reason for this changing estimate of the value of the status quo in the past few years is the perceptions that other states are becoming more assertive in challenging what the Chinese leaders believe are their legitimate interests. And so on.

If indeed security dilemma dynamics explain the evolution both of China's level of dissatisfaction *and* of regional perceptions of China's revisionist goals, then Joe Nye's argument about the self-fulfilling nature of the "China threat" is correct.[72] It is an argument that has had less appeal in the more traditionally realpolitik Bush administration, precisely because it requires policy makers to accept that definitions of interest are dynamic and that U.S. actions are in part an explanation of the conflicts in Sino–U.S. relations. Security dilemma arguments have rarely had appeal inside China because they require a recognition that China's own behavior has been counterproductive and has undermined its own security.[73] Thus Chinese and U.S. perceptions feed security dilemma dynamics precisely because both sides tend to ignore the existence of these dynamics.

In sum, a security dilemma explanation bridges the more empirically accurate end of the first explanation (that in Northeast Asia, China's revisionist goals are primarily limited to Taiwan and some minor territorial disputes) with the second explanation (that domestically-driven political changes in some regional players have reduced the perceived degree of shared interests with China).

CONCLUSION

This chapter has argued that in most respects Chinese diplomacy is more accepting of extant international institutions, international norms (such as they are), and U.S. dominance of the international and regional power structure than at any time since 1949. The most obvious and dangerous exception to this status quo-ization of Chinese diplomacy is the Taiwan issue. Here China reserves the right to use force to change the political and military facts on the ground in an effort to defend its symbolic claim to "name" the island of Taiwan. In an effort to stake this claim, Chinese leaders have taken military measures that have raised doubts outside of China about the overall status quo orientation of Chinese power in the region. These doubts have been magnified by changes in political ideologies and definitions of interests in some key capitals—Washington, Tokyo, and Taipei in particular. Their responses, in turn, have magnified doubts in Beijing that these three other players will accept China's self-perceived legitimate interests on questions of sovereignty and territorial integrity. The militarization of security interactions among these four players, this mutual construction of adversarial images, is best explained by security dilemma theory, not by some simplistic characterization of Chinese revisionism or American hegemonism.

The limited Sino–U.S. counterterrorism cooperation after September 11 has not changed these dynamics much. The tenor of Sino–U.S. relations improved somewhat after 9/11, as Chinese leaders realized that both countries shared an interest in defending sovereign states against violent non–sovereign state actors. There is, according to press reports, some limited sharing of intelligence. In addition, Chinese leaders were helpfully low key about Japan's unprecedented decision to send a small naval force to assist the United States in the Arabian Sea. The United States and China share an interest in seeing a multiethnic, more or less secular, Afghanistan. China and the United States also have every interest in seeing Pakistan survive as a unified, moderate Islamic state.

But precisely because so much of the U.S. perception of other states' levels of cooperativeness will be viewed through the 9/11 lens (for us or against us), the potential exists for speeding up security dilemma dynamics, perhaps even for transitioning China's interests into more overtly revisionist ones. If the United States allows states to choose from a wide menu of actions in support of the war against terrorism, then China can offer intelligence or assistance in tracking terrorists' financial networks. These would be less-demanding tests of China's cooperation. A narrow menu of choice (do not obstruct U.S. attacks on "rogue" states that may have WMD, for instance) will be a tougher test. In light of the ongoing debate over the nature of Chinese power, a failure to back the United States would add weight in determining that China is a fundamentally revisionist state. A Chinese "failure" would also contrast sharply with any Taiwanese support for the U.S. pre-emptive strategy against WMD proliferation and terrorism, however symbolic that support may be.

Even though it does not appear to be asking for any explicit or short-term quid pro quo for cooperation thus far, the Chinese leadership expects that the United States should become more sympathetic to China's "legitimate" interests. Yet the U.S. policies that worry the Chinese leadership most—arms sales to Taiwan, closer U.S.–Taiwan political and military relations, National Missile Defense, the China-directed elements of U.S. alliance policy in Northeast Asia, among others—are issues for which there is strong congressional and Pentagon support. Domestic critics of any strategy of cooperation with the United States will certainly be looking for, even while not expecting, U.S. concessions on these issues. The absence of any substantial U.S. overtures will be used as evidence of the failure of a concessionary approach to U.S. power. In other words, despite the improved tenor of relations, some of the perceived fundamental conflicts of interest remain. There is a sense among hard-liners in Beijing and Washington that any improvement in relations is tactical.

This leads to my final point. It should be noted that the decline in general revisionist interests in China does not mean their elimination nor the impossibility of their reappearance either globally or regionally. China moved from being a revolutionary, revisionist state to being a status quo one in forty-odd years. It isn't implausible that a more fundamental revisionism might emerge from disillusionment with marketization, from problems of internal secession, or from the domestic effects of Taiwan's gradual reconstruction as a U.S. ally in the containment of China. Indeed, because of external security dilemma dynamics and the internal negative effects of unrestrained marketization, in retrospect we may see the 1980s and 1990s as a period of relative

Chinese status quo-ness, sandwiched by Maoist revisionism and some post-Jiang quasi-fascism.

But that's the point. In both the academic world and the policy and punditry world (in both China and the United States) there is a tendency to forget that state interests are often in flux, contradictory, contingent, unstructured, and susceptible to the self-fulfilling prophecy effects of other states' behavior. Neither IR theory nor the policy world has shown much sophistication when determining whether a state is status quo or revisionist. Yet the implications of naming a state in these terms are monumental. In the IR theory world, the implications run from everything from coding (and thus for results in data analysis) to the reification of realist concepts of the timelessness of state-centric struggles for power under anarchy. In the policy world, the implications can lead to actions that produce the outcomes that they are designed to avoid. Mistakenly calling a revisionist actor a status quo one, of course, can lead to conflict via the appeasement of aggression. But mistakenly calling a status quo actor a revisionist one can lead to security dilemmas, or worse, the construction of "aggressors."

NOTES

1. For one of the few public scholarly debates over the status quo-ness of Chinese diplomacy, see the exchange between Xiang Lanxin and David Shambaugh in *Survival* 43, no. 3 (Autumn 2001): 7–30.

2. See Zhang Biwu, "China a Status Quo Country? Testing the China Threat" (Ohio State University, Department of Political Science, dissertation proposal), 10–15.

3. A. F. K. Organksi and Jacek Kugler, *The War Ledger* (Chicago: University of Chicago Press, 1980), 19–20, 23.

4. Robert Gilpin, *War and Change in World Politics* (Cambridge: Cambridge University Press, 1981), 34.

5. For a sophisticated summary of IR theory's definitions of revisionism, see Jay Lyall "The Revisionist State: Definitions and Measures" (unpublished paper, Cornell University, 2001).

6. Here I draw more directly on Gilpin's discussion of what constitutes the "rules of the game." I will discuss the central issue of indicators of challenging the "distribution of power" later in the chapter.

7. Calculated from the figures for international governmental organizations in the *Yearbook of International Organizations*, various years.

8. In 1999, 55 percent of states scored a 5 or more on the Polity IV index for overall level of democratic institutions; 64 percent scored 1 or more on this index. The index runs from –10 (autocracy) to 10 (democracy).

9. American critics of China's Taiwan policy exaggerate the degree to which democracy per se in Taiwan worries the Chinese leadership. The concern is not so much that democratic ideas in Taiwan will spread to the PRC. The concern is more that democracy

in Taiwan will unleash nationalist identity in Taiwan and cement U.S. ideological support for Taiwan.

10. *New York Times*, September 2, 2001.

11. See Allen Carlson, *Constructing a New Great Wall: Chinese Foreign Policy and the Norm of State Sovereignty* (Ph.D. dissertation, Yale University, 2000).

12. Margaret M. Pearson, "China's Integration into the International Trade and Investment Regime," in *China Joins the World*, ed. Elizabeth Economy and Michel Oksenberg (New York: Council on Foreign Relations, 1999), 161–205, and Nicholas Lardy, "China and the International Financial System," in *China Joins the World*, ed. Elizabeth Economy and Michel Oksenberg (New York: Council on Foreign Relations, 1999), 206–30.

13. On how decision rules can affect the ideology of an institution, see George W. Downs, David M. Rocke, and Peter N. Barsoom, "Managing the Evolution of Multilateralism," *International Organization* 52 (1998): 397–419.

14. My thanks to Marc Busch for this insight.

15. This index was developed by Kurt Signorino and Jeff Ritter and is a more accurate indicator of congruence in roll-call voting than is the traditionally used tau B. See Signorino and Ritter, "Tau-b or Not Tau-b: Measuring the Similarity of Foreign Policy Positions," *International Studies Quarterly* 43, no. 1 (1999): 115–44.

16. Department of Defense, *Quadrennial Defense Review Report*, September 30, 2001, at www.defenselink.mil/pubs/qdr2001.pdf (accessed July 2002).

17. See the *Report to Congress of the US–China Security Review Commission*, July 2002, at www.USCC.gov/anrp02.htm (accessed July 2002).

18. This claim is in the U.S. Department of Defense's annual "Report to Congress Pursuant to the FY2000 National Defense Authorization Act," at www.defenselink.mil/news/Jul2002/d20020712china.pdf, p. 9 (accessed July 2002). This goal is taken to be axiomatic by many commentators. See Aaron L. Friedberg, "The Struggle for Mastery in Asia," *Commentary* 110, no. 4 (November 2000): 17–27; Larry Wortzel, "China's Military Potential" (Carlisle, Pa.: Strategic Studies Institute, Army War College, October 1998), 16.

19. On the importance of preventing Taiwan's independence, see Thomas J. Christensen, "China," in *Strategic Asia: Power and Purpose, 2001–2002*, ed. Richard J. Ellings and Aaron L. Friedberg (Seattle: National Bureau of Research, 2001), 39–47; David M. Finklestein, "China's National Military Strategy" (Alexandria, Va.: C.N.A. Corporation, January 2000), 5–6; U.S. Department of Defense, "Report to Congress."

20. In reference to the Spratleys, one study argued that China's policy of "putting aside differences and jointly developing" the area was a "stratagem not a goal." Lu Jianren, "Nansha zhengduan ji duice" (Disputes in the Spratleys and countermeasures), in *Nansha wenti yanjiu ziliao* (Spratley issue research materials) (1996), 311 (this essay was originally published in *Nansha Wenti Yanjiu* in 1995).

21. See Robert Kagan, "What China Knows That We Don't: The Case for a New Strategy of Containment," *Weekly Standard*, January 20, 1997; Paul Wolfowitz, "Bridging Centuries—Fin de Siècle All Over Again," *National Interest*, no. 47 (Spring 1997): 3–9; Arthur N. Waldron, "China as an Ascending Power," testimony before the House National Security Committee on Security Challenges, 104th Cong., 1st sess., March 20, 1996. Needless to say, historical analogies are analogies, not causes or explanations.

Those who analogize tend only to look at the similarities across cases and neglect what could be important differences.

22. Even engagement sympathizers have reached this conclusion. See Evan A. Feigenbaum, "China's Challenge to Pax Americana," *Washington Quarterly* 24, no. 3 (Summer 2001): 31–43; David Shambaugh, "Sino-American Strategic Relations: From Partners To Competitors," *Survival* 42, no. 1 (Spring 2000); and Bates Gill, "Contrasting Visions: China, the United States, and World Order," remarks to the U.S.–China Security Review Commission, Washington, D.C., August 3, 2001, at www.uscc.gov/tesgil.htm.

23. For a thorough summary of this discourse, see Michael Pillsbury, *China Debates the Future Security Environment* (Washington, D.C.: National Defense University Press, 2000), 3–61.

24. For a good discussion of the ambivalence of Chinese strategists about the value of genuine multipolarity, see Christensen, "China," 30.

25. He Xin, "Guanyu dangqian guonei xingshi de yi feng xin" (A letter concerning the current domestic situation), May 4, 1992, in *He Xin zhengzhi jingji lunwen ji* (He Xin's collected essays on politics and economics) ed. He Xin (Harbin: Heilongjiang Education Press, 1993), 174–75. Fang Ning, Wang Xiaodong, and Qiao Liang, *Quanqiuhua yinying xia de Zhongguo zhi lu* (Beijing: Chinese Academy of Social Sciences Press, 1999), 47; Zhang Runzhuang, "Chong gu Zhongguo waijiao suo chu zhi guoji huanjing" (Re-estimating the international environment in which China's foreign relations are situated), *Zhanlue yu guanli*, no.1 (2001): 28.

26. See, for instance, Zhang Yunling's analysis of the strength of American unipolarity in "Bainian da guo guanxi de guiji" (The locus of one hundred years of great power relations), in *Huoban haishi duishou: tiaozheng zhong de Zhong Mei Ri E guanxi* (Partners or adversaries? Sino–U.S.–Japanese–Russian relations in transformation), ed. Zhang Yunling (Beijing: Social Science Documents Press, 2000), 24–30.

27. Wang Yizhou, "Guanyu duojihua de ruogan sikao" (A Few Thoughts Concerning Multipolarity) (unpublished paper, April–May 2000).

28. Zhu Feng, "Zai lishi gui yi zhong bawo ZhongMei guanxi," *Huanqiu Shibao Guoji Luntan* (*Global Times* international forum), February 28, 2002, at interforum.xilubbs.com/ (accessed 2002).

29. See Zhang Yunling, "Zonghe Anquan guan ji dui wo guo anquan de sikao" (The concept of comprehensive security and reflections on China's security), *Dangai Ya Tai* (Contemporary Asia–Pacific studies), no 1. (2000): 1–16; Wang Yizhou, "Duojihua bu deng yu fan mei" (Multipolarity is not equivalent to anti-Americanism), at memo.363.net/comment/duice09.htm (accessed 1999); Wang Yizhou "Xin shijie de zhongguo yu duobian waijiao" (The new century China and multilateral diplomacy) (paper presented to a research conference on "Theory of Multilateralism and Multilateral Diplomacy," Beijing, China, 2001); Zhang Yunling, "Bai nian da guo guanxi," 31.

30. See Yan Xuetong, *Zhongguo jueqi—guoji huanjing pingu* (An assessment of the international environment for China's rise) (Tianjin: People's Publishing House, 1999), 349–55.

31. The PLA estimates are taken from Michael Pillsbury, *China Debates the Future International Environment* (Washington, D.C.: National Defense University). The CICIR estimates are from CICIR, *Zonghe guojia liliang pinggu* (Estimation of comprehensive national strength) (Beijing: CICIR, 2000). For an insightful assessment of the estimates

of China's relative weakness vis-à-vis the United States, and the caution this has induced in Chinese diplomacy in East Asia, see David Finklestein, "Chinese Perceptions of the Costs of a Conflict," in *The Costs of Conflict: The Impact on China of a Future War*, ed. Andrew Scobell (Carlisle, Pa.: Strategic Studies Institute, October 2001), 9–27.

32. The former minister of foreign affairs, Qian Qichen, who is still influential in foreign policy making, recently listed some of the key issues in international relations research for China. First on the list was the "information society." Second was the question of globalization. Multipolarity was not among the issues. See "Dangqian guojiguanxi yanjiu zhong de ruogan zhongdian wenti" (Several key issues in current research on international relations), *Shijie jingji yu zhengzhi*, no. 9 (2000): 5–8.

33. For one of the few secondary analyses of the concept of globalization in China, see Thomas Moore, "China and Globalization," in *East Asia and Globalization*, ed. Samuel S. Kim (Lanham, Md.: Rowman & Littlefield, 2000), 111–18.

34. For these kinds of arguments see, Wang Xueyu, "Cong guojihua dao quanqiuhua" (From internationalization to globalization), *Shijie jingji yu zhengzhi* (World economics and politics), no. 8 (2000): 52; Wang Yizhou, *Dangdai guoji zhengzhi pouxi* (Analysis of contemporary international politics) (Shanghai: Peoples Publishing House, 1995), 15–16; Wang Yizhou, Zhubian shouji (Editor's note), in *Quanqiuhua shidai de guoji anquan* (International security in the era of globalization), ed. Wang Yizhou (Shanghai: Peoples Publishing House, 1999), 8; Liang Guangyan, "Quanqiu hua shidai: dangdai guoji anquan de beijing" (The era of globalization: the international security background), in *Quanqiuhua shidai de guoji anquan* (International security in the era of globalization), ed. Wang Yizhou (Shanghai: Peoples Publishing House, 1999), 25.

35. Jin Xide, "MeiRi tongmen guanxi de tiaozheng yu gengxin" (Adjustment and renewal in U.S.–Japan alliance relations), in *Huoban haishi duishou: tiaozheng zhong de Zhong Mei Ri E guanxi* (Partners or adversaries? Sino–U.S.–Japanese–Russian relations in transformation), ed. Zhang Yunling (Beijing: Social Science Documents Press, 2000), 297.

36. For an insightful study of the motives for and limits on Sino–Russian strategic cooperation, see Alexander Lukin, "Russian Images of China and Russia–China Relations" (Brookings Institution paper, 2001), at www.brookings.org/fp/cnaps/papers/lukinwp_01.pdf.

37. For a sophisticated analysis of Chinese interests on the Korean peninsula, see Tang Shiping, "A Neutral Reunified Korea: A Chinese View," *Journal of East Asian Affairs* (Seoul) 13, no. 2 (Fall–Winter 1999): 464–83.

38. See the analysis by PLA strategists in Zhu Yangming ed., *YaTai anquan zhanlue lun* (On security strategy in the Asia-Pacific) (Beijing: Military Sciences, 2000), 73.

39. See Zhang Yunling, "Peace and Security of Korean Peninsula and China's Role" (2001), at www.cass.net.cn/s28_yts/wordch-en/en-zyl/en-peace.htm (accessed July 2002).

40. The message is pushed with increasing urgency now, however, because of a real fear in Beijing that the DPRK's belligerence will provoke a hard-line American response, Japanese nuclearization, and a major military conflict in Korea followed by the collapse of the DPRK as a buffer state and its replacement by an economically strapped ROK that is allied to a United States that deploys its forces north of the 38th parallel.

41. To the extent that the DPRK uses *potential*, as opposed to deployed, WMD capabilities as a tool for extracting economic and political benefits from the ROK, the United States, and Japan, it may be that at least some DPRK extortion is in Beijing's interests.

42. According to the Beijing Area Study's feeling thermometer (0–100 degrees), the mean degree of feeling toward the ROK in 2001 was 58 degrees, in contrast to 47 degrees for the United States and 35 degrees for Japan.

43. Marcus Noland, Sherman Robinson, and Li-gang Liu, *The Costs and Benefits of Korean Unification* (Stanford, Calif.: Stanford University, Asia Pacific Research Center, March 1998).

44. On China's relatively relaxed view of the U.S.–ROK alliance, see Yu Bin, *Containment by Stealth: Chinese Views of and Policies toward America's Alliances with Japan and Korea after the Cold War* (Stanford, Calif.: Stanford University, Asia Pacific Research Center, September 1999), 10–11.

45. As of this writing, it is unclear whether Chinese assessments of a post-DPRK world are changing. In the context of growing Chinese worries that the DPRK may provoke a war on the peninsula, a growing anger at the North's reckless withdrawal from the Non-Proliferation Treaty, and a concern that China itself may be a target of DPRK nuclear weapons in the future, there are hints that Chinese analysts are thinking hard about whether an end to the DPRK might, under certain conditions, be in China's interests. One small example of movement on this issue is that in the spring of 2003 some Chinese analysts were beginning to openly discuss the need for regime change in the North with American interlocutors. The question for Chinese analysts is still whether the costs of a dramatic regime change—refugees, possible war on the peninsula, the loss of a buffer, among others—outweigh the benefits.

46. Zhao Zijin, "ZhongMei guanxi zhong de Riben yinsu" (The Japan element in Sino–U.S. relations), in *ZhongMei guangxi de fazhan bianhua ji qi qushi,* ed. Zhu Chenghu (Nanjing: Jiangsu People's Press, 1998), 362–63. Yang Bojiang, "Riben lengzhanhou de anquan zhanlue," (Japan's post–Cold War security strategy) in *Zhongguo yu YaTai anquan* (China and Asia-Pacific security), ed. Yan Xuetong (Beijing: Shishi, 1999), 160; Academy of Military Sciences (AMS) Strategy Department, *2000–2001 nian zhanlue pinggu* (2000–2001 strategic assessments) (Beijing: Military Sciences, 2000), 83.

47. See Jin, "MeiRi tongmen guanxi," 260–261, 269. Even some PLA analysts imply that the United States intends to use the alliance both to control Japanese power and to deal with Chinese and Russian power. See AMS, *2000–2001 nian,* 81.

48. See Wang Jianwei and Wu Xinbo, *Against Us or with Us? The Chinese Perspective of America's Alliances with Japan and Korea* (Stanford, Calif.: Stanford University, Asia Pacific Research Center, May 1998), 33. Beijing wants a statement excluding Taiwan from the scope of the U.S.–Japan treaty revisions. AMS, *2000–2001 nian,* 83.

49. As Christensen points out, this contingent view of the alliance is consistent with the Chinese practical preference that Japan not emerge as an independent pole in a future multipolar world. See his "China," 30.

50. Jin Xide "ZhongRi huoban guanxi de queli he weilai fazhan" (The establishment and future development of Sino–Japanese partnership relations), in *Huoban haishi duishou: tiaozheng zhong de Zhong Mei Ri E guanxi* (Partners or adversaries? Sino–U.S.–Japanese–Russian relations in transformation), ed. Zhang Yunling (Beijing: Social Science Documents Press, 2000), 205, 258; AMS, *2000–2001 nian,* 83.

51. See, for example, the opinion piece written by a PLA officer prominent in regional security policy, Sr. Col. Zhu Chenghu from the National Defense University, "Zhong-Ri

guanxi: liyi yu qinggan" (Sino–Japanese relations: interest and emotion), *Huanqiu shibao* (Global times), July 30, 1999. See also Feng Zhaokui, "Guanyu ZhongRi guanxi de zhanlue sikao" (Strategic thoughts on Sino–Japanese relations), *Shijie jingji yu zhengzhi* (World economics and politics), no. 11 (2000): 12. On the unconstructive *interactivity* in the relationship, see Feng, "ZhongRi quanxi," 15, and Jin, "ZhongRi huoban guanxi," 207.

52. Zhu, "Zhong-Ri guangxi." See also Jin, "ZhongRi huoban guanxi," 205, 207.

53. Zhu, "Zhong-Ri guanxi"; Feng, "ZhongRi guanxi"; Gilbert Rozman, "China's Changing Images of Japan, 1998–2001: The Struggle to Balance Partnership and Rivalry," *International Relations of the Asia-Pacific* 2 (2002): 113.

54. Jin, "MeiRi tongmeng guanxi," 301.

55. For example, some PLA analysts are worried that Japanese public opinion is no longer a constraint on Japanese military expansion. See Yang Yunzhong, "Riben jiashu xiang junshi daguo mubiao maijin" (Japan speeds up in forging ahead toward the goal of military great power) (2001), CASS Asia–Pacific Institute, at www.cass.net.cn/s28_yts/wordch-en/ch-ddyt2002/ch-qkddyt0205yyz.htm (accessed July 2002). Others want to retaliate for Japan's alleged lack of contrition on historical issues by shifting economic linkages away from Japan and toward Europe and the United States. See Feng Zhaokui's critique of this view in "ZhongRi guanxi," 12.

56. For a summary of a study of Chinese history textbooks and their hostile images of Japan, see Rozman, "China's Changing Images," 119–20.

57. Data from the 2001 Beijing Area Study.

58. Survey data from the Beijing Area Study from 1998 to 2001 show that wealth and education are positively correlated with higher levels of amity toward the United States, and that in absolute terms (prior to 2001) the middle class tended to have a higher level of amity toward the United States than toward most other states. See Alastair Iain Johnston, "Chinese Middle Class Attitudes Towards International Affairs: Nascent Liberalization?" (draft paper, June 2002).

59. Some concrete policy advice for promoting multipolarity includes diversifying China's economic interdependence to include Europe; improving relations with a diverse range of influential (status quo) middle powers; joining a strategic dialogue with the United States and Japan so as to pressure them to improve their transparency about Taiwan; and actively joining important multilaterals (including the G-8) so that China's voice is heard. See Wang Yizhou, "Guanyu duojihua de ruogan sikao" (Several thoughts on multipolarity) (unpublished paper, April–May 1998). These policies would fall under what Morgenthau might call "minor adjustments which leave intact the relative power positions of the nations concerned." See Hans J. Morgenthau, *Politics among Nations*, 5th ed. (New York: Knopf, 1978), 46.

60. Yong Deng "Hegemon on the Offensive: Chinese Perspectives on U.S. Global Strategy," *Political Science Quarterly* 116, no. 3 (Fall 2001): 359.

61. See for instance Thomas J. Christensen's argument about a Chinese limited blockade strategy against Taiwan, in "Posing Problems without Catching Up: China's Rise and Challenges for U.S. Security Policy," *International Security* 25, no. 4 (Spring 2001): 5–40.

62. Historically, in the Cold War era, for the United States the seamlessness of credible commitments to allies required a global military reach that, in turn, required political acquiescence/deference from a wide range of countries. The expansion of American

power in the Cold War, therefore, was to some extent a function of a conservative geopolitical goal of containment, combined with offensive military requirements dictated by the preservation of a global alliance system.

63. Michael Green, "Managing Chinese Power: The View from Japan," in *Engaging China: The Management of an Emerging Power*, ed. Alastair Iain Johnston and Robert S. Ross (London: Routledge, 1999), 152–75.

64. Gilbert Rozman, "Japan's Images of China in the 1990s: Are They Ready for China's 'Smile Diplomacy' or Bush's 'Strong Diplomacy'?" *Japanese Journal of Political Science* 2, no. 1 (2001): 97–125.

65. See *Report to Congress of the US–China Security Review Commission*, July 2002, at www.uscc.gov/anrp02.htm (accessed July 2002).

66. On the discourse of identity in Taiwan, see Su Qi, "Domestic Determinants of Taiwan's Mainland Policy" (paper presented at the Peace Across the Taiwan Strait Conference, May 23–25, 2002, Asian Studies Centre, Oxford University), at www.taiwansecurity.org/TS/2002/Su-0502.htm (accessed July 2002). For examples of the use of the identity card by Taiwan nationalists, see "Taiwan's Identity Crisis" BBC Report, May 17, 2002, at news.bbc.co.uk/1/hi/world/asia-pacific/1993608.stm (accessed July 2002); "Editorial: Taiwanese Must Make a Choice," *Taipei Times*, June 5, 2002, at www.taipeitimes.com/news/2002/06/05/story/0000139047 (accessed July 2002); and "Identity Crisis Eats at Nation: Lee" *Taipei Times*, June 8, 2002, at www.taipeitimes.com/news/2002/06/08/story/0000139436 (accessed July 2002).

67. Steven Goldstein and Randall Schriver, "An Uncertain Relationship: The United States, Taiwan and the Taiwan Relations Act," *China Quarterly* 165 (March 2001): 147–72.

68. Zalmay M. Khalilzad et al., *The United States and a Rising China: Strategic and Military Implications* (Santa Monica, Calif.: RAND Corporation, 1999).

69. See, for example, the interpretation of CINCPAC Admiral Dennis Blair's constructivist-influenced proposal for setting up a security community in East Asia in Song Yimin, "Yatai diqu de jige xin fazhan qushi" (Several new development trends in the Asia–Pacific region), *Shijie jingji yu zhengzhi* (World economics and politics), no. 9 (2000): 12–13.

70. Tom Christensen develops this logic in his insightful essay, "Windows and War: Changes in the International System and China's Decision to Use Force" (unpublished paper, March 2002).

71. These are two different goals and it is unclear which motivates Chinese behavior at the moment. In the 2000 white paper on Taiwan, the so-called third condition for the use of force—if Taiwan indefinitely postpones talks on unification—seemed to imply the Chinese leadership had shifted to the latter goal. But Beijing has downplayed this phrase of late, and it is possible that Jiang put the condition in with a domestic rather than foreign audience in mind.

72. For a recent restatement of his comment, see his, "The Case against Containment: Treat China Like an Enemy and That's What It Will Be," *Global Beat China Handbook* (June 22, 1998), at www.nyu.edu/globalbeat/asia/china/06221998nye.html (accessed July 2002). My claim about security dilemma dynamics in China–East Asian relations is not a novel argument. In addition to Nye's famous comment, see also Thomas J. Christensen, "China, the U.S.–Japan Alliance, and the Security Dilemma in East Asia," *International*

Security 23, no. 4 (Spring 1999): 49–80. Some of the components of a security dilemma argument are found even earlier, in Karl W. Eikenberry, "Does China Threaten Asia–Pacific Regional Stability?" *Parameters* (Spring 1995): 82–99.

73. There is a small but growing number of IR "new thinkers" in China, however, who are well aware of the security dilemma effects of China's own behavior on its own security. See, for instance, Zhang Yunling, "Zonghe Anquan guan," and Qin Yaqing, "Response to Yong Deng: Power, Perception and the Cultural Lens," *Asian Affairs* 28, no. 3 (Fall 2001): 155–58.

FURTHER READING

Christensen, Thomas. "Posing Problems without Catching Up: China's Rise and Challenges for U.S. Security Policy." *International Security* 25, no. 4 (Spring 2001).

———. "China, the US–Japan Alliance, and the Security Dilemma in East Asia." *International Security* 23, no. 4 (Spring 1999): 49–80.

Chu Shulong. "China and the U.S.–Japan and U.S.–Korea Alliances in a Changing Northeast Asia." Stanford, Calif.: Stanford University, Asia Pacific Research Center, June 1999.

Feigenbaum, Evan A. *Change in Taiwan and Potential Adversity in the Strait*. Santa Monica: RAND Corporation, 1995.

Finklestein, David M. "China's National Military Strategy." Alexandria, Va.: C.N.A. Corporation, January 2000.

Goldstein, Avery. "The Diplomatic Face of China's Grand Strategy: A Rising Power's Emerging Choice." *China Quarterly* 168 (December 2001).

Goldstein, Steven, and Randall Schriver. "An Uncertain Relationship: The United States, Taiwan and the Taiwan Relations Act." *China Quarterly* 165 (March 2001): 147–72.

Lee, Bernice. "The Security Implications of the New Taiwan." Adelphi Papers, no. 331. London: Institute of Strategic Studies, 1999.

Oksenberg, Michel. "Taiwan, Tibet, and Hong Kong in Sino–American Relations." In *Living with China*, edited by Ezra Vogel, 53–96. New York: Norton, 1997.

Pillsbury, Michael. *China Debates the Future Security Environment*. Washington, D.C.: National Defense University Press, 2000.

Ross, Robert S. "The 1995–1996 Taiwan Strait Confrontation: Coercion, Credibility and the Use of Force." *International Security* 25, no. 2 (Fall 2000): 87–123.

———. "The Geography of the Peace: East Asia in the Twenty-First Century." *International Security* 23, no. 4 (Spring 1999): 81–118.

Rozman, Gilbert. "China's Changing Images of Japan, 1998–2001: The Struggle to Balance Partnership and Rivalry." *International Relations of the Asia-Pacific* 2 (2002).

Tang Shiping. "A Neutral Reunified Korea: A Chinese View." *Journal of East Asian Affairs* (Seoul) 13, no. 2 (Fall–Winter 1999): 464–83.

Wang Jianwei and Wu Xinbo. "Against Us or with Us? The Chinese Perspective of America's Alliances with Japan and Korea." Stanford, Calif.: Stanford University, Asia Pacific Research Center, May 1998.

Whiting, Allen S. "Chinese Nationalism and Foreign Policy after Deng." *China Quarterly*, no. 142 (June 1995).

Yu Bin. "Containment by Stealth: Chinese Views of and Policies toward America's Alliances with Japan and Korea after the Cold War." Stanford, Calif.: Stanford University, Asia Pacific Research Center, September 1999.

3

China's International Relations: The Economic Dimension

Thomas G. Moore

By whatever measure one prefers, evidence of China's deepening participation in the world economy is undeniable. Multilaterally, Beijing holds membership in every significant global and regional economic forum for which it qualifies, including the World Trade Organization (WTO), the International Monetary Fund (IMF), World Bank, the Asia Pacific Economic Cooperation (APEC) forum, the Asian Development Bank, the Asia–Europe Meeting (ASEM) dialogue, and the ASEAN Plus Three (APT) process. (APT consists of the ten members of the Association of Southeast Asian Nations plus China, Japan, and South Korea.) Once a marginal actor in world markets for goods and capital, China is now a significant player. Indeed, China's foreign economic relations are defined today as much by its participation in globalized networks of production and exchange as by its participation in the aforementioned intergovernmental bodies. Put another way, China's experience as a latecomer in the world political economy has been profoundly influenced by both corporate-based hierarchies and state-based hierarchies. Led by the economic takeoff of its coastal areas, China's participation in transnational manufacturing networks has facilitated its emergence as a newly industrializing country. In industries as diverse as garments, footwear, and sporting goods, on the one hand, and power-generating machinery, computer hardware, and telecommunications equipment, on the other hand, China's profile as a producer (or, in many cases, as a partner in production) has risen swiftly.

Equally important, although somewhat underappreciated until recently, is the ongoing reform of China's economic system. Two decades before its WTO entry, Beijing began a significant (if incomplete) restructuring of the country's institutions, from the foreign trade system and investment laws to the foreign exchange regime and intellectual property standards. Perhaps most importantly to its leading economic partners, China's growing participation in the world economy has been accomplished without substantial compromises in the norms, principles, and rules that constitute the liberal international economic system. In this sense, China's current integration has been achieved both with minimal disruption to the overall management of the world economy and with minimal economic dislocation to individual members of the system, including its partners in Northeast Asia.[1] (As defined in this book, Northeast Asia consists of China, Japan, North Korea, Russia, South Korea, Taiwan, and the United States.)

ENTER THE DRAGON: CHINA'S EMERGENCE AS AN ECONOMIC POWER

China's March into the World Trade Organization

After fifteen years of arduous negotiations, China finally gained admission to the WTO in 2001. The decision by China's leaders to accept the stringent conditions offered for WTO entry demonstrated their commitment to accelerating domestic economic reform as part of the country's ongoing transition toward a market-based economy. A seminal event in several respects, Beijing's WTO accession represented a significant milestone in the history of the international economic system, to say nothing of China's integration into the community of nations. By any measure, WTO entry ranks as one of the most important developments in China since the reform era began after the death of Mao Zedong in 1976. As far as China's specific WTO commitments are concerned, only a few highlights can be mentioned here.[2] On market access issues, for example, China is required to slash both tariff and nontariff barriers (such as quotas and licenses) to imports of agricultural and industrial goods. With respect to exports, China has committed to eliminating its various subsidy programs. Other changes include a ratcheting-up of protection for intellectual property rights, increased availability of trading rights to foreign companies, and a dramatic opening to foreign investment of critical service sectors such as telecommunications, banking, insurance, securities, and distribution.

No one expects the implementation of China's WTO commitments to proceed easily, especially given the extremely ambitious set of changes outlined in Beijing's accession protocol. Compliance will also be complicated by factors such as the underdeveloped nature of China's legal system and the independent power wielded by industrial ministries and local governments. A further complication is the fact that China underwent a leadership transition in March 2003, as President Jiang Zemin and Prime Minister Zhu Rongji relinquished their posts to Hu Jintao and Wen Jiabao, respectively, after more than a decade at the top of China's political system.[3] Even if these (and other) high-level personnel changes do not significantly affect China's long-term commitment to pursuing deeper integration into the world economy, the succession process certainly raises questions about Beijing's shorter-term capacity to undertake substantial economic restructuring during a period of leadership consolidation. Potential crises such as the security environment on the Korean peninsula and the emergence of severe acute respiratory syndrome (SARS) only magnify the challenges facing China's leaders. Depending on the scope and pace of reform, a serious gulf could emerge between international expectations concerning China's WTO implementation and domestic political reality.

That said, China's WTO entry raises the prospect of major economic changes domestically, regionally, and globally. Successful implementation is expected to yield substantial gains not just in China's international trade flows and inward foreign direct investment (FDI), but perhaps most importantly, in the country's economic output, efficiency, and welfare.[4] By design, the core of China's economy was until now substantially insulated from competitive pressures in the world economy. For example, more than 40 percent of China's imports are still used as inputs in export processing arrangements rather than as competition for domestic producers. In this sense, China is perhaps best characterized as being heavily involved with, but only shallowly integrated into, the world economy. This is why Beijing's WTO accession is potentially so significant. Areas of especially shallow integration, such as agriculture and services, are at the forefront of China's WTO commitments. For this reason, China's entry could be code-named "Project Deep Integration."

Given China's size and potential, the world is watching carefully for signs of the eventual impact that China's WTO accession will have on the global economy. Particularly in East Asia, there is uncertainty about whether China's growth represents an opportunity or a challenge for the regional economy. (As used in this chapter, East Asia is simply shorthand for Northeast Asia and Southeast Asia.) On the one hand, the enhanced competitiveness of China's industries—especially as they increasingly excel in both labor-intensive and high-tech areas simultaneously—may displace exports from developing countries (ASEAN) and developed countries (Japan, South Korea, and Taiwan) alike. A related concern is that WTO entry will only increase the allure of the China market for foreign investors, further skewing capital flows in Beijing's favor. On the other hand, China's WTO entry is likely to increase the country's importance as an engine of growth for East Asia. From this perspective, Chinese modernization will generate a growing demand for goods and services from both ASEAN (natural resources, agricultural products, cheap labor-intensive goods) and Japan, South Korea, and Taiwan (capital-intensive goods and services). Furthermore, China may become a more constructive and committed participant in multilateral economic cooperation as its role in the regional economy changes over time. Even as regards FDI flows, China's gain may not be its neighbors' loss. Some experts predict that the overall investment pie in East Asia will grow as multinational corporations (MNCs) seek to locate other aspects of their operations in the region for proximity to their investments in China.

China in the Global and Northeast Asian Regional Economies

To understand China's evolving role in the world economy more fully, especially as regards its relations in Northeast Asia, a brief survey of China's participation as a foreign trader and FDI recipient is required.

Foreign Trade

By the time China joined the WTO, its integration into the world economy had already progressed further than most observers would have believed possible a quarter-century ago, when Deng Xiaoping became paramount leader shortly after Mao's death. As a result of consistently high growth rates in foreign trade, China rose from thirtieth place among world traders in 1977 to a rank of fifth in 2002. (If the European Union is counted as a single trader, China jumps to fourth place, trailing only the United States, the European Union, and Japan.) While much of the world has endured sluggish trade performance in recent years, China has continued to power ahead. In 2002, for example, China alone accounted for more than one-fifth of the growth in world trade. Indeed, its trade totals are now fast approaching those of the entire Middle East and Africa (combined) or Latin America. In a particularly telling statistic, China's exports in 2002 were virtually identical to the combined exports of India, Brazil, Indonesia, Malaysia, and Thailand. The scale of this export success has contributed significantly to the merchandise trade surplus Beijing has registered every year but one (1993) since 1990, surpluses that averaged $27 billion annually between 1995 and 2002. These surpluses have also helped China to maintain foreign-exchange reserves ($286 billion at the end of 2002) that have consistently ranked second behind only Japan's in recent years.

For trade data, this chapter relies almost exclusively upon statistics published by international agencies such as the WTO and IMF, which are based on customs reports submitted by China's trade partners.[5] Although the aggregate trade statistics published by the Chinese government are accurate, the country-specific data have some problems. For example, Chinese figures overstate trade with Hong Kong—the world's foremost economic entrepôt—and therefore also understate China's trade with countries such as the United States. Although Hong Kong has been under Chinese sovereignty since July 1, 1997, and is considered a special administrative region of the People's Republic of China (PRC), it retains its own currency and continues to function as a separate customs territory. Consequently, commerce between Hong Kong and mainland China is classified as foreign rather than domestic economic activity by all parties (Beijing, Hong Kong, and global actors such as international agencies and individual national governments). While this chapter does recognize that Hong Kong is an important (and largely independent) economic actor in Northeast Asia, it does not examine mainland China's relations with Hong Kong as a separate bilateral relationship. Nor does the chapter attempt to flout convention by reconfiguring the data to include Hong Kong's economic activity as a part of China's. Therefore, all references to China are explicitly to mainland China. Whatever the imperfections of the trade statistics presented here, they are still useful to identify trends in China's bilateral and regional trade relationships.

As a region, Northeast Asia has long served as the focal point of China's trade relations. In 1990, Japan, North Korea, Russia, South Korea, Taiwan, and the United States accounted for 47 percent of China's total trade. This figure rose to 56 percent in 1995, where it remained in both 2001 and 2002. The United States, Japan, South Korea, and Taiwan together accounted for 54 percent of China's total trade in 2002. By contrast, the European Union and ASEAN were responsible for only 14 percent and 9 percent, respectively. To underscore the importance of China's trade with the United States, it is worth noting that China's trade with its APT partners (ASEAN plus Japan and South Korea) accounted for 32 percent of its total trade, only 8 percent more than trade with the United States. Similarly, Japan, South Korea, and Taiwan accounted for 30 percent of China's trade, just 6 percent more than its trade with the United States. The significance of the United States is most apparent, however, as an export market. Although exports to one another among China, Japan, South Korea, and Taiwan have been steadily increasing in recent years, by 2002 they still equaled only 97 percent of their collective exports to the United States. Even this figure understates the importance of the United States as a market for finished goods, given the more substantial role of processing trade found in exports among China, Japan, South Korea, and Taiwan. These economies—both individually and collectively—have higher levels of exports to the United States than one would expect, given Washington's overall share of world trade. In China's case, exports to the United States represented 38 percent of its total exports in 2002. Although this figure has declined from its peak in 1999 (44%), it remains higher than at any time prior to 1998 (when it was 41%), when China's exports to its neighbors first fell in the wake of the Asian financial crisis (AFC). Seen from this perspective, China's dependence on the U.S. market has simply returned to a level consistent with the pre-AFC period, in which the share of Chinese exports taken by the United States doubled from 18 percent in 1987 to 36 percent in 1997.

Foreign Direct Investment

As spectacular as China's rise as a trading power has been, its success in attracting foreign capital has been equally impressive. From the time of Deng's landmark Southern Tour in 1992, after which China entered a new, more intense phase of reform and opening, FDI has accounted for approximately 75 percent of China's total foreign capital inflows (the rest has been primarily foreign loans).[6] In 2002, China surpassed the United States as the world's leading destination for FDI, absorbing nearly $53 billion. Previously, China had already stood for a decade as the world's leading recipient of FDI among developing countries. In 2001, for example, the last year for which comprehensive international data on FDI is available, China captured 23 percent of the total FDI received worldwide by developing countries. China received $47 billion in FDI compared with $3 billion for India. All told, China absorbed $448 billion in FDI between 1979 and 2002, more than $350 billion of which was recorded after 1990. By the mid-1990s, FDI accounted for sizable (and rapidly growing) percentages of domestic investment, industrial output, imports and exports, tax revenues, and jobs. By 2002, foreign-invested enterprises (FIEs) accounted for more than 53 percent of China's total trade, 25 percent of its industrial output, and 20 percent of national tax revenues. FIEs directly employed 23 million people, or roughly 10 percent of the working population in China's cities and towns.

Nearly four hundred of the world's Fortune 500 companies have FDI projects in China, including all the world's major producers of computers, electronics, and telecommunications equipment. For example, Microsoft announced a $750 million investment in 2002, the largest project to date by a foreign software company. Of particular relevance to this book, China now enjoys an increasing presence from MNCs based in Northeast Asia—such as JVC, Samsung, Panasonic, Mitsubishi, Motorola, AT&T, General Motors, IBM, Intel, and General Electric—as business investors have shifted their focus from Southeast Asia to China in recent years, particularly in the wake of the AFC and China's accession to the WTO. All of this suggests that FDI is an increasingly important mechanism for technology transfer as China attempts to "trade up" in the international product cycle. Indeed, 25 percent of exports by FIEs were already classified as high-tech exports by 2000. Perhaps most strikingly, these exports represented 81 percent of China's total exports in high-tech products, an increase of more than 20 percent since 1996. This trend stands to continue, given China's April 2003 accession to the WTO's Information Technology Agreement, which requires that China eliminate tariffs and other duties on most information technology imports from WTO members.

According to estimates by the Organization for Economic Cooperation and Development (OECD), China-bound FDI is projected to reach $100 billion annually by 2010 if Beijing fully implements its WTO agreements. If so, this would represent a doubling of current FDI inflows. Should it materialize, much of this growth is expected to come from Europe and North America, as investment projects increasingly gravitate toward the service sector, an area where FDI had lagged from the late 1990s to 2002, when it saw a 50 percent increase. According to the Investment Intensity Index, constructed by the United Nations Commission on Trade and Development (UNCTAD), Japan's investment in China is slightly below par, while the United States, Canada, and virtually all countries in Northern and Western Europe have very low intensities of investment in China. By contrast, Taiwan, South Korea, Hong Kong, and the members of ASEAN all have extraordinarily high intensities of investment in China. As staggering as the $100 billion a year projection may seem, studies have shown that China's current performance among developing country recipients of FDI ranks only in the middle of the pack relative to its potential based on factors related to economic size. According to UNCTAD's Inward FDI Index, China's revealed competitive advantage in attracting FDI is far from being exhausted. This may help to explain why China's FDI inflows have continued to grow, despite the fact that the share of total world FDI received by developing countries decreased by more than half from 1994 to 2000. In 2001 and 2002, moreover, China enjoyed substantial increases in FDI (15% and 13%, respectively) despite precipitous decreases in total world FDI (50% and 25%, respectively).

Identifying the source of FDI inflows by country of origin is very difficult for China.[7] Nominally, Hong Kong and the so-called Free Ports (the Virgin

Islands, the Cayman Islands, Bermuda, Samoa, and so forth) accounted for 50 percent of China's total FDI inflows in 2001, the last year for which detailed information is available. Obviously, the vast majority of this capital originated elsewhere. For example, some of Hong Kong's FDI to China is the result of so-called round tripping: funds sent from the mainland to be rerouted back into China to take advantage of tax breaks and other preferential treatment available to foreign investors. Additional sums represent the proceeds of funds raised by Chinese companies in Hong Kong capital markets. These count as "FDI" when they are moved into China. Still other "FDI" registered as coming from Hong Kong is, in fact, money originating from other countries or territories that prefer to use Hong Kong as a conduit. These phenomena help account for the amazing fact that tiny Hong Kong received $64 billion in FDI in 2000, the fifth highest total in the world for that year—substantially ahead of the mainland and trailing only the United States and three members of the European Union.

Using the nominal data available, China's partners in Northeast Asia collectively accounted for 30 percent of China's FDI inflows in 2001. If Hong Kong and the Free Ports are excluded, the United States, Japan, Taiwan, and South Korea are (in order) the four leading sources of FDI for China. All told, 87 percent of China's FDI inflows in 2001 came from the United States, the Free Ports, or Asia (including Hong Kong). Since most FDI from Hong Kong and the Free Ports is thought to come from China, Hong Kong, and Taiwan, this figure probably provides the most accurate picture of China's total FDI inflows from Asia plus the United States (although it still includes a certain amount of "FDI" that originates in China itself). By contrast, China relies upon Europe (including Russia), Canada, Australia, Latin America, Africa, and so forth, for only 13 percent of its FDI inflows.

China's Economic Relations in Northeast Asia: The Bilateral Dimension

Even in an age of economic globalization and expanding multilateralism in East Asia, bilateral relationships remain critical—especially given their centrality to Chinese strategic thinking and diplomacy. Another virtue of the bilateral dimension is how it underscores the fundamental connection between economics and politics. For China, mutually beneficial economic relations have often served as a bulwark against persistent political or security tensions with Japan, South Korea, Taiwan, and the United States. In this sense, their importance should not be underestimated. For reasons explained earlier, the data presented below exclude Hong Kong (for trade and FDI) and the Free Ports (for FDI).[8] It should also be noted that this chapter considers China only as a recipient of FDI, as Beijing is just beginning to emerge as an important source of capital flows. (Despite a 30 percent increase in 2002, China's outward FDI totaled only $2.3 billion—a fraction of its $52.7 billion inward FDI.)

North Korea

North Korea is a negligible trade partner for China, although China is North Korea's leading trade partner. In 1995, trade with China accounted for 24.3 percent of North Korea's total trade, a figure that declined slightly to 20.8 percent in 2001. By contrast, trade with North Korea represented only 0.2 percent of China's total trade in both 1995 and 2001. Not surprisingly, North Korea is a miniscule source of FDI for China, never exceeding 0.04 percent of China's inflows since 1995. All told, economic relations between China and North Korea are more significant politically than commercially, as Beijing remains Pyongyang's most important patron. Although estimates of its contributions vary widely, China is certainly North Korea's biggest provider of food and oil.

Russia

In 1992, the first year for which international agencies collected trade statistics for post–Soviet Russia, trade with China accounted for 21.3 percent of Russia's overall trade. That figure declined dramatically to 3.3 percent in 1995 before rebounding modestly to 3.5 and 7.1 percent in 2001 and 2002, respectively. For China, trade with Russia represented 3.5 percent of total trade in 1992, a figure that fell to 1.5 percent in 1995 before increasing to 1.9 percent in 2002. These low percentages notwithstanding, China and Russia still rank among one another's ten largest trade partners. Russia is not an important source of FDI for China, having provided only 0.06 percent of China's total FDI inflows in both 1995 and 2001. FDI to China accounted for an average of only 1 percent of Russia's total outward FDI from 1998 to 2001.

Although it has been estimated that unofficial trade (barter exchange and unrecorded border transactions) might nearly double the official statistics for two-way trade, commercial ties are a positive but limited aspect of Sino–Russian relations. Trade and investment linkages are decidedly secondary to political and military affairs, a reality only accentuated by events since September 11, 2001, as Russia's policies on NATO, the Anti–Ballistic Missile Treaty, counterterrorism, and the U.S. military presence in Central Asia have taken center stage, even as economic ties continue to expand. For

Beijing, civilian commerce has long received a much lower priority in dealing with Moscow than have arms sales (which make up about 25 percent of bilateral trade), the transfer of military technology, and political cooperation based on mutual opposition to U.S. policies, such as intervention in Kosovo and the Iraq War. Even in the commercial realm, the most significant developments in recent years have involved geostrategic projects, such as the much-ballyhooed oil pipeline between the two countries. At a multilateral level, the Shanghai Cooperation Organization (SCO) is the primary regional mechanism through which China now engages Russia on economic matters. Although the SCO—a six-member group of Central Asian nations established in June 2001—is primarily focused on strategic stability and international security in the region, it also convenes regular meetings among trade ministers and other economic officials. Although Russia is also a member of APEC, Beijing can be expected in the future to collaborate most closely with Moscow—even on commercial matters—through the SCO.

South Korea

China's economic relations with South Korea have expanded rapidly since the establishment of diplomatic relations in 1992. This has had the effect not only of facilitating China's economic development but also of advancing Beijing's strategic interests on the Korean peninsula by allaying (at least in part) concerns in Seoul about Beijing's support for Pyongyang. In 1992, the first year for which statistics on China–South Korean trade were collected by international agencies, trade with China accounted for only 2.7 percent of South Korea's total trade. That figure grew rapidly to 6.4, 9.4, and 13.1 percent in 1995, 2000, and 2002, respectively. Indeed, China has been the biggest source of trade growth for South Korea over the past decade, with Seoul's exports to Beijing growing at a rate of nearly 25 percent per annum from 1992 to 2002. For China, trade with South Korea represented only 3.8 percent of its total trade in 1992, a figure that rose to 5.9 percent in 1995 and 6.6 percent in both 2000 and 2002. In 2001, China surpassed Japan as South Korea's second-largest trading partner and trailed only the United States. South Korea is China's fourth-largest trading partner.

South Korea has also become an increasingly important source of FDI for China in recent years, accounting for 2.7, 3.7, and 4.6 percent of China's FDI inflows in 1995, 2000, and 2001, respectively. It is now the fifth-largest investor in China, and FDI to China averaged 45 percent of South Korea's total outward FDI from 1998 to 2001. In 2001, China supplanted the United States as South Korea's top destination for FDI.

To this point, economic tensions between Beijing and Seoul have been relatively modest. Although South Korea has been the most frequent target of Chinese antidumping actions in recent years, the two sides have for the most part managed to avoid the rancor sometimes found in Sino–American and Sino–Japanese trade relations. One issue of possible significance for the future is China's persistent trade deficit with South Korea, a subject of increasing displeasure in Beijing. On the South Korean side, there is growing concern about the implications of China's WTO entry for the competitiveness of Korean firms both at home and, especially, abroad.

Taiwan

Even as China and Taiwan push ahead with their respective military buildups and vie for political influence in foreign capitals, economic ties continue to grow and deepen. In 1990, trade with China accounted for 2.1 percent of Taiwan's total trade. That figure grew rapidly to 8.0 percent in 1995 and 18.0 percent in 2002. For China, trade with Taiwan represented 2.2 percent of total trade in 1990, a figure that thereafter rose, measuring 6.1 percent in 1995 and 7.2 percent in 2002. The result of this expanding trade is that Taiwan is now China's third-largest trade partner, and China is Taiwan's second-largest trade partner.

Despite various kinds of government restrictions, Taiwan has long been an important source of FDI for China. The official total of utilized FDI from 1989 to 2002 was $33.1 billion. In 2002, Taiwan ranked as China's second-largest source of FDI. Moreover, Taiwanese capital is understood to be a significant contributor to the huge increases of FDI inflows China has enjoyed from the Virgin Islands (and the Free Ports generally) in recent years. In 1995, FDI from the Virgin Islands accounted for less than 1 percent of China's total inflows. By 2001, that figure had risen to 10.8 percent. This undoubtedly explains why Taiwan's official share of Chinese FDI inflows decreased from 8.5 percent in 1995 to 6.4 percent in 2001, despite burgeoning commerce across the Taiwan Strait. By most estimates, Taiwan's total FDI in the mainland through all channels is at least double the official figure. Even that number shows Taiwan's FDI in China as averaging 56 percent of Taiwan's total outward FDI from 1998 to 2001. According to some estimates, one million or more Taiwanese now live on the mainland, as 50 percent of Taiwan's top one thousand companies have investments across the strait. Shanghai alone is said to host 300,000 Taiwanese.

With their linked accessions to the WTO in December 2001 and January 2002, respectively, China and Taiwan seem poised for even greater economic integration, given the trade group's rules on nondiscrimination. Reinforcing this logic, China's political strategy for dealing with Taiwan shifted in 2002, when Beijing removed the precondition that Taipei accept the "One China" principle before talks on direct links for trade, travel, and communications could progress. By deciding that those links could be classified as "cross-strait" rather than "domestic," Beijing demonstrated its belief that closer economic cooperation will enhance its leverage vis-à-vis Taipei and otherwise slow Taiwan's independence by making it more reliant upon the mainland for its economic well-being. Consequently, China is de-emphasizing, at least for now, the use of military force as a means to achieve reunification.

Although the requirements of WTO membership—to say nothing of the continued international competitiveness of Taiwanese MNCs—would seem to make further cross-strait economic liberalization inevitable, the pace of change will depend primarily on political developments in Taiwan, at least in the short run. These, in turn, will determine how fast Taipei opens its product markets to Beijing and on whether it eases further the investment restrictions faced by Taiwanese firms that wish to do business on the mainland—not to mention the fate of direct links. It is even possible, though perhaps not likely, that Taiwan might invoke Article 21, the WTO's so-called security exemption, in order to avoid conferring upon China the same benefits enjoyed by other WTO members.

As much as cross-strait commercial ties may appear to have their own economic logic, they will continue to be affected by the political atmosphere between Beijing and Taipei. Indeed, economic relations may become a more frequent source of political tension in the future. With both parties as WTO members, there is now a prospect that trade disputes may become multilateralized in the future, despite Beijing's clear preference that relations with Taipei remain strictly bilateral. Along the same lines, Taiwan has publicly expressed an interest in pursuing free-trade agreements (FTAs) with the United States, Japan, Singapore, and New Zealand as part of its ongoing strategy to avoid diplomatic isolation. Taipei is also worried about the economic implications of being excluded from the "FTA fever" that is currently gripping the world economy (especially in East Asia). For its part, Beijing has issued a series of stern warnings that other countries should not enter into FTAs with Taiwan.

Japan

In a relationship mired by historically rooted mistrust, ideological differences, geopolitical rivalry, and even cultural animosity, economic cooperation has served as a mainstay of mutual benefit between Beijing and Tokyo since the normalization of relations in 1972. Acting on their immense economic complementarities, both sides have allowed trade and investment ties to flourish despite a seemingly endless series of political tensions involving, inter alia, wartime accounts in Japanese history textbooks, visits by Japanese leaders to shrines paying homage to the country's war dead, Sino–Japanese territorial disputes, the Taiwan question, China's military buildup, the nature of the U.S.–Japan security alliance, and Japan's role in international affairs more generally.

As recently as 1990, trade with China accounted for only 3.5 percent of Japan's total trade. That figure grew rapidly to 7.4 percent in 1995 and 13.5 percent in 2002. Trade with Japan has been even more significant to China, representing 15.7 percent of total trade in 1990. After peaking at 20.6 percent in 1995, trade with Japan declined over time to 16.3 percent of China's total trade in 2002. Today, China and Japan each stand as the other's second-largest trading partner. (In 2002, China eclipsed the United States as the leading exporter to Japan.) Furthermore, Japan is China's second leading source of FDI, accounting for 8.5 percent of China's total inflows in 1995 and 7.2 and 9.3 percent in 2000 and 2001, respectively. FDI to China averaged 12 percent of Japan's total outward FDI from 1998 to 2001. Although final figures were not available at this writing, China was expected to become Japan's leading destination for FDI in 2002.

As much as commercial ties have served as a positive impetus in Sino–Japanese relations, the growing economic interdependence between the two giants has begun to produce political tensions of its own. Whereas the relationship three decades ago was one between an emerging economic superpower (Japan) and a desperately poor developing country (China), the dynamic today has changed substantially—especially at a perceptual level. While Japan's economy is still four times the size of China's, Japan has experienced a decade of stagnation that has seen its political as well as economic clout diminished both regionally and globally. During the same period, China's economy has continued its robust expansion, raising the country's international profile accordingly. With Beijing's entry into the WTO, China is now the one seen as an emerging economic superpower. Indeed, the prospect that China will continue its reform and opening, using the implementation of its WTO agreements as a prod for sweeping domestic change, only raises concerns among Japanese about their country's long-term competitiveness in world markets and its customary role as the region's economic leader.

To this point, any incipient economic rivalry has been limited mainly to a series of technical disputes involving trademark infringement, antidumping actions, and other allegations of unfair trade. What is changing, however, is the increased frequency of these disputes and the greater politicization of trade relations between Beijing and Tokyo. In December 2001, for example, China and Japan settled a nasty, nine-month dispute in which Beijing had threatened to place 100 percent tariffs on Japanese automobiles, mobile phones, and air conditioners in retaliation for Tokyo's decision to impose higher tariffs on Chinese agricultural goods under the so-called safeguard provisions of the WTO. Whatever the merits of Tokyo's case, it reinforced the growing international perception of Japan as a country looking to protect its farmers and otherwise insulate its economy while China relentlessly continues to open itself to foreign trade and investment.

Trade trends in 2001 illustrate well the changing fortunes of China and Japan described above.[9] While China's trade growth slowed to 7.5 percent from the breakneck rate of 15 percent it had averaged from 1990 to 2000, 7.5 percent was outstanding given that world trade declined by 4 percent overall in 2001, the largest annual decrease in two decades. On the export side, Asia as a whole contracted by 9 percent, with Japan registering a staggering 16 percent decline. For their part, South Korea, Taiwan, Singapore, Thailand, Malaysia, and the Philippines collectively experienced a 13 percent decline. This makes China's 7 percent increase look particularly impressive. On the import side, Asia as a whole saw a 7 percent decrease in imports, with Japan registering an 8 percent decline. South Korea, Taiwan, Singapore, Thailand, Malaysia, and the Philippines again collectively experienced a 13 percent decrease. From this perspective, China's 8 percent increase in imports was downright robust. Indeed, China was the only one of the world's top fifteen importers to register an increase in 2001. This of course underscores the increasingly important role China plays in the global economy. For example, whereas U.S. trade with Asia as a whole declined by 10 percent in 2001, including an 11 percent decrease with Japan, U.S. trade with China increased by 5 percent. Regionally, China's imports from (non-Japan) Asia were only 37 percent as large as Japan's imports from (non-China) Asia in 1990. That figure grew to 51 percent and 95 percent by 1995 and 2001, respectively.

Although China is classified as only a "medium development country" by the United Nations Development Program, its role as an engine of growth in the regional (and, indeed, global) economy increasingly belies that status. Although China accounts for only about 4 percent of the world's gross domestic product (GDP), it was responsible for more than 17 percent of global economic growth in 2002, making it second only to the United States. As explained in greater detail below, Japan and China have begun to compete more directly for regional economic leadership in Asia, particularly within the APT process. Although their economic strengths remain more complementary than competitive in a purely commercial sense, their efforts to influence regional economic affairs increasingly suggest a mix of cooperation and rivalry.

United States

Much like Sino–Japanese relations, Sino–American relations have long relied upon burgeoning economic ties as a bulwark against myriad tensions on political and security matters. China's paramount interest in preserving stable relations with the United States has, if anything, deepened since September 11, 2001, as the war on terrorism and Iraq war have, on balance, strengthened Washington's strategic position regionally and globally. On the economic front, Beijing continues to make allegations about American protectionism, with Washington's use of textile quotas, antidumping actions, safeguards on steel imports, and restrictions on high-tech exports high on the list of grievances. For its part, Washington continues to complain about the perennial trade surplus China enjoys with the United States. But the main focus of the economic relationship has now shifted to China's implementation of its WTO commitments, a task the United States asserts will further American and Chinese interests alike. With American extension of permanent normal trading relations status to China in 2000 and China's accession to the WTO in 2001, Sino–American economic relations are poised to expand the substantial ties built over the past two decades.

In 1990, trade with China accounted for only 2.3 percent of total U.S. trade. That figure rose progressively to 4.4, 6.7, and 7.8 percent in 1995, 2001, and 2002, respectively. For China, trade with the United States represented 21.6 percent of total trade in 1990, remained steady at 21.5 percent in 1995, and then rose to 23.7 percent in 2002. (As noted earlier, China is especially dependent on the United States as an export market, where it is poised to overtake Mexico in 2003 as the second leading supplier of goods after Canada.) Not surprisingly, the United States ranks as China's top trading partner. For its part, China is the United States' fourth-largest trade partner, trailing only Canada, Mexico, and Japan. The United States is less dominant as a source of FDI, but here, too, it ranks as China's leading partner. From 8.3 percent in 1995, the U.S. share of China's inward FDI grew, registering 9.5 percent in 2001. Unlike Taiwan, South Korea, and (to a lesser extent) Japan, the United States sends only a tiny share of its total outward FDI (an average of 3 percent from 1998 to 2001) to China.

As this profile suggests, mutual economic benefit has been an important counterweight for areas of conflict in Sino–American relations, such as nonproliferation, the Taiwan question, U.S. plans for missile defense, human rights, religious freedom, and the U.S.–Japan security alliance. Especially during a period of leadership succession and continued economic and social transition, China seeks to preserve stable relations with the United States both to enhance the country's security environment and as a means to facilitate domestic economic construction.

CHINA'S PARTICIPATION IN NORTHEAST ASIAN ECONOMIC REGIONALISM

China interacts with its Northeast Asian partners in several regional economic forums. Most prominent among these today (at least from a Chinese perspective) are APEC, APT, SCO, the Boao Forum for Asia, and the Tumen River Area Development Programme (TRADP).[10] In none of these forums, however, does each of the actors examined in this book (Japan, North Korea, Russia, South Korea, Taiwan, and the United States) participate. (APEC comes closest, with only North Korea failing to hold membership.) For China, this means that each regional forum has a slightly different political and economic dynamic. Except for a brief survey below, however, this chapter focuses mainly on China's participation in APT, as recent activity within this group has the greatest potential impact for both the future of economic regionalism in East Asia and for China's economic relations with its Northeast Asian partners.

Formed in 1989, APEC first gained prominence in 1993, when U.S. president Bill Clinton initiated an annual leaders' meeting by hosting a summit in Seattle. From China's perspective, the twenty-one-member group is most notable for its inclusion of Taiwan and Hong Kong as separate member economies and for the significant representation enjoyed by Western countries such as the United States, Canada, Mexico, Chile, Peru, Australia, and New Zealand. In 2001, China held the rotating chair of APEC, hosting the annual leaders' meeting in October in the wake of the terrorist attacks on the United States. Even without this heightened diplomatic visibility, the Shanghai summit would still have been the most important international gathering hosted by China since the founding of the PRC in 1949. Whatever its importance as a political "talk shop," APEC's progress as an economic forum committed to free trade and investment has been minimal. For its part, China has actively pursued a wide variety of economic, political, and security interests in APEC over the years, highlighted by its insistence that development issues receive equal priority with trade and investment liberalization. Beijing was also instrumental in obstructing periodic U.S.-led efforts to transform the forum into a more formal, rules-based economic organization.[11] During the 1990s, APEC was the most important multilateral trade forum to which China belonged. It now seems to be of diminishing importance to Beijing, however, with China's accession to the WTO and the emergence of APT as the most vital grouping in East Asia.

As mentioned earlier, China identifies the SCO as a regional mechanism for economic (as well as political and security) cooperation. That said, the SCO is focused primarily on strategic issues. Furthermore, Russia is the only significant economic partner of China's in the SCO. By contrast, participants in TRADP include Japan, North Korea, Russia, and South Korea (as well as Mongolia). Initially conceived around 1990, TRADP aims to develop the area around the conjunction of the Chinese, North Korean, and Russian borders on the Tumen River. China has long been an enthusiastic proponent of the project, actively supporting multilateral planning and working on infrastructure development within its territory.[12] That said, TRADP has not been able to sustain the intense activity it enjoyed in the early 1990s. Furthermore, most of its success has come in the form of improved transportation networks rather than the establishment of the Tumen River Delta area as a significant trade, financial, and communications center.

Among the various "dialogues" created to facilitate economic cooperation in the region, the Boao Forum for Asia enjoys especially enthusiastic support from China. Conceived as an Asian version of the global Davos World Economic Forum, the Boao Forum held its inaugural meeting in April 2002 with high-level representatives such as Prime Ministers Koizumi, Thaksin, and Zhu from Japan, Thailand, and China, respectively. In addition to top government officials, prominent businesspeople, scholars, and other dignitaries also attended the retreat on China's tropical Hainan Island, which will be the permanent site of the forum. In his keynote speech, Zhu reiterated Beijing's much-repeated assurance that China's rapid economic growth represents an opportunity for, rather than a danger to, its neighbors. Especially in the wake of its WTO accession, Beijing has redoubled efforts to allay concerns among its neighbors in both Northeast Asia and Southeast Asia that China poses an economic threat (or, for that matter, a political or security threat).

The "ASEAN Plus Three" Process

Since the AFC, the diplomatic center of gravity for economic regionalism has been steadily shifting away from APEC toward APT. The first APT summit was held in Kuala Lumpur in December 1997, with subsequent annual summits in Hanoi (1998), Manila (1999), Singapore (2000), Brunei (2001), and Phnom Penh (2002). In practice, APT is the reincarnation of the East Asian Economic Group (EAEG), an idea first proposed by Malaysian prime minister Mahathir Mohammed in 1990 that failed to take root, even as a loose consultative forum, after being renamed as the East Asian Economic Caucus in October 1991. At that time, the United States, Japan, South Korea, and Singapore threw their weight behind APEC as the regional forum most deserving of their diplomatic attention. With the fallout over the AFC, however, interest in an East Asian (rather than a broadly Asia–Pacific) dialogue was rekindled in many capitals across the region. To varying degrees, Japan, South Korea, and Singapore have now converted to the APT faith. (For its part, the United States has largely silenced its objections.) South Korea was especially active under President Kim Dae Jung, making a series of proposals that led to the formation of the East Asian Vision Group and the East Asian Study Group. At the Phnom Penh summit in November 2002, APT leaders received the final report of the East Asian Study Group and, in the words of the official press statement, "agreed with the . . . vision for ASEAN + 3 summits to evolve in the long term into East Asian summits and eventually an East Asian Free Trade Area."[13] The tentative nature of this declaration is worth noting: the commitment is still one of principle (vision) rather than decisive action (concrete steps). As reported elsewhere in the official statement, the "leaders expressed willingness to explore the phased evolution of the ASEAN + 3 summit into an East Asian summit." In equally noncommittal fashion, the leaders instructed their economic ministers "to study and formulate options on the gradual formation of an East Asia Free Trade Area."

While China's vision is less grand than South Korea's notion that closer regional economic integration can serve as the basis for an emerging "East Asian Community" in social, political, and security affairs, Beijing's growing support for APT is unmistakable. In his November 2001 speech at the Brunei summit, which has served as the basis of subsequent Chinese policy on regional cooperation, Zhu identified APT as "the main channel of East Asia cooperation," signifying its importance relative to other forums.[14] Indeed, Zhu argued that the "10 + 3 mechanism" should serve as the framework within which subregional cooperation should proceed. (Conveniently, this stance was fully consistent with China's proposal, made at the Singapore summit in 2000, to explore an FTA with ASEAN under the "10 + 1" process.) Taking care not to alienate those outside APT unnecessarily, Zhu argued that "10 + 3 cooperation should retain its openness and be ready to explore ways of establishing contacts with other regional cooperation mechanisms in the world as may be appropriate."

That said, APT's membership is one of its main virtues from China's perspective. Perhaps most importantly, the interstate framework of APT marginalizes Taiwan significantly, unlike APEC and the WTO, where Taipei enjoys status as a member economy and a customs territory, respectively. (The same comments apply to Hong Kong's status in APT, although its absence is certainly less important to Beijing than Taipei's.) In addition to Taiwan, the United States, Australia, and New Zealand—all countries with significant interests in East Asia—are also excluded from APT (to say nothing of remaining APEC members Canada, Mexico, Chile, Papua New

Guinea, and Russia). And in contrast to APEC, APT includes Myanmar, Laos, and Cambodia. China's preference for the current composition of APT was also made clear by its vigorous opposition to the idea, floated at the Singapore summit in 2000, of an expanded ASEAN Plus Four format that would have included India.

Although China's proposed FTA with ASEAN, which is discussed below in greater detail, has garnered most of the headlines as far as Beijing's participation in APT is concerned, the "10 + 3" process has also provided a mechanism for a growing subregional dialogue among China, Japan, and South Korea. At the annual APT summit, leaders from Beijing, Tokyo, and Seoul hold a separate "Plus Three" meeting. A parallel set of trilateral meetings has also been launched at the foreign minister level. At the Phnom Penh summit in November 2002, Zhu proposed that a feasibility study be undertaken by Beijing, Tokyo, and Seoul on a trilateral FTA, with a goal of beginning talks on a three-way pact after China's negotiations with ASEAN were concluded. Although the trio agreed to conduct a joint study, Koizumi expressed Japan's preference for pursuing a bilateral FTA with South Korea before considering any kind of agreement with China.

By all accounts, FTAs among APT members will not come easily. Even the China–ASEAN FTA currently under negotiation is a major undertaking whose fate cannot be predicted at this time. Because prospects for a larger East Asian FTA seem remote at present, it is difficult to place too much stock in Beijing's advocacy of this cause. Indeed, many observers have dismissed it as political theater designed to make Beijing look good at Tokyo's expense. While this analysis may be true, there are also indications that China genuinely seeks improved regional dialogue (and action) through APT. Especially interesting in this regard is Beijing's willingness to undertake political and security dialogue within the 10 + 3 and 10 + 1 processes. Here again Zhu's speech at the Brunei summit in November 2001 laid down an important policy marker by arguing that "efforts should be made to gradually carry out dialogue and cooperation in the political and security fields."[15] Citing dangers such as terrorism, AIDS, and cross-border crimes, including drug trafficking, illegal immigration, and cybercrimes, Chinese officials have subsequently called for the expansion of regional cooperation in APT to include consideration of nontraditional security issues. For example, APT adopted a proposal at the Phnom Penh summit (originally made by Zhu in Brunei) to hold a ministerial meeting on combating transnational crime. For now, China clearly wishes for APT to focus on regional economic cooperation, with ancillary attention to nontraditional security issues. That said, statements by Chinese officials have hinted at the possibility of a more expansive agenda in the long run.[16]

China's support for APT has been profoundly influenced by lessons gleaned from the AFC. Unlike the Europeans, who were able to handle their own monetary crisis in 1992–1993 relatively ably, East Asians found themselves "excessively dependent" upon external actors (i.e., the IMF, the United States, and private-market actors)—this despite possessing large shares of both world economic output and foreign exchange reserves. Much like the fairy-tale character Goldilocks, East Asia has long been searching for a suitable regionalism. Neither ASEAN nor APEC provided the necessary leadership during the AFC. What this failure did for China, as it did for many countries in East Asia, was to underscore a shared interest in developing a greater (albeit still limited) regional capacity to act. This sentiment was captured well by the Chinese media during the November 2000 APT summit in Singapore:

> East Asian cooperation is an inevitable trend. One of the lessons learned by the various countries in the region from the East Asian financial crisis is the heavy price that they paid for acting on their own. In the face of a financial storm, the strength of a single country is limited. Only through multinational coordination and regional cooperation will it be possible to avoid any "domino" effect and minimize damages.[17]

For all the rhetoric about pursuing an East Asian FTA, APT has indeed made its greatest strides in the area of monetary cooperation. These efforts date back to Japan's suggestion in 1997 that an Asian Monetary Fund (AMF) should be established to better manage the region's financial affairs in response to the AFC. China, like the United States, thought Japan was trying to take advantage of its neighbors' weakness during the crisis to assert regional monetary hegemony. Undaunted, Japan continued to work quietly behind the scenes to lay the foundation for heightened, but less institutionally ambitious, regional cooperation. This included initiatives such as the influential Miyazawa Plan, which proved to be the precursor to more elaborate currency swap arrangements developed under the so-called Chiang Mai Initiative (CMI), an agreement reached by APT members in May 2000. Under the CMI, APT members are working to create an enhanced network of swap schemes that will provide the currency borrowing necessary to finance foreign-exchange interventions in future crises. The plan has three basic elements: first, to expand the existing \$200 million ASEAN Swap Arrangement among the five founding ASEAN members (Indonesia, Malaysia, Singapore, Thailand, and the Philippines) and eventually extend participation to all ten ASEAN members; second, to establish bilateral swap arrangements (BSAs) among Japan, South Korea, and China; and, third, to establish BSAs between the five founding ASEAN members and Japan, South Korea, and China.

To date, China has concluded BSAs with Thailand (December 2001), Japan (March 2002), South Korea (June 2002), and Malaysia (October 2002). The agreement with Japan, which was largely symbolic, given the vast foreign exchange reserves held by both countries, was notable for being the first yen-denominated currency swap concluded under the CMI. The fact that Beijing was willing to countenance such an agreement with Tokyo only four years after it had resisted Japan's proposal for an AMF—as a bid for yen hegemony—is significant indeed. However modest it remains, monetary cooperation in APT today outstrips both the preexisting ASEAN Swap Arrangement and Japan's provisions under the Miyazawa Plan. While still falling short of a full-fledged regional liquidity fund like the AMF would have provided, the new BSAs could nonetheless represent a preamble to greater Asian monetary integration in the long run. Indeed, APT countries are now regularizing their cooperation through frequent ministerial meetings and various monitoring activities. For its part, Beijing has been uncharacteristically proactive in working for the institutionalization of these cooperative efforts.

Competing to Cooperate: China's Proposal for a China–ASEAN Free Trade Area

As mentioned above, China has worked assiduously to explore the possibility of a China–ASEAN FTA since November 2000, when Zhu Rongji first proposed the creation of a joint ASEAN–China panel to study the impact of China's impending WTO accession and consider ways to enhance China–ASEAN economic cooperation. This suggestion, made during meetings with ASEAN officials at the APT Singapore summit, caught observers by surprise, given Beijing's previous criticism of subregional trade agreements. Wary of China's growing power, Malaysia, Indonesia, and Vietnam, among others, resisted the idea of a China–ASEAN FTA. Singapore and Thailand were reportedly more supportive, but ASEAN as a whole approached the concept cautiously. Regardless, the ASEAN–China Expert Group on Economic Cooperation was formed to assess the feasibility of an FTA. The resulting study, which was submitted in October 2001, recommended that the two sides work toward a formal agreement to forge closer economic relations. When Chinese officials arrived in Brunei for the APT summit, they offered to open some of their own markets before ASEAN countries would be scheduled to reciprocate. To sweeten the pot further, Beijing offered additional concessions to ASEAN's least-developed members. Some observers questioned whether these gestures were more symbolic than real, given the trade liberalization commitments China had already made under its WTO accession protocol, but they proved sufficient to win agreement from ASEAN officials to begin formal discussions on an FTA. After a year of occasionally difficult dialogue, the two sides signed a Framework Agreement on Comprehensive Economic Co-operation at the Phnom Penh APT summit in November 2002. This document sets a goal for completion of FTA negotiations in 2004, with the objective of establishing free trade between China and the original five ASEAN members by 2010 and between China and ASEAN's four newest members (Cambodia, Laos, Myanmar, and Vietnam) by 2015. To secure the approval of their ASEAN interlocutors, Chinese officials agreed to reduce tariffs effective January 2004 on certain (mainly agricultural) imports from ASEAN countries as an "early harvest" phase of trade liberalization. This concession reflects Beijing's determination to pursue a China–ASEAN FTA.

Although Beijing's pursuit of an FTA with ASEAN is ostensibly about economics (trade liberalization) and Chinese relations with Southeast Asia more generally, a closer look reveals that it is actually driven more by politics (regional influence) and China's relations with Japan, South Korea, and the United States. To be sure, China has several motivations for seeking closer economic relations with Southeast Asia, but the overriding dynamic is arguably competition with its Northeast Asian economic partners over the shape of regionalism generally and ties with ASEAN specifically. Washington has long championed APEC as its preferred vehicle for economic regionalism, favoring an emphasis on Pan-Pacific membership that includes key trade allies such as Canada and Australia. Without abandoning multilateralism, the United States has also shown signs of catching the bilateral "FTA fever" that has swept much of the region, as demonstrated by Washington's May 2003 agreement with Singapore. This pact is envisioned as the first of several FTAs to be negotiated as part of the Enterprise for ASEAN Initiative introduced by President Bush at the October 2002 APEC summit. Under the program, the United States will also support efforts by Cambodia, Laos, and Vietnam to join the WTO. As a signal of the importance that Washington places on this initiative, President Bush held a separate meeting with ASEAN leaders on the sidelines of the APEC summit. This was the first such group meeting between a U.S. president and ASEAN leaders since 1984. For its part, Japan has supported both APEC and APT as forums for enhanced multilateral economic cooperation, but in recent years Tokyo has also explored numerous bilateral FTAs in East Asia and cross-regional FTAs with Latin America. South Korea's modus operandi has been similar to Japan's, working both multilaterally and as a participant in the region's "FTA fever."

Although there are several "contestants" in the game of competitive regionalism in East Asia, the most salient rivalry is arguably that between China and Japan. It is no coincidence, for example, that Koizumi's proposal for a "Comprehensive Economic Partnership" with ASEAN, made during a weeklong tour of Southeast Asia in January 2002, came on the heels of China's November 2001 agreement with ASEAN to begin formal discussions on an FTA. Trying to keep pace with Beijing, Tokyo did in fact sign a joint declaration on a Comprehensive Economic Partnership with ASEAN at the Phnom Penh APT summit in November 2002. Unlike China's agreement with ASEAN, however, the Japanese initiative refers only to "elements of a possible free trade area" being completed in ten years and, most notably, it does not include agricultural products.[18] While there would be considerable benefit to ASEAN from closer economic relations with Japan, the accord envisioned by Tokyo is less comprehensive than Beijing's offering to ASEAN.

More broadly, Japan has sought to provide a vision for regional economic cooperation distinct from China's. For example, Koizumi has touted a long-term concept of East Asian Community that would include not just the current APT membership but also Australia and New Zealand. Within APT, Tokyo has become more active in hosting workshops and meetings on issues such as oil security and economic development. At the Asian Development Bank, Japan has set forth policy proposals on development financing and poverty alleviation that promote its own leadership in the region. Despite continued monetary cooperation under the auspices of the CMI, the competitive dynamic in trade initiatives and other economic issues raises questions about the implications of an East Asian regionalism in which China and Japan, as France and Germany in the postwar period, might end up vying for influence as competing poles more than they work together as collaborators.

Managing the Twin Forces of Globalization and Regionalism: The View from China

Although a thorough discussion of China's views of, and behavior toward, globalization is beyond the scope of this chapter, a few points are in order.[19] First, most Chinese observers conceive of globalization as an increasingly competitive struggle among national economies over the means to create wealth within their territories. In this sense, the mainstream view among leaders, bureaucrats, and scholars alike is that globalization has not changed the fundamental nature of international relations as a state-centric system of competition for power and security. What has changed, as reflected in both Chinese views and Chinese behavior, is that the underlying basis of national power and security has shifted significantly toward economic strength at the expense of the previously more single-minded focus on military strength. Furthermore, the relevant instruments of state power are also seen as being increasingly economic in nature (financial, technological, and industrial). In short, economic factors enjoy a higher profile in Chinese strategic thinking than at any other time since the PRC was established in 1949.

Second, the main significance of globalization is its implication for the objective of making China rich and strong: modernization can be achieved only by increasing China's (economic) interdependence with other countries. As expressed by Jiang in June 2000, economic globalization is a "natural outcome of world economic development . . . [and] the external environment for the economic development of all countries in the future."[20] This analysis is consistent with the surprisingly resolute position he took in August 1998 during the AFC, when globalization had become a political bogeyman throughout much of East Asia:

> Economic globalization, being an objective tendency of the development of the world's economy, is independent of man's will and cannot be avoided by any country. The world today is an open world and no country can develop its own economy if isolated from the outside world. We must firmly implement the policy of opening up, keep in line with economic globalization, energetically take part in international economic cooperation and competition, and make full use of various favorable conditions and opportunities brought by economic globalization.[21]

While Jiang, Hu, and other Chinese leaders have also routinely noted—sometimes quite passionately—the negative aspects of globalization, they seem to believe that globalization, if properly managed by appropriate national policies, affords latecomers the chance to achieve significant economic gains by integrating themselves into transnational production and financial structures.[22] Specifically, China is seen both as one of the world's main recent beneficiaries of globalization and as a country well positioned to take further advantage of globalization in the future. This view, of course, is consistent with China's epochal decision to enter the WTO. As explained by Jiang, "Joining the WTO is a strategic policy decision by the Chinese government under the situation of economic globalization; it is identical with China's objective of reform, opening up, and establishing a socialist market economic structure."[23]

That said, Beijing remains concerned about external challenges to national economic sovereignty, as well as the possibility that deeper economic integration could lead to the transmission of undesirable political values. Consequently, China's participation in the WTO and other multilateral economic forums is also designed to allow Beijing to exert greater influence over the course of globalization. Its sweeping reform commitments notwithstanding, Beijing is still trying to achieve a controlled opening to the outside world consistent with the idea of "managed" globalization. Put another way, the goal remains a strategic opening rather than an indiscriminate opening that could jeopardize China's economic security. Although national economic competition is not necessarily seen as zero sum in a literal sense—one side's gain being another's loss—the dynamic remains one in which there are relative winners and losers internationally, even if the game is positive sum overall. In this sense, development is a national challenge—rather than a collective endeavor—in which economic competition determines which countries will enjoy "comprehensive national strength" *(zonghe guoli)* in the long run.

For the most part, regionalism and globalization are seen in China as complementary rather than contradictory forces. In April 2002, the official media described greater economic integration with China's neighbors in East Asia as "the globalization of the regional economy." Specifically, this article called the idea of a China–ASEAN FTA "an inevitable move suited to economic globalization," arguing that a "free-trade region is a form of economic globalization . . . compatible with the WTO."[24] The author, director of the State Council's Development Research Center, maintained that regional groups can further the liberalization of world trade (and advance globalization generally) as long as they seek to minimize the exclusive nature of such arrangements. As these examples suggest, China has now largely converted to the view—at least in its official rhetoric—that regional economic groups are "building blocks" rather than "road blocks" in facilitating international cooperation. As explained by Finance Minister Xiang Huaicheng at a January 2001 APT meeting, East Asian "cooperation is in line with the world's current regionalization development. It and globalization complement and promote each other, and so they are not in conflict with each other."[25]

That said, Chinese leaders do sometimes portray regionalism as a response to globalization, a mechanism by which countries can work together (although in pursuit of their own individual interests) in coping with the rigors of the contemporary world economy. Indeed, Jiang presented precisely this sort of reasoning in a May 2002 speech to the Asian Development Bank:

> Economic globalization, while generating development opportunities, has added uncertainties to the world economic environment and made it harder for the developing economies within the region to restructure and fend off the external shocks. In order to seize the opportunities, meet the challenges, and accelerate development, Asian countries should step up their own efforts and work in closer regional cooperation with Asian characteristics. . . . Such cooperation will help Asian coun-

tries further expand their market and use their resources more extensively, promote a rational development of world multipolarization and economic globalization, and contribute to greater peace and prosperity in the world.[26]

These qualifications aside, globalization has not generally suffered from the higher profile regionalism has enjoyed recently in China. Globalization remains, in official parlance, "an irreversible objective trend and an unavoidable reality." Although countries must proceed with caution, "actively participating in the process of economic globalization is not equal to accepting 'Westernization' and entering a 'trap.'" To the contrary, to resist globalization is to "face the danger of 'marginalization.'"[27]

INTERDEPENDENCE AS A SOURCE OF CHINESE FOREIGN POLICY

Interdependence is an increasingly important context for understanding Chinese foreign policy, as Beijing now has a substantial interest in, inter alia, rising levels of world trade, vibrant international financial markets, and relative exchange-rate stability. China's ability to achieve its ambitious economic growth targets—and thereby maintain the domestic stability that the top leadership regards as a prerequisite for pursuing further economic reform—depends to an unprecedented degree on international developments such as changing macroeconomic conditions among its major trading partners, especially the United States and Japan, but also the European Union and China's smaller neighbors in East Asia, such as South Korea. Even as a continent-sized economy, China is certainly not immune from the vagaries of the world economy.

The challenge for China's decision makers, of course, has been to balance these new economic interests with longstanding concerns about sovereignty, independence, and socialist virtue. It is not the case, therefore, that one set of interests has simply replaced another; rather, new interests have to be reconciled as effectively as possible with preexisting interests. One concept that illustrates the meshing of old and new interests is the idea of economic security. Chinese behavior, especially since the AFC, suggests recognition by the country's leaders that national economic security cannot always be achieved unilaterally or even bilaterally; in some cases, it may require de facto multilateral coordination or even formal cooperation. In this sense, the "independence" of Chinese domestic and foreign policy is somewhat constrained by the country's increasing economic interdependence. This dynamic was certainly evident in Beijing's response to the AFC, where international economic and political considerations weighed heavily in the formulation of China's currency policy.[28]

Another good example of China's "interdependence predicament" is its recent support for enhanced monetary cooperation in APT, a policy shift that reflects the greater weight Beijing now places on regional financial stability as an important objective of Chinese economic security. Indeed, it is doubtful that China supports the CMI primarily for benefits that Beijing itself will enjoy, as the *renminbi* is not convertible on the capital account and China maintains very large foreign-exchange holdings. Consequently, it is not likely that China will need liquidity from its neighbors in the foreseeable future. While it could be argued that Beijing has warmed to the idea of monetary cooperation in anticipation of the *renminbi's* future convertibility, plans for this development have been put off indefinitely (ten to fifteen years). A more compelling argument is that China's perception of its self-interest in regional stability has grown in the wake of the AFC. Indeed, China's words and actions over the past two years suggest that its decision makers are convinced that greater (albeit still limited) monetary cooperation is a critical safeguard for regional stability. As such, mechanisms such as the BSAs provided for under the CMI are now viewed as increasingly necessary. In 2000, Finance Minister Xiang Huaicheng described China's support for the CMI as a defensive measure against future speculative attacks of the kind that led to the AFC, saying that his government backed the idea "because it contributes to the financial and economic stability of this region."[29] As a Japanese finance official later explained Beijing's change of heart about monetary cooperation, "China realizes that regional stability is important and that it is to their benefit to participate in such a mechanism."[30]

This discussion raises a question about the extent to which the "national interest" has come to be defined in China by idealist conceptions such as cooperative security, institutionalized interdependence, and community building. While it is certainly true that China's new, more complex set of interests vis-à-vis the world economy has produced deeper and more sustained cooperation within a variety of regional and global forums, these developments should not be mistaken for either a thoroughgoing transformation in China's worldview or a substantial change in its strategic focus on national power. In this sense, the pursuit of economic security and national development through multilateral cooperation could be characterized as a (neo-)liberal means to realist ends.

Seen from this perspective, China's acceptance of stringent terms for its WTO entry should not be interpreted as an embrace of economic interdependence as an independently valued goal. The decision to join the WTO occurred despite concerns about national sovereignty, not as the result of a newfound preference for institutionalized multilateralism per se. Even the staunchest domestic advocates of China's WTO accession typically acknowledge the tradeoffs involved in Beijing's strategic choice, but they believe membership will be the most effective means for continuing the massive overhaul of the economy necessary to make China rich and strong in the long run. Any resulting restraints on sovereignty have been accepted only as necessary steps to accrue more fully the benefits of deeper participation in the world economy. In this sense, China's instrumental acceptance of interdependence as a collective means to a national end differs from what has happened in the European Union, where some members seem to value interdependence—especially as manifested in regional and global institutions—for its own sake.

This assessment is not meant to discount the possibility that a substantial change in China's basic worldview could occur over time. Indeed, the literature on foreign policy "learning" in international relations theory would suggest that interdependence may have a profound impact on China's worldview in the long run, if changes in China's declared policies and actual external behavior continue to advance ahead of shifts in its weltanschauung. According to this perspective, norms often follow behavior. One can certainly imagine a nontrivial transformation in worldview over time if China gravitates toward the view that economic security is best pursued cooperatively through multilateral entities such as APT or a China–ASEAN FTA. (In a July 2002 speech, Foreign Minister Tang Jiaxuan noted the utility of "multi-form regional economic cooperation" for safeguarding economic security.)[31] For now, however, China's declared policies and actual behavior still seem to have changed more than its worldview. On a wide variety of economic issues, China cooperates when its interests—still defined quite narrowly in terms of national power—are served by cooperative action. The furtherance of interdependence per se is not seen as an independent goal to be pursued by Chinese foreign policy.

FUTURE PROSPECTS

One of the more pronounced shifts in Chinese foreign policy over the past decade has been Beijing's more positive view toward formal modes of regional economic cooperation in East Asia, such as APEC, APT, and the proposed China–ASEAN FTA. In the past, China had exhibited a strong preference for informal modes of economic cooperation based upon ethnic ties, geographical proximity, or transnational manufacturing networks. Beijing was particularly comfortable with the idea of "economic circles" *(jingji quan)* popularized in East Asia in the 1980s and early 1990s, a "natural" arrangement whereby mutually beneficial integration was achieved among complementary economies through private, market-based trade and investment ties rather than through agreements made by intergovernmental bodies.[32] With the passage of time, however, China has begun to view interstate forums (regionalism) more favorably under certain circumstances.

As noted earlier, Beijing's motivations for this shift have included a heightened awareness of mutual economic vulnerability. As the AFC demonstrated so painfully in East Asia, informal cooperation is sometimes inadequate to meet the challenges of contemporary globalization. At the same time, Beijing has been increasingly burdened by a fear of exclusion, as regionalism has advanced in seemingly every corner of the world. From the adoption of a single currency in the Europe Union and the outbreak of "FTA fever" in East Asia, to plans for a Free Trade Area of the Americas and discussion of cross-regional FTAs between several of China's neighbors and Latin American countries, China has found cause to worry both about its own leverage in the region and about that of East Asia vis-à-vis Europe and North America. Even while it concluded tortuous negotiations to gain membership in the WTO, Beijing understood that the multilateral trading system was in danger of weakening. As the Chinese media put it in 2001, "The WTO may well end up as a secondary international economic and trade organization, large but diffuse, while the functions of regional economic organizations increase."[33]

As argued earlier, however, the central motivation behind China's selective support for regional initiatives—for example, its promotion of a China–ASEAN FTA while generally resisting concerted progress toward trade liberalization in APEC—is competition, albeit a restrained competition, with its Northeast Asian partners over the shape of regionalism. In this sense, Beijing's pursuit of an FTA with ASEAN is part of a larger diplomatic effort to increase its influence in Southeast Asia vis-à-vis Japan and the United States while at the same time trying to allay local fears that China's economic growth will leave ASEAN on the regional sidelines. This strategy, which was in place well before the war on terrorism adversely affected Beijing's security environment, is designed to use foreign economic relations as an instrument of geopolitical statecraft. If China were able to conclude an FTA with ASEAN, it would greatly elevate its profile as a regional leader. Notably, China's behavior vis-à-vis ASEAN seems little motivated by conventional economic interests, as a China–ASEAN FTA, in terms of welfare and trade effects, would produce the least economic benefit for China of any regional liberalization scenario that has been studied (e.g., APEC, an East Asian FTA, or a China–Japan–South Korea FTA).[34] Indeed, standard economic analysis suggests that, among the alternatives, China has the most to gain in relative economic terms by pursuing an FTA with Japan and South Korea at the *exclusion* of ASEAN. According to the report submitted by the ASEAN–China Expert Group on Economic Cooperation, a China–ASEAN FTA would have rather modest effects, increasing ASEAN's GDP by 1.0 percent while raising China's GDP by only 0.3 percent.[35]

In keeping with its overall foreign policy approach, China's priority for economic relations in Northeast Asia is to maintain international stability while focusing on the paramount domestic objective of economic development. Toward both of those ends, Beijing assiduously pursues cooperative economic ties throughout the region. For all their frustration with recent exercises of U.S. power, China's leaders still apparently believe that the international environment is sufficiently peaceful that they can continue to concentrate on their modernization agenda. Aside from Taiwan, which seemingly is the only issue that could trump this assessment, Beijing appears committed to maintaining constructive relations with Washington. In this sense, China's relatively quick re-engagement with the United States after serious bilateral incidents (such as the May 1999 U.S. bombing of the Chinese embassy in Belgrade and the April 2001 spy-plane affair) is strong evidence that concerns about U.S. hegemony—raised most recently by the September 2002 publication of *The National Security Strategy of the United States of America* and the ensuing Iraq War—have been at least partially subordinated to the pursuit of economic security, as defined in terms of high economic growth and improved access to the developmental resources available in the world economy. This focus is likely to persist in the near future, especially given the still uncertain economic impact of the SARS crisis.

Although China seeks to increase its political influence in the region, it has generally tried to do so without unnecessarily challenging the influence of others—especially the United States. That said, China's recent support for monetary cooperation in APT and its pursuit of an FTA with ASEAN—both of which have come indirectly at the expense of APEC—raise the question of how far Beijing can proceed without appearing to challenge U.S. economic interests in East Asia. Indeed, the economic realm is already the policy arena in which China's foreign relations have arguably most violated Deng's dictum that China should "never take the lead, keep a low profile, and watch changes with a cool head."

Despite its clear preference for APEC, the United States has been fairly neutral toward APT, plans for a China–ASEAN FTA, and other endeavors that advance economic liberalization in East Asia. Compared with its decidedly negative reaction to proposals for the EAEG and AMF in the 1990s, Washington's response to recent initiatives that exclude it—such as the

CMI—has been noticeably measured. As long as Washington takes the view that economic cooperation in East Asia is consistent with a U.S. interest in regional stability and liberalization, the economic realm is likely to remain one mainly of cooperation rather than conflict. Similarly, as long as China remains focused primarily on internal matters such as economic development and leadership succession, it is unlikely to promote schemes for regional economic cooperation that would be especially threatening to U.S. interests, for this could jeopardize constructive relations with Washington. In the same vein, Beijing can be expected to proceed pragmatically with each of its partners in Northeast Asia, cooperating economically where doing so does not violate China's core political–security interests such as territorial integrity and state sovereignty.

Despite China's increasingly positive view of regional economic integration, it still sees regional dynamics in Northeast Asia (and elsewhere) primarily in terms of bilateral relations. Accordingly, the institutionalization of regional economic cooperation still elicits resistance from Beijing in certain respects. Like many countries in East Asia, China remains most comfortable with informal modes of cooperation unless the added value of formal regionalism significantly outweighs the perceived costs. Consequently, Beijing supports the CMI as fulfilling a functional need that could not otherwise be met. Similarly, it pursues a China–ASEAN FTA as an instrument of Chinese statecraft vis-à-vis its partners in Northeast Asia. For this same reason, however, it remains skeptical about the need to upgrade the informal APT summit to a more institutionalized East Asian summit aimed explicitly at community-building. This caution notwithstanding, China's current enthusiasm for regional economic multilateralism is unprecedented and may continue to grow as Beijing finds itself with more muscles to flex in the future. Riding the momentum of its long-sought WTO accession, China is now actively seeking the opportunity to shape its regional environment in a way that would have been unthinkable only a few years ago. While there are good reasons for skepticism about whether a China–ASEAN FTA can ultimately be achieved, Beijing's bold maneuver is revealing all the same. One thing is clear: an important evolution is underway in Chinese strategies for managing the economic interdependence that increasingly characterizes the country's foreign relations.

NOTES

1. For more on these themes, see Margaret Pearson, "China's Integration into the International Trade and Investment Regime," in *China Joins the World: Progress and Pros-*

pects, ed. Elizabeth Economy and Michel Oksenberg (New York: Council on Foreign Relations, 1999); and Pearson, "The Major Multilateral Economic Institutions Engage China," in *Engaging China: The Management of an Emerging Power*, ed. Alastair Iain Johnston and Robert S. Ross (London: Routledge, 1999).

2. For comprehensive treatment of this issue, see Nicholas Lardy, *Integrating China into the Global Economy* (Washington, D.C.: Brookings Institution, 2002), and *China in the World Economy* (Paris: OECD, 2002), Annex 1.

3. These moves, which were carried out at the National People's Congress, were preceded by a sweeping transition from so-called third generation leaders, in their seventies, to fourth-generation leaders, in their fifties and sixties, at the Sixteenth Congress of the Chinese Communist Party in November 2002. It was at this conclave that Hu replaced Jiang as the party's general secretary. At this writing, Jiang remains the chairman of the Central Military Commission, the last of his three official leadership posts.

4. For an excellent review of the many studies that estimate the impact of WTO membership on China's economy, see *China in the World Economy*, Annex 2.

5. The trade figures presented in this chapter are drawn from two annual volumes: *Direction of Trade Statistics Yearbook* (Washington, D.C.: International Monetary Fund, various years) and *International Trade Statistics* (Geneva: World Trade Organization, various years). In some cases, the figures result from calculations made by the author based upon the published data. For 2002, provisional statistics were obtained from the WTO press release of April 22, 2003, "World Trade Figures 2002," World Trade Organization website, at www.wto.org/english/news_e/pr337_e.htm.

6. The figures presented in the next three paragraphs are drawn from one book, *China in the World Economy*, and three annual volumes, *Yearbook of China's Foreign Economic Relations and Trade* (Beijing: China Foreign Economic Relations and Trade Publishing House, various years), *China Statistical Yearbook* (Beijing: China Statistical Publishing House, various years), and *World Investment Report* (Geneva: UNCTAD). In some cases, the figures result from calculations made by the author based upon the published data.

7. The FDI figures used in the next two paragraphs were calculated by the author from data available in two annual volumes: *China Statistical Yearbook* and *World Investment Report*.

8. Unless otherwise noted, the data presented in this section are drawn from *Direction of Trade Statistics Yearbook*, *China Statistical Yearbook*, and *World Investment Report*.

9. The data presented in this paragraph are drawn from *World Trade Developments* (Geneva: WTO, 2002).

10. China also participates in forums such as ASEM, the Asian Cooperation Dialogue, the Pacific Economic Cooperation Council, the Pacific Basin Economic Council, and the United Nations Economic and Social Commission for Asia and the Pacific.

11. For more detail on China's participation in APEC, see Thomas G. Moore and Dixia Yang, "China, APEC, and Economic Regionalism in the Asia-Pacific," *Journal of East Asian Affairs* 13, no. 2 (Fall–Winter 1999): 361–411.

12. For more on China's participation in TRADP, see Jean-Marc F. Blanchard, "The Heyday of Beijing's Participation in the Tumen River Area Development Programme, 1990–95: A Political Explanation," *Journal of Contemporary China* 9, no. 24 (July 2000): 271–90.

13. All quotations in this paragraph are from the "Press Statement" on the Phnom

Penh APT summit, November 4, 2002, Association of Southeast Asian Nations website, at www.aseansec.org/13188.htm.

14. Zhu Rongji, "Strengthening East Asian Cooperation and Promoting Common Development," November 5, 2001, at www.fmprc.gov.en/21861.html.

15. Zhu, "Strengthening East Asian Cooperation."

16. For example, Tang Jiaxuan once acknowledged that "traditional and non-traditional security factors are intertwined" and suggested that a comprehensive "multilateral security and cooperation framework will eventually take shape" in the region. Tang Jiaxuan, "Speech by Chinese Foreign Minister Tang Jiaxuan at 9th ARF Foreign Ministers' Meeting," July 31, 2002, at www.fmprc.gov.eng/33228.html.

17. *Wen Wei Po* (Hong Kong), November 24, 2000, in Foreign Broadcast Information Service, *China Daily Report* (Internet version; hereafter FBIS-CHI) 2000-1124.

18. "Joint Declaration of the Leaders of ASEAN and Japan on the Comprehensive Economic Partnership," November 5, 2002, Association of Southeast Asian Nations website, at www.aseansec.org/13191.htm.

19. For more detailed analysis, see Stuart Harris, "China and the Pursuit of State Interests in a Globalising World," *Pacifica Review* 13, no. 1 (2001): 15–29; Banning Garrett, "China Faces, Debates the Contradictions of Globalization," *Asian Survey* 41, no. 3 (2001): 409–27; and Thomas G. Moore, "China and Globalization," in *East Asia and Globalization*, ed. Samuel S. Kim (Lanham, Md.: Rowman & Littlefield, 2000).

20. Jiang Zemin, "Address to the 21st Century Forum," in FBIS-CHI-2000-0613.

21. "Jiang Zemin, Zhang Wannian Meet Diplomats," *Xinhua*, August 28, 1998, in FBIS-CHI-98-242.

22. In his limited public comments on globalization, Hu has deviated little from the analysis provided by Jiang, Zhu, and other Chinese officials in recent years. See, for example, excerpts from Hu's speech "Jointly Write a New Chapter in Asia's Peace and Development," *Xinhua*, April 24, 2002, in FBIS-CHI-2002-0424.

23. "Seize Opportunity, Meet Challenge, and Participate in Economic Globalization," *Renmin Ribao*, December 19, 2001, in FBIS-CHI-2001-1220.

24. "China's Regional Economic Relations in Asia Following Its Accession to WTO," *Ta Kung Pao* (Hong Kong), April 20, 2002, in FBIS-CHI-2002-0420.

25. *Xinhua*, January 14, 2001, in FBIS-CHI-2001-0114.

26. Jiang Zemin, "Unity and Cooperation in Asia for Peace and Development in the World," *Xinhua*, May 10, 2002, in FBIS-CHI-2002-0510.

27. *Renmin Ribao*, December 16, 2000, in FBIS-CHI-2000-1218.

28. Thomas G. Moore and Dixia Yang, "Empowered and Restrained: Chinese Foreign Policy in the Age of Economic Interdependence," in *The Making of Chinese Foreign and Security Policy in the Era of Reform, 1978–2000*, ed. David M. Lampton (Stanford, Calif.: Stanford University Press, 2001).

29. *Financial Times*, May 8, 2000, 10.

30. *Bangkok Post*, August 10, 2000.

31. "Speech by Chinese Foreign Minister Tang Jiaxuan at 9th ARF Foreign Ministers' Meeting."

32. Dajin Peng has written extensively on this topic. See, for example, Peng, "Subregional Economic Zones and Integration in East Asia," *Political Science Quarterly* 117, no. 4 (2002–2003): 613–41.

33. *Ta Kung Pao* (Hong Kong), May 10, 2001, in FBIS-CHI-2001-0510.

34. See, for example, Robert Scollay and John P. Gilbert, *New Regional Trading Arrangements in the Asia Pacific?* (Washington, D.C.: Institute for International Economics, 2001).

35. *Forging Closer ASEAN–China Economic Relations in the Twenty-First Century*, October 2001, Association of Southeast Asian Nations website, at www.aseansec.org/newdata/asean_chi.pdf.

FURTHER READING

Economy, Elizabeth, and Michel Oksenberg, eds. *China Joins the World: Progress and Prospects*. New York: Council on Foreign Relations, 1999.

Garrett, Banning. "China Faces, Debates the Contradictions of Globalization." *Asian Survey* 41, no. 3 (2000): 409–27.

Harris, Stuart. "China and the Pursuit of State Interests in a Globalising World." *Pacifica Review* 13, no. 1 (2001): 15–29.

Lampton, David M., ed. *The Making of Chinese Foreign and Security Policy in the Era of Reform, 1978–2000*. Stanford, Calif.: Stanford University Press, 2001.

Lardy, Nicholas R. "China and the International Financial System." In *China Joins the World: Progress and Prospects*, edited by Elizabeth Economy and Michel Oksenberg. New York: Council on Foreign Relations, 1999.

———. *Integrating China into the Global Economy*. Washington, D.C.: Brookings Institution, 2002.

Moore, Thomas G. "China and Globalization." In *East Asia and Globalization*, edited by Samuel S. Kim. Lanham, Md.: Rowman & Littlefield, 2000.

———. *China in the World Market: International Sources of Reform and Modernization in the Post-Mao Era*. New York: Cambridge University Press, 2002.

Moore, Thomas G., and Dixia Yang, "Empowered and Restrained: Chinese Foreign Policy in the Age of Economic Interdependence." In *The Making of Chinese Foreign and Security Policy in the Era of Reform, 1978–2000*, edited by David M. Lampton. Stanford, Calif.: Stanford University Press, 2001.

Pearson, Margaret. "China's Integration into the International Trade and Investment Regime." In *China Joins the World: Progress and Prospects*, edited by Elizabeth Economy and Michel Oksenberg. New York: Council on Foreign Relations, 1999.

Pearson, Margaret. "The Major Multilateral Economic Institutions Engage China." In *Engaging China: The Management of an Emerging Power*, edited by Alastair Iain Johnston and Robert S. Ross. London: Routledge, 1999.

———. "The Case of China's Accession to GATT/WTO." In *The Making of Chinese Foreign and Security Policy in the Era of Reform, 1978–2000*, edited by David M. Lampton. Stanford, Calif.: Stanford University Press, 2001.

Zweig, David. *Internationalizing China: Domestic Interests and Global Linkages*. Ithaca, N.Y.: Cornell University Press, 2002.

4

Japan's International Relations: The Political and Security Dimensions

Thomas Berger

Japan presents the student of international relations with a paradox. By most conventional measures of power, Japan is one of the strongest nations in Asia, if not the strongest. Its economy is the second-largest in the world and by far the largest in Northeast Asia. Although other nations are catching up, Japan's GDP still represents 67 percent of the region's total.[1] Japan's technological capabilities are exceeded only by those of the United States. Japan's armed forces are among the largest and best equipped in the world, replete with F-16 combat aircraft, *Aegis*-class destroyers, and an annual defense budget that, at approximately $40 billion dollars,[2] is the world's second largest. Only in the area of nuclear weapons does Japan lag behind if compared with Russia and the People's Republic of China (PRC). Even in this respect, there is little doubt that were it to choose to do so, Japan could develop a formidable nuclear arsenal in a relatively short period of time.[3]

Despite these assets, Japanese national security policy making since 1945 has been marked by an extraordinary degree of circumspection, even timidity, when it comes to the actual exercise of military power. Japan has gone out of its way to avoid assuming an active military role in security affairs, restricting its armed forces primarily to the defense of its own territory. Although Japan is aligned with the United States and relies on the United States for key aspects of its security, including nuclear security, it has repeatedly resisted providing more than token shows of military support for U.S.

military operations, most notably during the 1991 Gulf War. Japan has deliberately eschewed developing weapons systems that could be construed as offensive in character, including aircraft carriers and long-range bombers. Japan's basic approach to national security could be described as a quasi-isolationist strategy of limited rearmament, limited alignment, and maximal distancing of Japan from any potential military conflict.

At times this strategy has provoked bitter charges of "free riding" from the United States, which felt that Japan was enjoying the fruits of America's efforts to contain communism in Asia while paying only a small part of the costs. In response, Japan countered that it had provided the United States with the bases it needed to support American strategy in Asia, and it pointed out that it had consistently followed America's lead on most important foreign policy issues. Despite recurring rounds of mutual recrimination, the relationship between Tokyo and Washington proved highly stable over the course of the Cold War, and Japan's strategy of relying on the United States turned out to be a highly successful one. Not only was communism contained in most of Asia, but Japan rebuilt its economy and emerged by the 1980s as one of the richest and most influential nations in the world.

Since the end of the Cold War, however, Japan's cautious approach to national security has come under pressure. With the collapse of the U.S.–Soviet military rivalry, Japan can no longer take American strategic support for granted. At the same time, the global and regional security environment remains unstable. Tensions continue to simmer on the Korean peninsula, with an added element of danger for Japan created by North Korea's acquisition of long-range missiles capable of reaching Japan's major cities. The PRC, with its vast population, rapidly expanding economy, and assertive territorial claims on Taiwan and the South China Sea, looms as a potential regional rival. Finally, the global war on terrorism offers a new challenge for Japan's security policy and its already complicated relationship with the United States, one that Japan is constitutionally ill prepared to meet. In many respects, the Japanese security environment is more fluid today than it has been at any time since the end of World War II.

There are a number of ways in which Japan could respond to its new environment. One would be for it to increase its military capabilities and assume a more active security role, both in Asia and beyond. Such a policy would not necessarily preclude maintaining its strategic partnership with the United States. On the contrary, it might even strengthen it, as Japan could reduce the burden on the United States of maintaining security in the region. A Pax Nipponica could supplement a larger Pax Americana. At the same time, it would enable Japan to chart a more independent course in world affairs and give it a stronger fallback position were the United States ever to decide to scale back its commitments in Asia. Such a muscular, nationalist foreign policy has been referred to as a "normalization" of Japanese foreign policy and has been advocated by a number of conservative politicians and commentators in Japan. Realist scholars of international relations in the United States have tended to see this as the most likely scenario for Japan's future.[4]

Alternatively, Japan could maintain its low profile in political–military affairs while strengthening its security ties with the outside world through the creation and promotion of regional and global multilateral security institutions. Again, such a policy need not mean a termination of Japan's ties with the United States. To the extent that an intensified security dialogue among Asian nations increases regional stability, it might well serve U.S. strategic interests as well. At the same time, such a policy would also require Japan to pay greater heed to the interests and wishes of other nations, including Russia, the two Koreas, and the PRC. In such a scenario, Japan might no longer follow the American lead on foreign policy issues as closely as it did during the Cold War. Such a multilateralist approach to security affairs has been advocated by many Japanese commentators and policy makers and would be consonant with a more liberal international relations vision of the world.[5]

At the time of this writing (Spring 2003), Japan has pursued neither of these two options. While Japan has modernized its military forces and begun to engage in a limited range of military missions beyond a limited defense of its own territory, it continues to rely overwhelmingly upon the United States for its security. Although Japan has actively sought closer security ties with other nations by engaging in extensive bilateral and "minilateral" (i.e., involving a limited number of partners on an ad hoc basis) security dialogues and promoting the creation of new regional security institutions, these multilateral initiatives are clearly designed to merely supplement the U.S.–Japanese security relationship.

These apparently contradictory policy initiatives are based on what can best be described as Japan's "cautious liberalism."[6] On the one hand, Japan is too wedded to a civilianized, nonmilitary foreign policy to go down the realist path toward "normalization." In this sense, Japan's foreign policy vision remains quintessentially liberal, eschewing military power in favor of diplomacy and peaceful cooperation. On the other hand, events since the end of the Cold War have demonstrated to Japanese leaders and the broader public that Northeast Asia (in contrast to Western Europe and North America) remains a realist world where power politics are central and military confrontation is a very real possibility. The liberal ideals motivating Japanese national security policy have thus been tempered by a pragmatic realism that in recent years has led to an increased willingness to expand Japan's military capabilities and support the use of force.

In the years ahead, Japan's cautious liberalism is likely to be severely tested. Will Japan be able to continue to muddle through with an incremental reform strategy? Or will it be compelled to seek a qualitatively different approach to national security, whether along the lines of a more muscular, normalized attitude toward military power or a more cooperative, multilateralist set of policies? To answer these questions, this chapter will briefly explore the ways in which geography, history, and Japan's strategic environment have shaped Japanese national security policies since 1945. The chapter will then turn to the ways in which Japan's strategic environment has changed as a result of the end of the Cold War and examine how Japan has responded to those changes. In conclusion, it will hone in on some of the central problem areas that confront Japanese policy makers today, before offering some speculations on the directions in which Japanese policy is likely to develop in the future.

THE BURDENS OF GEOGRAPHY, HISTORY, AND STRATEGY

Japanese national security has been decisively shaped by an unusual combination of strength and fragility. This seemingly contradictory combination is attributable to three factors: a geographic position that makes it extremely vulnerable to being cut off from foreign markets and supplies of strategic resources; lingering historical memories in Japan and other parts of Asia that create a high level of domestic and international political sensitivity to any increase in Japanese military power; and a geostrategic environment that makes Japan highly dependent on the United States for security while at the same time encouraging it to avoid involvement in external security affairs.

Geography has played a large role in shaping Japan's strategic outlook. As a relatively small, resource-poor island nation, Japan is highly dependent on access to world markets for raw materials. Above all, it is almost entirely dependent on the outside world for its oil and natural gas, and it is more than 50 percent dependent for its supply of food. To pay for the import of such goods, Japan must be able to export manufactured products to world markets. Although in theory Japan could sustain itself without trade, it could do so only at great cost to its standard of living and at the risk of falling economically behind other nations.

Maintaining access to raw materials and world markets, however, is no easy task. Most of Japan's trade with the outside world takes place along lines of communication that stretch for many thousands of miles through the South China Sea, Southeast Asia, the Indian Ocean, and the Middle East. Sovereignty in some of these areas, such as the Spratley Islands in the South China Sea, is the object of international dispute. Other areas, such as Indonesia and the Middle East, are prone to crisis and instability. Were shipping disrupted anywhere along the route to these areas—for instance in the Straits of Malacca between Malaysia and Indonesia, through which approximately 70 percent of Japan's oil imports flow—the consequences for the Japanese economy would be severe.

To meet these challenges, in theory Japan could develop its political–military capabilities and assume a larger security role in the Asian region and beyond. This was precisely the strategy that it adopted in the pre-1945 period, when it engaged with the outside world from a position of strength, building a powerful military and creating a vast empire in Asia. This strategy, however, proved disastrous, eventually bringing Japan into conflict with much of the rest of the world and resulting in its devastating defeat in World War II. Consequently, post-1945 Japanese leaders have tried instead to secure access to outside markets through nonmilitary means—diplomacy, trade, and foreign aid. While Japan allied with the United States against the Communist powers, it tried to maintain diplomatic and trade relations with all nations as much as possible.

Japan labors under a *burden of history* as well as of geography. Japanese imperial expansion between 1890 and 1945 has left behind bitter memories in much of Asia, especially in Korea, which was under Japanese colonial rule for thirty-five years, and in China, where it is estimated that 20 million people died following the Japanese invasion beginning in 1937. This history left behind the widespread perception that Japan is by nature a militaristic and aggressive society that, if given the opportunity, could easily revert to its expansionist ways. Such fears are exacerbated by the unrepentant stance of many prominent right-wing Japanese politicians and opinion leaders who deny that Japan bears any moral responsibility for the Pacific war and paint an idyllic picture of the Japanese empire and the motives behind its creation. As a result, throughout the region, any steps taken by Japan to expand its military or to take on a larger security role tend to be greeted with trepidation. As Lee Kuan Yew once famously remarked, encouraging Japan to increase its military capabilities is like offering chocolate liqueurs to a reformed alcoholic.

The fact that Japan possesses the capability to become a serious threat to its neighbors means that such fears cannot be regarded as entirely unfounded.[7] Regardless of whether Japan is ready to revert to aggressive nationalism or not (and below I will argue that it is not), the very fact that such a perception exists has consequences. Were Japan to increase its military power significantly, it would certainly be viewed with alarm by its Asian neighbors. China, South Korea, and possibly other nations might well undertake a military buildup of their own, sparking a general arms race in the Asian–Pacific region.[8]

The burden of history has a domestic side as well. Japan is often accused—with some justification—of suffering from "historical amnesia" regarding its modern history.[9] "Amnesia," however, is a misleading term. In fact, the Japanese have very strong memories of the war. These memories, however, have focused more on the suffering the Japanese people themselves endured than on the suffering they inflicted on others. By the end of the war of the Pacific, three million Japanese soldiers and civilians had died, Japan's economy had collapsed, and its cities lay in ruins. The Japanese people blamed these losses on the wartime Japanese leadership, especially the Imperial Army and Navy. In post-1945 Japan, it was widely believed the military, and their ill-considered expansionist policies, had recklessly led the nation into a war it could not win and had prosecuted the war without respect for the immense losses it inflicted on ordinary Japanese.[10]

Traumatized by their defeat, ordinary Japanese and many influential elites came to reject the prewar approach to national security and the nationalist ideology on which it was founded. Instead of trying to cope with the strategic dilemmas posed by Japan's geography by building its military power, Japan's postwar leaders chose the opposite approach. Japan would engage the outside world through peaceful means, through trade and diplomacy, while maintaining as low a profile as possible militarily in order to reassure its neighbors as to its peaceful intentions. U.S. hegemony in the Western Pacific was the critical enabling factor that made this strategy possible. By closely aligning itself with the United States and primarily relying on American power to provide for its external security, including access to foreign markets and raw materials, Japan was able to focus its energies on economic development. This strategy was closely associated with the most important politician of the early postwar period, Prime Minister Yoshida Shigeru, and is still referred to today as the "Yoshida doctrine."[11]

During the Cold War, Japan did create a highly sophisticated military establishment, the Japan Self Defense Force (SDF), with 250,000 highly trained personnel equipped with technologically advanced weapons systems. However, historically grounded domestic and international political neuralgia concerning the military led Japan to place the SDF under a highly restrictive system of safeguards *(hadome)*. A tight regime of civilian control was imposed on the SDF, with a powerful civilian bureaucratic apparatus—the internal bureaus of the Japan Defense Agency (JDA) set up to monitor the armed forces.[12] The armed forces were sharply limited in the types of equipment and missions in which they could engage. Weapons of mass destruction were forbidden, as were weapons systems that could be construed as being offensive in character. Defense spending after 1960 was held to approximately 1 percent of GDP.[13] The SDF could not be dispatched overseas, even on UN-sponsored peacekeeping missions. Furthermore, an extraordinarily restrictive set of rules of engagement was adopted to prevent the military from creating a military incident. Prior to being allowed to fire their weapons, the Self Defense Forces would first have to receive approval from the Japanese prime minister himself. In theory, were Japanese fighter pilots to encounter a squadron of unauthorized Russian bombers flying toward Tokyo, they would have to wait for permission before being able to open fire.[14]

On the surface, the limitations placed on the SDF may seem excessive. Yet they were perfectly understandable in light of Japan's unhappy history with the military. The primary purpose of the armed forces was to provide a first line of defense and delay a potential attacker long enough for help to arrive from the United States. In addition, the SDF was in certain respects a cadre army, one that could be used as the basis for a much larger military should the need to create one arise. For similar reasons, Japan also developed a substantial indigenous arms industry capable of producing the most advanced weapons technology available without having to rely on overseas suppliers.[15]

The third set of factors contributing to Japan's strategic fragility was rooted in its *geostrategic position*. Every nation in an alliance is torn between two opposing fears. On the one hand, there is the fear of abandonment, that in a military contingency one's ally will fail to provide the level of military support that has been expected or promised. On the other hand, there is fear of entanglement, the worry that by committing to an alliance the nation risks being drawn into conflicts in which it has no national interest.[16]

As an island nation, for Japan the threat of a direct Soviet invasion during the Cold War was relatively small. The United States, as the dominant naval power in the world, could protect Japan and its vital sea lanes of communication with relative ease. At the same time, the bases that Japan provided the United States were vital to the American strategy of containing Communism. Therefore, on the balance, the threat of abandonment by the United States was relatively small.

At the same time, the threat of entanglement seemed relatively large. While the Cold War in Europe was relatively peaceful, if tense, the Cold War in Asia was frequently violent and dangerous. The United States fought two large-scale limited wars, in Korea and Vietnam, and found itself embroiled in numerous lower-intensity conflicts, in the Taiwan Strait, on the Korean peninsula, and throughout Southeast Asia. As a result, the fear of entanglement loomed relatively large in Japanese strategic thinking.[17]

Fears of entanglement in the Japanese case were reinforced by the historical memory of the rise of militarism. Having experienced the military's exploitation of overseas emergencies to undermine Japanese democracy in the 1930s, Japanese elites and the general public in the postwar period were doubly sensitive to the possible costs of military commitments overseas. Since 1945, the Japanese defense debate has been persistently haunted by the fear that, were Japan to become involved in foreign military adventures again, even within the framework of a larger American-led military campaign, reactionary forces within Japanese society might exploit the situation by declaring a military emergency and recreate an authoritarian political system.[18]

Because of the fear of entanglement, Japan took great pains to keep its American allies at arms length. Under the terms of the Mutual Security Treaty (MST), originally signed in 1952 and revised in 1960, the United States tentatively committed itself to the defense of Japan. In return, Japan recognized that it had a strategic interest in the stability of East Asia. In a separate agreement, Japan agreed to provide the United States with strategic bases in order to help the United States maintain regional order. Yet, while Japan relied on the United States to come to its aid in an attack, it was under no such obligation with respect to the United States. Unlike Korea or the European members of NATO, Japan did not establish a joint command structure with the United States, and cooperation between the two nations' armed forces was restricted to the defense of Japan. Until the mid-1980s, Japanese leaders explicitly avoided using the word "alliance" with reference to the security relationship with the United States.

Despite its peculiarities and many internal contradictions, this limited approach to national security served Japan well throughout the Cold War. While changes in the international environment, such as the development of Soviet naval power in the Pacific in the 1970s and 1980s, forced adjustments, the system proved adaptable. After 1989 and the fall of the Berlin Wall, however, Japan's strategic environment began to change fundamentally.

CHALLENGES OF THE POST–COLD WAR

The end of the Cold War did not have the same, immediate impact in Asia that it did in Europe. There was no Soviet Empire in Asia comparable to the vast territories under Moscow's control in Europe. While Communist regimes collapsed from Berlin to Moscow, Marxism–Leninism continued to be the ruling orthodoxy in the PRC, North Korea, and Vietnam. In Europe, the fall of the Berlin Wall led to German reunification, removing what had been arguably the greatest source of tension in European politics between 1945 and 1989. In Asia, however, disputes over national boundaries remained widespread, from the demilitarized zone between the two Koreas to the Spratley Islands in the South China Sea. Although the collapse of the Soviet Union led to a considerable reduction in military tensions in Asia, the potential for conflict, if anything, increased on the Korean peninsula and in the Taiwan Strait. Japan continued to be confronted with the strategic dilemma of protecting the vital sea-lanes along which the lifeblood of its economy flowed. Historically rooted fears of Japanese military power eased somewhat, at least in Japan and Southeast Asia. Nonetheless, the Japanese public remained profoundly uncomfortable with the notion that Japan should assume a larger military role, and in Northeast Asia—especially in China and Korea—historical animosities emerged all the stronger.

Yet, despite the relative degree of continuity in the Asian security environment, beneath the surface the political tectonic plates on which the regional order rested were shifting. In the immediate wake of the Cold War, the United States seemed increasingly preoccupied with its internal affairs.[19] The disappearance of the Soviet military threat undermined the primary rationale for the United States' commitment to its overseas alliances. Consequently, the threat of abandonment began to loom larger in Japan's strategic calculus, even though the fear of entanglement remained.

A number of options were theoretically available to Japan in this changed international environment. One possible response would have been for Japan to increase its military capabilities, taking over more of the burden of maintaining regional order from the United States. Such a policy, however, would have cut against the grain of established Japanese policy and would have generated considerable political opposition both at home and abroad, and there were no serious voices within the Japanese political establishment calling for a military buildup.

A second option, and one that was more reflective of the Japanese establishment's instinctive liberalism (at least when it comes to matters of international security), was to promote the development of multilateral security institutions that might defuse tensions and prevent conflict. In the early to mid-1990s, this strategy did enjoy prominent backers on the Japanese political scene, including Foreign Minister Nakayama Taro and the members of the prime minister's Special Advisory Committee on Defense (the Higuchi commission).[20] During this period, Japan launched a series of initiatives, including a bid for a permanent seat on the United Nations Security Council. To support that bid Japan increased its contributions to the United Nations and allowed its forces for the first time to participate in UN-sponsored peacekeeping missions.[21] Japan also took the lead in promoting regional security institutions, most notably the ASEAN Regional Forum (ARF), a multilateral institution dedicated to improving communication and building confidence between its member nations, including virtually all the nations of the Asia–Pacific region. Likewise, the Japanese government began to intensify bilateral and "minilateral" security dialogues with its Asian neighbors, including China, South Korea, Russia, and most of Southeast Asia.[22]

Japan's bid to for a permanent seat on the Security Council, however, soon floundered in the face of bureaucratic inertia and great power resistance.[23] At the same time, the Asian region proved only marginally ready to create a wider security community. Despite some successes, most notably in Cambodia, tensions remained and a number of countries, most notably China, continued to build up their military.[24]

Given Japan's continued vulnerability to outside pressures, and its unwillingness to become a more active military power, the only remaining alternative was to strengthen its alliance with the United States. It took some time, however, before Japan realized that the end of the Cold War meant it would have to strengthen its security relationship with the United States, rather than try to outgrow it. Faced with a faltering economy and wracked by a series of political scandals that ended the Liberal Democratic Party's one-party domination of Japanese politics, Japanese political elites had little time or inclination to face difficult policy-making decisions. Moreover, a half a century of reliance on the United States for its external security had created a certain popular complacency about military matters in Japan as well as in the United States. As U.S. undersecretary of defense Joseph Nye memorably put it, , "security is like oxygen—you tend not to notice it until you begin to lose it, but once that occurs there is nothing else that you will think about."[25]

It would take a succession of crises in the first half of the 1990s to get the Japanese political system to recognize that the air was getting thin in the wake of the Cold War. The first crisis was the Gulf War, during which Japan was conspicuous for its absence. Although Japan made a substantial monetary contribution to the American-led war effort (more than $13 billion), it failed to send even token forces to the region. This led to bitter criticism of Japan in the American press and the U.S. Congress. Why, it was demanded, if Japan shared our ideals, values, and interests, was it unwilling to risk the lives of its citizens alongside the American, British, French, and other allied nations fighting in the Gulf? Did the Japanese view American soldiers as nothing more than mercenaries, twentieth-century Hessians, as some of the most severe critics put it? In response to these accusations, the Japanese government desperately sought some way to dispatch forces to the region, if only in a noncombat support role. Popular pressures and resistance in the Diet, however, thwarted these efforts.

In the end, the United States won the war with only a minimum of casualties and the intra-alliance acrimony subsided. Many Japanese political commentators at the time, however, felt that Japan had had a narrow escape. If American forces in the Gulf had suffered the kind of casualties many American commentators, including former heads of the American Joint Chiefs of Staff and many leading military analysts, had predicted at the start of the conflict, the political backlash against Japan could well have wrecked the U.S.–Japanese alliance.[26]

After the Gulf War, Japan sought ways to go beyond "checkbook diplomacy" and make a "human contribution" (i.e., provide personnel) to the international security order. It was in this context that in 1992 Japan lifted the ban on the overseas dispatch of Self Defense Forces, allowing them to participate in UN-sponsored peacekeeping operations. Yet the fear of entanglement remained strong, and stringent conditions were placed on the types of missions that the SDF could be sent on and the type of weapons they could carry.[27] More significantly, the alliance with the United States continued to be neglected.

The next crisis came in 1994. The United States and North Korea appeared to be on a collision course over the refusal of the North Koreans to allow the inspection of its nuclear facilities to ensure that it was not developing nuclear weapons. As diplomatic negotiations broke down and tensions mounted, the U.S. government became increasingly convinced that it would have to launch a preemptive military attack on North Korea's nuclear facilities, probably sparking an all-out war. As U.S. forces were rushed to the region and nonessential U.S. personnel were evacuated from Korea, the American government was shocked to discover that Japan was unwilling to clarify what level of logistical support it would provide in the event of a conflict. Japanese diplomats were even unable to promise that Japanese hospitals would be made available for wounded American soldiers being evacuated from the front. Once again, fortune smiled on Japan, and a settlement of the conflict was negotiated. If U.S.–Japanese alliance can be said to have dodged the bullet in the Gulf War, in Korea it had narrowly avoided being hit by a surface-to-surface missile.[28]

Soon after the Korean crisis, public protests erupted over the continued presence of U.S. bases in Japan, sparked in 1995 by the brutal rape of a Japanese schoolgirl by three U.S. marines stationed in Okinawa. While the Japanese government was eventually able to contain the protests, the incident demonstrated that not only American but also Japanese public support for the alliance was in danger of eroding.[29] By the mid-1990s, the U.S.–Japanese relationship, so central to Japan's post-1945 approach to national security, had appeared to become, in the words of noted Japanese commentator Funabashi Yoichi, an "alliance adrift."[30]

After the near debacle in Korea, the two governments were finally galvanized into action. A series of bilateral talks took place on improving the ability of the alliance to respond in a military emergency. These discussions culminated in 1997 with a revision of the 1978 Guidelines for U.S.–Japanese Defense Cooperation. In addition to reemphasizing the importance of the alliance in general, for the first time the Japanese government promised to provide rear-area, logistical support to U.S. forces during a regional security crisis. The SDF was authorized to provide food and fuel to U.S. forces both in Japan and in "areas surrounding Japan." The United States was also promised access to Japanese facilities, including ports, air bases, and storage facilities. Beyond logistical missions, the SDF also was to be allowed to coordinate with the U.S. armed forces on a wide variety of other missions, including refugee relief, noncombatant evacuation, search-and-rescue missions, and activities in support of economic sanctions.[31]

The new guidelines represent a major step forward in the U.S.–Japan strategic relationship. For the first time, Japan has taken concrete measures to allow its military forces to be used for regional security missions and not merely for the defense of its own territory. The Japanese government has followed these measures up with a variety of changes in the SDF structure. The Japanese Maritime Self Defense Forces are now exploring the possibility of acquiring light aircraft carriers with helicopters and VTOL (vertical take-off and landing) warplanes for use in peacekeeping missions, as well as armored landing craft that could be used to evacuate Japanese and allied nationals in situations in which domestic order has broken down. Similarly, the Air Defense Forces have acquired tanker planes that can refuel military aircraft while in flight, thus nearly doubling their effective operational range. The acquisition of these types of systems makes perfect sense in terms of the expanded regional security role that Japan has committed itself to. Yet it also feeds fears among neighboring states that Japan may be remilitarizing, and it represents a significant loosening of the system of tight institutional safeguards *(hadome)* that have been put in place to keep the Japanese armed forces in check.[32]

The revitalization of the U.S.–Japan alliance is a major development in Japanese national security policy. It was probably a necessary adjustment to the changed circumstances of Japan's security environment after the Cold War. Certainly, it has been hailed by the security-policy community in Japan and the United States as heralding a new era in the relationship between the two countries. At the same time, it is important to appreciate that it represents very much a continuation of the Yoshida doctrine and the basic philosophy that has informed Japanese national security policy during the Cold War. It allows Japan to continue to pursue a basically liberal vision for the future of the region—one that seeks to create a growing community of nations tied together by trade and commerce and free of the fear of war, while operating in an environment that remains basically realist in character.

Nonetheless, many points of potential tension remain. Although Japan is now far better equipped to respond to a new crisis on the Korean peninsula than it was in 1994, there remain questions concerning how it might respond to other regional crises, such as a Sino–U.S. confrontation over Taiwan or a conflict in the South China Sea. Moreover, the Asian security environment remains complex and potentially fluid. Three areas in particular stand out as potential challenges in the future: the Korean peninsula, relations with China, and the war on terrorism. In each of these three areas pressures may arise that will test Japan's cautious liberal approach to national security and lead to further, possibly more far-reaching changes.

THE KOREAN PENINSULA—THREATS AND OPPORTUNITIES

Nowhere are the threats and opportunities for Japanese foreign policy greater than on the Korean peninsula. On the one hand, a crisis in the peninsula could place Japan's security relationship with the United States under intense strain. Under certain circumstances, it could even force Japan to recalculate its fundamental approach to national security issues, pushing it in a far more realist direction. On the other hand, no other issue has so pushed Japan over the past decade toward closer cooperation with its allies, not only the United States, but also the Republic of Korea (ROK, or South Korea). Dealing with North Korea has also led, to a lesser extent, to closer contacts with the People's Republic of China. Successful multilateral management of the Korean situation could provide the strongest boost to Japan's liberal goals of achieving a more peaceful regional security environment in Northeast Asia, moving it from its present cautious liberalism to a more confident and robust form of liberalism.

Dealing with North Korea, or the Democratic People's Republic of Korea (DPRK), has long been one of the most intractable issues in the Northeast Asian region. Over the past decade, problems with the DPRK have clearly gotten worse. Since the end of the Cold War, the North Korean military has engaged in a massive military expansion, increasing its standing forces from around 400,000 in the 1980s to around 1.1. million today, equipped with 3,500 tanks, 2,500 armored personnel, 10,600 artillery, and 500 combat aircraft, all forward based and apparently configured for offensive action.[33] In addition to its conventional force capabilities, North Korea has accelerated its efforts to acquire weapons of mass destruction and the capability of delivering them over long distances. While the framework agreement that ended the 1994 crisis served to slow down efforts by the North to acquire nuclear weapons, the North Korean regime continued to develop more advanced delivery capabilities, as was demonstrated by the 1998 Taepodong missile test, when North Korea fired a three-stage missile over Japan.

In the winter and spring of 2002–2003, the crisis reintensified when Korea revealed that it had started a separate secret uranium enrichment program in 1998 capable of producing the fissile material needed for the creation of nuclear weapons. Thereafter, tensions grew geometrically when Pyongyang first announced that it was backing out of the 1994 agreement, then closed down the monitoring mechanisms that had been placed on its nuclear facilities as part of the framework agreement and finally notified the United States that it was beginning to extract plutonium that could be used to make nuclear weapons. U.S. intelligence estimated that North Korea already had enough material for two devices and warned that it could soon produce enough for dozens more. By the summer of 2003, as the United States, Japan, and South Korea scrambled to find some way of rolling back the North Korean program without starting an all-out war that could kill hundreds of thousands of Korean civilians and lead to attacks on U.S. facilities in Japan, East Asia faced the most dangerous crisis that it has seen since the end of the Cold War.

There is considerable disagreement among analysts over how to interpret the North Korean actions. Some see it as the prelude to a last, desperate military assault to achieve reunification, others as a diplomatic club for extorting concessions and desperately needed material resources from the outside world. Yet others argue that the main purpose of the buildup is to bolster the legitimacy of the Kim Jong Il regime.[34] Given the paucity of information available to the outside world about the thinking of the North Korean leadership, there is no way to determine what the reality is. Certainly North Korean rhetoric toward Japan, as well as toward the United States and South Korea, has been highly belligerent in tone and content.

Regardless of what North Korean intentions may in fact be, the fact remains that North Korea has the capability to trigger a major, destructive conflict on the peninsula. Although the prospects for a successful North Korean invasion of the South appear dim,[35] North Korea has been willing in the past to continue to engage in provocative behavior. In addition to the Taepodong missile launch, there have been numerous incidents of North Korean incursions into South Korean territory, sometimes resulting in armed clashes between North and South Korean troops. Of particular concern to Japan has been the activities of North Korean spy ships *(fushinsen)* in Japanese territorial waters, ships that are believed to be engaged in spying, kidnappings of Japanese citizens, and other nefarious activities. Reports that possibly hundreds of North Korean agents are in place in Japan, possibly equipped with weapons of mass destruction, including poison gas, dramatically raise the risk of confrontation for Tokyo.[36] While the United States has worked closely with Japan, South Korea, and China to try to defuse the crisis peacefully, the perception that the North has reneged on its previous agreements makes it difficult to achieve a lasting diplomatic solution, and within the U.S. defense establishment there is a strong sentiment that a forceful approach may be the only realistic solution. As a result, the possibility that war may break out on the Korean peninsula, whether as a result of a planned invasion from the North or as the result of an inadvertent escalation of a more limited incident, is frighteningly real.

North Korean actions over the past decade have had a huge impact on Japanese defense policy and the way in which Japan thinks about defense. If war on the peninsula were to erupt, Japan would come under immense pressure to assume a far greater military role than ever before. Fortunately, Japan today is far better prepared to respond to such pressures than it was in 1994. There is little doubt that Japan would provide logistical support to the United States and its South Korean allies, and SDF might well assist in various important noncombat, and possibly even some limited combat, roles. Nonetheless, a number of risks remain. First, there exists a very high likelihood that U.S. facilities in Japan, and perhaps Japanese military and even civilian targets, would be attacked by the North using commandos or missiles. There is even the possibility of attacks using biological, chemical, or nuclear weapons. Japanese civilian casualties are likely to result, possibly in high numbers.[37]

It is impossible to predict how Japan would react were it to suffer a foreign attack on its soil for the first time since 1945. The impact on Japanese perceptions would undoubtedly be great, on the same order of magnitude as, and possibly even greater than, the American response to the September 11 terrorist attacks. In the eyes of many Japanese, Japan's postwar approach of avoiding military confrontations and seeking to engage potential adversaries would be decisively discredited. Furthermore, the U.S. alliance's ability to insulate Japan from a devastating attack would be called into question. Extended deterrence would have failed. In the wake of such a catastrophe, the Japanese populations would, in all likelihood, move toward a far tougher, possibly more nationalistic stance on defense and security issues than before.

Even if such a nightmare scenario never materialized, there is the danger that tensions with North Korea still may over time erode Japan's cautious liberalism. North Korean actions have clearly been highly provocative to Japan. The Japanese political leadership's reaction to the Taepodong launch was little short of apoplectic. The missile test seemed to convey as much a message to Japan as to the United States that the North remained a potential threat. More importantly, it demonstrated that North Korea had developed the capability to directly threaten the Japanese home islands. The initial response of the government of Prime Minister Obuchi Keizo was to suspend politically sensitive Japanese support to the Korean Peninsula Energy Development Organization (KEDO), an organization that had been set up as part of the agreement to defuse the 1994 crisis. Intense diplomatic pressure from the United States was needed to induce Japan to resume its support.

The Taepodong shock galvanized the Japanese government into action. The Obuchi government decided to develop and deploy its own spy satellite system in order to improve its ability to monitor, independently of the United States, developments on the Korean Peninsula and elsewhere in the Northeast Asian region.[38] Political support increased for the revised Guidelines for U.S.–Japanese Defense Cooperation. The Japanese government also authorized the Japanese navy and coast guard to pursue and if necessary use force against unidentified ships entering Japanese territorial waters. These instructions resulted, in December 2001, in an armed clash between an unidentified ship *(fushinsen)*—believed to be of North Korean origin—and the Japanese Coast Guard and Maritime Self Defense Forces, resulting in the sinking of the unidentified ship and the death of all fifteen crew members. Remarkably, this incident, the first deliberate and open use of force by the Japanese armed forces since 1945, met with general public approval, something that would have been all but unthinkable ten years earlier. This shift in public opinion was undoubtedly fed by popular antipathy toward North Korea in the wake of the missile crisis and the reports (later confirmed) of North Korean kidnappings of Japanese citizens. Such sentiments, if they developed further, could lay the basis for a much tougher, more realist approach to national security policy.

Perhaps most importantly, after a great deal of domestic debate, Japan agreed to support the development, if not yet the deployment, of a Theater Missile Defense (TMD) system for East Asia.[39] The deployment of a TMD system is likely to be highly provocative to the PRC. Not only might China's nuclear deterrent be neutralized by such a system, but its ability to apply military pressure on Taiwan to forestall a possible bid for independence might be eroded as well.[40] At least as important, were a TMD system jointly developed and deployed in Northeast Asia, Japan would be compelled to integrate its command and control structure with those of the United States and South Korea.[41] The strategic significance of such a development is obviously great, and so by extension are the implications for the Japanese approach to national security. Japanese preferences for a cautious liberal approach to regional security would run the risk of being swept away in the event of a crisis. If the United States found itself in a confrontation with China over the Taiwan Strait, or prepared to launch a preemptive strike on North Korean weapons of mass destruction, Japan would have no choice but to follow along.

The 2002–2003 crisis has further accelerated the Japanese push to acquire greater capabilities. In response, Japan finally launched two reconnaissance satellites over North Korea, moved to acquire advanced Patriot missile-defense systems, and deployed naval forces in the Sea of Japan on heightened alert status. After fierce domestic debate, the Japanese Diet finally passed Emergency Law legislation that would enable the Japanese military to respond more effectively in the event of a military contingency.[42] The Koizumi government continued to advocate a negotiated solution and clearly preferred a strategy of engagement rather than confrontation with Pyongyang. However, other voices inside the Japanese government—most notably the outspoken director general of the Japanese Defense Agency, Ishiba Shigeru—called for a more far-reaching revamping of Japanese defense policy, including the acquisition of offensive Tomahawk missiles and development of the capacity to launch preemptive attacks on North Korean missile sites.[43]

While the Korean situation holds great risks for Japan's cautious liberalism, it also holds out great hopes as well. Nowhere is this more evident than in the context of Japanese–South Korean relations. Historically, relations between the two countries have been marred by an intense antagonism rooted in feelings of historical injustice. Modern Korean nationalism defined itself in opposition to Japan. The Japanese for their part have long looked down on their former colonial subjects.[44] Commercial rivalry and strategic suspicion further complicated an already very complicated Japanese–South Korean relationship.[45]

Despite these obstacles, there has been significant cooperation between Korea and Japan in a number of different areas. Japanese economic assistance and investment has been of particular importance in the development of Korean industry, especially after the two nations normalized relations in 1965. Japan and the ROK have worked together in the area of national security as well, especially during periods when there appeared a danger that the United States might pull back from the Asian region.[46] This trend toward cooperation has greatly accelerated since of the end of the Cold War. The two countries have intensified military-to-military talks since 1991, and the two militaries held their first joint exercises in 1998. In 1994 Japan joined South Korea in managing the KEDO initiative. In the wake of the Taepo-dong incident, Japan joined South Korea and the United States in creating a little-known, but quite effective, Trilateral Coordination and Oversight Group (TCOG), which has coordinated the three countries' policies toward North Korea.[47] Economic cooperation between Japan and South Korea has also continued apace, particularly in the wake of the 1997 Asian financial crisis (AFC), when Japan was instrumental in helping prop up the stricken South Korean economy.

These trends toward policy coordination have been paralleled by efforts to address the roots of feelings of historically based antagonisms between the two sides. Despite numerous setbacks, the two sides have struggled to overcome these feelings of antagonism, culminating in a historical summit in 1998 between Prime Minister Obuchi Keizo and Korean President Kim Dae Jung. At the summit, not only did the Japanese prime minister offer a strong apology for Japanese misdeeds during the colonial period, but also, just as importantly, Kim Dae Jung appeared to accept these apologies and committed his country to moving on beyond the acrimony of the past. While these efforts faltered during the summer of 2001, they received fresh impetus during 2002, especially after Korea and Japan successfully comanaged the 2002 World Cup soccer games. Public opinion data in each country showed unprecedented levels of favorable popular perceptions of the other.[48] In December 2001 the Japanese emperor even went so far as to publicly admit the long-rumored, but never officially confirmed belief that the Japanese imperial household is of at least partial Korean descent.[49]

If the trend toward Japanese–Korean reconciliation and policy cooperation continues, the long-term consequences could be immense. Potentially, it could be a development as important as Franco–German reconciliation in the 1950s. The two countries could serve as the core of a larger East Asian community of nations linked together by deepening ties of commerce and common political interests. If they together can manage a successful, peaceful reunification of the Korean peninsula, the entire Northeast Asian region would enjoy a significant increase in stability, and Japan's liberal instincts would no longer be confronted with as harsh a realist world, as it has been for the past five decades. Movement toward a more genuinely liberal regional order would become possible.

In the meantime, resolution to the North Korean situation clearly remains some way off. Even were such a resolution to be achieved, the need for a U.S.–Japanese alliance would not necessarily disappear.[50] The possibility of conflict involving China or a resurgent Russia remains. Likewise, the new challenges posed by global terrorism would not be solved. Nonetheless, Japan would no longer be as dependent on the U.S. alliance as it has been in the past, and it would be able to more effectively and openly pursue a more liberal national security policy.[51]

CHINA—SLOUCHING TOWARD CONTAINMENT

In many respects, Japan's relationship with the People's Republic of China holds out similar hopes and perils as its relationship with Korea. Improvement in atmosphere between the two nations, to say nothing of a full-blown reconciliation, is potentially of even greater importance than improved relations between Japan and Korea. Such a development would go even further in turning Northeast Asia into a liberal security environment. However, if Japan and China found themselves locked in armed confrontation with one another, the implications for Northeast Asian and world politics would be severe. Although a Sino–Japanese confrontation is by no means inevitable, there are far less grounds to be optimistic with respect to the future of Sino–Japanese relations than there are in the Japanese–Korean case. The feelings of historically rooted animosity between China and Japan are more intractable, and the clash in basic interests is greater. Above all else, over the past five years the trend seems to be one of slouching toward a containment of China by the United States and its allies, including Japan. If this is the case, it is likely to sharply constrain the possibility of further movement of Japanese foreign policy in a liberal direction. Under certain conditions, tensions with the PRC could push Japan toward full-blown realism.

For much of the Cold War, there was strong Japanese popular sentiment in favor of maintaining ties with the People's Republic of China. In 1952, opinion data showed that 57 percent of the Japanese public favored restoring diplomatic relations with China. In 1960, those favoring normalization increased to 75 percent.[52] Japanese business interests in reopening commercial ties with the Chinese mainland, historically one of modern Japan's strongest markets, were similarly strong. Despite strong U.S. disapproval and the presence of a small but active pro-Taiwan lobby inside of Japan, a relatively low but significant level of trade between the two countries was maintained, even at the height of the Cold War.[53] The Japanese government of Yoshida Shigeru agreed to recognize the Nationalist government of Taiwan instead of the Communist government in Beijing, but only under intense pressure from the United States at the time of the signing of the San Francisco Peace Treaty of 1951.[54]

Following the resumption of diplomatic ties in the 1970s, Japan emerged as one of the PRC's major economic partners. Trade and investment between the two countries soared. The Japanese government helped infuse the Chinese economy with large sums of foreign aid in the form of low-interest yen loans. During the 1990s, China was consistently the number one or two recipient of Japanese aid, receiving more than 20 billion dollars worth over the course of the decade.[55] After the Tiananmen incident of 1989, Japan became the target of considerable criticism for being the first country to resume normal diplomatic relations with the People's Republic.[56]

After the Cold War, opening a security dialog with China became an important priority of Japanese diplomacy, both bilaterally and within a multilateral framework. The Nakayama initiative leading to the creation of ARF was in no small measure motivated by the desire to engage the PRC, and it was followed by a series of bilateral initiatives, including contacts between the two nations' armed forces. Behind these efforts was an essentially liberal strategy of engagement. By embedding China into a network of trade and diplomatic relations with the outside world, Japanese leaders hoped to defuse the potential for conflict and to assist in the eventual transformation of the PRC into a peaceful, cooperative member of the international community.

These diplomatic efforts reaped some successes, most notably when China helped broker an end to the Cambodian civil war in 1992. As the 1990s progressed, however, Sino–Japanese relations began to sour. The steady increase in Chinese defense spending, and evidence that China was attempting to develop a more modern military replete with power projection capabilities that could affect Japanese interests, sparked protests from the Japanese government.[57] Chinese nuclear tests in 1995 and 1996 were even more provocative from a Japanese perspective, especially as the 1996 tests took place despite worldwide criticism.[58]

Chinese willingness to forcefully assert territorial claims in the region, particularly in the South China Sea and with respect to the Senkaku/Diaoyu Islands, claimed by both China and Japan, further added to rising tensions.[59] Chinese use of missile launches around Taiwan in 1996 to intimidate proindependence sentiment on the island alarmed the Japanese public and outraged Japanese political leaders.

After the 1996 Taiwan Strait crisis, Japanese public-opinion data showed that for the first time fewer than 5 percent of respondents held a positive view of China.[60] Even traditionally pro-PRC politicians, such as influential LDP (Liberal Democratic Party) faction leader Kato Koichi, warned the Chinese leadership that their actions risked permanently alienating Japan.[61] The crisis, together with developments on the Korean peninsula, contributed to the Japanese decision to revise the Guidelines for U.S.-Japanese Defense

Cooperation and encouraged Japan to support joint research and development of a regional TMD system, despite strenuous Chinese objections.[62]

At the same time as these developments, there is a growing trend toward nationalism in the PRC, stimulated by the Chinese Communist Party's search for a new way to legitimate its rule now that the old Marxist–Leninist–Maoist ideology has lost its credibility.[63] This nationalism is strongly anti-Japanese and feeds recurring bouts of acrimony between the two countries over historical issues since the 1980s. Public opinion in China shows a growing level of antipathy toward Japan, with more than 50 percent of Chinese respondents in a 2002 poll indicating that they disliked Japan.[64] Historically grounded suspicions regarding Japan seem rampant among the Chinese foreign-policy elite, with Japan generally portrayed as a potentially aggressive, militaristic power.[65] In response, Japanese public opinion has become increasingly negative toward China. One concrete consequence of this trend is growing pressure on the Japanese government to reduce the amount of foreign aid that it provides to the PRC.[66] Unlike in Japan's relations with South Korea, there is little sign that these tensions are likely to subside at any point soon, and there is good reason to believe that they may even intensify.[67]

There exist a number of countervailing factors to these generally negative trends. First, at the start of the twenty-first century, China does not yet pose a conventional military threat to Japan. Its navy and air force are still at least a decade or more away from the point where they could pose a serious threat to Japanese regional interests.[68] More importantly, the Chinese leadership is overwhelmingly technocratic in orientation and is therefore far more amenable to participation in international institutions than the reclusive Pyongyang regime.[69] This is particularly true with respect to economic and environmental issues, where despite frictions Japan and China cooperate extensively, and there is a widespread perception that cooperation is in both nations' long-term interests.

There is thus considerable uncertainty over the future direction of Chinese foreign policy. In the main, the Japanese leadership remains committed to pursuing an engagement policy toward China and avoiding actions that could be interpreted as provocative. At the same time, a growing and vocal part of the Japanese government and the broader intellectual and political elite is taking a skeptical view of the future of Japanese–PRC relations.[70] In the 1960s, the split between pro-PRC and pro-Taiwan factions was one of the bitterest fights inside the LDP.[71] Today there is evidence that such splits could reemerge. During the Diet debates over the guidelines, a fierce battle broke out over the definition of the geographical area in which the new policy would be operative. Chief Cabinet Secretary Kajiyama Seiroku insisted that Taiwan could be included. LDP general secretary Kato Koichi, however, insisted that Taiwan should be specifically excluded. In the end, the Japanese government of Prime Minister Hashimoto Ryutaro worked out the uneasy compromise that the terms "Far East" and "areas surrounding Japan" did not in fact refer to specific geographical areas.

Consequently, unlike in Korea, if a conflict were to break out in the Taiwan Strait between the United States and China, it is far from certain what Japan's response would be. Given Okinawa's close proximity to Taiwan, and the presence of the large American military bases on Okinawa, it is likely that Japan would be pushed to act. If Japan failed to provide adequate support to the United States, and if the United States sustained significant casualties, the Mutual Security Treaty system would suffer a potentially mortal blow. But if Japan were to intervene forcefully, it would run the risk of making Japanese forces and facilities, and the American bases in Japan, the targets of Chinese attack.[72] In either case, the impact on Japanese attitudes toward national security is likely to be enormous and could tip Japan decisively in a more realist direction, whether as an ally of the United States or as a strong, independent actor.

THE TERROR OF THE WAR ON TERRORISM

The war on terrorism has added a new and complicated dimension to Japan's security environment. The long-term impact of coping with the threat of terrorists willing to use weapons of mass destruction to inflict large numbers of civilian casualties is impossible to predict. In the short term, however, terrorism is likely to exacerbate many of the strategic problems that Japan already faces on the Korean peninsula, in its relations with China, and with respect to its security relationship with the United States. Moreover, the normative and institutional restrictions that Japan suffers with regard to external security overlap with and compound similar problems in the area of internal security counterterrorism. As a result, the already strong Japanese penchant for immobilism on security issues is likely to be reinforced.

The situation on the Korean peninsula is made potentially even more explosive by President George Bush's designation of North Korea as part of the "axis of evil." Many of the criteria used for mounting an attack on Iraq apply even more strongly to North Korea: it is one of the world's most odious regimes and brutally represses its own people; the North Korean atomic and missile programs are considerably more advanced than those of Iraq were; and North Korea has a history of support for terrorist groups (including, it is rumored, the Aum Shinrikyo doomsday cult).[73] The greatest fear in the context of the 2002–2003 crisis is not that North Korea might launch an unprovoked attack on its neighbors, but that it might be willing to sell weapons of mass destruction, including possibly nuclear weapons, to terrorist groups. Fears voiced by many Japanese and South Korean commentators that North Korea could be the next target in the war on terrorism are far from groundless.[74]

The PRC supported the U.S. campaign in Afghanistan and used the war on terrorism as a useful cover for cracking down on Muslim minority Uighur organizations resisting Chinese rule in Xinjiang.[75] In the long run, however, the U.S. presence in Central Asia may increase Chinese fears of encirclement, and could lead to new tensions in Sino-American and thus, indirectly, Sino–Japanese relations. Japan's greater willingness to send its forces abroad, and its sinking of a North Korean spy ship in December 2001, has reinforced Chinese fears of a potential revival of Japanese militarism.[76] Chinese leaders may also be emboldened to take a tougher stance on the Taiwan issue, calculating that China's diplomatic leverage has increased as a result of American efforts to build a coalition against terror. Chinese diplomatic support is widely viewed as the critical element in forcing the North Korean regime to abandon its nuclear program.

Finally, Japanese fears of entanglement have been revived by the evident American penchant for unilateral action in pushing for attacking rogue states. Initially, Japanese support for the American action was swift and decisive. Under the leadership of Prime Minister Koizumi Junichiro the Japanese Diet passed new legislation authorizing the SDF to dispatch a small flotilla of ships, including three destroyers, to provide rear area support for the U.S. forces fighting in Afghanistan. Japan was also among the leading donors of aid and supplies to Afghanistan and Pakistan.[77]

Public opinion was generally supportive of the U.S. campaign, with 71 percent of Japanese polled in October 2001 favoring Japanese support of the United States in the war on terrorism. Public opinion was less positive, however, on the dispatch of Japanese forces overseas, with 49 percent in favor and 40 percent opposed.[78] Traditional concerns over possible overseas entanglement resurfaced in the debate over what type of escort ships should be sent to the Indian Ocean. Despite heavy U.S. pressures, the Japanese government decided not to send its *Aegis*-class destroyers for fear of inciting public criticism and that Japan could be overly drawn into American military operations through the *Aegis*'s high-tech radar and communications systems.[79]

Japanese resistance was even greater on the subject of supporting a U.S. campaign against Iraq. Opinion data in the summer of 2001 showed that 77 percent of the Japanese population opposed dispatching Japanese forces to support a U.S. campaign in the Gulf.[80] Despite strong urgings from Washington, Japanese officials warned their U.S. counterparts that it would be difficult legally and politically to provide military support.[81] Nonetheless, once the war commenced, the Koizumi government went out of its way to support the United States, dispatching military ships to the region and providing vigorous diplomatic support to the American-led campaign, in marked contrast with many of America's traditional NATO allies. An important factor in Koizumi's thinking has been reportedly the desire to secure U.S. support on North Korea.[82]

The war on terrorism promises to be difficult for Japan in terms of not only its foreign relations, but also its domestic politics. Terrorism for Japan is not a new problem. In the prewar period, Japanese right-wing terrorism was instrumental in destroying the fledgling Japanese democracy of the Taisho period. In postwar Japan, terrorism from both the political right and the left continued, albeit in somewhat more muted forms. The most spectacular instance of terrorism, however, came from neither the left nor the right. Rather, it came from the Aum Shinrikyo doomsday cult, which on March 20, 1995, launched a devastating poison gas attack in the Tokyo subway system, killing twelve persons and injuring more than six thousand.[83]

The Aum case is illuminating with respect to the difficulties that Japan may have in responding to terrorism. The Aum sect had thousands of members. It accumulated significant military resources, including caches of automatic weapons and a stockpile of poison gas, and had developed a surprisingly advanced bacteriological and chemical weapons research program. The cult engaged in a string of violent crimes, including possibly dozens of murders, and engineered another poison gas attack in the town of Matsumoto in which seven people were killed.

Despite this astounding record, the Japanese police were largely oblivious to the cult's activities, due to strongly engrained norms against intervening in the internal affairs of religious organizations. During the prewar period, the Japanese state had actively regulated religious organizations in a bid to unite the nation behind the state cult of Shinto and the worship of the emperor as a living god. Under the direction of the powerful Internal Ministry *(Naimusho)*, which controlled local government and police functions as well as religious affairs, the police were an omnipresent factor in everyday life in Imperial Japan. After 1945, the *Naimusho* was dismantled, the police forces were decentralized, and the government's ability to intervene in civil society was sharply curtailed. While the Japanese police remained relatively well integrated on the local level, and quite effective in countering ordinary crime, they no longer had the broad range of social regulatory authority they enjoyed in the prewar period.

In the wake of the Aum attacks, the Japanese government moved to enact legislation that would have enabled the police to more closely monitor and clamp down on potential terrorist groups, including ones designated as religious organizations. These initiatives, however, were eventually watered down or abandoned in the face of determined opposition from an alliance of civil libertarians and mainstream religious organizations, especially the Buddhist Clean Government Party, which was part of the governing coalition at the time.

In dealing with terrorism in the future, similar antiauthoritarian norms of postwar Japan are likely to combine with antimilitary norms to significantly impede Japanese counterterrorist strategy.[84] One reflection of these difficulties can be seen in the fate of the Emergency Law legislation, designed to enable the Japanese military, working together with the police and local authorities, to mobilize effectively in response to a military or terrorist event. Despite being a top priority of the Koizumi administration, during the spring and summer of 2002 the Emergency Law legislation became bogged down in the Japanese Diet, as questions were raised over the law's constitutionality and potential endangerment of civil liberties. In the end, the Japanese government was compelled to postpone deliberation of the bill indefinitely.[85] More than a year after the September 11 incident, and despite ample evidence of an Al Qaeda–related terrorist network operating in Southeast Asia,[86] Japan's ability to respond to terrorism remains sharply constrained.

To be sure, as past shifts in Japanese defense policy would suggest, such obstacles can be overcome. After 9/11, the Koizumi government was able to provide an unprecedented support for Operation Enduring Freedom in Afghanistan. The Japanese government was among the first to enact legislation to cut off the flow of funds to terrorist organizations. A new Division of International Counterterrorism Cooperation was established in the Ministry of Foreign Affairs.[87]

Yet change in Japan's counterterrorist strategy and its national security policies in general is likely to be slow and incremental, creating the possibility of a catastrophic policy failure. If Japan becomes the target of a major, foreign-based terrorist attack, it is impossible to predict how it will respond. Much will depend on whether the United States and other allied nations are perceived as providing a credible and supportive response to such an attack. If so, Japan's alliance with the United States might well be further strengthened and turned into a much deeper partnership. If not, a feeling of betrayal, leading to an aggressive isolationism, might result.

Regardless of whether Japan ever falls victim to such an attack (and at present the probability would seem relatively low), the war on terrorism poses more immediate problems in all the critical areas of Japan's foreign affairs. If the United States, together with other powers, is able to hammer out a viable international coalition to combat terrorism, Japan will be drawn in a liberal foreign policy direction. Japan would seek to join counterterrorist international institutions and in this way would be drawn further out of the semi-isolationism on security issues that characterized Japanese foreign policy during the Cold War. But if international cooperation should break down and there is increased acrimony over what is perceived as U.S. unilateral efforts to combat terror, the strain on Japan's existing security policies may be too great to bear. The crisis in transatlantic relations during the run-up to the war in Iraq revealed the potential for intra-alliance acrimony over how to respond to the threat of terrorism. Similar tensions are apparent in differences between Seoul and Washington over how to handle North Korea. If such tensions continue and worsen, they could erode the political basis for the entire alliance structure that was slowly built up in the wake of World War II. Japan would then find itself in the situation it has dreaded since the 1950s; it would be confronted with a bleak and hostile world of great power politics and the constant specter of violence. Under such circumstance, a tougher, more realist approach to national security would be well nigh impossible to avoid.

CONCLUSION

As this survey makes clear, Japanese security policy today faces a number of significant challenges. Japan is confronted with the constant threat of a major military crisis emerging on the volatile Korean peninsula. Japanese leaders have to worry about the erosion of its relationship with China. Above all, Japan continues to struggle with the threat that its security relationship with the United States may lead it to become entangled in conflicts in which it has no interest. This latter threat has become more tangible in the wake of September 11, with America's determination to wage war on international terrorism.

Japan has made significant strides toward meeting these challenges. Moreover, as the richest and most technologically advanced nation in Northeast Asia, Japan continues to enjoy important strategic advantages over its potential rivals and enemies. Nonetheless, Japanese foreign policy is hampered by a legacy of normative anxiety regarding national security issues. Japan's historically rooted distrust of the coercive apparatus of the state, whether represented externally by the armed forces or internally by the police, has served to keep the police and military institutionally weak and makes it very difficult for Japanese leaders to take forceful action on security issues.

As a result, Japanese leaders are strongly inclined toward a liberal approach to international relations, one that favors trade and diplomacy over force or the threat of force as a means of achieving foreign policy objectives. In the past, this approach has been sustainable in the often harsh world of Northeast Asian international relations because of the insulating presence of the United States and the Mutual Security Treaty system.

Whether this essentially liberal outlook on international relations will survive in the future depends on factors that are at least in part beyond Japan's control. As the junior and highly dependent alliance partner, Japan can exert only limited influence on the United States. Likewise, its ability to affect the development of democracy in China or the stabilization of the Korean peninsula is also constrained. There are a number of more or less plausible scenarios under which Japan may be forced toward a tougher, more realist stance on national security. The most serious danger derives from a possible U.S. withdrawal or a significant downscaling of its presence in Asia, possibly in the wake of renewed controversy over burden-sharing issues sparked by a crisis involving Korea, China, or the war on terrorism. Likewise, an attack on the Japanese mainland, a Japanese Pearl Harbor if you will, could galvanize Japan toward a more realist foreign policy, possibly independently of the United States.

There are also a number of scenarios that can be envisioned in which Northeast Asia evolves in a more peaceful direction. Successful management of North Korea and the war on terrorism will be vital if such a future is to be realized. The transformation of China into a peaceful liberal society fully integrated into the international system would greatly enhance the likelihood of such a development. Under such circumstances, Japan would be able to move more fully toward a liberal foreign policy.

Astute Japanese diplomacy can play a key role in nudging the region in one direction or the other. While Japan cannot control its environment, it is a crucial, even indispensable player. Japanese diplomacy, however, can no longer avoid dealing with security issues as it has in the past. In order to have influence, Japan will in all likelihood have to assume a larger regional, and possibly international, security role. Ironically, if Japan wishes to move the world in a more liberal direction, it will have to resort—judiciously but with firm resolve—to more realist tools of foreign policy. To do so, external pressures and strong Japanese leadership will be required to overcome the institutional and normative-cultural obstacles discussed above. Unfortunately, while the external pressures are present in abundance, leadership is a commodity that is in short supply in present-day Japan. Whatever energy Japanese leaders have left over from their internecine, factional struggles and bureaucratic battles is likely to be absorbed by Japan's looming economic crisis. In the interim, Japan is likely to continue to make halting, incremental changes to its national security policies in response to pressures from the outside. One can only hope that the world will continue to allow Japan to muddle through.

NOTES

1. According to World Bank data, Japan's GDP in 2001 was $4.1 trillion, out of a Northeast Asian regional total (Japan, China, South Korea, North Korea, Russia, and Taiwan) of approximately $3 trillion. World Bank, World Development Indicators database, World Bank website, at www.worldbank.org/data/databytopic/GDP.pdf.

2. For fiscal year 2001, the Japanese defense-related expenditures are approved at 4.94 trillion yen, which at the 2003 exchange rate of 120 yen to a dollar rounds to $41 billion.

3. Selig Harrison, *Japan's Nuclear Future: The Plutonium Debate and East Asian Security* (Washington, D.C.: Carnegie Endowment for International Peace, 1996).

4. Classic formulations of the realist position include Hans J. Morgenthau, *Politics among Nations: The Struggle for War and Peace*, 5th ed. (New York: Knopf, 1978); and Kenneth Waltz, *Theory of International Politics* (Reading, Mass: Addison–Wesley, 1979). For an example of an explicitly realist thinking applied to Japan, see for instance Christopher Layne, "The Unipolar Illusion: Why New Great Powers Will Rise," *International Security* 17, no. 4 (Spring 1993): 5–51 especially 41–45; and Kenneth Waltz, "The Emerging Structure of International Politics," *International Security* 18, no. 2 (Fall 1993): 44–79. A number of Japan experts make similar arguments. See Chalmers Johnson, "Rethinking Asia," *National Interest* 32 (Summer 1993): 21–28, and in a more sensationalist vein, George Friedman and Meredith Lebard, *The Coming War with Japan* (New York: St. Martin's, 1992). For prominent examples of Japanese calls for a more realist foreign policy, see Ozawa Ichiro, *Blueprint for a New Japan: The Rethinking of a Nation* (New York: Kodansha International, 1994); and Okazaki Hisahiko, *Kokusaijosei Handan: Rekishi Kyokun Senryaky to Tetsugaku* (Tokyo: PHP Kenkyujo, 1996).

5. For useful recent overviews of liberal views of international relations, see Andrew Moravschik, "A Liberal Theory of International Politics," *International Organization* 51, no. 4 (Autumn 1997): 513–53; Mark W. Zacher and Richard A. Matthew, "Liberal International Theory: Common Threads, Divergent Strands," in *Controversies in International Relations Theory*, ed. Charles W. Kegley Jr. (New York: St. Martin's, 1995); and David Baldwin, "Neoliberalism, Neorealism, and World Politics," in *Neorealism and Neoliberalism: The Contemporary Debate*, ed. David Baldwin (New York: Columbia University Press, 1993). Perhaps the best-known examples of a liberal interpretation of Japanese foreign policy are Hanns Maull, "Germany and Japan: The New Civilian Power," *Foreign Affairs* 69, no. 5 (1990–1991): 91–106; and Richard Rosecrance, *The Rise of the Trading State* (New York: Basic, 1986). For examples of Japanese exponents of a more liberal foreign policy, see Yoichi Funabashi, "Japan and the New World Order," *Foreign Affairs* 70, no. 5 (1991–1992): 58–74; and Tsuru Shigeto, *Nichibei Ampo: Kaisho e no Michi* (Tokyo: Iwanami Shoten, 1996).

6. In this respect, the analysis here differs from that offered by Michael Green in his excellent book, *Japan's Reluctant Realism* (New York: Palgrave, 2001). Green argues that Japan is moving slowly but surely toward a more realist position. While I agree with much

of Green's analysis, I maintain that Japan's realism is more of a tactical than a strategic nature. The majority of Japanese leaders as well as the Japanese public remain philosophically committed to an essentially liberal view of international relations. They hope and believe that in the long run the world can be steered toward a more peaceful future. At the same time, they reluctantly recognize that in the interim they need to prepare for the very real possibility of armed conflict.

7. For an analysis along these lines, see Robert S. Ross, "The Geography of Peace: East Asia in the Twenty-first Century," *International Security* 23, no. 4 (Spring 1999): 81–118.

8. On the impact of its reputation on Japanese strategy, see Paul Midford, "Making the Best of a Bad Reputation: Reassurance Strategies in Japan's Security Policy," *Social Science Japan* 11 (November 1997): 23–25. For its impact on Japan's relations with China, see Thomas Christensen, "China, the U.S.–Japan Alliance and the Security Dilemma in East Asia," *International Security* 23, no. 4 (Spring 1999): 49–80.

9. See George Hicks, *Japan's War Memories: Amnesia or Concealment?* (Aldershot: Ashgate, 1997); Ian Buruma, *The Wages of Guilt: Memories of War in Germany and Japan* (New York: Farrar, Straus and Giroux, 1994); Iris Chang, *The Rape of Nanjing: The Forgotten Holocaust of World War II* (London: Penguin, 1997).

10. On the formation of Japan's memories of the war, see, in addition to Hicks, *Japan's War Memories*, John Dower, *Embracing Defeat* (New York: Norton, 1999); James J. Orr, *The Victim as Hero: Ideologies of Peace and National Identity in Postwar Japan* (Honolulu: University of Hawaii Press, 2001); and Yoshikuni Igarashi *Bodies of Memory: Narratives of War in Postwar Japanese Culture, 1945–1970* (Princeton, N.J.: Princeton University Press, 2000).

11. See John Dower, *Empire and Aftermath: Yoshida Shigeru and the Japanese Experience, 1875–1954* (Cambridge, Mass: Harvard University Press, 1979).

12. For a thorough discussion of the organizational constraints placed upon the JDA through the end of the Cold War, see Peter Katzenstein and Nobuo Okawara, *Japan's National Security: Structures, Norms and Policy Responses in a Changing World* (Ithaca, N.Y.: Cornell University Press, 1993).

13. For a discussion of defense-spending issues during the Cold War, see Joseph P. Keddell, *The Politics of Defense in Japan* (Armonk, N.Y.: Sharpe, 1993).

14. In 1979, a senior Japanese military man, General Kurisu Hiromi, was forced to resign after he stated in a press interview that in such a hypothetical situation Japanese pilots would be forced to take illegal action.

15. The arms industry also served as a means of procuring technology from the United States. See Michael J. Green, *Arming Japan: Defense Production, Alliance Politics, and the Postwar Search for Autonomy* (New York: Columbia University Press, 1995); and Richard Samuels, *Rich Nation, Strong Army: National Security and the Technological Transformation of Japan* (Ithaca, N.Y.: Cornell University Press, 1994).

16. For a theoretical elaboration of this argument, see Glenn Snyder, "The Security Dilemma in Alliance Politics," *World Politics* 36, no. 4 (July 1984): 461–95.

17. For an application of the concept of abandonment versus entanglement to the Japanese case, see Jitsuo Tsuchiyama, "The End of the Alliance? Dilemmas in the U.S.–Japan Relationship," in Peter Gourevitch et al., eds., *United States–Japan Relations and International Institutions after the Cold War* (San Diego: Graduate School of International Relations and Pacific Studies, 1995).

18. For an extended discussion of the politics of Japanese defense, see Thomas U. Berger, *Cultures of Antimilitarism: National Security in Germany and Japan* (Baltimore, Md.: Johns Hopkins University Press, 1998).

19. For an insightful treatment of this trend and the dilemmas that it eventually generated, see David Halberstam, *War in a Time of Peace: Bush, Clinton, and the Generals* (New York: Scribner, 2001).

20. One of the best overviews of Japanese multilateral diplomacy during this period is Green, *Japan's Reluctant Realism*, chapter 6.

21. See Reinhard Drifte, *Japan's Quest for a Permanent International Security Council Seat: A Matter of Pride or Justice?* (London: Palgrave, 1999).

22. For an overview of Japan's role in creating ARF, see Paul Midford, "Japan's Leadership Role in the East Asian Security Multilateralism: The Nakayama Proposal and the Logic of Reassurance," *Pacific Review* 13, no. 3 (2000).

23. See Drifte, *Japan's Quest*.

24. For a useful overview of Japan and multilateral security institutions in general during the 1990s, see Green, *Japan's Reluctant Realism*, chapter 7.

25. Joseph S. Nye Jr. "East Asian Security: The Case for Deep Engagement," *Foreign Affairs* (July–August 1995): 90–102, quote on 91.

26. See Thomas Berger, *Cultures of Antimilitarism*, 171–77. For a more detailed discussion of the Japanese government's reactions to the Gulf War, see *Asahi Shimbun*, "Wangankiki" Shuzaihan, *Wangan Senso to Nihon* (Tokyo: Asahi Shimbunsha, 1991).

27. See Bill Heinrich, Akihiko Shibata, and Yoshihide Soeya, *Guide to Japan and UN Peace Keeping Operations: A Guide to Japanese Policies* (Tokyo: United Nations University, 1999).

28. Author's interviews with U.S. and Japanese officials involved in bilateral discussions at the time. For an overview of the crisis, see Don Oberdorfer, *The Two Koreas: A Contemporary History* (New York: Basic, 1997). On Japan's reaction to the crisis, see Christopher W. Hughes, "The North Korean Crisis and Japanese Security," *Survival* 28, no. 2 (Summer 1996): 79–103.

29. For a description of the Okinawa crisis and the Japanese and American efforts to cope with it, see Yoichi Funabashi, *An Alliance Adrift* (New York: Council on Foreign Relations, 1999), chapters 6 to 10. See also Sheila Smith, "Challenging National Authority: Okinawa Prefecture and the US Military Bases," in *Local Voices, National Issues: The Impact of Local Initiative on Japanese Policy-Making*, ed. Sheila Smith, Michigan Monograph Series in Japanese Studies, no. 31 (Ann Arbor: Center for Japanese Studies, University of Michigan, 2000).

30. This apt description was coined by *Asahi* newspaper journalist Funabashi Yoichi in a volume detailing the creeping sense of crisis that emerged during the period. See Funabashi, *An Alliance Adrift*.

31. For an overview of the development of U.S.–Japanese defense cooperation, see Sheila A. Smith, "The Evolution of Military Cooperation in the U.S.–Japan Alliance," and Paul S. Giarra and Akihisa Nagashima, "Managing the New U.S.–Japan Security Alliance," both in *The U.S.–Japanese Alliance: Past, Present and Future*, ed. Michael J. Green and Patrick M. Cronin (New York: Council on Foreign Relations, 1999).

32. On Korean fears sparked by the guidelines, see the lead editorial in *Korean Times*, September 25, 1997.

33. Victor Cha, "North Korea's Weapons of Mass Destruction: Badges, Shields or Swords?" *Political Science Quarterly* 117, no. 2 (Summer 2002): 225–26.

34. Cha, "North Korea's Weapons."

35. For a detailed and persuasive military analysis, see Michael O'Hanlon, "Stopping the North Korean Invasion: Why Defending South Korea Is Easier than the Pentagon Thinks," *International Security* 22, no. 4 (Spring 1998): 135–70.

36. See "Will Japan Become a Battlefield in War with North Korea?" *Weekly Post*, March 17–23, 2003. The authors' discussions with former Japanese military men suggest that these agents are a far greater source of concern than are Korean missiles, which are inaccurate, or Korean planes and ships, which military leaders are confident can be intercepted.

37. A number of analysts argue that Japan, not the United States, is the immediate target of any strategic deterrent capability that North Koreans may be developing. See Victor Cha, "North Korea's Weapons," 220.

38. This has been a long-sought goal of Japanese military men, who argue that without its own satellite system, Japan will be unable to access its security interests. From this perspective, the ability to gather and analyze strategic information is a prerequisite for an expansion of Japan's security role. Without it, Japan constantly fears that it is being manipulated by the United States. Author interviews with senior Japanese military officers, fall 1989.

39. Green, *Japan's Reluctant Realism*, 125–28.

40. Thomas Christensen, "Theater Missile Defense and Taiwan's Security," *Orbis* 44, no. 1 (Winter 2000): 79–90, and Kori Urayama, "Chinese Perspectives on Theater Missile Defense: Policy Implications for Japan," *Asian Survey* 15, no. 4 (July–August 2000): 599–621.

41. Patrick Cronin, Paul S. Giarra, and Michael J. Green, "The Alliance Implications of Theater Missile Defense," in *The U.S.–Japan Alliance: Past, Present and Future*, ed. Michael J. Green and Patrick M. Cronin (New York: Council on Foreign Relations, 1999); Michael D. Swaine and Loren H. Runyon, "Ballistic Missiles and Missile Defense in Asia," *NBR Analysis* 13, no. 3 (June 2002).

42. At the time of this writing, the upper house had yet to pass the legislation. For more details and analysis of the debate, see *Asahi* and *Yomiuri*, May 15, 2003.

43. On Ishiba's string of controversial comments on defense issues, and Koizumi's repeated efforts to reign him in, see *Asahi*, March 15, 2003.

44. On the impact of these views on Japanese–Korean relations during the Cold War, see Cheong Sung-Hwa, *The Politics of Anti-Japanese Sentiment in Korea: Japanese–South Korean Relations under American Occupation, 1945–1952* (Westport, Conn.: Greenwood, 1991), and Brian Bridges, *Japan and Korea in the 1990s: From Antagonism to Adjustment* (Brooksfield, Vt.: Elgar, 1993).

45. Jin-Young Chung, "The Eagle, the Goose and the Dragon: Cagemates in the Asia–Pacific Trade Order?" in *East Asia's Potential for Instability and Crisis: Implications for the United States and Korea*, ed. Jonathan D. Pollack and Hyun-Dong Kim (Santa Monica, Calif.: RAND, 1995).

46. See Victor Cha, *Alignment Despite Antagonism: The U.S.–Korea–Japan Security Triangle* (Stanford, Calif.: Stanford University Press, 1999).

47. On the background of TCOG, see Green, *Japan's Reluctant Realism*, 128.

48. In July 2002, 79 percent of both the Korean and Japanese publics felt that their countries were moving in a positive direction. For more details of the long and complicated process of Japanese–Korean conciliation, see Thomas Berger, "The Construction of Antagonism: The History Problem in Japan's Foreign Relations," in *Reinventing the Alliance: U.S.–Japan Security in an Era of Change*, ed. John Ikenberry and Takashi Inoguchi (New York: Palgrave, 2003).

49. *Japan Times*, March 11, 2002.

50. For a strongly argued case, from a Japanese point of view, for the continuation of the alliance even after Korean unification, see Narushige Michishita, "Alliances after Peace in Korea," *Survival* 41, no. 3 (Autumn 1999): 68–83.

51. On the significance of the Koizumi mission to Pyongyang as an effort to forestall a possible move on North Korea as part of the war on terrorism, see John Larkin, "Japan–North Korea Ties: Breakthrough," *Far Eastern Economic Review*, September 26, 2002.

52. Prime minister's office polling data quoted in Kamiya Masataka, "Japanese Foreign Policy toward Northeast Asia," in *Japanese Foreign Policy Today*, ed. Takashi Inoguchi and Jain Purendra (New York: Palgrave, 2000), 227.

53. See Ogata Sadako, *Sengo Nichu, Bei Chu Kankei* (Tokyo: University of Tokyo Press, 1992); Soeya Yoshihide, *Nihon Gaiko to Chugoku 1945–1972* (Tokyo: Keio Tsushin, 1995).

54. On the background of this event, as well as Prime Minister Yoshida's strong personal preference for closer ties with the mainland, see John Dower, *Empire and Aftermath: Yoshida Shigeru and the Japanese Experience 1878–1954* (Cambridge, Mass.: Council on East Asian Studies, Harvard University Press, 1979), 400–14.

55. Kamiya, "Japanese Foreign Policy," 232; Tanaka Akihiko, *Nichu Kankei, 1945–1990* (Tokyo: University of Tokyo Press, 1991), 108–15.

56. See David Shambaugh, "China and Japan towards the Twenty-First Century: Rivals for Pre-eminence or Complex Interdependence," in *China and Japan: History, Trends and Prospects*, ed. Christopher Howe (Oxford: Oxford University Press, 1996); Michael Oksenberg, "China and the Japanese–American Alliance," in *The United States, Japan and Asia: Challenge for U.S. Policy*, ed. Gerald L. Curtis (New York: Norton, 1994).

57. Already in 1992, the Japanese government had urged China not to acquire aircraft carriers from Ukraine. See Eugene Brown, "Japanese Security Policy in the Post–Cold War Era," *Asia Survey* (May 1994): 437.

58. See Green, *Japan's Reluctant Realism*, 80–82.

59. For a review of China's stance on the South China Sea, see Eric Heyer, "The South China Sea Disputes: Implications of China's Earlier Territorial Settlements," *Pacific Affairs* 68, no. 1 (Spring 1995). Regarding the dispute with Japan, see Green, *Japan's Reluctant Realism*, 82–88. Actions by Japanese rightists helped provoke this dispute.

60. Kamiya, "Japanese Foreign Policy," 240.

61. Qingxin Ken Wang, "Taiwan in Japan's Relations with China and the United States after the Cold War," *Pacific Affairs* 73, no. 3 (Fall 2000): 364.

62. Green, *Japan's Reluctant Realism*, 88–93.

63. See Allen S. Whiting, "Assertive Nationalism in China's Foreign Relations," *Asian Survey* 23, no. 8 (August 1983).

64. *Asahi*, September 27, 2002, 9. In 1997, 34 percent of Chinese respondents indicated that they disliked Japan. By 2002, that figure had increased to 53 percent.

65. See Thomas Christensen, "China, the U.S.–Japan Alliance and the Security Dilemma in East Asia," *International Security* 23, no. 4 (Spring 1999), and Allen S. Whiting, *China Eyes Japan* (Berkeley: University of California Press, 1989).

66. *Yomiuri*, September 10, 2002. Of Japanese surveyed, 55 percent indicated that China could not be trusted, as opposed to 37 percent who felt it could be. *Yomiuri* first asked this type of question in 1988, when 76 percent indicated they felt China could be trusted.

67. See Berger, "Construction of Antagonism."

68. One Japanese military officer who has observed Chinese military exercises told me that in his estimation it will be twenty years at least before the PRC's military forces can begin to approach Western or Japanese standards of training. Conversation in Makuhari, Japan, October 1996.

69. For an overview of China's willingness to integrate itself in global institutions, see Elisabeth Economy and Michael Oksenberg, eds., *China Joins the World: Progress and Prospects* (Washington, D.C.: Council on Foreign Relations, 1999).

70. See, for example, Komori Yoshihisa, *Nichu Kankei Saiko* (Tokyo: Sankei Shimbunsha, 2001); and Satoshi Amako, ed., *Chugoku wa Kyoi Ka?* (Tokyo: Keiso Shobo, 1997). For an overview of the development of these trends in Japanese thinking, see Michael J. Green and Benjamin Self, "Japan's Changing China Policy: From Commercial Liberalism to Reluctant Realism," *Survival* 38, no. 2 (Summer 1996): 34–58.

71. See John Welfield, *An Empire in Eclipse: Japan in the Postwar American Alliance System* (London: Athlone, 1988), chapter 5.

72. Some analysts suggest that China hopes to deter the United States by threatening Japan. See Thomas Christensen, "Posing Problems without Catching Up: China's Rise and Challenges for U.S. Security Policy," *International Security* 25, no. 4 (Spring 2001): 21.

73. See David E. Kaplan and Andrew Marshall, *The Cult at the End of the World* (New York: Crown, 1996), 68. There is some circumstantial evidence that North Korea had extensive connections with the Aum Cult. A number of the top members of the cult were drawn from the ranks of the resident North Korean population in Japan, which in turn has close links to North Korean intelligence. The chief scientist of the cult, a resident North Korean, was assassinated by unknown assailants while in police custody. Finally, analyses of the poison sarin gas used by the cult indicated it was made using vintage 1950s Soviet technology, the same sort of technology that is believed to be used by North Korea. Japanese and U.S. officials are closemouthed on a possible link, and the general suggestion is that no conclusive evidence is available. Given the delicate situation on the Korean peninsula and the powerful popular sentiments generated by the Aum Shinrikyo issue in Japan there are good reasons for neither government pursuing this issue further. However, were it so desired, even this circumstantial evidence could be used to help make a case for a U.S. preemptive operation aimed at Pyongyang.

74. For an early voicing of these concerns, see Kyung Yoon, "North Korea: Coming in from the Cold?" *Far Eastern Economic Review*, October 25, 2001. See also, *New York Times*, January 31, 2002,

75. David Murphy, "Uighurs: No Afghanistan," *Far Eastern Economic Review*, November 29, 2001.

76. See *Japan Times*, January 24, 2002.

77. For an overview of Japanese support for the U.S. operation in Afghanistan, see www.mpfa.gp.jp/region/n-america/terr-109/policy.campaign.html. These measures are not without precedent. During the Korean War the United States secretly mobilized former Japanese soldiers to man minesweepers that were sent on missions off the Korean coast. These forces engaged in combat and sustained casualties. See James Auer, *The Postwar Rearmament of Japan's Maritime Forces, 1945–1971* (New York: Praeger, 1971). What distinguished the post–September 11 Japanese efforts, however, was that support was provided openly and with public approval.

78. See *Asahi*, October 16, 2001. These results marked a significant increase over earlier polls, which showed a plurality of 46 percent opposing the dispatch of the SDF. See *Asahi*, October 4, 2001.

79. *Asahi*, October 28, 2001, and November 15, 2001. Such fears are far from baseless. One of the precedents that paved the way to eventual German participation in military operations outside of the NATO area was the support provided by German AWACS (airborne warning and control system) crews in guiding NATO fighter planes against Serb targets during the air war in Bosnia in 1994.

80. *Asahi*, September 4, 2002.

81. See *Asahi*, December 8, 2001, and *Asia Times*, May 1, 2002.

82. *Yomiuri*, March 13, 2003.

83. On Japanese counterterrorism policy in general, see Peter J. Katzenstein and Yutaka Tsujinaka, *Defending the Japanese State: Structures, Norms and the Political Response to Terrorism and Violent Social Protest in the 1970s and 1980s* (Ithaca: N.Y.: East Asia Program, Cornell University); Isao Itabashi and Masamichi Ogawara, with David Leheny, "Japan," in *Combating Terrorism: Strategies of Ten Countries*, ed. Yonah Alexander (Ann Arbor: University of Michigan Press, 2002); and Michael J. Green, ed., *Terrorism: Prevention and Preparedness: New Approaches to U.S.–Japan Security Cooperation* (New York: Japan Society, 2001). On the Aum Shinrikyo cult, see David E. Kaplan and Andrew Marshall, *Cult at the End of the World*; Robert Lifton, *Destroying the World to Save It: Aum Shinrikyo, Apocalyptic Violence and the New Global Terrorism* (New York: Holt, 1999); and Ian Reader, *Religious Violence in Contemporary Japan: The Case of Aum Shinrikyo* (Honolulu: University of Hawaii Press, 2000).

84. See Itabashi, Ogawara, and Leheny, "Japan"; David Leheny, "Tokyo Confronts Terror," *Policy Review* (December 2001–January 2002); and Peter J. Katzenstein, "September 11 in Comparative Perspective: The Counter-Terrorism Campaigns of Germany and Japan" (forthcoming).

85. *Japan Times*, September 23, 2002.

86. Singapore has twice arrested groups of suspected Muslim militants, once in December 2001 and once in September 2002, who were accused of planning attacks on U.S. targets in Southeast Asia. See www.reuters.com/StoryIFD + 1469736 (accessed September 19, 2002). See also Barry Wain and John McBeth, "War on Terrorism: A Perilous Choice for the Presidents," *Far Eastern Economic Review*, September 3, 2002.

87. www.mofa.go.jp/policy/terrorism/division.html (accessed March 12, 2002).

FURTHER READING

Berger, Thomas. *Cultures of Antimilitarism: National Security in Germany and Japan*. Baltimore: Johns Hopkins University Press, 1998.

Cha, Victor. *Alignment Despite Antagonism: The United States–Japan–South Korea Security Triangle*. Stanford, Calif.: Stanford University Press, 1998.

———. "Japan's Engagement Dilemmas with North Korea." *Asian Survey* 41, no. 4 (July–August 2001): 549–63.

Christensen, Thomas. "China, the U.S.–Japan Alliance and the Security Dilemma in East Asia." *International Security* 23, no. 4 (Spring 1999): 49–80.

Funabashi, Yoichi. *An Alliance Adrift*. New York: Council on Foreign Relations, 1999.

Green, Michael. *Arming Japan: Defense Production, Alliance Politics and the Postwar Search for Autonomy*. New York: Columbia University Press, 1995.

———. *Japan's Reluctant Realism: Foreign Policy Changes in an Era of Uncertain Power*. New York: St. Martin's, 2001.

Green, Michael, and Patrick M. Cronin, eds. *The U.S.–Japan Alliance: Past, Present and Future* New York: Council on Foreign Relations, 1999.

Harries, Meirion, and Susie Harries. *Sheathing the Sword: The Demilitarization of Japan*. New York: MacMillan, 1987.

Harrison, Selig. *Japan's Nuclear Future: The Plutonium Debate and East Asian Security*. Washington, D.C.: Carnegie Endowment for International Peace, 1996.

Heinrich, Bill, et al. *Guide to Japan and UN Peace Keeping Operations: A Guide to Japanese Policies*. Tokyo: United Nations University, 1999.

Hughes, Christopher. "The North Korean Security Crisis and Japanese Security." *Survival* 38, no. 2 (Summer 1996): 79–103.

Katzenstein, Peter J. *Cultural Norms and National Security: Police and Military in Postwar Japan*. Ithaca, N.Y.: Cornell University Press, 1996.

Katzenstein, Peter J., and Nobuo Okawara. *Japan's National Security: Structures, Norms and Policy Responses in a Changing World*. Ithaca, N.Y.: Cornell University Press, 1993.

Midford, Paul. "Japan's Leadership Role in the East Asian Security Multilateralism: The Nakayama Proposal and the Logic of Reassurance." *Pacific Review* 13, no. 3 (2000): 367–97.

Pyle, Kenneth B. *The Japanese Question: Power and Purpose in a New Era*. Washington, D.C.: AEI, 1996.

Rozman, Gilbert. *Japan and Russia: The Tortuous Path to Normalization*. New York: St. Martin's, 2000.

Samuels, Richard J. *Rich Nation, Strong Army: National Security and the Technological Transformation of Japan*. Ithaca, N.Y.: Cornell University Press, 1994.

Samuels, Richard, and Eric Heginbotham. "Mercantile Realism and Japanese Foreign Policy." *International Security* 22, no. 4 (Spring 1998): 171–203.

Schaller, Michael. *The American Occupation of Japan: The Origins of the Cold War in Asia*. New York: Oxford University Press, 1985.

Wang, Qingxin Ken. "Taiwan in Japan's Relations with China and the United States after the Cold War." *Pacific Affairs* (2001): 353–73.

Weinstein, Martin. *Japan's Postwar Defense Policy, 1945–1968*. New York: Columbia University Press, 1971.

Welfield, John. *An Empire in Eclipse: Japan in the Postwar American Alliance System*. London: Athlone, 1988.

5

Japan's International Relations: The Economic Dimension

William W. Grimes

Japan's economic power and interests pervade virtually all aspects of its foreign relations. Increasingly moving away from economic relations centered purely on the United States, Japan has turned more and more toward Northeast Asia. In particular, its economy has become increasingly enmeshed with the economies of China, South Korea, and Taiwan. (Russia and North Korea are much less factors in the Northeast Asian regional economy, at least from Japan's point of view, although there has been some Japanese interest in Siberian resources such as oil. Meanwhile, Japan's main form of economic relationship with North Korea is still remittances home from North Korean citizens resident in Japan.)

The rise of Northeast Asia in Japanese economic calculations is a major development in Japan's postwar foreign and economic policies. For all of the period, its alliance with the United States has been crucial in guaranteeing access to resources, technology, and international markets. The long Cold War, meanwhile, severely constrained Japanese economic relations with its Northeast Asian neighbors, especially China, Russia, and North Korea. Thus, for many years Japan's economic relations with Northeast Asia were limited, with far deeper bonds having developed with the United States. But while the United States remains Japan's most important economic partner in every respect, Taiwan, South Korea, and more recently, China have become key to Japan's international economic posture at the beginning of the twenty-first century.

The Japanese Miracle

From devastation in the wake of World War II, Japan's economy has grown to be second in size only to the United States, and the nation possesses one of the highest standards of living in the world. Japan is the world's second-largest trading nation, with persistent surpluses in its trade and current account balances, and it is by far the largest creditor nation. Despite virtually no economic growth from the early 1990s through the early years of the twenty-first century, Japan remains the postwar world's greatest economic success story and the dominant economic power of Northeast Asia, dwarfing all of its neighbors.

As it grew in wealth, Japan also became ever more involved in the international economy. In the early postwar years, Japan had been cut off from its former main markets in Asia, as it lost its colonial possessions and encountered the hostility of states whose territories it had invaded during the war. Virtually its only major trading partner was the United States, and the vast majority of its exports were in light industry products such as textiles and toys. Over time, Japanese exports have moved toward high value-added and high-technology goods, and its trading patterns have diversified.

In particular, its trade with East Asia expanded much more rapidly than its trade with North America, such that by the early 1990s both imports from and exports to East Asia exceeded those to North America—although the United States remained the largest single trading partner. Japan's trade with Northeast Asia alone was almost 90 percent of the size of its trade with the United States by the mid-1990s (fig. 5.1).

In tandem with the expanded magnitude and scope of trade came Japanese direct investment and development assistance. Reflecting its precarious balance-of-payments situation in the 1950s and 1960s, Japan was not a major exporter of capital in the first few postwar decades. Foreign investments in that period were mainly to support manufactured trade or to secure access to raw materials. But as Japanese trade surpluses grew, so too did net capital outflows (albeit with very low levels of inward capital flows). Over time, Japanese outward foreign direct investment (FDI) grew very large, strengthening Japanese firms' market positions around the world and creating regional and even global production networks based on intrafirm or intraenterprise group trade.[1]

The Japanese government provided considerable support for these activi-

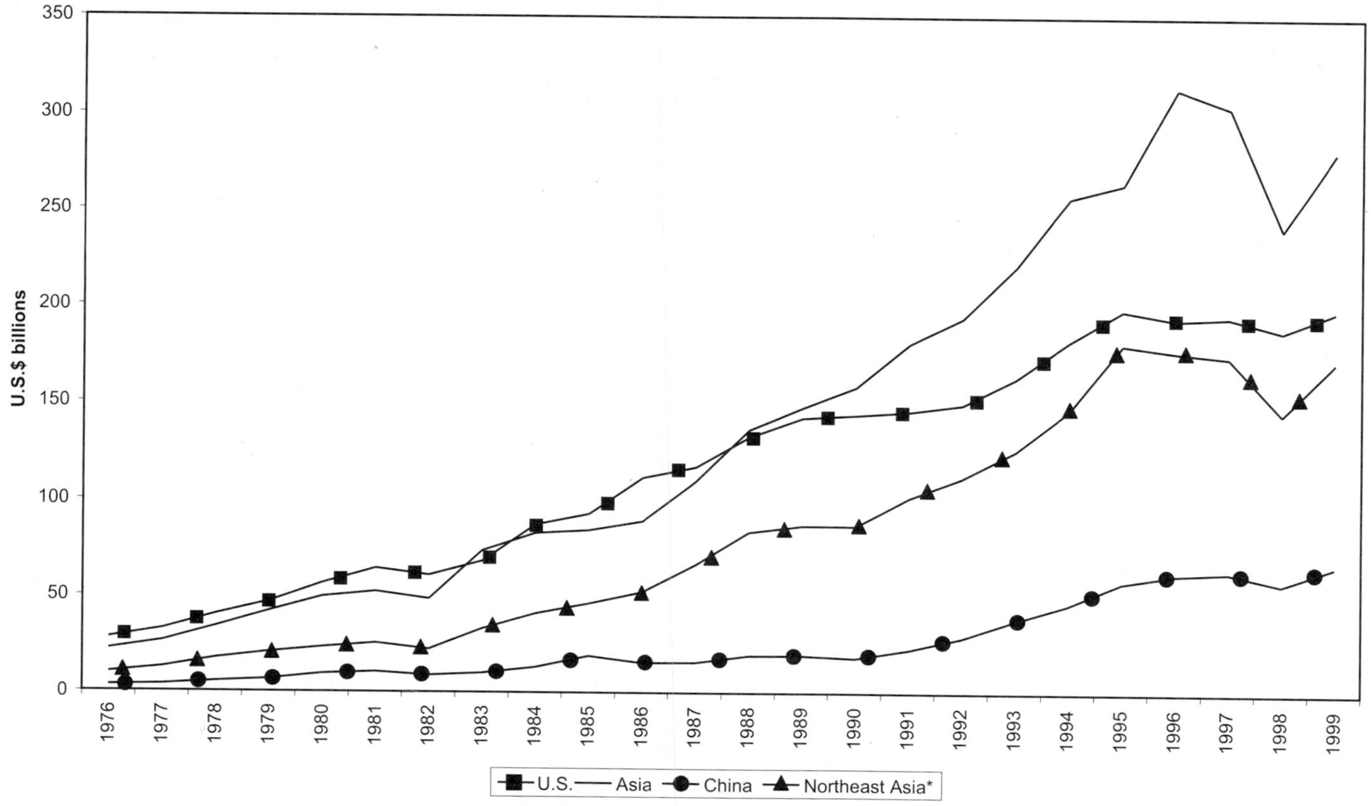

Figure 5.1. Japan's Trade, 1976–1999

Source: International Monetary Fund, *Direction of Trade Statistics Yearbook,* various years.
*Northeast Asia data calculated as the sum of trade with China, Taiwan, South Korea, and Hong King.

ties. Japan's aid program early on emphasized support for resource extraction in Southeast Asian countries that in turn contributed to the needs of Japanese industry. By the 1980s, an increasing amount of Japanese development assistance went to other economically productive projects such as harbors, power plants, telecommunications infrastructure, and export processing zones throughout East Asia.[2] In Northeast Asia, the bulk of Japanese aid currently goes to China (in most years the largest recipient of Japanese aid), since Taiwan's and South Korea's impressive economic development means that they have long since graduated from the ranks of Japanese aid recipients. They did continue to benefit from nonconcessional official lending and FDI support programs that helped to tie them more closely to the Japanese economy; such funds have also flowed in large amounts to China and to a much more limited degree to joint resource extraction projects in the Russian Far East. Japanese aid has generally also accompanied normalization of relations with its neighbors (in lieu of war reparations) and contributed to industrial development in both Taiwan in the 1950s and South Korea in the 1960s. Today as well, Japanese aid is a major incentive for North Korea and Russia to establish or improve diplomatic relations.

Aid projects were often helpful to Japanese firms, both because Japanese firms were often the contractors on them and because improved infrastructure contributed to the efforts of Japanese firms producing goods and services within the target countries. Japanese production networks have had considerable influence in the Northeast Asian economies of Taiwan, South Korea, and China. In particular, Japanese firms have used all three as destinations for manufacturing processes that were no longer competitive in Japan's higher wage environment. While the style of technology transfer has differed considerably among those countries—with licensing agreements dominating in South Korea and FDI of greater importance in China—the economies of Northeast Asia have been of crucial importance in the strategies of Japanese firms and government alike.

Frictions

The speed and scale of Japan's successes were unprecedented, but they also contributed to international frictions with Japan's trading partners and competitors. In Europe and North America, industries injured by the new Japanese competition called for—and in many cases received—protection from their Japanese competitors through tariffs, quotas, "voluntary export restraints," and other trade policies. As the Japanese economy industrialized and became more and more advanced, the sectors in question shifted from textiles to color televisions to steel and automobiles to semiconductor chips and satellites.

Japanese trade barriers also contributed to trade frictions. Although Japan abandoned most of its quotas in the early 1960s and by the 1980s had among the world's lowest tariffs (except in agricultural products and processed food), its trading partners often accused it of being an "unfair trader." Access to Japanese markets was difficult for firms from Northeast Asia as well as the industrialized West, as seen for example in the relatively low levels of imports from South Korea, even in areas such as basic materials, where Korean firms clearly held a comparative advantage. Only where Korean and Taiwanese firms have formed long-term alliances with Japanese firms—either as joint venture partners or as manufacturers of Japanese name-brand products—have they enjoyed reasonable market access.[3] Japanese subsidiaries (especially in China), by contrast, have had much better luck in exporting their goods to Japan.

More recently, Japan has found itself on the other side in some trade disputes. Concerned about increasing inexpensive imports of clothing and agricultural products from China, the Japanese government has found itself imposing explicit import restrictions on China. Most surprising have been "safeguard" provisions imposed on several minor agricultural products and the decision to mount antidumping cases in steel and textiles in 2000–2001. China's angry reaction and imposition of painful trade restrictions have lain bare the trade-offs for Japan of protecting its declining sectors against its neighbors. China particularly loomed large for Japanese firms, policy makers, and pundits who feared the erosion of Japan's economic position as a result of the rise of Chinese industry.

MERCANTILISM AND JAPAN'S INTERNATIONAL ECONOMIC RELATIONS

Japan has virtually none of the basic raw materials needed in a modern economy, and thus has had to purchase all of its needed resources (except for coal in the early postwar years) on international markets. The only way to do this has been by emphasizing the export of manufactured products.

Given the importance of exports to Japan's postwar growth, the Japanese government sought to promote private-sector exports through a variety of methods, including tax policy and preferential access to foreign currency. Thus, exporters were able to grow more quickly than nonexporting firms. Export promotion was one of the foundations of Japanese economic and industrial policy in the postwar period. Many authors have argued that Japan is in fact a "mercantile" economy, privileging producers over consumers and associating national security with trade surpluses.[4] This tendency has contributed to many of Japan's disputes with its trading partners.

Mercantilism and Trade

Japan's rise as a trading nation in the postwar era paralleled its rapid economic growth. As the Japanese economy became stronger and more efficient, its exports became more and more competitive with the products of the most-developed economies. Consequently, trade has been a consistent source of international friction for Japan, even as it has been a key element in its economic development.

The rapid rise of Japanese manufactured exports was related to Japanese export promotion policies. However, as trade surpluses grew and trading partners complained, export promotion and protectionism were renounced over time. By the early 1980s, most formal protectionist measures had been eliminated, and many (but not all) of the remaining, hidden protectionist measures were eroded over the course of the 1980s and 1990s. More importantly for Northeast Asia, protection shifted over time from advancing sectors to declining ones. This meant that countries at earlier levels of development, such as Taiwan, South Korea, and China, have often found their exports to Japan blocked, except when the exporters have been local subsidiaries of Japanese firms.[5]

Japan's trade relations with developed countries have generally improved in recent years, as Japan's rapid growth has leveled off and its industrial policy has become far less intrusive. However, new areas of trade friction have bubbled up with Japan's less-developed Northeast Asian neighbors—especially China, which enjoys massive bilateral trade surpluses with Japan.

Characteristics of Japanese Trade

Two characteristics of Japanese trade are most distinctive when compared with those of other economies. One is the sheer size of the trade and current account surpluses that developed after the 1970s and averaged more than $100 billion per year in the 1990s.[6] The other is the very low levels of intraindustry trade that have persisted for the entire postwar period. Both have contributed to tensions with Japan's trading partners.

In the aggregate, trade and current account balances reflect the net savings (private-sector savings, minus investment, plus government revenue, minus government spending) of an economy. If an economy has negative net savings, that means that it is borrowing from the outside world and thus has a deficit in its current account.[7] Japanese private sector savings have been high, which from the late 1960s led to persistent trade surpluses. Japan has particularly tended to have large bilateral trade surpluses with the developed countries because such a large share of its imports are of raw materials and energy resources. Japan's persistent trade surpluses with its Northeast Asian neighbors of South Korea and Taiwan (as well as the major Southeast Asian economies) have stemmed from these countries' dependence on Japan for capital goods, which exceeds their exports of finished goods to Japan. To some extent, trade surpluses with a specific country can also reflect specific Japanese trade barriers.

The other distinctive pattern of Japanese trade has been very low intraindustry trade. This means that if Japan is a major exporter in a given industry, it imports very little in that industry. This is unusual for an industrialized economy, since manufactured products are much more differentiated than commodities. Also, a considerable amount of trade in any given product area is usually made up of components rather than just finished products. The only major industrialized economy that does not have high rates of intraindustry trade has been Japan. Despite the apparent beginnings of a shift in the mid-1990s, the data do not yet conclusively show a permanent trend toward higher intraindustry trade.[8]

Japan's distinctive trade patterns result from both its government policies and its industrial structure. While Japanese tariffs are now among the lowest in the world, less formal barriers often remain. Nontariff barriers to trade (NTBs) include regulations that are not formally aimed at restricting trade, such as costly or time-consuming inspections of imported products and excessive sanitary or safety requirements.[9] There is considerable econometric and anecdotal evidence that NTBs significantly raise the prices of imports.[10] These barriers are increasingly found in declining industries, which is where most Korean, Taiwanese, and Chinese competition is to be found. A 1984 example, while more blatant than more recent cases, is instructive: South Korea's Ssangyong Cement attempted to export a large amount of cement to Japan, but found that the Japanese Customs Bureau insisted on weighing all the cement (instead of calculating it based on ship displacement, the normal method), which took months to complete. Not surprisingly, despite huge cost advantages, imported cement has not made major inroads into the Japanese market.[11]

Japan's low intraindustry trade appears also to stem from the country's distinctive patterns of industrial organization. Many Japanese firms are affiliated with one another in groups known as *keiretsu*. A given company tends to maintain long-term supplier or vendor relations with a set of companies, making it very difficult for foreign firms to break into the supply chain and thus reducing intraindustry trade.[12] A similar dynamic holds in distribution, where many products, including automobiles and electronics, are sold by dedicated stores, which do not carry products of competing manufacturers. Even as intraindustry trade finally began to increase slowly in the late 1980s and early 1990s, many of the imports were actually from Japanese firms that had located factories abroad. Thus, the *keiretsu* system has been extended internationally, although exclusive relations appear to be weakening in the face of global competition and opportunity.[13]

A more insidious aspect of Japanese industrial organization has been the persistence of cartels. A number of Japanese product markets are effectively controlled by cartels that exclude potential competitors.[14] Examples that have led to trade disputes since 1990 include steel (especially affecting South Korea and China), flat glass, telecommunications, petrochemicals, and cement. Cartels are not legal, but antitrust regulation has traditionally been weak in Japan, and cartels are pervasive in declining industries.

In addition to nurturing "winners," Japanese economic policies also have laid the groundwork for serious inefficiencies in other sectors. As noted above, an increasing proportion of protection has gone to sustain firms that could not stand up to competition. The continued protection of declining sectors has contributed to Japan's economic stagnation in the 1990s and early twenty-first century, since it encourages excessive investment and employment in nonproductive activities.

Trade Frictions

Japan's trade surpluses, apparent protectionism, and export competitiveness in several major manufacturing sectors have combined to create considerable trade frictions in the postwar period. Indeed, Japan has found itself embroiled in trade disputes with the developed economies almost constantly since at least the 1970s, in both bilateral and multilateral forums.

Restraining Japanese exports has been an important goal of developed country trade policy. These states have pressured Japan to accept a number of so-called voluntary export restraints (VERs) in which Japan has agreed to restrict exports of a specific product to a specific number or amount.[15] Japanese policy makers and firms have consistently used VERs to ease trade frictions with the United States and European countries; more recently, they have begun to use them in dealing with less-developed economies as well. For example, news reports in the summer of 2002 stated that Japanese steelmakers were restraining their exports to China to prevent China from imposing unilateral trade barriers.

Market access has been a second major focus of Japan's trade negotiations with foreign governments, especially the United States. Other countries, including those in Northeast Asia, have had less leverage over Japan and thus have been less publicly active, even though their grievances were often considerable. An important exception could be seen in a trade dispute with China in 2001 in which Japanese agricultural import barriers provoked a strong Chinese response. More generally, since the mid-1990s the Japanese government has consistently fought to have bilateral trade disputes contested only in the international legal environment of the World Trade Organization's (WTO's) dispute settlement mechanism. This shift also reflects an ongoing debate in Japan regarding whether its international relations should be pursued at bilateral, regional, or multilateral venues.

Finally, "managed trade" has been an important theme in Japan's economic relations. "Managed trade" means negotiating market shares of each country's products rather than allowing them to be determined by market forces, and it can encompass both export restraints and market access. While most attention has been focused on managed trade with the United States and Europe, it has probably been more prevalent in Japan's trade with South Korea, Taiwan, and China. Prior to China's market reforms of the late 1970s and early 1980s, essentially all Sino–Japanese trade was subject to governmental negotiations. As for South Korea, Taiwan, and post-1980 China, the *dirigiste* nature of their economic policies has combined with Japan's own protectionist tendencies to make many aspects of their trade relations subject to negotiation on a de facto basis. In a related vein, considerable anecdotal evidence suggests that Korean firms in particular have negotiated with their Japanese counterparts to privately manage Korean market share in Japanese basic industries.

Refocusing on East Asia

Japan's export-based strategy of resource access was largely dependent on the existence and stability of the U.S.-established postwar trading system. As long as natural resources were freely traded and major markets remained open to Japanese exports, lack of access to key raw materials, energy sources, and food would not be a problem. In the 1980s and 1990s, increasing Japanese fears of European and North American trade restrictions prompted interest in redeveloping East Asian markets. At the same time, consistently rapid growth in much of East Asia meant that those economies offered more promise as destinations for both trade and investment. In practical terms, the bulk of Japanese flows of FDI and technology transfer went to the Northeast Asian economies of Korea, Taiwan, China, and Hong Kong, because of their greater sophistication and ability to absorb capital and technology relative to the economies of Southeast Asia.

From the 1980s, Japanese official development assistance (ODA) and other official flows (OOF) increasingly focused on improving economic infrastructure in East Asia. In helping to increase power generation, communications networks, roads, and harbors, these funds made it easier for Japanese firms to expand their commercial ties with those countries. Indeed, most aid projects were carried out by Japanese contractors, giving them important footholds in new markets. Thus, official funds supported considerable Japanese private investment, which came to far exceed official flows.

Japanese government policies have supported these developments in several ways. Japanese government officials argued for years that Japan played a key role in helping the rest of Northeast and Southeast Asia to develop. They used the analogy of "flying geese," in which the lead goose reduces air resistance on the geese behind it, the second-tier geese do the same for the third-tier geese, and down the line. In this paradigm, Japan was the lead "goose," and as its comparative advantage shifted it would shed industries that would then be taken up by South Korea and Taiwan, then Malaysia, Thailand, and China, and so on throughout East Asia. In this view, Japanese trade and investment in the region was to be promoted for the good of Japan's neighbors. (The 2001 Ministry of Economy, Trade, and Industry white paper on Asia argues that the era of the flying geese is over, as the old second-tier economies as well as China increasingly compete on the same level as Japan, although other analyses belie that conclusion.)[16]

Levels of both ODA and OOF have generally tracked Japanese economic interest in a given country; thus, once China became a major destination for Japanese investment, its share of ODA and OOF expanded considerably. More generally, about 40 percent of aid goes to East Asia, with 8.5–13.5 percent of bilateral flows going to China in 1996–1998.[17] Especially after the 1997 Asian financial crisis, the Japanese government provided massive amounts of ODA and OOF to try to stabilize the economies of East Asia. The other major use of official money has been to support overall Japanese diplomatic aims throughout the world; in this respect as well, China was a major target, as Japanese leaders tried to entice Chinese friendship with money. Aid has been largely a reward for good behavior and seldom a punishment for bad behavior, with only a few exceptions, such as a partial withdrawal of funds to China following the 1989 Tiananmen incident and a 1995 nuclear test and a similar withdrawal of funds to India and Pakistan after their nuclear detonations in 1998.

Another form of government financial support for Japanese investment in developing countries is FDI finance. Several government programs offer lending and risk insurance to Japanese firms that invest abroad, dwarfing the amounts provided by other national governments.[18] In earlier years, these were mainly used to promote investment in extractive industries such as mining, but particularly since the mid-1990s, they have been focused on moving inefficient manufacturing out of Japan. The bulk of such FDI goes to East Asia, and in recent years especially to China.[19]

Finally, Japanese diplomacy in East Asia has been supportive of the needs of Japanese firms. Thus, the Japanese government has sought to persuade regional governments to loosen rules on foreign investment and repatriation of profits, to lower trade barriers, and to harmonize regulations to reduce the costs of doing business.[20] Governments have been generally receptive to such recommendations, although it is by no means obvious that changes in policies have been the result of Japanese pressures. And historical memory has ensured that the Japanese government has tread lightly in its relations with its Northeast Asian neighbors.

The Japanese government has also sought to integrate the country's economic interests in its neighbors with its activities in global institutions. For a number of years, Japan strongly supported the accession of China and Taiwan to the WTO, which finally occurred in 2001. However, in the process of bilateral negotiations between prospective and existing members, Japan pushed China to agree to reforms in the way that foreign firms and trade would be handled, above and beyond China's specific WTO obligations. Similarly, in the 1997 International Monetary Fund (IMF)-led negotiations to support the South Korean economy following the Asian financial crisis, Japan supported the efforts of the United States to force market-opening measures on Korea as a condition of aid. More generally, Japan has been eager to see countries—especially China—adhere to WTO rules concerning investment, trade, and intellectual property protection, and China's WTO accession has contributed to an upsurge in investment by Japanese firms hoping to take advantage of the new opportunities.[21] Breaking down resistance to foreign trade and investment in Northeast and Southeast Asia has become increasingly important to the Japanese government over the past two decades as a means of supporting the activities of Japanese firms.

Investment Issues

Together with trade, investment issues have been the most important element of Japan's economic relations with East Asia and the West alike. Japan's foreign investment patterns, like its trade patterns, are distinctive. They reflect a combination of developmental tendencies, foreign pressures, and straightforward macroeconomics.

Outward Investment

Net capital outflows are essentially the mirror of current accounts. If an economy is in current-account surplus, that means that it is a net provider of capital (investment) to the rest of the world. Thus the rapid rise of Japan's current account in the 1980s made for huge net outflows of capital. This does not mean that Japan was the world's largest foreign investor in gross terms, however, because one of the most striking characteristics of Japan's investment patterns has been the very low level of *inward* investment. Thus, as in trade in manufactured goods, Japan's capital position has been highly skewed.

The 1980s were a critical time of change for Japanese outward investment, not only because of Japan's large current account surpluses, but also because of the near-doubling of the value of the yen between 1985 and 1987.[22] The rapid appreciation of the yen meant two things for Japanese investors. First, it meant that investments in foreign countries looked extremely inexpensive and thus much more attractive to Japanese firms and individuals. (In contrast, it made Japanese assets all the more out of reach for foreign investors, despite relaxed regulations on inward capital flows.) Second, it fundamentally altered the comparative advantage of many Japanese manufacturing firms. In particular, the rapidly developing newly industrializing economies of South Korea and Taiwan were well placed to compete with Japanese firms. In response, Japanese firms began to engage in large-scale direct investment in plants and equipment throughout East Asia. This has contributed significantly to regional economic integration and the development of a regional division of labor. In Northeast Asia, cooperation with Taiwanese and South Korean firms has been seen especially in joint ventures or manufacturing partnerships from relatively early on; Japanese corporate activity in China started later and has involved more activity by subsidiaries.[23]

Japanese outward investment had been rather low through the 1970s and had mostly been focused on FDI by firms that were establishing overseas subsidiaries, factories, mining operations, and similar investments. With the rapid rise in excess capital in the 1980s, however, Japanese outward investment increased rapidly. While much of that capital was initially portfolio investment (especially in the form of U.S. government bonds), from the mid-1980s onward FDI accounted for an increasing share of Japan's outward capital flows.

Japanese outward FDI (JFDI) has been closely related to trade in both East Asia and Western industrialized economies.[24] Producing goods or having a marketing or service presence in a foreign country can be useful in ensuring that products fit the needs of that market, or in making use of advantages such as cheap or educated labor, good transportation facilities, access to suppliers or technology, and proximity to natural resources. In general, FDI of this sort is a *complement* to exports, meaning that it tends to increase exports from the firm's domestic factories.

JFDI has also been a *substitute* for trade when Japanese exports faced trade barriers or the threat of barriers. By investing in production abroad, Japanese firms can sell in closed markets. For example, in order to sell automobiles in the domestic Chinese market, all the major Japanese auto makers have sought to establish subsidiaries or joint ventures within China. Following a different strategy, Japanese electronics firms have aggressively invested in East Asian "export platforms"—factories in countries such as Thailand and China, which export much of their production to North America, Europe, and increasingly, Japan.[25] Japanese firms' East Asian export platforms were able to exploit cost advantages in countries with low-wage, good-quality workforces and relatively well-developed infrastructure and administration. At the same time, by exporting production to North America and Europe from sites outside Japan, these operations could circumvent trade barriers or threatened trade barriers against Japanese-made products.

In parallel, an important strategy in South Korea and Taiwan, both of which have relatively highly developed local corporations (and where inward investment restrictions have limited opportunities for Japanese FDI), has been original equipment manufacturing (OEM), in which local firms or Japanese joint ventures produce goods that are shipped under Japanese nameplates.

Inward Investment

In contrast to Japan's rapid increases in outward investment after the 1970s, inward investment—particularly inward FDI—remained low. Low levels of inward investment at first reflected strict legal regulation based on Japan's mercantilist style of economic management. In its quest for national economic autonomy, the Japanese government actively discouraged not only imports of goods that could be manufactured in Japan, but also foreign ownership within the Japanese economy. Even after legal changes in 1981 that eliminated the need for government approval of FDI, foreign entry remained low. The exclusive nature of *keiretsu* along with the cost effects of yen appreciation and the rapid rise in land prices after 1985 effectively discouraged foreign firms looking to invest in Japan.

Inward investment only began to grow rapidly after around 1995. Financial deregulation in the 1980s and early 1990s led first to rapid increases in portfolio investment. Deregulation also made FDI easier legally, but with relatively little initial effect on inward investment. Economic weakness in Japan since 1995 (as well as a general weakening of the yen) has meant rapid increases in the years since, but almost entirely from the United States and Europe.[26] Less significantly, there have been a small number of well-publicized Chinese and Taiwanese direct investments in Japan in recent years. Also, a number of Hong Kong and South Korean banks have established branches in Japan, often to finance trade by Chinese or Korean firms with Japan.

Probably the main "foreign" direct investment in Japan from Northeast Asian sources has been by long-term (in some cases, third- or fourth-generation) Korean and Taiwanese residents of Japan who have not taken on Japanese citizenship. Most of these businesses are relatively small, such as restaurants and *pachinko* parlors (a sort of legalized gambling), but two important regional Northeast Asian aspects exist. First, there are a very small number of regionally important large businesses such as Lotte, a Korean–Japanese conglomerate that operates in both countries as a local firm. More pervasively, legal and illegal remittances from North Korean–affiliated small firms and financial institutions in Japan constitute one of North Korea's largest sources of foreign exchange.

Trade and Investment with Northeast Asia

While much attention has understandably concentrated on Japan's relations with the developed world, developing economies have become increasingly important to Japan's economy and foreign economic relations. This is particularly true of the main economies of Northeast Asia, with which Japan has become intimately linked. Moreover, there has been a vigorous debate within Japan since the late 1980s over whether Japan's economic and diplomatic energies should be more focused on Asia or toward the developed economies of the West.[27] This has had practical effects in Japan's decisions about whether to pursue formal cooperation at bilateral, regional, or global levels (see below).

Since 1979, Japan has imported more from East Asia than from North America, and since 1990 more of its exports have gone to East Asia as well. (About 60 percent of Japan's East Asian trade is with Northeast Asia, which has been equivalent to 80–90 percent of Japan's trade with the United States since 1994.)[28] While the United States is still clearly Japan's largest single trading partner, the growth of Asia as market and supplier has been extraordinary since the mid-1980s, with a significant downturn only in the crisis years of 1997–1998.

In terms of composition, Japan's trade with Northeast Asia has changed substantially over the past two decades as regional economies have industrialized and improved the quality of their manufactured production. That shift is particularly notable in the case of China, which until the late 1980s was not seen as a manufacturing location for products for sale outside China itself. By the mid-1990s, China was primarily importing capital goods and components from Japan for manufacture within its rapidly industrializing economy and exporting lower-end manufactured components or assembled products back to Japan. For the more developed economies of Taiwan and South Korea, exports of higher and higher value-added products—produced, in many cases, on an OEM basis—have come to compete with Japanese-made products both in Japan and in global markets. In turn, they were importing some of Japan's highest-end equipment and technologies. More recently, Japanese firms have been transferring increasingly high-technology manufacturing to their subsidiaries and joint ventures in China (for example in optoelectronics), despite the reputation of Japanese firms as reluctant to transfer technology abroad.[29]

A result of this pattern of Japanese exports of capital goods and technology on the one hand and imports of consumer goods or lower value-added components on the other has been that Japan has maintained trade surpluses with virtually all the industrialized or industrializing economies of East Asia. The one major exception is China in recent years—and it is indeed a major exception, as China has by far the largest bilateral trade surplus in the world with Japan. One important reason appears to be that domestic Chinese labor-intensive manufacturers account for a large share of Chinese exports to Japan.

The shift in trade patterns was inspired not only by industrialization outside Japan, but also by the rapid appreciation of the yen that began in 1985. As Japanese products became more and more costly relative to those of other countries, it naturally became less and less profitable for Japanese firms to be producing more labor-intensive (or later on, less technology-intensive) products at home, and Northeast Asian neighbors soon took up the slack. Japanese firms increasingly sought to move their least competitive operations abroad, either by sourcing through existing Asian (usually Korean or Taiwanese) companies or by investing throughout East Asia in their own factories and offices. In both cases, Japanese firms became ever more enmeshed in a regional network of production.[30]

It is virtually impossible to discuss Japan's trade with its Asian neighbors since the mid-1980s without also considering Japanese direct investments in those countries. In Southeast Asia, JFDI shifted its previous focus from extractive industries such as mining, forestry, and plantations to manufacturing. More recently, China has emerged as both Japan's largest trading partner and the largest recipient of Japanese FDI and ODA in East Asia. More generally speaking, despite the profound Japanese economic influence in Southeast Asia, Northeast Asia has been the recipient of the bulk of regional Japanese FDI and technology transfer as well as trade.

Manufacturing investment in those countries has been attractive for several reasons in addition to the high-quality, low-cost labor that became so important with yen appreciation. Since the 1980s, governments in the region have been receptive to foreign investment as a means of rapid industrialization and have worked to lower barriers and encourage Japanese and other firms. Moreover, growth within East Asia meant that those markets were becoming more and more profitable. Finally, Japanese firms, facing barriers to trade in Europe and North America, used some of their operations in other East Asian economies as "export platforms," with the bulk of production being sold to the West.

Japanese investment has had profound effects on trade patterns in Northeast Asia, and indeed throughout East Asia more generally. Not only did it lead to new export markets and new products, but it also contributed to a new regional division of labor. Japanese manufacturers have developed regional networks in which various components are produced in different countries according to their comparative advantages, then assembled either in Japan or another country and sold either within the region or globally. Japanese subsidiaries also dominate East Asian exports to Japan, although Japanese subsidiaries have been less prevalent in Northeast Asia, which has more sophisticated domestic and foreign firm operations. (Japanese firms have been a relatively less important source of FDI, licensing, and joint ventures in China than in South Korea, Taiwan, or Southeast Asia, due to the Chinese economy's large size and the extensive presence of other foreign firms. Therefore, China's integration into the regional and global economies has been less based on a Japanese-driven regional division of labor.)

While some non-Japanese firms have been able to participate in these networks, Japanese business activities in most of East Asia have replicated Japanese domestic economic organization to a remarkable degree. Many Japanese manufacturers have essentially invested as groups, with long-term suppliers and financial institutions investing in the region to service their long-term customers, although there is some evidence that *keiretsu* are more open to non-Japanese suppliers when they are operating outside Japan than when they are operating domestically.[31]

Japanese firms have thus been central to the growing integration of East Asian economies. Their regional production strategies have, moreover, provided models that have been followed by South Korean, Taiwanese, other "overseas Chinese," and even U.S. and European firms in the region. Despite the remarkable progress in economic integration since the mid-1980s, however, *formal* institutions of regional integration have been limited—particularly in Northeast Asia. The contrast between de facto and formal integration creates serious questions for Japan and other states in the region regarding how to promote further mutual economic benefits and whether to build toward greater political cooperation, as discussed below. (North Korea and Russia have largely been left out of regional integration—and more specifically, out of Japanese regional integration strategies—due to historical animosities, political risk, and territorial issues. The only real exception has been limited attempts at cooperative resource extraction in the Russian Far East.)

Shadows on the Horizon

While the development of a regional division of labor has clearly improved economic efficiency and growth in Japan and among Japan's Northeast Asian economic partners, it has also created potentially serious frictions. This is particularly true in Sino–Japanese relations.

Perhaps the single greatest fear among Japanese policy makers and the public concerns the role of Northeast Asia, and especially China, in contributing to the "hollowing out" of Japan's industrial economy.[32] Chinese manufactured goods have made major inroads into Japanese markets. This has been particularly notable at the labor-intensive and agricultural end, where inexpensive textiles and other products have an enormous price advantage against Japanese-made goods. Increasingly, however, the Japanese have begun to fear that Chinese goods (computers, for example) will kill off Japanese producers in higher value-added sectors as well. Ironically, in many cases, the threatening Chinese-made goods are produced by Japanese companies' subsidiaries, as in the case of cameras. Such deindustrialization would not be a major issue if the Japanese economy were developing new, higher value-added industries and jobs, but economic stagnation since the early 1990s has meant that such replacement has been limited at best.

At least some Japanese policy makers have also begun to worry about the implications of economic dependence upon a potentially hostile neighbor. While Japan's dilemma in this regard is clearly less severe than South Korea's—let alone Taiwan's—the link between economy and security may be increasingly difficult to ignore in coming years.

BILATERALISM, REGIONALISM, AND GLOBALISM IN JAPAN'S INTERNATIONAL ECONOMIC RELATIONS

All states carry out their foreign relations at multiple levels—bilateral, regional, and global. Japan has for most of the postwar period dealt with its

Northeast Asian neighbors primarily in a bilateral manner. East Asia generally, and Northeast Asia in particular, are strikingly "uninstitutionalized," meaning that there are very few established, effective organizations in which states cooperate. This is true not only of security organizations, as Berger shows in chapter 4, but also of economic and functional matters. Nonetheless, all of the Northeast Asian states are members of one or more global organization with specific rules for how states should interact within specific policy areas.

Participation in global organizations has empowered Japan by guaranteeing it secure access to markets and resources without recourse to military power, even though it has not always followed all the rules of postwar liberalism. In this atmosphere of acquiescence by its major trading partners, Japanese international economic policy grew in distinctive ways. In terms of Northeast Asian economic relations, the most important of these have been the relatively one-way (outward) orientation of Japanese trade and investment, a deep sensitivity to bilateral U.S. demands, and avoidance of contentious bilateral negotiations with its neighbors. In the third of these three areas, Japan has often "piggybacked" on the market access and economic reform demands made on East Asian economies by the United States and IMF rather than aggressively pushing its own agenda.

As regional ties slowly develop around formal organizations and de facto economic integration, however, Japan and its neighbors increasingly have a choice as to the level at which they should deal with any given issue. The Japanese government, which for much of the postwar period found its economic relations dominated by bilateral negotiations with the United States, has begun to vary the levels at which it interacts for both strategic and tactical reasons.[33] It has sought advantage at some times in the legalism of global organizations, at others in informal bargaining at the bilateral level, and at others in the vagueness or hierarchy of regionalism.

Japan's Strategy in International Organizations

Japan's anomalous position in the world has had profound effects on its behavior in international organizations. Japan has been the world's second biggest economy since the 1970s, but has not built military capabilities to match. Moreover, the suspiciousness of its neighbors (not to mention the sheer size of near neighbors such as China and Russia) has meant that despite the regional economic importance of Japan, it has not for the most part been a regional leader, no matter how its region is defined. And with the United States—the world's preeminent economic, military, political, and technological power—as its closest partner in virtually every respect, Japan's ability to exert political influence has been strikingly limited.

Prior to the mid- to late 1970s, Japanese foreign policy professionals saw international organizations as an extension of Japan's relations with the United States and generally supported U.S. positions. This first started to change following the 1973 oil shock. Gradually, a relatively coherent strategy emerged, with Japan trying to gain authority within international organizations to influence other states as an alternative to using traditional power politics.

As Japan has become less willing to follow an exclusively U.S.-oriented foreign policy, it has tried to develop influence at the global level, through international organizations. For the past quarter century or so, Japan has been the second-largest contributor to virtually every major global organization, from the United Nations (and many of its specialized agencies) to the IMF to the World Bank. In the IMF, the World Bank, the Bank for International Settlements, the General Agreement on Tariffs and Trade (GATT, now WTO), and the Group of Seven, Japan has been an indispensable nation. The Asian Development Bank (ADB) was actually established at Japanese initiative; Japan is its largest shareholder and has supplied every president of the ADB since its founding.

The Japanese government has seen global-level organizations as particularly useful in terms of their legal functions. Japan's major problem in international diplomacy and economic negotiations has been that it has often been at a disadvantage in bilateral terms. This has particularly been true of trade negotiations with the United States, on whose markets and overall cooperation Japan has been more dependent than the other way around. Negotiations with China and South Korea have also been complicated, although primarily for historical/political reasons. (Negotiations with North Korea are even more complicated.) Japanese government officials see international law and multilateral dispute resolution as potentially reducing the effects of political asymmetries in bilateral negotiations, increasing transparency, and stabilizing expectations. This is best seen in Japan's attitude toward GATT and the WTO. Since the early 1990s, Japan has become much more assertive in insisting that international trade disputes be handled through the WTO. Most strikingly, it has taken or threatened to take the United States to the WTO dispute-settlement procedure on several occasions, often with success.[34]

Now that China has been confirmed as a WTO member, it is likely that Japan will also seek to use that multilateral commitment to pressure China to follow global trade and investment rules. More broadly, many Japanese diplomats and businesspeople speak of the need to integrate China into regional and global economic orders so as to raise the costs to it of political or military aggression.

Japan has not simply accepted international obligations as they are, but has been active in shaping the rules of the game. In negotiations to establish and expand the capabilities of the WTO (the Uruguay Round of 1986–1994 and the Doha Round, which began in 2000), Japan has consistently sought to push forward its own agenda. That agenda has included a strong dispute-settlement mechanism and strict standards on when antidumping rules apply (American misuse of these rules has been a major Japanese complaint regarding U.S. trade policy) in order to ensure that its exporters are treated fairly in global markets. At the same time, Japan's global trade agenda has maintained important elements of protectionism as well—most prominently, its efforts to keep agricultural trade and domestic antitrust laws off the international agenda. It has thus sought to protect its politically important (but extremely inefficient) agricultural sector, as well as firms that use cartelistic or monopolistic business practices to protect their markets within Japan.

Regional Efforts

Between the bilateral and global levels, Japanese economic and functional diplomacy has increasingly focused on regional cooperation. Actually, the very concept of "region" is very complicated in Northeast Asia (and in East Asia more generally), as reflected in the membership of the various groups of which Japan is a member. To begin with, the extraordinary U.S. economic and security role in postwar East Asia, in addition to the long-time mutual hostility among regional states, has created deep economic linkages between the United States and every major East Asian economy. The development of Japanese (and to a lesser extent South Korean and Taiwanese) export platforms outside Northeast Asia has in some ways compounded those linkages. Thus, by virtually any measure the United States must be considered a member of any meaningful economic region that includes East Asia.[35] Indeed, most of the key "regional" organizations in East Asia of which Japan is a member specifically include the United States in a leading role, including the Asia Pacific Economic Cooperation (APEC) forum and the ADB in the economic realm and the ASEAN (Association of Southeast Asian Nations) Regional Forum and the Korean Economic Development Organization in the security realm. Japan has for the most part resisted regional organizations that exclude the United States, at least until 1997, when it joined the informal ASEAN Plus Three (APT) grouping, comprising Japan, China, and South Korea, and the Southeast Asian states.

While keeping in mind the delicate issue of relations with the United

States, Japan has been increasingly active in regional cooperation since the late 1980s. A key example is APEC, formed in 1991 at the initiative of the Australian and Japanese governments.[36] APEC includes twenty-one members on both sides of the Pacific, including Japan, China, South Korea, Russia, the United States, Canada, Australia, and six of the ASEAN nations. The purpose of APEC is to propose and to aid in the implementation of policies to promote greater regional economic interaction. It is different from existing trade blocs in two significant ways, however. First is its stated goal of "open regionalism," which means that any liberalization achieved within the group will not exclude outsiders. Second, APEC does not produce binding legal decisions as one might see in a standard free-trade area. Instead, it seeks to create goals for its members and then to provide assistance in carrying them out. Some of its activities are as mundane as trying to promote common product classifications for tariff schedules or providing technical assistance to developing country members to harmonize their trade regulation with WTO rules. The most ambitious effort was the 1994 Bogor Declaration, which called for completely free trade in the APEC region by 2020.

Japan's role in APEC has been an interesting one. Its original interest in establishing the forum followed overtures by Malaysia for a more exclusive East Asian Economic Group. The Japanese government, fearing that such a group would alienate the United States, demurred in favor of a more inclusive grouping. Although it was a primary backer of APEC, however, Japan's actual role in the group has been an ambiguous one. For example, in 1998 the Japanese government chose to allow an ambitious trade promotion round known as Early Voluntary Sectoral Liberalization to founder in order to keep protecting Japan's inefficient agricultural sector. This preference for protection gained Japan the resentment of developing country members and the United States, Canada, and Australia alike. Whether Japan can maintain a leading role in APEC remains to be seen; however, in several more recent initiatives in the APT, Japan seems to be moving toward building up more purely East Asian cooperation rather than trying to reinvigorate APEC. Particularly in APT, the Sino–Japanese relationship is key to the success of the effort. Whether the movement toward regional economic cooperation can survive (or perhaps even improve) that often-contentious bilateral relationship remains to be seen.

Historical Memory

Complicating efforts at promoting regionalism, or even improving relations with its neighbors, Japan's history of imperialism in East Asia has colored its relations with all its neighbors in the postwar period. Indeed, while

Japan established diplomatic relations with the Republic of China (Taiwan) immediately after the former's reemergence from U.S. occupation in 1952, it had no diplomatic relations with other major neighbors such as South Korea, the People's Republic of China, Indonesia, and Malaysia until much later. In Northeast Asia, Japan still has not extended diplomatic recognition to the government of North Korea, and it has yet to sign a peace treaty with Russia, despite the passage of nearly sixty years since World War II.

Japan's diplomatic isolation put a damper on its regional economic relations for many years, and the Japanese government has consistently worked to improve its relations throughout East Asia. Establishing and maintaining these relations has had considerable costs. For one thing, establishment of relations has tended to involve commitments of Japanese aid.[37] The stunning joint communiqué between Japanese prime minister Junichiro Koizumi and North Korean leader Kim Jong Il in September 2002 continued this pattern, although subsequent events have put a temporary stop to moves toward normalization. The allure of Japanese money—so important for the economically prostrate North Korean economy—undoubtedly helped to overcome Kim's reluctance to admit to his government's abductions of eleven Japanese citizens. Of course, the practical economic benefits to Japan of normalizing relations with North Korea would be small—the real payoff would be in reducing one of the most profound sources of tensions in Northeast Asia.

The effects of Japanese sensitivity to historical memory can be seen in both patterns of ODA and in the unwillingness of Japan to criticize actions of its Asian neighbors—examples of the latter include human rights abuses in China and elsewhere and political misuse of Japanese aid by East Asian governments. By the late 1980s, however, the spread of Japanese production networks and official funds had helped to eliminate many of the economic complaints of East Asian governments.[38] This has been particularly true in Southeast Asia, where Japanese occupation was brief, albeit often brutal. Issues of historical memory have been more intractable in Northeast Asia, where China and the two Koreas hold deep animosity toward Japan. These feelings are fueled in part by the different historical experiences of those countries as compared to Southeast Asia (which had essentially traded European colonialism for Japanese) or Taiwan (where resistance to Japanese rule had been slight). At the same time, various Chinese and Korean governments have appeared to promote anti-Japanese feeling either as a means of domestic legitimation or to gain leverage in negotiations with Japan.[39]

Recent Developments

Recent developments have both accentuated and bucked some of the trends described above. The most important economic event of the past two decades in East Asia was the Asian financial crisis (AFC) of 1997–1998. While Japan was the Asian economy least affected by the crisis, the AFC proved to be an important impetus for Japanese policies toward the region. Most obviously, the Japanese government contributed large amounts of money to addressing the problems of the economies that were most directly affected. This included a total of $19 billion to the IMF rescue packages to Thailand, Indonesia, and South Korea, as well as the $30 billion New Miyazawa Plan, which sought to reinforce regional currencies in the short term and reinvigorate investment and growth over the longer term.[40]

Even these amounts of money could not fully make up for the pullback of Japanese firms and financial institutions, although it is undeniable that no other government in the world contributed nearly as much to resolving the AFC. By stepping in to support its neighbors, Japan gained a new credibility in the East Asian region that it has brought to subsequent ventures. The crisis also persuaded Japanese policy makers of the need to vastly expand cooperation in handling regional trade and capital flows.

Japan's new attitude toward cooperation with its regional economic partners has been evidenced by two main sets of initiatives. One of these has been the effort to build regional institutions to deal with problems of financial instability, such as those that occurred in the AFC. The reason was the disappointment of Japanese (and many other East Asian) policy makers with the response of the IMF and the United States to the crisis. Realizing that global-level institutions were insufficient to deal with the kind of crisis suffered by East Asian economies in 1997–1998, Japan has sought to build regional institutions that can address any future crisis more quickly and forcefully, and in a way that recognizes the special characteristics of the East Asian economies.[41]

In the fall of 1997, with the crisis ongoing, Japan proposed the formation of an Asian Monetary Fund (AMF) that would have ready access to $100 billion with which to support regional currencies in crisis. Japan itself would supply half the money and other East Asian countries would commit a portion of their foreign exchange reserves to support neighbors facing currency crises. The proposal failed in the face of opposition from the United States, the IMF, and China, but the idea of a regional support fund remained attractive to many in East Asia.

Two and a half years later, at a meeting in Chiang Mai, Thailand, in May 2000, Japan, China, South Korea, and the ten members of the ASEAN declared their intention to establish "swap lines" (official lines of credit in dollars and other major currencies) to help support each others' currencies in times of crisis. The Chiang Mai Initiative was seen by many as a first step toward a regional currency bloc similar to the European Monetary System, which led to the establishment of the euro. This was still only a very preliminary step, with limited financial obligations, and as of autumn 2002 not all the swap lines had been established. Nonetheless, the initiative constituted the first real concrete action of a purely Asian economic group in which Japan was involved. This effort by the APT states has helped to expand on their existing informal cooperation within APEC.[42]

While Japan has shown leadership in proposing and funding the AMF and its successors, it has not been an undisputed leader. In particular, the Chinese government has been wary of Japanese hegemony, and it strongly opposed the original AMF proposal. Only when China signaled its willingness to cooperate in regional currency arrangements did the Chiang Mai Initiative become possible. Even then, regional sensitivities meant that the initiative was formally proposed by the ASEAN states, which sought guarantees that the arrangements would not favor the larger, more powerful economies of Japan and China. Japan's leadership in this area, as in others, has largely been based on its ability to shape the incentives facing its partners and on its ability to convince Chinese leaders that the plan would not threaten China's interests.[43]

The other set of new Japanese initiatives in the post-AFC period has been the move toward forming bilateral free-trade areas (FTAs). While FTAs had been widely used elsewhere in the world, including Europe, North America, the Caribbean, South America, and ASEAN, Japan had always avoided such arrangements. In part, this has been because Japan has been so dependent upon the global trading system. Also, the persistence of Japanese trade barriers has made it difficult even to contemplate free-trade agreements. Nonetheless, in 1999 the Japanese government announced its intention to pursue FTAs, starting with Singapore and then moving on to South Korea. The oddly named Japan–Singapore Economic Agreement for a New Age Partnership, signed on January 13, 2002, constitutes Japan's first bilateral FTA; negotiations with South Korea continue.[44]

A Japan–South Korea FTA will not necessarily be easy to achieve and its benefits may in any event be marginal for Japan. Several obstacles remain that go to the very core of both Japan's and South Korea's economic identities. Primary among these would be the need for each country to accept unbuffered competition from the other, which would create severe economic pain for declining industries in Japan and several cutting-edge industries in South Korea. Neither fate is likely to be politically attractive to leaders. Moreover, WTO rules require that FTAs not exclude large parts of the economy, which would mean agricultural competition between the two countries, both of which have heavily protected that sector. Moreover, the benefits are questionable, as several econometric simulations have shown.[45] Only when

China or the United States is included in the FTA are major gains predicted; however, economic gains would be the result of exactly the kind of economic adjustment that Japan and South Korea have generally tried to avoid.

All of these initiatives point to an increasing Japanese focus on economic integration with East Asia, often without including the United States. However, the path to formal Northeast Asian (or, more generally, East Asian) economic integration has not been and will not be smooth. An example of the difficulties facing Japan in leading such cooperation can be found in the Early Voluntary Sectoral Liberalization (EVSL) negotiations held under APEC auspices in 1998.[46] EVSL sought to lower trade barriers in several specific sectors among all the APEC countries. This would have been a major step in the evolution of Asia–Pacific regionalism and would also have improved the credibility of the free-trade area that APEC states had agreed to in 1994. However, EVSL died when Japan refused to make any meaningful concessions on agricultural trade, preferring to protect its inefficient farming sector rather than make a sacrifice for the sake of regional economic integration. Japan's intransigence on the agricultural issue greatly undermined Japan's pretensions to leadership in the eyes of the Southeast Asian countries, many of which depend on agricultural exports. Agricultural issues also complicate Japan's ability to form FTAs, even with a country such as South Korea that also protects its inefficient agricultural sector.

A significant recent twist in Japan's relations with its neighbors has been the advent of trade frictions with China. Japan has had trade deficits with China since 1988, which by the late 1990s were averaging $16–20 billion per year on total trade of about $60 billion. Behind these numbers were several important trends. One of these was the rapid development of industry in China, which made Chinese exports competitive with not only low-end Japanese goods but also higher-end ones (although not the highest end). This has made many Japanese firms nervous about an onslaught of cheap imports that will wreck them—a fear that has been effectively propagated through Japanese society by the media.

Nonetheless, the greatest effect has been at the lowest end of manufacturing (particularly textiles) and in agricultural products. In April 2001, the Japanese government imposed "safeguard" quotas (a WTO-legal form of temporary trade barrier) to protect Japanese producers of shiitake mushrooms, leeks, and a kind of reed that is used in traditional Japanese flooring. None is a major part of the Japanese economy, to say the least, but the safeguard remained in place until that December, despite Chinese retaliatory trade barriers levied against a variety of major Japanese exports, including electronics and automobiles. Both the brinkmanship of the Chinese government and the ability of special interests in Japan to gain safeguard protection seemed to bode poorly for bilateral trade relations.

Through 2002 and 2003, word of bilateral trade tensions with Northeast Asia continued to appear in the news. Two examples in particular seemed instructive. In July 2002, the major Japanese steel firms announced voluntary cuts in exports to China in order to persuade China not to impose long-term safeguard restrictions. (In May, China had already imposed a 180-day provisional safeguard quota.) On the import front, the Japanese government decided to impose dumping duties on imports of South Korean and Taiwanese polyester following complaints by domestic manufacturers.[47]

CONCLUSION: JAPAN IN THE NORTHEAST ASIAN POLITICAL ECONOMY

Japan has been critical in developing a regional division of labor and increasing economic integration in Northeast Asia. Its unique blend of government policy and firm behavior have meant, however, that while Japanese firms and products have penetrated its East Asian neighbors deeply, there has been relatively little penetration in reverse.

At the same time, formal integration through the development of regional organizations has been limited. This lack of formal cooperation reflects several factors, including the effects of the Cold War, Japan's own prewar and wartime imperialism, the difficulties of defining Northeast Asia (or even, more generally, East Asia) as a meaningful economic area, the mercantilist economic development strategies of Japan and its neighbors, and the ubiquitous influence of the United States in Northeast Asian international relations. Meanwhile, economic frictions between Japan and its regional trading partners complicate the process of formal cooperation even as they demonstrate the need for better coordination of economic policies and activities.

Japanese policy makers thus face serious challenges in contemplating how to build on the success of regional economic development to date. One such challenge is to walk the fine line between improving Northeast Asian cooperation and keeping the United States committed to open markets. Another is to figure out how to deal with China, which may threaten large parts of Japan's manufacturing economy and its regional leadership, not to mention (at least potentially) its security. Finally, the Japanese government must make decisions about how to weigh the respective desires to create greater regional wealth, to be a regional leader, and to protect the weakest sectors of its economy.

In the face of these challenges, perhaps the likeliest result will be continued eclecticism, as Japan seeks to embrace Northeast Asian economic integration through limited regional efforts (such as a Japan–Korea FTA and APT), to minimize specific frictions through bilateral negotiations with each of its major economic partners, and to keep Northeast Asia embedded in the global economy through its activities in the WTO and IMF. Whether such an approach will be effective in supporting further beneficial integration—and thus perhaps even reducing political and security threats for Japan—remains to be seen.

NOTES

1. Patricia Nelson, "Integrated Production in East Asia: Globalization without Insulation?" in *Japan's Managed Globalization*, ed. Ulrike Schaede and William Grimes (Armonk, N.Y.: Sharpe, 2002).

2. Robert Orr, *The Emergence of Japan's Foreign Aid Power* (New York: Columbia University Press, 1990).

3. Bernard, Mitchell, and John Ravenhill, "Beyond Product Cycles and Flying Geese," *World Politics* 47 (January 1995): 171–209.

4. Robert Gilpin, *The Political Economy of International Relations* (Princeton, N.J.: Princeton University Press, 1987); Eric Heginbotham and Richard Samuels, "Mercantile Realism and Japanese Foreign Policy," *International Security* 22, no. 4 (Spring 1998): 171–203.

5. Mark Tilton, *Restrained Trade: Cartels in Japan's Basic Materials Industries* (Ithaca, N.Y.: Cornell University Press, 1996); Bernard and Ravenhill, "Beyond Product Cycles."

6. International Monetary Fund (IMF), *International Financial Statistics* (Washington, D.C.: IMF, various years).

7. The current account includes the trade balance (exports and imports of goods and services) as well as royalties, repatriated profits, and other earnings.

8. Edward Lincoln, *Troubled Times* (Washington, D.C.: Brookings Institution, 1999), chapter 2.

9. Lincoln, *Troubled Times*, chapter 6.

10. Yoko Sazanami, Shujiro Urata, and Hiroki Kawai, *Measuring the Costs of Protection in Japan* (Washington, D.C.: Institute for International Economics, 1995).

11. Tilton, *Restrained Trade*, chapter 4.

12. Lincoln, *Troubled Times*; Michael Gerlach, *Alliance Capitalism* (Berkeley: University of California Press, 1992).

13. Bernard and Ravenhill, "Beyond Product Cycles."

14. Tilton, *Restrained Trade*; Ulrike Schaede, "Industry Rules: From Deregulation to Self-Regulation," in *Japan's Managed Globalization*, ed. Ulrike Schaede and William Grimes (Armonk, N.Y.: Sharpe, 2002).

15. Aaron Forsberg, *America and the Japanese Miracle* (Chapel Hill: University of North Carolina Press, 2000), chapter 8; Lincoln, *Troubled Times*.

16. Ministry of Economy, Trade, and Industry, *Tsusho Hakusho 2001* (Tokyo: METI,

2001); C. H. Kwan, *Yen Bloc: Toward Economic Integration in Asia* (Washington, D.C.: Brookings Institution, 2001).

17. Ministry of Foreign Affairs, *ODA Annual Report 1999* (Tokyo: MOFA, 2000), charts 42, 44.

18. Mireya Solis, "Adjustment through Globalization," in *Japan's Managed Globalization*, ed. Ulrike Schaede and William Grimes (Armonk, N.Y.: Sharpe, 2002).

19. Japan External Trade Organization (JETRO), *JETRO White Paper on Foreign Direct Investment 2002* (Tokyo: JETRO, 2002).

20. Walter Hatch and Kozo Yamamura, *Asia in Japan's Embrace* (Cambridge: Cambridge University Press, 1996).

21. JETRO, *JETRO White Paper*.

22. For more information on the causes of the rapid yen appreciation, see William Grimes, *Unmaking the Japanese Miracle* (Ithaca, N.Y.: Cornell University Press, 2001).

23. Peter Katzenstein, "Introduction: Asian Regionalism in Comparative Perspective," in *Network Power: Japan and Asia*, ed. Peter Katzenstein and Takashi Shiraishi (Ithaca, N.Y.: Cornell University Press, 1997), 1–45; Bernard and Ravenhill, "Beyond Product Cycles"; Hatch and Yamamura, *Asia in Japan's Embrace*.

24. Dennis Encarnation, *Rivals beyond Trade* (Ithaca, N.Y.: Cornell University Press, 1992).

25. Bernard and Ravenhill, "Beyond Product Cycles."

26. JETRO, *JETRO White Paper*.

27. Ming Wan, *Japan between Asia and the West* (Armonk, N.Y.: Sharpe, 2001).

28. International Monetary Fund, *Direction of Trade Statistics* (Washington, D.C.: IMF, various years).

29. Nelson, "Integrated Production"; on Japan's reputation for reluctance in technology transfer, see Hatch and Yamamura, *Asia in Japan's Embrace*, chapter 6.

30. Bernard and Ravenhill, "Beyond Product Cycles"; Nelson, "Integrated Production."

31. Nelson, "Integrated Production"; Takabumi Suzuoki, *From Flying Geese to Round Robin: The Rise of Non-Japanese Asian Companies* (Cambridge, Mass.: Harvard US–Japan Program, 1997).

32. Nelson, "Integrated Production."

33. Ellis Krauss, "The U.S., Japan, and Trade Liberalization: From Bilateralism to Regional Multilateralism to Regionalism" (unpublished paper presented at Sophia University, Tokyo, June 21, 2002).

34. Saadia Pekkanen, "Sword and Shield: The WTO Dispute Settlement System and Japan," in *Japan's Managed Globalization*, Ulrike Schaede and William Grimes, ed. (Armonk, N.Y.: Sharpe, 2002).

35. Akira Kohsaka, "Interdependence through Capital Flows in Pacific Asia and the Role of Japan," in *Financial Deregulation and Integration in East Asia*, ed. Takatoshi Ito and Anne Krueger (Chicago: University of Chicago Press, 1996), 107–46.

36. Vinod Aggarwal and Charles Morrison, eds., *Asia Pacific Crossroads: Regime Creation and the Future of APEC* (New York: Palgrave MacMillan, 1998).

37. Forsberg, *America and the Japanese Miracle*; R. K. Jain, *Japan's Postwar Peace Settlements* (Atlantic Highlands, N.J.: Humanities, 1978).

38. Wan, *Japan between Asia and the West*, 74–76.

39. See Komori Yoshihisa, *Nitchu saiko* (Tokyo: Sankei Shimbun, 2001), for an influential Japanese journalist's view of how China has manipulated Japan to gain advantage in obtaining aid, investment, and other concessions.

40. William Grimes, "Internationalization as Insulation: Dilemmas of the Yen," in *Japan's Managed Globalization*, ed. Ulrike Schaede and William Grimes (Armonk, N.Y.: Sharpe, 2002).

41. Saori Katada, *Banking on Stability* (Ann Arbor: University of Michigan Press, 2001); Saori Katada, "The Purposes of Asian Monetary Regionalization," *Geopolitics* 7, no. 1 (Summer 2002): 85–112.

42. Grimes, "Internationalization as Insulation"; Katada, "Asian Monetary Regionalization."

43. Katada, *Banking on Stability*; Katada, "Asian Monetary Regionalization"; William Grimes, "Purchasing Credibility in East Asia, But at What Cost? Japan and Regional Currency Arrangements" (unpublished paper presented at Sophia University, Tokyo, June 21, 2002).

44. Jeffrey Schott and Benjamin Goodrich, "Economic Integration in Northeast Asia," *Joint U.S.–Korea Academic Studies* 12 (2002): 103–39.

45. Schott and Goodrich, "Economic Integration."

46. Krauss, "U.S., Japan, and Trade Liberalization."

47. *Weekly Japan Digest*, July 22 and 29, 2002.

FURTHER READING

Bernard, Mitchell, and John Ravenhill. "Beyond Product Cycles and Flying Geese: Regionalization, Hierarchy, and the Industrialization of East Asia." *World Politics* 47 (January 1995): 171–209.

Funabashi, Yoichi. *Asia Pacific Fusion: Japan's Role in APEC*. Washington, D.C.: Institute for International Economics, 1995.

Hatch, Walter, and Kozo Yamamura. *Asia in Japan's Embrace: Building a Regional Production Alliance*. Cambridge: Cambridge University Press, 1996.

Katzenstein, Peter, and Takashi Shiraishi, eds. *Network Power: Japan and Asia*. Ithaca, N.Y.: Cornell University Press, 1997.

Kwan, C. H. *Yen Bloc: Toward Economic Integration in Asia*. Washington, D.C.: Brookings Institution, 2001.

Lincoln, Edward. *Troubled Times: U.S.–Japan Trade Relations in the 1990s*. Washington, D.C.: Brookings Institution, 1999.

Schaede, Ulrike, and William W. Grimes, eds. *Japan's Managed Globalization: Adapting to the 21st Century*. Armonk, N.Y.: Sharpe, 2002.

Wan, Ming. *Japan between Asia and the West*. Armonk, N.Y.: Sharpe.

6

Russian Foreign Policy in Northeast Asia

Gilbert Rozman

Moscow's relations with Russia's neighbors in Northeast Asia remain perched between balance-of-power politics and economic integration. Despite recurrent promises since Mikhail Gorbachev's Vladivostok speech in 1986 to open the Russian Far East and Eastern Siberia to large-scale foreign investment and regionalism, Moscow's leaders long leaned toward power politics. This can be seen in five policy choices: (1) a priority to China as regional partner and to a geopolitical rather than an economic relationship with it; (2) a lack of urgency about resolving the territorial dispute with Japan and a refusal to establish the conditions necessary to attract Japanese investment; (3) frustration of South Korea's enthusiasm for close ties with and increased determination to support North Korea in order to gain leverage on the process of reunification on the Korean peninsula; (4) lethargy in addressing the problems of the Russian Far East in a way that would build trust and cooperation with other countries; and (5) suspicion of globalization and the U.S. role in Northeast Asia. For ten years after the collapse of the Soviet Union, old images of potential threats and national interests overshadowed new strategies of mutual benefit,[1] but after 9/11 there were signs of significant change that persisted in 2002.

From the time Russians traversed Siberia and reached the Amur River and the Pacific Ocean in the seventeenth century, they have felt that their settlements were exposed in this populous region.[2] Until the 1850s, Russians pleaded for trade and access, while being refused entry to Japan and Korea and allowed only an ecclesiastical mission and caravan trade through a single point into China. After joining in the humiliation of China through unequal treaties that ceded the area around what would become Vladivostok, Russia focused on military expansion and influence in the region.[3] It competed with Japan for control of Korea and built the Trans-Siberian Railroad with a shortcut through Manchuria. As the pace of settlement accelerated, Chinese and Korean labor and small business was essential; yet fear of being overwhelmed gave rise to extreme nationalist warnings against the "yellow peril." Heterogeneity did not bring shared communities or trust.

The international communist movement's expansionism into China coupled with Japanese militarism spreading from Korea into China reinforced a psychology of Russian adventurism amid insecurity. Memories of the short-lived Far Eastern Republic after the Bolshevik Revolution and the brief presence of a Japanese expeditionary force left fears of separatism. Stalin was late to impose his suffocating controls, but when he did they came with an added dose of xenophobia: expulsion of all Chinese residents, forced migration of all Koreans to Central Asia, hysteria over alleged Japanese spies, and a purge of cosmopolitan elites. When foreigners reentered the Russian Far East in 1945, they were Japanese prisoners of war kept in forced labor after the Soviet Union's last-minute entry into the Pacific war. Success in imposing communism on North Korea and supporting the communist revolution in China created an atmosphere of superpower arrogance, not openness through easy cross-border interactions with trusted neighbors.

In the Cold War era, insecurities quickly resurfaced. The 1950s brought the Korean War, and the 1960s the Sino–Soviet split and an intense military buildup along a disputed border.[4] In the 1970s and most of the 1980s, Moscow encouraged a psychology of reliance on one's own country in everything, military prowess as the key to regional influence, and fear of neighboring nations whose real motives were alleged to be direct or indirect expansionism. Only North Korea was a friend, but ties were circumscribed by an extreme version of Stalinism. Although trade in lumber and coal through a few Pacific ports had boosted economic ties with Japan, Vladivostok and most of the Russian Far East stayed closed to the world. Moscow paid heavily to fortify its eastern flank, but did little to prepare it for cooperation rather than confrontation. In the first half of the 1980s, ties with Japan were at their nadir since the 1956 reestablishment of relations, and the BAM (Baikal–Amur) railway construction well north of the Trans-Siberian line was hopelessly mired in cost overruns. Above all, China's economic dynamism and openness were outpacing Russia's stagnation and leaving closed and heavily fortified borders a relic of a bygone era. It was obvious that Russia would have to change.

In 1987, Gorbachev announced a massive investment program for the

Russian Far East that would draw heavily on foreign capital and aimed at integrating this area with the Asia–Pacific region. A year later, Evgenii Primakov was named to head a new national committee on developing ties with the region. Negotiations to normalize relations with China made progress as the Soviets agreed to remove their troops from Afghanistan, stop support for the Vietnamese occupation of Cambodia, and reverse the military buildup along the Chinese border, including in Mongolia. Glasnost came late to coverage of Japan and South Korea. In 1986–1987, glasnost opened many sensitive subjects, but only from 1988 to 1990 did one revelation after another cast doubt on the shibboleths of Soviet ideology concerning this region: that South Korea had started the Korean War, that Japan's workers and opposition were ripe for revolution, that China had damaged itself in capitalist reforms, and that the U.S. role harmed the region's prospects. New thinking and policy reversals laid a foundation for a revised approach to Northeast Asia, but after three centuries of different assumptions and in an atmosphere of regional flux the emergent Russian state found itself torn on how to proceed.[5]

Through the Yeltsin era, several basic questions stood in the forefront of Russian debates over policy toward Northeast Asia. One was the question of whether Moscow should give priority to the West or balance its foreign policy by looking also to the East. In fact, answers usually took the form of calling for more priority for the East in anger over some slight or another from the United States or the EU. Rarely did Russia look realistically at the role Western countries and their allies would be likely to play if economic integration in the East actually proceeded. Another question was whether Russia should rely on China as its principal partner in Northeast Asia or aim for balance in the region. Actually, this issue had more to do with the global great power balance, for which China was favored, than any serious discussion of a regional balance of power. Finally, Russians asked how they could best safeguard the Russian Far East in the face of worrisome transportation, economic, and demographic conditions. This issue also was tinged with unrealistic assumptions that ignored possibilities for integrating the area into the dynamic regional economy in favor of far-fetched schemes to avoid a doomsday scenario.[6] Until the end of the 1990s, few Russians were asking the practical questions about what needed to be done in Northeast Asia. Yet in the background there was unease because of an inherent orientation to the West, a fear of overreliance on China, and a sense of economic crisis in the Russian Far East. As rhetorical consensus intensified, it rested on a fragile foundation without any long-term strategy for economic reconstruction and increased security.

In his first year in power, Vladimir Putin also hesitated to focus on tough foreign policy decisions, while he concentrated on rebuilding state capacity, centralizing domestic power, and making Russia's presence felt. In 2001, as Putin faced a crossroads in the choices he could make for his country, it was clear that he would decide on the overall global framework and national recovery program before setting the direction for each of the five elements that stood in the forefront of Russia's Northeast Asian policy. As long as policy toward the United States awaited the outcome of negotiations, Putin kept his options open by strengthening ties with China first, holding ties with Japan in abeyance, keeping momentum with North Korea without alienating South Korea, and delaying on plans for regionalism. Without a strategy for domestic recovery through large-scale investment, Putin would also keep the Far Eastern governors guessing about how far centralization would proceed and how much Moscow would press them to integrate their economies with those of neighboring countries. Yet after September 11 Putin sided with the United States in the war against terrorism, setting in motion a course that could reshape Russia's role in Northeast Asia as well as its economic development strategy.

Having made a bold decision to support the U.S. war on terrorism and to quiet objections to the Bush administration's decisions on the Anti-Ballistic Missile (ABM) treaty and even NATO expansion, Putin could be expected to display similar pragmatism on the vexing issues facing his country in Northeast Asia: (1) a breakthrough in relations with Japan; (2) a showdown over North Korea's weapons of mass destruction and reluctance to reform; and (3) the failure of the Russian Far East in coordination with Moscow to create an environment for regional integration. To appreciate the possibilities, we need not only review the nationalist rhetoric on these issues prior to September 11, but also look for clues about how national interests are being redefined. Relations with China will be a byproduct of decisions on these matters as much as they will be a result of what happens on bilateral issues.

RUSSIAN POLICY TOWARD CHINA

At the birth of the Russian Federation, relations with China were shaky. Eager to distance itself from a regime shunned by the international community after June 1989, Moscow had done little to build on the normalization reached as student demonstrators milled around Gorbachev's summit venue. The fact that the Chinese government showed its sympathy to the abortive August 1991 coup did not endear it to Boris Yeltsin, the hero of the resistance. Chinese experts intensely debated whether the loss of power by the Communist Party of the Soviet Union and the early tilt by Yeltsin to the

West meant a severe setback for China's foreign policy. Yet they correctly concluded that Moscow would quickly become disillusioned with the West, and China beckoned to Russia with a vision of a multipolar world driven by great power rivalries as much as economic globalization.

Russian relations with China improved in stages over a decade. At the end of 1991, Yeltsin reassured Beijing of continuity, building on a border demarcation agreement and cross-border trade ties recently approved. A year later, Yeltsin visited Beijing and made it clear that China was Russia's principal partner in the region, shunting Japan to the sidelines and lowering expectations for South Korea only two months after his visit to Seoul. Through 1994, Moscow pursued Beijing not from concern about the peril to economic ties after a precipitous drop in cross-border trade, but from a desire to create a partnership in order to put pressure on the United States and Japan.[7] After Primakov became foreign minister in 1996, Moscow called for a strategic partnership for a multipolar world in order to block so-called hegemonic power. The joint rhetoric in response to the U.S. war over Kosovo further exposed the fact that Moscow's Northeast Asia policy was more driven by the negative goal of warning NATO than by any positive ideas for a region in need of cooling hot spots and integrating peripheral economies. Putin took little time in carrying this logic further in 2000–2001 by rebuilding ties with North Korea and signing a friendship treaty with Beijing that stopped just short of pledging an alliance in case of war over Taiwan or NATO expansion along Russia's borders.

The logic of great power relations drew Moscow, which still had a superpower appetite despite a stomach reduced to the size of a second-level European state, to China.[8] So too did the enormity of the challenge it faced along its vast Asian borders. China's deferential behavior in Central Asia and self-restraint toward the Russian Far East enabled Russia to cope better with pressing concerns from Afghanistan to Chechnya. Along with Russia, it feared Islamic fundamentalism as a threat to its territorial integrity. The result was stability that enabled Moscow to turn its attention elsewhere. Yet many in Russia, especially in the Far East, saw a worrisome divergence: China was rising as the continental colossus as Russia's status sunk. Demographically, economically, and even politically, Russia would be likely to slip into some sort of dependency relationship.[9]

Moscow's goals for Sino–Russian relations hinted at grandiose possibilities but often held only modest expectations. Strategically, the two were placed at the nucleus of Eurasianism, with the possibility of adding India and Iran and creating a new bloc against the maritime Atlantic and Asia–Pacific alliances. But Sino–Indian relations were strained further by Indian nuclear tests and Russia was wary of increased bilateral military ties that could transfer its most advanced weaponry to China or draw it into a clash over Taiwan. Yet the sale of fighter planes, submarines, and other weapons became indispensable for Russian military suppliers and constituted as much as one-fifth of recorded two-way trade. Economically, talk of unlimited complementarities, with Moscow supplying the natural resources and Beijing the labor, stumbled before Russian fear of becoming a kind of colony for a dynamic nation whose irrepressible entrepreneurship and diligent workforce would leave Russia with no assets except its resources. Trade stagnated until 2000, as Russians stripped Chinese joint ventures of their assets, rejected proposals for Chinatowns or even shopping centers, forced Chinese merchants to work under tight restrictions or even harassed them, and kept Chinese imports to levels far below Russian exports. Only in 2000–2001, as Russia's economy revived through high oil prices and a devalued ruble, did it become easier to accept a normal trading relationship with China. Culturally, even as China's top leaders chattered away in Russian and evoked nostalgia for the golden era of fraternal relations in the 1950s, young people in the two countries drew further apart. Study of the other's language and way of life had little appeal to the younger generation in either country. Trust would have to be rebuilt between business interests and a new generation of pragmatic leaders, with little help from cultural affinity.

Russian attitudes toward China are filled with contradictions. For twenty years, brave voices of reform argued first that Moscow should learn from Beijing's excesses under Mao that reform is necessary and then that Beijing's openness and market reforms under Deng offered a positive model.[10] After the Tiananmen turning point in June 1989, these reformers cooled on China's example, while opponents, in support of their position, focused on China's resistance to political reform. China's image as a model keeps shifting even today. An even sharper reversal occurred when reformers advocating normalization of relations with China in the 1970s and 1980s as part of a general attenuation of international tensions were replaced at the start of the 1990s by conservatives favoring some sort of alliance with China in order to keep tensions at a level supportive of Russia's great power aspirations. China may be the power most feared over the long run, even as it is recognized as the power most needed in the short run.[11] Indeed, some people embrace both ways of thinking.

After a strategic partnership was declared in April 1996, relations seemed shaky and without much momentum.[12] Leaders put the best face on, making high-sounding declarations at summits, but many of their goals were not reached. At first the Chinese side hesitated, recognizing that its economic interests were elsewhere and believing that Russia should remain a balancing force in triangles, not an ally whose existence would revive fears. The Yeltsin leadership seemed able to do little more than mark time, as it lacked a foreign policy strategy and Yeltsin himself faced bad health and low popular support. As late as the start of 2000, when Putin assumed the presidency, Moscow vacillated on whether to strengthen relations with Beijing. Through most of 2001, despite the shallowness of relations, there were signs that they would grow stronger. Trade at last was nudging upward, as Russians prepared to supply a gas pipeline across Western China and Chinese products gained some ground in the Russian market. Hopes were growing for another pipeline to Daqing in Northeast China with possible extension to the Pacific at Nakhodka that could make it possible for Russia to develop large energy deposits north of Lake Baikal. Meanwhile, the new Bush administration's penchant for unilateralism appeared more likely to push Moscow and Beijing closer than to pull them apart. Both countries eyed U.S. plans for missile defense warily, although Russia was ready to negotiate changes in the ABM treaty and, in the aftermath of closer relations in response to the terror attack on the United States, muted its criticism of the U.S. decision to withdraw from the treaty. Even after Putin's turn to the West persisted, it was still not easy to imagine that Russian foreign policy would begin to show signs of moving away from reliance on China as its centerpiece in Northeast Asia. When Moscow and Washington split over the war in Iraq in March 2003, Beijing's quiet agreement with Moscow gave added reason for the two to work together.

RUSSIAN POLICY TOWARD JAPAN

In the Gorbachev era, progress in normalizing relations with Japan trailed every other diplomatic initiative. Although in the first half year of the Yeltsin era there was much talk of an impending agreement over the territorial dispute and of a peace treaty, the difficulty of resolving these matters again became a symbol of diplomatic frustration. Efforts to achieve a breakthrough in relations with Japan faced three serious obstacles on the Russian side. First, Russians absorbed three decades of Soviet criticisms of Japanese demands for four islands of what Japanese called the Northern Territories and Russians called the Kuriles. This followed Moscow's unilateral abrogation in 1960 of the 1956 treaty promising to return two of the disputed islands closest to Japan. Russia contended that Japan's demand for four islands meant overturning the Yalta agreement and yielding to nationalist pressure. Without looking closely at the historical record or Japan's case for the islands, Russians branded Japan as a threat to sovereignty and national strength. Second, Russians saw Japan as too closely linked to the United States to expect much leverage on the global arena from giving it priority. Only after Japan announced its Eurasian diplomacy in 1997 did some begin to take seriously the prospect of using Japan to balance both the United States and China. Third, although Russians understood that there would be an economic payoff from normalizing relations with Japan, they failed to envision the rise of regional economic integration embracing the Russian Far East. No image developed of how Japanese capital and multinational companies would transform the Russian economy as they had the economies on an arc from South Korea to Thailand. In fact, some erroneously saw economic motives in Japan's desire for the islands, as if their recovery would bring a bonanza to Japan and an economic debacle to Russia.

Although Russian expectations remained low, relations with Japan fluctuated over the 1990s. Rumors of a possible deal whereby Japan would "purchase" the islands for more than $25 billion preceded Mikhail Gorbachev's visit to Tokyo in April 1991, but neither side was particularly hopeful after the modest results of the first formal summit in eighteen years between the two countries. Japan pressed Boris Yeltsin to act quickly after he became the president of the Russian Federation, and his diplomats secretly explored the possibility of reviving the formula of returning the two small islands nearest Japan. Yet the Japanese insisted on more and gained a reputation as holdouts on economic assistance in the G-7, while calling for international backing for their territorial claims. Even as Japan relented on aid, Russian politicians made it the target in the revival of nationalism. A weakened state, they insisted, had to make a stand against being pushed around; resisting Japan's arrogance was where the line should be drawn. While Yeltsin had agreed to visit Japan in September 1992, he followed the advice of these nationalists by canceling the trip on very short notice. When he traveled to South Korea a month later and then to China in December, the unmistakable message to Japan was that Russia could manage without it. Although Yeltsin finally made the trip to Tokyo in October 1993 and agreed to a declaration that listed all four islands as disputed while calling for a solution on the basis of "law and justice"—the very terms Japanese believed would favor their case—Russian pessimism toward Japan showed no sign of lifting through the mid-1990s.[13]

Lethargic relations finally gave way to a burst of negotiations and upbeat rhetoric. For four years leading up to the Irkutsk summit of March 2001, a forward-looking mood prevailed between the leaders of Japan and Russia. The Japanese side had chosen a new approach, and Yeltsin responded in November 1997 at a "no necktie summit" in Krasnoyarsk with so much optimism that the process was dubbed the "countdown to the year 2000," pointing to a territorial agreement and the conclusion of a peace treaty in that year. The Russian media saw things differently from the Japanese. They lauded the "Hashimoto–Yeltsin plan" for economic cooperation as the true achievement reached, explaining that Japan was alarmed enough by the rise of China and its own recent economic stagnation to relax its demands and predicting that a peace treaty could be signed without the territorial dispute being resolved. In contrast, the Japanese side depicted Yeltsin as virtually committing Russia to the return of all four islands, confirming that at last the country's economic desperation as well as the danger of China's rise had been carefully assessed. Wishful thinking on both sides obscured the fact that each needed the other in order to be taken more seriously in great power maneuvering, even if neither side was giving much thought to the compromises the other side would expect.

In 1997–1998 and again in the first year of Putin's presidency, diplomatic contacts proceeded at a furious pace. Japanese officials courted Russia's leader, hoping for a personal decision from the top. The two states reached a fishing agreement to stop Russian patrol boats shooting at Japanese vessels near the disputed islands. They expanded visa-free travel for groups of Japanese visiting ancestral graves on the disputed islands and Russian locals seeing nearby Hokkaido. Yet as much as both sides sought to convey an image of momentum, negotiations over the islands essentially ground to a halt after the fall of 1998, just as Russia's economic crisis scuttled most investment hopes.[14] Only secretive talks led by a few Japanese leaders kept alive the hope that Yeltsin would act and led to a fresh burst of energy to persuade Putin immediately after his election. After talks intensified, Liberal Democratic Party potentate Suzuki Muneo, with authority vested by Prime Minister Yoshiro Mori, gave Moscow hope that a deal could be reached with the return of only two islands, which elicited Putin's statement that Moscow recognizes the 1956 treaty to be in effect. Yet, when Junichiro Koizumi replaced Mori, Tokyo returned to the stance that it was not interested in "two islands first," but rather in "four islands in a batch." In 2002, Japanese attention was diverted by scandal that implicated Suzuki and others working with him at the Foreign Ministry in "hijacking" negotiations for illicit gains. Another stalemate in relations had occurred.

Although the countdown had ended unsuccessfully, some aspects of relations had improved. Tokyo had championed Moscow's entrance into APEC, while Moscow had pledged to back Tokyo's effort to become a permanent member of the UN Security Council. Visits by military leaders had built confidence between the two states. Plans had been vetted for building a gas pipeline connecting the deposits already being extracted off the coast of Sakhalin by a multinational consortium including companies from both sides, along with ExxonMobil, to the residential and industrial consumers in the northeastern half of Japan. Neither side wanted relations to sink back to the oblivion they faced five years earlier.

If Japan's worsening economic plight caused it to lose some of its luster for Russia, the more significant concern was Russian uncertainty over both its great power strategy and its economic course. Relations with the United States and domestic politics would be the decisive factors in settling those concerns. Putin did not consider Japan a determining force in making the most fundamental decisions for his country, but he might be expected to follow such turning points with initiatives directed at Tokyo. Once a positive climate for investment was established, he would likely target Japan to assist in the manufacturing, energy, and transportation sectors. Having decided not to protest loudly the U.S. decision on national missile defense, Putin could also make security ties a springboard for closer relations. Once again the United States held the key to Russo–Japanese relations, assuming the Japanese could overcome a chaotic swing in their foreign policy and the Suzuki scandal.

Since the 1950s, leaders and analysts in Moscow had drooled at the idea of turning Tokyo from a passive supporter of U.S. diplomacy into an independent power willing to defy Washington and look for balance from Moscow. While hopes had been dashed on various occasions, they continued to flicker. In 2001, rising Japanese nationalism was accompanied by new tensions in Sino–Japanese relations over Japanese middle-school history textbooks that whitewashed Japan's past depredations. Particularly those who warned of risks in Moscow's relations with Beijing had no choice but to make room for Japan in visions of balanced great power relations in the Asia–Pacific region.[15] Somehow the two nations would have to find a formula for quieting the territorial dispute in order to make possible serious exploration of closer ties that would give both more strategic leverage.

After September 11, the logic of normalization between Japan and Russia became more compelling. Japan saw the switch in Russian policy to the United States, and it wanted to take advantage of the momentum. Koizumi Junichiro had begun his tenure as prime minister with a nationalist bent, including rejection of the posture, assumed by Japan at the Irkutsk summit, to split negotiations in two. With Japan's relations with China and South Korea troubled over the summer, Koizumi had few options. He responded to the U.S. war on terrorism by pushing legislation to authorize sending Japanese warships in a supportive role, but also by resuming talks with Putin, heralding the chance for an energy pipeline while leaving vague how the territorial issue might be addressed.. The outlines of a possible deal were left unspoken on both sides: Russia would return two islands, as promised in 1956, and agree to joint management and development of the other islands;

Japan would sign an interim treaty without conceding its claim to the remaining islands. Diehard nationalists on both sides would be dissatisfied, even as great power aspirations for both nations would be boosted.

If such a deal could be reached, Russian foreign policy would take a dramatic turn in Northeast Asia that was favorable to the United States and regional integration but worrisome to China's great power strategy and to North Korea. Russian diplomats were waiting for Japan to make the next move, but such a move would be unlikely before Russia's 2004 elections, which could give the Japanese confidence that Putin is not becoming vulnerable before strident nationalists skeptical over the earlier tilt toward the West. In 2002, the Japanese were prepared to wait two years before making a new push for negotiations, while the Russians expected little from such talks.

RUSSIAN POLICY TOWARD THE KOREAN PENINSULA

The Korean peninsula, dangling from Russia and Northeast China toward Japan, evokes for some the promise of a corridor for a new Iron Silk Road or energy pipeline and for others the danger of a hot spot that could erupt in war or stand poised for the launching of missiles with weapons of mass destruction. After discarding the North in the process of normalizing relations with the South, Moscow reconsidered this "rash" decision. In return for this switch in allegiance that took root in renewed contacts around the Seoul Olympics in 1988 and was finalized while Gorbachev held power, the South promised $3 billion in loans and partnership with a dynamic, modern economy. The North had been a drain on Soviet resources, offering only barter in shoddy goods in repayment for weapons, energy supplies, and a lifeline to the Soviet economy. Its debts had been mounting and its international isolation did not serve the new image of Gorbachev's perestroika. Indeed, Pyongyang had furiously opposed his reforms and the new thinking that could enliven diplomacy in Northeast Asia. By breaking away from its grip, Moscow changed the regional environment, but Moscow was unprepared for market-based economic ties.

It did not take long for Russia's anticipated scenario to be thwarted. The loans from Seoul as part of its "northern strategy" were not put to use transforming the Russian economy, since the legal, political, and economic structures for that were not in place. The funds disappeared without any prospect of repayment, and Seoul realized that it would have to withhold new loans or simply lose everything. Initial investments by Korea companies, often based on political rather than economic calculations, proved as susceptible to Russian expropriation as those of other foreign investors. In addition,

Pyongyang failed to follow the example Moscow set by undertaking serious reforms. Instead, it turned to the unilateral path of diverting nuclear materials toward construction of bombs and accelerating the development of intermediate and long-range missiles. After insisting that further exports would require cash payments, Russia lost its leverage there. At the same time, it was becoming irrelevant to the search by the South and the United States for a way to deter the North's military buildup. When an agreement was reached in 1994 for Pyongyang to suspend operations of its nuclear reactor in return for oil supplies and construction of new reactors as well as to proceed with the Four-Party Talks, including Washington and Beijing but not Moscow, Russians felt slighted and betrayed. Not only were they relegated to observer status, but also their plan to build a nuclear reactor in the North was effectively over. A defiant Russian elite wanted to make its voice heard again.

From the mid-1990s, Russian foreign policy experts fixated on the idea of gaining influence over developments on the Korean peninsula. This did not mean support for regional economic integration that would entice the North, such as the Tumen River area project backed by China and, since 1991, the United Nations Development Program. Along with North Korea, Russia paid only lip service to this project for fear that a new port and growth center would drain resources away from Vladivostok and other Russian cities along the Pacific. Moscow turned instead to regaining the trust of Pyongyang, sympathizing with its fear of becoming a target of military or economic pressure and of Beijing's call for gradual change that does not allow the United States or Japan geostrategic advantage. The fate of millions of North Koreans suffering from severe famine and human rights abuses was not a major concern. As in the Cold War era, Russians again treated Korea as a pawn in the struggle among great powers, but it offered little to the North and placed its relationship with the South in the framework of globalization, including plans for large energy deliveries.

Seoul quickly reconciled itself to Moscow's shift to neutrality. When Kim Dae Jung launched his "sunshine policy," he made improved relations with Moscow a vital element in the effort to persuade Pyongyang to engage in direct talks. Putin obliged by advocating this position even as he was resuming weapons sales to the North and upgrading relations with a visit by his foreign minister early in 2000 and his own trip in July shortly after the summit of the Koreas. When talks between Pyongyang and Seoul stalled in 2001, Putin hosted Kim Jong Il in Moscow and offered additional support. Since Pyongyang was keen on obtaining advanced weapons supplies on credit and Moscow found it advantageous to use it as a proxy in keeping the heat on Washington and Tokyo, Seoul may have been getting more reassurance from Moscow to Pyongyang than it wanted. Yet Russia's leaders understood that as long as the North did not launch reforms and make a deal with the United States over weapons of mass destruction, it would remain a liability as a partner with no economic prospects and few diplomatic options.

Several of South Korea's strategies regarding Russia had floundered in the face of the usual obstacles. One approach had centered on nearby Primorskii Krai in order to create a sympathetic and economically affiliated area on the border of North Korea. Efforts included: (1) an industrial park in Nakhodka that would have taken advantage of a free economic zone and employed diverse types of people, from female textile workers to high-tech intellectuals; (2) a hotel and convention center in Vladivostok to become the centerpiece of the krai's opening to the world; (3) support for Koreans returning to the Khasan area after more than a half century of exile in Central Asia; (4) close ties to the Russian military, including arms purchases; (5) intensive monitoring of intelligence to keep track of continuing links to North Korea; and (6) cultivation of an image as Russia's most dependable partner in Northeast Asia. When others pulled back, Koreans became known in the mid-1990s as the most tenacious foreign businessmen in the Russian Far East. But they too lost heavily from the endemic corruption, and when the dual shock of 1997's Korean financial crisis and 1998's Russian economic crisis struck, Korean business had to admit defeat. Projects failed. The movement of Koreans to Khasan was blocked, and even in Vladivostok there were barriers. The battle of intelligence services led to the murder of a South Korean agent, perhaps by North Koreans, without an adequate Russian investigation. Then a Russian foreign ministry official was charged in Moscow with spying for South Korea. In 1998, under Kim Dae Jung, Seoul repaired its ties with Moscow centered on a more limited focus on facilitating direct talks with Pyongyang, which opened the way for Putin to flex Moscow's muscles over Korean diplomacy.

In August 2001, Kim Jong Il took an armored train across the Trans-Siberian Railroad to meet Putin in Moscow. Colin Powell, the U.S. secretary of state, appealed to Putin to persuade Kim to honor his promise to pay a return visit to Seoul as well as to resume talks with the United States. With Jiang Zemin scheduled to travel to Pyongyang in October and the recent signing of a friendship treaty by Putin and Jiang, Russia had resumed its role as a central actor in the drama over the Korean peninsula. By deciding how many weapons and how much oil to provide the North and on what conditions, Putin could strengthen Kim's hand in maintaining a military threat. Alternatively, by concentrating on the need for economic reform and cooperation under projects such as the Iron Silk Road connecting Pusan, South Korea, to the Trans-Siberian Railroad, Putin could give a boost to regional economic integration. In contrast to the mid-1990s, now Russia felt it had a say in the most important regional drama. Abruptly, the context changed after 9/11.

The Bush plan to press ahead with a missile defense program that required withdrawal from the ABM treaty in defending first of all against North Korean weapons left Moscow with an urgent decision. Having already thrown his support behind U.S. forces dislodging the Taliban, Putin decided not to resist very loudly. Clearly, support for North Korea was not a top priority. In the year 2000, the Korean peninsula had already become the centerpiece in regional diplomacy, with Kim Dae Jung in the lead. After the U.S. military offensive in Afghanistan, there was talk of targeting North Korean weapons of mass destruction at the third stage in the war against terrorism. If the United States should proceed unilaterally, that would put Russia in an awkward situation. After all, it did not share the U.S. image of threat and had been cultivating relations with both Koreas in order to influence a different endgame on the peninsula. If instead North Korea should take a threatening step, such as resuming testing of medium-range missiles, Russia would still be in a bind, since it would be inclined to a multilateral approach with reassurances to the North. As in the case of Russo–Japanese relations, the state of Russo–U.S. relations would likely determine the degree of cooperation Putin would offer in the event of a showdown over North Korea.

Having boosted ties with South Korea, including surprisingly robust direct contacts between the armed forces of the two countries, Moscow could also shape the outcome on the Korean peninsula by trying to find a common position with Seoul as well as Beijing. If the United States did not adhere to the spirit of the joint posture against terrorism since September 11, Moscow's options remained open. Eventually, reconciliation is likely to be explored in which Moscow's improved ties with the United States as well as carefully cultivated relations with China and South Korea may give it leverage on the outcome. For the time being, it would likely sustain the improved ties recently achieved with Pyongyang as one guarantee that its voice will be heard.

THE RUSSIAN FAR EAST AND NORTHEAST ASIA

In the first half of the 1990s, the eight administrative regions of the Russian Far East fell precipitously from their Soviet-era pedestal. Long subsidized by inexpensive transportation across long distances, they suddenly faced market prices. Reliant on industrial production for the military, they could not convert plants to civilian use. Key exports such as marine and wood products were transferred to private owners, whose large profits escaped taxation through payoffs to local officials and capital flight. Living standards for the majority of people sunk rapidly, accompanied by arrears in payments for electricity and eventually blackouts. In the north, even in the diamond-rich Sakha republic, desperation drove out-migration. Along the Amur and Ussuri Rivers in the south, cheap Chinese consumer goods made it easier for the large poverty-stricken population to survive; yet many felt cheated by the poor quality of these goods and humbled by their new dependence on people long viewed as much needier. The most promising seaports, such as Vladivostok and Nakhodka, were soon branded as the "wild east," where criminal groups in cahoots with local administrations squandered some of the best opportunities in Russia to open the door to foreign economic ties.

Debates on foreign policy in Asia began to take into account the future of the Russian Far East. In 1992–1993, threats by local assemblies to declare independence in order to gain at least the rights of republics to the profits from their own exports led to concern that nearby countries would welcome the fragmentation of Russia. Yet no other country showed any interest, and the struggle inside Primorskii Krai proved to be about economic resources and not in any way related to ethnic nationalism.[16] Through the middle of the decade, a scare arose about the depopulation of the Russian Far East, caused by out-migration even more than the negative natural increase in population seen across Russia. Analysts extrapolated a drop from 8.0 million to 7.2 million residents in the huge expanse of the Far East, while warning of the more than 100 million inhabitants of Northeast Chinese seeking relief from overcrowding. Newspapers outdid each other in exaggerating the numbers of illegal Chinese living on the Russian side of the border, as security forces launched campaigns to find them and send them back. Mostly, they discovered traders who had overstayed their restrictive visas to make a little money, but the hysteria served the purposes of demagogic leaders who played on the fears of a newly insecure electorate. Defense of Russian sovereignty now took the form of forcing China to accept tough visa requirements and calling for a program of domestic migration to this exposed area. Of course, memories of Chinese territorial claims led to suspicions of "quiet expansionism."

Five of the administrative territories of the Russian Far East faced the new reality that as borders really opened, their location would make them dependent on foreign states more than on their own neighboring Russian territories. Blagoveshchensk, the capital of Amur Oblast, looked across the Amur River at Heihe in Heilongjiang Province. While the latter had emerged quickly in the 1990s as a commercial center focused on the Russian market, its twin city was so frightened of a Chinese influx that it kept stalling on plans to build a bridge. The agricultural lands on the Russian side could increase their yields appreciably when Chinese tenants were hired, but this occurred only sporadically. Further east, Khabarovsk, one of the two largest cities in the Russian Far East and seat of the regional association as well as the krai administration, looked across with even greater trepidation at a more populous part of Heilongjiang. Governor Viktor Ishaev tried to block navigation by Chinese ships along the river, to restrict Chinese traders to one or two specially designated markets, and to limit migration severely. (The small Jewish Autonomous Region was essentially an appendage of Khabarovsk that was even more exposed to, and afraid of, China.) By the end of the decade, however, sales to China of the Sukhoi fighter planes (produced in Komsomolsk-na-Amur further north in Khabarovsk Krai) had done a lot to smooth relations as well as keep production lines going. Best situated to expand contacts with Northeast China, including Jilin Province, was Primorskii Krai. But Governor Evgenii Nazdratenko, during eight years in office (1993–2001), outdid all others in stirring emotions against the Chinese. He rounded up illegals in campaigns called "foreigner," slowed plans for developing a corridor to the sea, fought for years until the end of 1997 to stop the border demarcation from being completed, and became a symbol of hysteria over improving relations. Yet after he finally yielded to Moscow's pressure on the demarcation his tone changed amid reports that he had found additional sources of financial gain from ties to China. Compared to Moscow's welcome to Beijing as a close partner, however, the borderline administrations kept Chinese at a distance as potential threats and largely won popular support for their efforts.

Treatment of Japan was more varied. If suspicions prevailed in the early years of the Russian Federation, the mood was changing in some areas by the turn of the century. The Japanese courted Ishaev, who began to visit regularly, and drew some indication of his support for a compromise on the territorial dispute. This contrasted to the intense hostility from the leadership of Sakhalin, which administered the disputed islands. With Sakhalin close to Japan and exposed to Japan's prosperous economy, its officials were preoccupied with keeping the ample proceeds of their marine exports and gaining a large share of the budding oil and gas developments while holding Japanese interests at bay. Further away, also isolated from the Russian mainland, and with Japanese cities the logical metropolitan focus, Kamchatka had to overcome powerful naval and fishing interests if it was to open its doors to normal contacts. Fear of becoming the hinterland of Japan drove areas with rich resources to spurn many types of cooperation that would have eased worsening economic crises. While some governors saw an advantage in using Japan to balance China, the general pattern in the Russian Far East was to treat close neighbors as a threat. This led to organized crime and security services playing a large role in shaping relations.

Many in the population of the Russian Far East benefited from their location on the periphery of the world's most dynamic countries in the last quarter of the twentieth century. From prosperous Japan they obtained used cars and trucks that often had been discarded after only a few years of use and found no domestic buyers even at prices as low as several hundred dollars. Instead of seamen and tourists bringing back one car each for personal use, organized crime soon took control of the trade. The costs rose. Turf battles erupted with car merchants in other parts of Russia. Although the streets of Vladivostok and other cities were filled with vehicles that had steering wheels on the right, the benefits were far less than they might have been, and eventually restrictions sacrificed consumer interests. Along with the fact that marine exports brought little tax revenue to cover public costs, the used-car story was proof that state policies were not targeted at public well-being or economic growth, but at boosting the fortunes of a small elite. A region divided between small, personalized fiefdoms had squandered a chance for economic development at a large cost to local residents and the Russian state.

In Putin, the Far East faced a force for centralization unlike anything seen since the collapse of the Soviet Union. This could be observed not only in the appointment of an activist presidential representative, Konstantin Pulikovskii, stationed in Khabarovsk and in efforts to control critical territories exemplified by the arranged resignation of Nazdratenko, but also in a new assertiveness over foreign policy. The era of one governor after another shaping cross-border relations independently and insisting on a final say over issues such as border demarcations was probably ending. No longer would presidential programs for the region, such as the one announced by Yeltsin in 1996, be dead on arrival, except as a means to extract a little more money from Moscow. Putin, with his close ties to security forces, promised less but carried a bigger stick. It was unlikely that he would wait long before setting a new, more realistic challenge for the units of the Far East working together to take advantage of their Northeast Asian regional location. Yet Putin's penchant for tight control could leave too little initiative in local hands to respond flexibly once a course of regional integration is chosen. Alongside his political moves, Moscow financial circles also were acquiring assets that could tip the balance toward central guidance.

RUSSIA, THE UNITED STATES, AND THE ASIA–PACIFIC REGION

Moscow has a penchant to think big about an emergent region that others see differently. In the days of the Cold War, the area east and southeast of

Russia became identified as a battleground between Moscow and Washington as part of the struggle between socialism and capitalism. Japan and South Korea did not need to be taken seriously, since they were pawns in a global confrontation. Only China appeared caught in the middle, but Moscow analysts insisted that this was an illusion obscuring the reality that China was becoming a dupe of the United States in a bipolar world. The very notion of regionalism in Asia, which drew widespread interest by the early 1980s, was anathema to Soviet ideology with its simplifications aimed at rejecting reform thought at home and serious détente abroad. Only under Gorbachev did Moscow change course and accept regionalism as a positive force that must include Russia, but there was little realistic discussion of how.

In the late 1980s, Japanese publications became enamored with the prospect of the Sea of Japan rim as a new economic region embracing the Russian Far East. By 1990, Chinese journals were trumpeting the notion of Northeast Asian regionalism with a somewhat broader geographical range than Japan's thinking, boosting China's presence. Russian writings kept using the very broad concept of the Asia–Pacific region to include all of Russia. This reasoning was laced with fear that inclusion of only a periphery of Russia would undermine national integration and create an appendage for supplying natural resources to East Asian nations with little benefit to the Russian people. Suspicions prevailed that spontaneous regionalism without the strong arm of Moscow would boost the national power of other countries, but not Russia.

Having long perceived the Russian Far East as a valuable treasure chest and an ideally situated frontier for boosting comprehensive national power, Russians had trouble conceiving it in any other fashion. They were realistic about these local areas' lack of the necessary entrepreneurial acumen and efficient government to allow them to compete, so this limited their dreams. Recognizing the drive of Chinese merchants and the experience and capital behind Japanese multinational corporations, Russians were right to doubt that their own efforts would meet with much success in regional economic integration. They could not bring themselves to allow foreigners to buy land or buildings, to gain unrestricted access to markets, or even to win control over natural resources through investments. That logic left oft-repeated plans for regionalism no more than wishful thinking.[17]

Over the course of a decade, Moscow could have been enticed by at least four models of regionalism: (1) the Tumen River Area Development Project for creating a new "dragon's head"; (2) the Gore–Chernomyrdin commission's interest in the Russian Far East as part of globalization; (3) the Hashimoto–Yeltsin plan for Japanese investment in resources and management; and (4) the Shanghai Cooperation Organization's focus on regional security. Each received the backing of external forces and gained some support inside

Russia, but none reflected a domestic consensus on what served the national interest.

The Tumen proposal was favored by China's Jilin Province and reached its height of popularity in the early 1990s. Its impetus came from the deep desire in a landlocked area of Northeast China to gain access to the sea and the urgency of following in the footsteps of Southeast China in opening to the outside world and identifying key points to lead the way in attracting foreign investment. The message to Russians was to build a new city on the border of three countries and let its spillover effects bring along successive concentric circles in the hinterland. When opposition arose in Primorskii Krai, advocates modified the plan. Not only would the Russian share of the city be located in this krai, but it would also not lose its sovereignty to some international body and it would become only one part of a development triangle to reach north to Vladivostok. Russians still balked. Vested interests feared loss of their power and jobs. Few expected to be able to compete with cheap and diligent Chinese labor in the export industries, with Chinese merchants in the development of the service sector, or with multinational corporations in providing the capital and management. Many also saw the outcome in geopolitical terms: China would gain access to a port on the Sea of Japan and be able to project its military power close to Russia's naval fortresses. Instead of proposing an alternative plan for Tumen, Russians just waited for the idea to die. If Moscow allowed some cautious exploration of the idea to continue despite the reservations of local Russians, it did not really back the project. Fear of starting with a new city left Russians to champion the use of existing assets. In the mid-1990s, the Gore–Chernomyrdin commission, established between Russia and the United States and headed by the number two leader in each country, was placing priority on the Russian Far East. This area, with its few major cities, could become the proving grounds for efforts to bring modern economic practices to the Russian Federation. In fact, corruption abounded in the area and little was done to make a reality of high-sounding rhetoric. If residents of the Far East welcomed this countervailing economic force to China and other nearby nations, they did not expect any amount of assistance to help. Indeed, the more money provided to change the culture of monopolies and crime, the more opportunity for those very forces. While some Russians charged that NATO expansion and paltry U.S. assistance caused the Russian people to feel betrayed, there was little the United States could have done to raise trust in globalization in areas dominated by elites draining money away and pointing the blame elsewhere. U.S. leverage was limited; trust in the United States was inadequate. Lacking any notion of their own for regionalism to complement globalization, American officials, even when the proximity of Alaska was taken into account along with Seattle's early interest, never fired the imagination of Russians in the Far East.[18]

After floating ideas about huge amounts of development assistance in return for four islands and about a Sea of Japan network building for economic integration, Japan tried anew in 1997 with the Hashimoto–Yeltsin plan, placing emphasis on the Russian Far East. If the plan's exact contents remained vague, at least three themes already tested figured into the mix. First, multinational corporations would invest in megaprojects, especially energy extraction and pipelines and energy conservation measures through trading in compliance with the Kyoto accords on climate change. The Sakhalin-1 and Sakhalin-2 projects, under development by that time, would become models for other projects. Second, management training and assistance to small businesses would be accelerated. Business centers operating in a few cities of the region would become the backbone of an expanded effort. Third, humanitarian assistance, which had begun with powdered milk and medical supplies in 1992–1993, would be expanded to alleviate widespread poverty. Yet Russians understood that large-scale assistance was contingent on a peace treaty after the return of the islands was resolved. Ordinary Russians had no reason to assume that any such assistance would be of much use beyond fattening the overseas bank accounts of the elite, who in turn did not welcome the controls and transparency that could accompany serious foreign investment. Yet the Japanese appeal found some support, for instance from Governor Ishaev in Khabarovsk, who as head of the Far East regional association had a mandate to look at the development needs of the region as a whole.[19]

China's initiative for regionalism took a different form. After years of also trying to impress upon the Russians that closer bilateral ties could boost the economy of the Russian Far East, the Chinese side found that efforts at security cooperation received the most enthusiasm. In 2001, China proposed to transform the group known as the Shanghai 5 into a more formal and wide-ranging entity called the Shanghai Cooperation Organization. The focus would be on Central Asia, including four states that eventually joined, rather than the Russian Far East. They would target armed Islamic fundamentalist movements as the common enemy. The six members would share intelligence and even conduct joint military exercises. After years of trouble with economic cooperation in Central Asia, where corruption and criminality only seemed to worsen, it was unclear how this kind of regionalism could boost the economy of Russia or China. It catered to hopes for energy security in China and control in Russia, which corresponded to the outlook on what the purposes of regionalism should be. After September 11, U.S. forces moved into Central Asia with Russian approval, casting doubt on the future of special Sino–Russian ties and the Shanghai Cooperation Organization.

After a decade of dangling the carrot of regionalism before increasingly impoverished and frustrated Russians, other nations should have understood what was required. Appeals to idealistic reformers in Moscow or restless local elites on the border do little good. Decisions will be made by central leaders after they have consolidated power and decided on a long-term economic development strategy that they think can be implemented. As a strong president, Putin may be in a position to act soon, assuming relations with the great powers have stabilized. If so, he will be driven more by calculations about national power than by living standards, and more by effectiveness in balancing other countries than by benefits from integration under one country's leadership. Regionalism is not a priority; it is a means to ends set in Moscow. It may be helpful to refine an optimistic vision of regionalism to entice the Russian people, but that will not be the deciding factor in Russia's choice. Yet if Putin continues to lean toward the United States and the EU and if a new economic strategy succeeds in capitalizing on the economic upturn of 1999–2002, regional economic integration could become another means to create a secure environment for Russia within a global community.[20]

CONCLUSION

Russians have no choice but to approach Northeast Asia from a position of weakness. The Soviet military juggernaut has been reduced to but a fraction of its old power and nobody worries any longer about offensive actions by remnants of the Pacific Fleet or the Red Army. Yet by teaming with China and assisting its arms buildup, Russia could keep military tensions high around the Taiwan Strait and add to its own relevance. Likewise, by resuming weapons supplies to North Korea and supporting its right to maintain military options on land and by missile, Russia may boost its own position as an essential power in the region. By reminding the world of the danger from hot spots, Russia thought it had a chance to be taken seriously again at the end of the 1990s. This may have temporarily sufficed for a country intent on giving vent to frustrations, but it did little to produce economic growth and long-term hope. Putin preferred another option for a weak Russia after 9/11.

The scope of the compact between Putin and Bush waited to be tested. While in 2002 it was being applied across South and Southwest Asia as well as Europe, Northeast Asia remained on the sidelines. Increased arms sales from Russia to China clashed with closer military cooperation between the

United States and Taiwan. If Washington pushed for Moscow's acquiescence to the emerging U.S. framework for dealing with China or North Korea, there was no reason to be confident that Putin and other leaders would comply.

For its sense of national purpose and the satisfaction of powerful interest groups, Russia is unlikely to abandon preoccupation with boosting its great power status. Along with Europe, Moscow may look to Asia as a promising arena for exerting leverage on great power relations. China is unlikely to do anything for the next decade that would undermine its close geopolitical ties to Russia, considering that the United States will remain China's foremost concern. Meanwhile, long-term concerns about the rise of China will not suffice for Russia to undercut the ties that form its strongest bulwark against U.S. power. Unable to compete effectively on its own, Russia may allow its "eternal passion" to see itself as a great power to drive it in many directions for balance in Asia.[21] Closer U.S. ties now diminish the need for such balance, but this way of thinking is likely to persist.

Over the next few years, Russia's relationship with Japan may set the tone for the region. A new opportunity looms to reach an interim agreement on the territorial issue, sign a peace treaty, and make a dramatic improvement in bilateral ties. The United States and Japan would welcome Russia's cooperation on North Korea and the limiting of their weapons of mass destruction at the same time that Russia may at last be able to implement a strategy for regional economic integration while feeling satisfied that its great power status is confirmed. Yet it will take bold leadership and skilled diplomacy for Russia to succeed in this.

When the nuclear crisis erupted between the United States and North Korea in October 2002, Moscow tried to position itself as the indispensable force for bringing the two to the negotiating table. Yet when, as the war in Iraq was ending, the two sides met it was Beijing that offered the venue and the appearance of multilateral talks. Moscow's leverage on Pyongyang proved to be insufficient even as its standing had declined in Washington as a result of the Iraq war. While the outcome remained unpredictable, Moscow would be left on the sidelines without the economic or military clout to shape events in Northeast Asia.

As the WTO embraces China and sets a framework for economic regionalism in Northeast Asia as well as the world, Russia is eager to seek membership, too. In 2001, it began making its case, although it sought many exceptions from the strict standards for entry. With regional economic integration accelerating and a national decision to meet WTO standards, the Russian Far East may be obliged to abandon many of its barriers. After a decade of vacillating over opening borders, the center and the localities may at last have to agree on forward-looking policies with a specific timetable. Once Moscow has sorted out its great power strategy, it can be expected to turn to solving the crisis of the Russian Far East and regionalism as another strategy long left in abeyance.

NOTES

1. M. L. Titarenko, *Rossiia litsom k Azii* (Moscow: Respublika, 1998).

2. John J. Stephan, *The Russian Far East: A History* (Stanford, Calif.: Stanford University Press, 1994).

3. S. C. M. Paine, *Imperial Rivals: China, Russia, and Their Disputed Frontier* (Armonk, N.Y.: Sharpe, 1996).

4. Lowell Dittmer, *Sino–Soviet Normalization and Its International Implications, 1945–1990* (Seattle: University of Washington Press, 1992).

5. Gilbert Rozman, "Ajia-taiheiyo chiiki e mukete takamaru Soren no kitai," *Soren no kiki to Nisso kankei* (1991): 86–96, 243–69.

6. *Rossiiskii Dal'nii Vostok i Severo-Vostochnaia Aziia* (Moscow: Editorial URSS, 1998).

7. Gilbert Rozman, "China, Japan, and the Post-Soviet Upheaval: Global Opportunities and Regional Risks," in *The International Dimension of Post-Communist Transitions in Russia and the New States of Eurasia*, ed. Karen Dawisha (Armonk, N.Y.: Sharpe, 1997), 147–76.

8. Gilbert Rozman, "Sino–Russian Relations in the 1990s: A Balance Sheet," *Post-Soviet Affairs* 14, no. 2 (Spring 1998): 93–113.

9. V. L. Larin, *Kitai i Dal'nii Vostok Rossii v pervoi polovine 90-x: problemy regional'nogo vzaimodeistviia* (Vladivostok: Dal'nauka, 1998).

10. Gilbert Rozman, *A Mirror for Socialism: Soviet Criticisms of China* (Princeton, N.J.: Princeton University Press, 1985).

11. Alexander Lukin, "Russia's Image of China and Russian–Chinese Relations," *East Asia* 17, no. 1 (Spring 1999): 5–39.

12. Sherman W. Garnett, ed., *Rapprochement or Rivalry? Russia–China Relations in a Changing Asia* (Washington, D.C.: Carnegie Endowment for International Peace, 2000).

13. Tsuyoshi Hasegawa, *The Northern Territories Dispute and Russo–Japanese Relations*, Vol. 2, *Neither War Nor Peace, 1985–1998*, International and Area Studies Research Series, no. 97 (Berkeley: International and Area Studies, University of California, 1998).

14. Gilbert Rozman, ed., *Japan and Russia: The Tortuous Path to Normalization, 1949–1999* (New York: St. Martin's, 2000).

15. A. D. Bogaturov, *Velikie derzhavy na tikhom okeane* (Moscow: Konvert—MONF, 1997).

16. Mikhail A. Alexseev, ed., *Center–Periphery Conflict in Post-Soviet Russia: A Federation Imperiled* (New York: St. Martin's, 1999), 205–46.

17. Judith Thornton and Charles E. Ziegler, eds., *Russia's Far East: A Region at Risk* (Seattle: University of Washington Press, 2002).

18. Michael J. Bradshaw, ed., *The Russian Far East and Pacific Asia: Unfulfilled Potential* (Richmond, U.K.: Curzon, 2001).

19. V. I. Ishaev, *Mezhdunarodnoe ekonomicheskoe sotrudnichestvo: regionai'nyi aspect* (Vladivostok: Dal'nauka, 1999).

20. Gilbert Rozman, Mikhail C. Nosov, and Koji Watanabe, eds., *Russia and East Asia: The 21st Century Security Environment* (Armonk, N.Y.: Sharpe, 1999).

21. E. P. Bazhanov, *Rossiia kak velikaia derzhava (traditsii i perspektivy)* (Moscow: Nauchnaia kniga, 1999), 42.

FURTHER READING

Akaha, Tsuneo, ed. *Politics and Economics in Northeast Asia: Nationalism and Regionalism in Contention*. New York: St. Martin's, 1999.

Chufrin, Gennady, ed. *Russia and Asia–Pacific Security*. Stockholm: Sipri, 1999.

Green, Michael J. *Japan's Reluctant Realism: Foreign Policy Challenges in an Era of Uncertain Power*. New York: Palgrave, 2001.

Inoguchi, Takashi, ed. *Japan's Asian Policy: Revival and Response*. New York: Palgrave, 2002.

Inoguchi, Takashi, and Purnendra Jain, eds. *Japanese Foreign Policy Today*. New York: Palgrave, 2000.

Kimura, Hiroshi. *Distant Neighbors, Vol. 2. Japanese–Russian Relations under Gorbachev and Yeltsin*. Armonk, N.Y.: Sharpe, 2000.

Menon, Rajan, Yuri E. Fedorov, and Ghia Nodia, eds. *Russia, the Caucasus, and Central Asia: The 21st Century Security Environment*. Armonk, N.Y.: Sharpe, 1999.

Minakir, Pavel A., and Gregory L. Freeze, eds. *The Russian Far East: An Economic Handbook*. Armonk, N.Y.: Sharpe, 1994.

Trenin, Dmitri. *The End of Eurasia: Russia on the Border between Geopolitics and Globalization*. Washington, D.C.: Carnegie Endowment for International Peace, 2002.

Verbitsky, Semyon, Tsuyoshi Hasegawa, and Gilbert Rozman. *Misperceptions between Japan and Russia*. Carl Beck Papers, no. 1503. Pittsburgh: University of Pittsburgh, Center for Russian and East European Studies, 2000.

Zhang Yunling and Guo Weihong, eds. *China, US, Japan, and Russia in a Changing World*. Beijing: Social Sciences Documentation, 2000.

7

U.S. Foreign Policy in Northeast Asia

Kent E. Calder

For America's future, most students of international relations would agree, Northeast Asia will inevitably be a region of major importance. With around 20 percent of global GNP, 30 percent of world savings, and a third of the world's prospective industrial manpower, the economic potential of the region is beyond doubt. In geopolitical terms, stable relations with China, Japan, and Korea are indispensable as the "Far Eastern anchor" of U.S. global strategy.[1]

Yet in America's past, Northeast Asia has been consistently misperceived and all too often underappreciated, with disastrous consequences. A misreading of regional dynamics in 1949 led U.S. secretary of state Dean Acheson to place continental Asia outside the U.S. defense perimeter, leading to the Korean War.[2] A misreading of mainland China by Douglas MacArthur in late 1950 led to Chinese intervention and a bloody escalation of that conflict.[3] John Foster Dulles was but the first in a long line of American policy makers showing great interest in Northeast Asia who nevertheless misread the subtle interactions within the region.

To understand American policy toward Northeast Asia—especially its distinctiveness within the broader sweep of American foreign policy as a whole—one must go back to its unusual political–economic origins. In contrast to Europe, Latin America, the Middle East, or even Southeast Asia, the United States never had a dominant economic or political presence in Northeast Asia before World War II. Korea and Taiwan were Japanese colonies. In China, American influence was generally subordinate to that of the

European powers. American investment, with a few exceptions like the AIG insurance firm in China and the American auto industry in Japan, was quite limited in this region.[4]

DISTINCTIVE, NONECONOMIC ORIGINS OF U.S. INVOLVEMENT

The American presence was concentrated in more idealistic spheres. There were many American missionaries in China, Korea, and Japan.[5] They and other Americans played a role in developing the educational systems of the region. Americans also provided technical advice on everything from rectifying Japan's unequal treaties with the West to building Seoul's first subway.[6] Yet their direct political–economic involvement in Northeast Asia was minimal.

Not surprisingly, Americans generally were naïve and somewhat detached about Northeast Asia until the 1930s. They could afford to be. In contrast to the interests of Japanese and the Europeans, U.S. economic and geopolitical interests were only mildly engaged. Most Americans could afford idealism, and even a bit of naïveté, about a truly distant corner of the world that rarely intruded much into their consciousness.

Then the United States was blindsided from Northeast Asia—twice within the bloody 1941–1951 decade: first at Pearl Harbor and then in the Korean conflict. As the smoke settled, the United States still lacked transcendent economic interests in a decimated Northeast Asia, although its banks and oil companies established a foothold in Japan during the U.S. postwar occupation. Nevertheless, the United States gained, through its jarring military involvement with the region, a hard-won and deeply felt set of security stakes, reinforced by the deepening Cold War.

Limited economic consciousness and a high military profile—this distinctive, historically grounded configuration to the American presence and to American policies in Northeast Asia was institutionalized in the San Francisco Peace Treaty of September 1951, which formally ended World War II in the Pacific. Indeed, the set of political–economic relationships embodied in the treaty has proven to be so enduring that one can speak of a "San Francisco System" of trans-Pacific relations as the defining paradigm for U.S. association with this tumultuous region, persisting to this very day.

KEY TRAITS OF THE SAN FRANCISCO SYSTEM

Constructed as the Korean War was raging, in an effort to integrate Japan into a network of U.S. Pacific alliances through a nonvindictive peace, the San Francisco System had five basic features:

1. *Bilateral*, highly asymmetric U.S. *security alliances* with key nations of the Pacific, including Japan, South Korea, the Philippines, Taiwan, and Australia/New Zealand. These alliances, still mostly intact, generally obligate the United States to the defense of the local partner, with only limited converse obligations;
2. *American military bases* in most nations with whom the United States concluded bilateral security treaties;
3. *Asymmetrical economic arrangements* that opened U.S. markets to American security partners without commensurate foreign access for U.S. firms;
4. *Selective exclusion* of American military adversaries—chiefly mainland China and the Soviet Union—from the web of asymmetrical and reinforcing political–economic relationships between America and its allies;
5. *Little multilateral security or economic architecture*. Europe has developed a rich institutional fabric of both security and economic institutions, ranging from NATO to the European Union. The Western Hemisphere has the Organization of American States, Africa has the Organization of African Unity, the Middle East has the Arab League, and Southeast Asia has had the South East Asian Treaty Organization and the Association of Southeast Asian Nations (ASEAN). Yet Northeast Asia has never had any significant regional institutions.

In the early 1950s, John Foster Dulles was enthusiastic about a Northeast Asian regional security body; it was Japan's Yoshida Shigeru and South Korea's Rhee Syngman who were opposed.[7] Despite its formidable regional supremacy in the early Cold War years, the United States was unable to forge a Northeast Asian equivalent to NATO. Yet by the early 1990s the United States had come to appreciate the "hub and spokes" architecture of the San Francisco System. The spokes, after all, radiated out from Washington in a network of asymmetrical ties that reinforced American dominance. U.S. leaders of the 1980s and early 1990s such as George H. W. Bush and James Baker saw little need for supplementary multilateral frameworks in Northeast Asia.[8]

EMERGING CHALLENGES TO THE SAN FRANCISCO ARCHITECTURE

The "hub and spokes" of the San Francisco System were for over four decades reinforced by the Cold War structure of international relations in Northeast

Asia. All of America's regional allies—Japan, South Korea, and (indirectly) Taiwan—desired strong, bilateral security ties with Washington to reassure them in the face of a looming communist threat, even if those ties were highly asymmetric in favor of the United States. The lack of multilateral institutions in the region reinforced this reliance on American power.

Yet when Kim Dae Jung of South Korea and Kim Jong Il of the North met on the tarmac of Pyongyang on June 13, 2000, the region's past and present tensions seemed to be giving way to the promise of future cooperation. The remarkably positive chemistry of the initial meetings produced tangible results. Within little more than two months, North and South Korea had agreed to rebuild roads and railways across the demilitarized zone (DMZ), resolved to reestablish a liaison office in Panmunjom (a village in the DMZ used as a neutral setting for international discussions), and completed an emotional series of visits between family members who had been separated for nearly fifty years. Soon afterward, their athletes marched under a common flag at the Sydney Olympics.

These initiatives marked a significant shift in regional diplomacy. For the first time since World War II, Seoul and Pyongyang—rather than Washington, Moscow, or Beijing—were driving events. The two Koreas sensed that they were on center stage and relished their new place in the sun.

A glance at the map, and its geopolitical implications, suggests the power of the forces potentially unleashed by a Korean rapprochement. Korea is the strategic pivot of its region. With a hostile, communist North Korea lying between it and the rest of the Asian continent, South Korea has long been a geostrategic island. Yet peninsular cooperation could potentially transform North Korea from a barrier into a bridge—to Russia, China, and the world beyond.

A lack of domestic energy resources, coupled with a rapidly rising demand for energy, gives North and South Korea a shared economic motive to develop common railways and pipelines northward to exploit Siberian gas and trans-Siberian shipment opportunities. In 1999, South Korea's primary energy consumption rose more rapidly than any other nation's, driven by heavily increased demand for natural gas.[9] The country is eager to reduce its already heavy energy dependence on the Middle East by diversifying toward new suppliers, such as gas-rich Siberia. As North Korea's economy strengthens, its demand for Russian energy could also rise sharply.[10]

The Cold War, epitomized in the San Francisco System of Northeast Asia, created a static, stable, oddly comfortable world; antagonistic political affiliations implanted conflict in Northeast Asia, but at least they were strong and predictable. The new geopolitics, by contrast, threatens to be much more fluid, particularly at its Korean vortex. The architect of change was clearly Kim Dae Jung, a visionary leader who won the 2000 Nobel Peace Prize for his efforts at North–South reconciliation. Kim simultaneously enticed the North out of isolation, reassured Japan, and stimulated Russian interest in mutually beneficial contacts in trade, transportation, and energy, before running into geopolitical complexities and diplomatic backlash in the spring of 2001.

The two Koreas and Russia could benefit more than others from a peninsular thaw. Subtly capitalizing on the potential economic and diplomatic benefits for his country, Russian president Vladimir Putin has been a highly active new geopolitical force in the region. Only weeks after the Pyongyang summit, he visited both Pyongyang and Beijing, where he strengthened the security ties that already gave Russian manufacturers 90 percent of the substantial and growing Chinese arms market. After attending the Okinawa summit of the Group of Seven highly industrialized nations (G-7) plus Russia in late July 2000, Putin visited Japan again in early September and then invited Kim Jong Il to Moscow. During the summer of 2002 he strongly encouraged Kim to finalize North–South railway arrangements and to be forthcoming with Japanese prime minister Koizumi. Russia has been alert to the fact that resource-rich Siberia and Russia's neighboring Far Eastern regions could profit from the endemic and voracious Korean and Japanese needs for energy and raw materials, which could encourage a broad range of commercial exchanges at various levels.

For China, the Korean conciliation had mixed implications. China reportedly helped engineer the rapprochement by encouraging Kim Jong Il to adopt a more pragmatic policy toward his southern neighbor.[11] China also seems to have encouraged Kim's later steps toward economic liberalization, although it proved ambivalent when a Chinese entrepreneur, with North Korean support, tried to establish a special economic zone on its border without prior official consultation.[12]

The prospects of change in Korea could, to be sure, ultimately rekindle the long-term rivalry between China and Japan for influence on the peninsula, as did Korean internal turbulence before the Sino–Japanese War of 1894–1895.[13] Yet in the short run China is benefiting from intensified local pressure against U.S. bases in the region, especially in Korea. These facilities appear less necessary to local citizens, to the extent that regional tensions relax.[14]

THE INITIAL U.S. AND JAPANESE RESPONSES

Washington was arguably left behind in the early aftermath of the Pyongyang summit, after dominating Korean diplomacy for more than five decades.

Even after the Cold War ended, Washington had continued to set the pace and direction of regional discussions. From late 1998 to early 2000, former secretary of defense William Perry made a series of visits to countries in the region as President Clinton's special envoy to North Korea, a diplomatic process marked by Perry's crucial Pyongyang discussions of May 1999.[15] These were followed in September 1999 by North Korea's agreement to a moratorium on missile tests, followed by a relaxation of most U.S. sanctions on exports to and imports from North Korea. But a year later, the historic North–South summit temporarily eclipsed Perry's bilateral U.S.–North Korea efforts and shifted diplomatic initiatives toward the two Koreas themselves.

The United States, however, naturally recouped some influence through its sway with multilateral bodies potentially crucial to the North's reconstruction, such as the International Monetary Fund, the World Bank, and the Asian Development Bank (ADB). Indeed, it exercised this leverage to veto, jointly with Japan, Pyongyang's application for ADB membership late in the year 2000. The United States also has continuously remained central to strategically important missile and satellite talks, as the high-level exchange of visits between North Korean military leader Jo Myong Rok and U.S. secretary of state Madeleine Albright in October 2000 so clearly showed.

Washington obviously also stands to gain, in the short run, by stopping the new geopolitics in its tracks. This was apparently the early strategy of the George W. Bush administration, beginning with the March 2001 U.S.–South Korea summit. Following the 9/11 terrorist attack on the World Trade Center, the Bush administration's geopolitical impulse to slow North–South détente was intensified by its suspicions of North Korean complicity with Middle East pariah states, as epitomized in the "axis of evil" remarks in the 2002 state of the union address.[16]

The most unfortunate victim of the new geopolitics was initially Japan, which is ironic, given that it is the economic giant of Asia. As an island on Northeast Asia's periphery, without the deep involvement with that region's commerce that it has with Southeast Asian trade, Japan is relatively detached from the direct economic benefits of the relaxation of tensions in Korea that its continental neighbors anticipate. As the largest and most affluent economic power in the region, however, Japan could easily be saddled with the costs.

Questions of national security, compounded by flagrant kidnappings of Japanese citizens by North Korean intelligence agencies during the 1980s—to which Kim Jong Il admitted in September 2002—make many Japanese quietly uneasy about increased collaboration between the Koreas. They sense that South Korean and Japanese interests may be diverging on such sensitive issues as economic assistance and North Korean Nodong mobile missiles capable of reaching Japan. Prime Minister Koizumi Junichiro, to be sure, jumpstarted Japan's relations with the North through a dramatic one-day visit to Pyongyang in September 2002 that secured North Korean agreement to an indefinite missile-test ban.[17] Yet deep underlying divisions within the Japanese polity—exacerbated by the high-profile kidnapping issues—impede rapid agreement on the large-scale financial assistance from Japan that the North so desperately seeks. American ambivalence could well strengthen the domestic hand of Japanese conservatives. In any event, Japan's cumbersome decision-making processes, hindered by bureaucratic rivalries and political factionalism, tend to keep its responses to developments on the continent consistently a step behind other nations' reactions.

Japan's ambivalent relations with China compound its other problems. Recent Chinese naval activities, including several contentious visits to disputed areas in the East China Sea and the first circumnavigation of the Japanese archipelago in more than fifteen years, have accelerated this deterioration. During the past twenty years, $23 billion in Japanese aid has helped neutralize bilateral tensions. But now a combination of steadily rising Chinese military expenditures (a 17.7 percent increase in 2001 alone, the twelfth double-digit jump in a row)[18] and Japanese aid fatigue is eroding this long-standing pillar of interdependence. China's trade surplus with Japan, which was U.S.$25 billion by Japanese figures in 2000, increased to $27 billion in 2001.[19] Additionally, the nine-month trade row from April to December 2001, in which Japan imposed safeguards on three Chinese agricultural products, followed by a Chinese retaliation of 100 percent punitive tariffs on Japanese cars and other products, did not help.[20]

The initial burst of diplomatic activity across Northeast Asia following the Pyongyang summit was remarkable. Yet basic political and economic forces in the region could, in the absence of strong discouragement from the outside, provoke even more sweeping and unexpected change. Progress on North–South railway ventures, special economic zones in North Korea,[21] and signs—however tortured and partial—of Japanese reconciliation with North Korea all point to an erosion in the San Francisco System that has undergirded the U.S. political–economic position in Northeast Asia for more than half a century.[22]

THREE LONG-RUN PRESSURES FOR CHANGE IN NORTHEAST ASIA

Leaders in the broader region face three long-term challenges that transcend Korea's current evolution: the emergence of democracy, rapid changes in defense technology, and transformations of long-standing international political and economic relationships. Many of the political and technological changes, to be sure, began quietly reshaping Asia a decade or more ago. Yet it was the Pyongyang summit that catalyzed change and suddenly intensified the immense challenges that now confront the region, inevitably shaping the agenda for U.S. Northeast Asia policy.

The Populist Challenge

In the long run, democratization in Northeast Asia will help bring about a more peaceful world. Yet in the short run, making governments more accountable to people introduces new uncertainties and limits into diplomacy. Opening foreign policy decisions to the public—especially at times of regional transition—makes national security a more central topic of public debate. Northeast Asian governments remain unprepared for this emerging reality.

Recent regime changes in South Korea and Taiwan, for example, brought advocates of political reform to power. In South Korea, former long-time dissident Kim Dae Jung (whom military rulers tried to eliminate for a quarter century) is now nearing successful completion of his five-year term as president. In May 2000, Taiwan elected to the presidency Chen Shui-bian, a radical civil-rights lawyer and advocate of independence from China for two decades. In both cases, however, government and opposition are locked in a precarious balance, with neither side enjoying a broad mandate. Indeed, Chen garnered only 39 percent of the vote in a three-way race and confronted controversial impeachment proceedings only months into his term.

The reform governments' fragility subjects their foreign policy to more intense scrutiny and pressure from domestic public opinion. It also has given outside actors—notably mainland China and North Korea—greater incentive to manipulate democratic politics for their own ends. Both on the Korean peninsula and in the Taiwan Strait, the result is delicate, volatile, and often paranoid political interaction, with reformers trying simultaneously to transform domestic politics and to adapt diplomacy and foreign policy to the new geopolitics of the surrounding region.

The more delicate and dangerous of the two situations, particularly from the standpoint of American policy, clearly lies in the Taiwan Strait. The ambiguity of Taiwan's international status, deepened by the gradual U.S. derecognition of an erstwhile ally during the 1970s, is further complicated by the mutual lack of trust. Beijing seems wary of Chen's intentions on the all-important independence issues. Chen, supported by only a weak plurality of the presidential vote and confronted by Beijing's active efforts to isolate him, may be tempted to take the locally popular course of confrontation with China to solidify his domestic support base. Chinese president Jiang Zemin, moving toward the end of his leadership tenure, cannot actively seek compromise. Were both sides in the confrontation less beset by domestic pressures, accommodation would undoubtedly come easier.

In South Korea, in contrast to Taiwan, popular sentiment favors détente rather than confrontation. More than 7.5 million South Koreans—roughly 15 percent of the population—have relatives in the North. The initial round of family reunions, heavily covered in the media, seems to have awakened a deep yearning for renewed social ties between North and South, although some skepticism about Northern intentions later emerged. Transportation breakthroughs such as the August 2000 North–South agreements to build freeway and railway links across the DMZ, as well as a proliferation of tourism and contract-manufacturing ventures, will also provide new economic incentives for deeper integration if and when these measures are implemented. As in the case of Taiwan, any substantial change in the status quo could stir complex reactions in the United States.

In Japan, where declared reformer Koizumi Junichiro took power within the ruling Liberal Democratic Party (LDP) in April 2001, public opinion is becoming more influential in foreign policy formation generally, and more vocal on Northeast Asian issues in particular, although the public is divided with respect to preferred policy outcomes. A rash of financial scandals at the Ministry of Foreign Affairs (MOFA), uncovered just as Koizumi was taking office, stirred grassroots resentment against MOFA that was inflamed further by Foreign Minister Tanaka Makiko. Following Tanaka's forced resignation in early 2002, MOFA and LDP politicians tried to recoup influence with a bold secret overture to North Korea, which culminated in Prime Minister Koizumi's Pyongyang visit of September 2002. The formal revelation to Koizumi in Pyongyang that eleven Japanese had indeed been kidnapped by the North, and that eight of them were dead, set off another broad-based backlash and a hardening of the Japanese negotiating stance with the North, demonstrating again the rising influence of populist sentiment on foreign policy in Northeast Asia.

Juche *Twilight*

One nation, of course, remains immune to the populist tendencies sweeping across much of the region. Despite new signs of apparent pragmatism in foreign policy, North Korea's people remain hermetically sealed off from the outside world. The regime's ideological rationale for this isolation has been *juche*, or self-reliance. This approach is clearly now in its twilight—thanks to a severe famine and a North Korean manufacturing production capacity and energy supply that have shriveled by 50 percent in the past decade. Deepened economic, if not political, interdependence with the outside world has a powerful logic that could well be further reinforced by détente across the Northeast Asian region as a whole.

The decline of *juche*, or a "*juche* twilight," in North Korea is a complex political and economic reality with fateful implications for the neighboring nations and for the United States as well.[23] It has three key elements: a precarious North Korean economic situation; a political order that, although highly repressive, continues to be surprisingly stable under Kim Jong Il's consolidation of power; and economically pragmatic but military-oriented leadership in Pyongyang. For example, Kim Jong Il's government tolerates, and even promotes, economic interdependence with other nations at levels low enough not to threaten political stability at home, as through the establishment of special economic zones on its borders. At the same time, North Korea continues to expand its capacity to project military power against the outside world.

Juche twilight is, to a greater extent than many outside observers realize, compatible with greater North Korean economic cooperation with the surrounding world. Broad economic and political liberalization, to be sure, could sound the death knell of the current North Korean regime (and thus spread chaos and substantial economic adjustment costs across the region). Yet this is not the sort of economic interdependence that either Pyongyang or many of its prospective regional economic partners have in mind. Provided that political interaction with the outside world remains controlled, the North Korean regime could still be able to survive if, for example, it allows energy and transportation infrastructure projects to pass through its territory en route from South Korea to Russia and beyond. Indeed, such transit projects could very well help perpetuate *juche* twilight by providing North Korea with the revenue to alleviate its severe current economic crisis. Special economic zones such as the one wealthy Chinese-born Dutch businessman Yang Bin attempted to open[24] in late 2002 at Sinuiju on the Chinese border should be similarly functional, from Pyongyang's perspective.

Virtually all the key actors of Northeast Asia have an economic interest in the indefinite persistence of *juche* twilight, which is essentially an enervated, pragmatic version of the vigorous North Korean militancy of recent years. South Korea, in particular, would prefer to defer the challenge of a merger until its economy grows stronger. President Kim Dae Jung has clearly suggested that full integration of the Northern and Southern economies should take twenty to thirty years. Surrounding nations, for various reasons, have a similar economic stake in an extended *juche* twilight.

The danger in *juche* twilight obviously comes on the security side. Among North Korea's few sources of leverage with the world are the military threats that it poses, on land against South Korea as well as through its missile, chemical, biological, and nuclear capacities against Japan and even the United States, either directly or in collaboration with others. Economic relations with the outside world may provide Pyongyang with new technologies and the economic resources to amplify those threats. The longer *juche* twilight persists, and the more effort that the North puts into military programs to increase its international leverage, the more provocative and threatening these challenges could become, even as the North Korean political economy slowly crumbles. One troubling prospect is the possibility, for which there appears to be little or no evidence (in the public domain at least) of North Korean cooperation with Islamic terrorists.

The Bush administration, particularly since 9/11, has highlighted these security dangers of *juche* twilight, especially the possibility of North Korea–Middle East interactions that might aid the cause of terrorism. Without directly threatening to destabilize the North's regime, the Bush administration radically shifted the terms of discourse on North–South issues soon after taking office, proposing to make virtually all regional economic cooperation with the North contingent on military steps that the North would likely find difficult to take. The Bush administration also used the leverage of its enhanced military credibility, flowing from the successful Afghan campaign of 2001–2002, to inhibit the North from cooperating with its implicit Middle Eastern strategic allies, as epitomized in President George W. Bush's "axis of evil" phrasing in his January 2002 state of the union speech. The Bush doctrine of strategic preemption against rogue regimes, declared in September 2002, increased the pressure on North Korea. Following Koizumi's Pyongyang visit, however, and the commencement of North–South railway construction, U.S. policy moved back marginally to a pragmatic mode more in step with its allies.

Confronting Technological Change

The most serious technological danger for Northeast Asian leaders today, and arguably for the United States as well, is missile proliferation.[25] Every government in the region is now both a large-scale consumer and a major producer of missiles. This unsettling reality, unique among the major regions of the world, is a disturbing product of the past decade—and the consequent dangers have been growing more pronounced over the past three years.

Technological advances and rapid deployment in China are a major part of the picture: the fastest developments have occurred in short-range missiles, such as the Dong Feng 11, which China tested near Taiwan in 1996 and has since deployed along the Taiwan Strait. These deployments grew from twenty missiles in the mid-1990s to two hundred by 1999 and have recently been increasing by roughly a missile per week. This short-range missile buildup has ranked among the most destabilizing elements of the overall Northeast Asian political–military situation, from an American perspective.[26]

China has also been developing and deploying longer-range missiles capable of hitting other locations in Asia, including U.S. bases in Japan and South Korea. In August 1999, it tested the solid-fuel, road-mobile, 8,000-km range Dong Feng 31. A longer-range variant is reportedly being planned. In May 2000, China also began importing Russian Sunburn SSN-22 supersonic cruise missiles for its twenty-four new *Sovremenny*-class destroyers.[27]

China's steady buildup of short-range missiles increases the prospects of multiple waves of attacks launched in many directions. This development is potentially destabilizing because it has naturally provoked a counterresponse from across the Taiwan Strait. Taiwan has already deployed American Patriot antimissile defenses while developing its own Skybow surface-to-air missile and Cheng Kung missile frigates. A new Taiwanese strategy to offset the Chinese buildup would reportedly involve preemptive long-range strikes on major Chinese command, communications, logistics, and economic centers. Taiwan has also begun large-scale research and development on a theater missile-defense system and upgraded its information-warfare capabilities.

North Korea, of course, has further exacerbated regional missile proliferation—and protracted *juche* twilight threatens to make matters worse. After starting with basic Soviet Scuds, North Korea test fired the indigenous, mobile Nodong I in 1993. Since 1997, it has deployed the Nodong in substantial numbers. Simple in design and difficult to preempt due to its mobility, the 1,300-km range Nodong is widely viewed as a credible terror weapon against large cities in western Japan. Indeed, Japanese analysts continue to see the Nodong as the principal North Korean missile threat to Japan, despite possible problems with its accuracy.

And Japan is not the only country threatened. In one of the most provocative recent developments in the region, North Korea also tested the Taepodong I missile, which has a 3,500–6,000-km range, over Japanese airspace and international aircraft routes into the Pacific Ocean during August 1998.[28] Although the missile landed well short of its maximum range, conservatives in the United States saw it as validating Rumsfeld Report projections of a potential long-term North Korean missile threat to parts of the United States. In any event, the fact of the North Korean threat to Japan, coupled with a steady long-term Chinese missile buildup, appears to figure increasingly in American strategic planning, helping provoke a Bush administration withdrawal from the global Anti-Ballistic Missile treaty. The Northeast Asian missile race, in short, clearly has consequences well beyond the region.

Japan, limited by constitutional constraints and a gridlocked political system, has responded in a relatively moderate, defensive fashion. In December 1998, three months after the North Korean tests, it approved joint ballistic-missile defense research with the United States. It has also made plans to launch eight observation satellites by 2008. So far, the United States has concentrated its attention on the longer-range Taepodong missile issues. Yet the strategic threat that Japan confronts from North Korean Nodongs, not to mention recent Chinese missile advances, also remains real.[29]

A Changing Geopolitical Calculus

The third major challenge confronting Northeast Asian leaders is the prospect of a rapidly changing international environment. This challenge's complex interaction with the demographic, political, and technological challenges noted above would make such a hurdle particularly difficult to manage. The rapidly shifting leverage of key parties also means that continuous international consultation is more necessary than ever.

Three challenges distinguish the prospective new international context. First, and most frustrating for the United States, no single power would be clearly in charge. Perry's negotiating efforts put regional change under Washington's direction, but the two Koreas, rather than the United States, thereafter drove the pace of regional change until the end of the Clinton administration. Russian and Chinese diplomacy has also shaped the emergent détente. And Japan, particularly in the wake of Koizumi's dramatic Pyongyang visit of September 2002, remains a force to be considered.

The advent of the Bush administration and the terrorist attacks of September 2001 on the United States clearly deepened American hesitancy at accommodating a North Korean regime with demonstrable chemical, biological, and possibly nuclear capabilities, not to mention a history of state-sponsored terrorism. This U.S. reluctance, together with some South Korean disillusionment at the lack of reciprocity from Pyongyang, slowed the short-term momentum of North–South reconciliation. Military clashes in the summer of 2002, coupled with the waning of Kim Dae Jung's presidency, compounded this tendency. Yet rising financial surpluses and trade interdependence on the Northeast Asian continent, especially between China and South Korea, are gradually shifting the crucial locus of decision making on issues of long-term regional economic interdependence away from Washington and toward Seoul, Tokyo, and Beijing.

A second, related feature of the post-Pyongyang situation is the passivity of those, including the G-7 powers and international financial institutions, with the resources to actually undertake the massive economic restructuring that diplomatic developments may provoke. Some caution is clearly warranted as long as North Korea equivocates on key security issues. Yet as contact between the Koreas deepens, including the reconnection of the severed Kyonggui railway line from Seoul to Sinuiju and the establishment of a Sinuiju Special Administrative Region in the fall of 2002, the world must prepare for the possibility of major, unanticipated economic change.

The prospective burden of a Korean merger would be much greater than what West Germany faced a decade ago in absorbing the East. According to a recent Bank of Korea study, the North's 1999 GDP was less than 4 percent of the South's and its per capita income of $714 was just 8 percent of South Korea's. By contrast, in 1989 East Germany's GDP was about 20 percent of West Germany's. Combining the North and South Korean economies could cost anywhere from $100 billion to $500 billion. A South Korea just recovering from the Asian financial crisis simply does not—despite its recent $80 billion trade surplus—have the money to undertake this task alone.[30]

Northeast Asia's institutions are startlingly inadequate for coping with regional problems, given the enormity of the dislocation that prospective changes in Korea could provoke. The ASEAN Regional Forum (ARF) is a useful venue for casual dialogue, but it is not the solution. ARF has not even been able to mediate issues in ASEAN's backyard, such as the East Timor question. In this dearth of capable institutions, long-standing bilateral treaties still provide the crucial backbone of military deterrence. Yet now something more is clearly needed to smooth the wrenching transition to a new era and marshal the massive resources needed for reconstruction, if and when the serious security issues posed by *juche* twilight are addressed. In stark contrast with Europe, which has a rich organizational infrastructure, including NATO, the European Union, and the Organization on Security and Cooperation in Europe, Northeast Asia still lacks institutions to help it adjust to new challenges.

IMPERATIVES FOR THE FUTURE

The nations of Northeast Asia, together with the United States, need to fashion a new North Pacific framework that builds on the considerable strengths of the past to stabilize a potentially volatile future. The single most important imperative for the United States is to strengthen its military and political alliance with Japan in a way that helps stabilize the region. The United States and Japan together hold nearly 40 percent of global GDP, lead the world in technology, and contain nearly half of the world's savings. They thus make up a critical mass that can guide otherwise fluid, uncertain developments in Asia in a productive, stabilizing direction.

A central feature of American policy toward Northeast Asia is the presence of more than eighty thousand U.S. troops based in Japan, in South Korea, and aboard the Seventh Fleet in the Pacific. These are by far the largest non-NATO American forces outside the United States and constitute the great bulk of American troops in the entire Pacific. The value of forward-deployed forces to the United States is undeniable, particularly given the high levels of financial support—roughly $5 billion a year in the case of Japan—that allies provide to keep them in the region.[31] Yet two important, related issues remain to be resolved.

First, whether existing deployments remain strategically optimal needs serious review. Communications, information processing, air defense, and mobile naval capabilities are gaining importance, given the missile buildups, revolutionary information-technology changes, and rising Northeast Asian dependence on oil and gas from the Middle East. Changes that make room for these new capabilities and spread U.S. forward deployments more fully across the Pacific need study. Changing defense technologies, coupled with local political currents, make a bottom-up review of the U.S. force structure in Northeast Asia imperative.

Second, deeper consideration must also go to sustaining the strategically vital (if not yet most favorably configured) American military deployments across the region in the face of intensifying populist and international pressures. Popular calls for a reduction of the U.S. military footprint in Northeast Asia are already strong and may well grow more vociferous in the coming years. Yet the receptivity of local communities to the American military presence varies enormously across the region, and U.S. policy makers need to be conscious of local sentiment, even when it cannot readily be accommodated. Continued and intensified efforts to broaden the perceived benefits that U.S. bases give to local communities are a crucial priority. Facilities made more available for joint civilian–military use, disaster-relief cooperation, international education centers, on-base internship programs, and efforts to reduce tensions between base personnel and the community are all helpful. So is cultivating a deeper, more balanced sense of partnership with local military units.[32]

To strengthen the political credibility of the alliance, both Washington and Tokyo must devote much more attention to explaining to their general publics the comprehensive security goals they hold in common, as well as the substantial progress in civil–military relations that they have already achieved at the local level. A new, more articulate elaboration of shared interests is needed to legitimize their joint defense commitments, while building a much more dynamic program that addresses mutual concerns beyond defense. A deepened common agenda between the two countries should focus more on high-profile issues that attract widespread public interest, such as energy, mass transit, earthquake research, and education for the information age. The Cold War and the Korean rivalry legitimized and sustained a U.S.–Japan alliance based on narrow economic and security interests. In the post–Cold War era, partnerships must also draw strength from a shared worldview.

Economic policy can also reinforce the broader alliance in creative ways. For example, the United States and Japan should seriously study the feasibility of reviving comprehensive open-market negotiations, focusing on the high-technology and service sectors. They should encourage still further the recent surge of foreign direct investment into Japan by pressing Japanese policy makers to seriously implement declared changes in the commercial code (which regulates how business is conducted in Japan), consolidated taxation, and corporate governance. Given the political gridlock in Tokyo and the high levels of Japanese public debt, it will be difficult for government programs alone to open and revitalize the Japanese economy. Transforming the incentive structure of the private sector through technical but microeconomically important steps that would encourage direct finance and greater business efficiency would be far more effective.

A related imperative is reinforcing American relations with South Korea, which stands at the vortex of Northeast Asia's potentially volatile new geopolitics. Such an effort could include five basic elements. First, a more comprehensive U.S.–South Korean policy-coordination process should build on the recently initiated Trilateral Coordination and Oversight Group of the United States, Japan, and South Korea. Second, policy makers should undertake a broad review of U.S.–South Korea security relations, parallel to the Guidelines for U.S.–Japan Defense Cooperation process just completed. Third, the North needs to take concrete good-faith steps regarding infrastructure investment in North Korea, technical training of officials involved in international commercial transactions, and other measures to make previous nonaggression pledges irreversible. Fourth, Washington and Seoul should initiate working-level studies on appropriate coordination and sequencing of joint U.S.–South Korean responses to inter-Korean developments. And fifth, there should be joint exploration of options for reconfiguring ground-force deployments in the event of a serious, verifiable reduction of North–South tensions, while retaining residual air and naval capacities and prepositioned equipment.

Given the complexity of trans-Pacific dealings among massive political economies with different cultures and histories, forging a more coherent relationship among the United States, Japan, and South Korea is easier said than done. All sides clearly have divergent, as well as shared, interests. Yet they must see the value in strategically pursuing concrete priorities. Sustaining an alliance in the face of growing populist pressures will require cooperative steps, fundamental strategic reviews, and economic initiatives that build common collateral in the trans-Pacific future.

REFORMING JAPAN

Northeast Asia's new geopolitics badly needs Japan to be a more active player, both in its alliance with the United States and in global affairs more generally. Japan is the real colossus of Northeast Asia and a potential force for both stability and prosperity. The Japanese economy remains nearly five times the size of China's, and this imbalance is unlikely to change decisively for at least a generation, despite China's higher prospective growth rates. With 30 percent of global savings, Japan—the largest capital exporter on earth—can contribute crucially to global financial and political projects; China could be a marginal financial contributor at best.

While U.S. policy has been broadly supportive of Japanese activism in international affairs over the past decade, especially in the military and foreign aid areas, it has on occasion found such activism inconvenient and tried to inhibit or counteract it. This was clearly true in the case of Japan's proposal for an Asian Monetary Fund (AMF), presented by Vice Minister of Finance for International Affairs Sakakibara Eisuke during the 1997 Asian financial crisis. Maintaining that the AMF notion undermined the International Monetary Fund in its efforts to encourage reform in indebted nations, the U.S. Treasury teamed up with China, an unlikely partner, to forestall this unusual Japanese initiative. Yet three years later, a less ambitious variant was approved by the ASEAN Plus Three leaders in the 1990 Chiang Mai financial swap agreement.

To play a truly meaningful and active international role, on a more than episodic basis, Japan requires massive political and economic reform. Given the explosive pace of change and the rising fluidity of foreign affairs, three priorities deserve particularly serious consideration.

First, Japan must reform its overly regulated economy. The serious fragmentation in Japanese politics and administration means that a shift to new standards of corporate governance and direct finance would be far more effective in restructuring the Japanese economy than would any government program. Since 1998, Japan has been moving toward a new business paradigm with its "Big Bang" in financial affairs, new bankruptcy legislation, consolidated accounting, and the advent of new venture-capital markets.[33] These reforms, if fully implemented, could in turn accelerate Japanese growth, deepen its interdependence with foreign trading partners, and make Japan a more viable competitive environment for many foreign firms.[34]

Political restructuring is also necessary. Japanese politics, like its economy, is suffering a quiet crisis. The general elections in June 2000 graphically demonstrated voters' substantial frustration with the ruling conservatives, especially among urban and younger Japanese. The emergence of Koizumi Junichiro as a seemingly determined reform prime minister within the LDP in the spring of 2001 momentarily defused this frustration and helped generate an LDP victory in the 2001 House of Councilors election. Yet Koizumi's ultimate success remains far from assured.

Japan's high levels of political regulation, the large financial resources available for the government to dispense, and the weak social base for pluralist politics in a largely homogenous society still make it difficult for political parties themselves to spearhead much-needed change. Market incentives and pressure from the outside world need to carry more of the burden of change in Japan than they do elsewhere.[35]

Finally, the innovative decisions and diplomacy required by the new geopolitics make the Japanese political parties' sluggishness in changing a more urgent problem. Thus decisive individual leadership has become an imperative for Japan. Koizumi's success is of enormous importance to Japan's future.

A FRAMEWORK FOR THE NEW GEOPOLITICS

The greatest danger posed by the new shape of Asia, especially for status quo powers such as the United States and Japan, is that populist pressures and changing technology will incite a destabilizing struggle over the regional balance of power. The perils implicit in such a power struggle are especially acute because Northeast Asia, unlike Europe or even Southeast Asia, has no well-established regional institutions capable of muting paranoid perceptions and setting mutual goals.

The region, to be sure, has the U.S.–Japan and the U.S.–South Korea security alliances, which are reinforced by U.S. forward deployments and are a vital cornerstone of stability.[36] Yet the fluid world now emerging needs broader cross-regional support mechanisms. The world of "hub and spokes," implicit in the San Francisco System, is comfortable in the short run but unsustainable over time, the impressive U.S. military victories of 2001–2002 in Afghanistan notwithstanding.

U.S. policy has been ambivalent about confronting this new reality. The Clinton administration clearly backed the strengthening of APEC as an overall framework for Pacific relations, beginning with the Blake Island Summit of 1993. Within Northeast Asia specifically, it put priority on formalizing trilateral consultation among the United States, Japan, and South Korea, particularly after the North Korean missile shot of August 1998. The Bush administration continued this trilateral dialogue, and indeed, top-level U.S. participation in the APEC summits, while placing generally less emphasis on multilateralism than its predecessor.

Overall, U.S. policy concerning the establishment of Northeast Asian economic and security institutions has been reactive—an atypical stance for U.S. foreign policy as a whole, and one at sharp variance with Dulles's pronounced activism of the early 1950s with respect to the region. This reactive approach has been inspired, by and large, by a feeling that traditional structures more effectively articulate American interests and offer less scope for "balance-of-power" manipulations adverse to those interests to manifest themselves.

The United States has seen no obvious reason why ASEAN, based half a continent away from Northeast Asia, should be central in the process of multilateral institution building, although ARF is, as noted earlier, a useful venue for casual dialogue and U.S. diplomats have been reluctant to antagonize Southeast Asia. The four-party framework of the Koreas, the United States, and China, created to formalize a Korean War peace settlement, leaves out two key players and is therefore poorly equipped to address the most fundamental issues of Northeast Asia's future. U.S. negotiating experience within this framework has been difficult.

Russia under Putin has become a dynamic player in Asian politics, and Japan will also inevitably play a crucial role in Korean reconstruction. Both deserve a seat at a table of expanded, six-party talks on Korea, and recent U.S. policy has encouraged such a development. Periodic meetings in this format, supplemented by a formalization of the U.S.–Japan–South Korea policy coordination processes that have evolved since 1998, should gradually, in the U.S. estimation, create an institutional basis for deeper and more stable regional interactions, supplementing existing security arrangements.

American policy makers have warily watched the emergence since the late 1990s of the ASEAN Plus Three (APT) diplomatic framework, which excludes the United States. In the world of embedded global multilateralism that has begun to emerge since the establishment of the World Trade Organization, the second Bush administration, to be sure, does not seem to find the APT as threatening as the first Bush administration felt Mahathir Mohammed's East Asian Economic Caucus proposals to be in the early 1990s. Still, the APT, strongly supported by both China and South Korea within Northeast Asia, has a strong brain power and has proven more effective than any other alternative to the Washington-centric San Francisco System.[37]

Beyond the issue of multilateral organization, a greater role in directing the North Pacific's future clearly should also be reserved for "Track II" institutions and processes (unofficial contacts among nongovernmental actors), especially those that deepen triangular understanding among Washington, Tokyo, and Beijing. The Bush administration, like the Clinton administration before it, has encouraged Track II activities, partly because many of its key East Asia policy makers, such as Assistant Secretary for East Asian and Pacific Affairs James Kelly, have been heavily involved previously in Track II operations. On issues of comprehensive security in particular—such as energy, food, and the environment—a remarkably sophisticated set of such institutions, including the Council for Security Cooperation in the Asia Pacific, has begun to evolve. Partially because formal intergovernmental bodies have been so weak and diplomatic processes so complicated, these private-sector groups have come to play an important role. Track II processes could vitally help moderate what could otherwise be volatile, paranoid, destabilizing tendencies in the new geopolitics of Northeast Asia, especially on Taiwan-related issues.

From a set of static, rigid, Cold War relationships in continental Northeast Asia has emerged, with remarkable speed, a fluid, deceptive new world. That world poses particular challenges to an American diplomacy heretofore so heavily reliant on the "hub and spokes" San Francisco System of asymmetrical bilateral alliances. Post-9/11 developments, of course, suggest a common, intensified antiterrorist focus congruent with American interests. Yet those recent developments cannot roll back the fundamental post-Pyongyang geopolitical changes. Unanticipated dangers are becoming clear even as new prospects for cooperation and reconciliation materialize. American policy seems likely to be proactive in dealing with the dangers, while deferring to the market as the catalyst for economic cooperation.

As the economies of Northeast Asia continue to grow and to deepen their linkages with the broader world, the importance of Northeast Asia to the global economy, including the United States, will continue to rise. With growing technological sophistication in the region, its importance to the security calculus will also likely increase. Until war exploded across the Korean peninsula in 1950, this volatile region was somewhat peripheral to the mainstream of American foreign policy. Yet along both the economic and security dimensions, Northeast Asia will need to play an increasingly central role in American diplomatic thinking across the challenging years to come.

NOTES

1. See Zbigniew Brzezinski, *The Grand Chessboard: American Primacy and its Geostrategic Imperatives* (New York: Basic, 1997), 151–93.

2. Dean Acheson, *Present at the Creation: My Years at the State Department* (London: Hamish Hamilton, 1969), 354–61.

3. Allen S. Whiting, *China Crosses the Yalu: The Decision to Enter the Korean War* (Stanford, Calif.: Stanford University Press, 1960); and Thomas J. Christensen, *Useful Adversaries: Grand Strategy, Domestic Mobilization, and Sino–American Conflict, 1949–1958* (Princeton, N.J.: Princeton University Press, 1996).

4. G. C. Allen and Audrey Donnithorne, *Western Enterprise in Far Eastern Economic Development: China and Japan* (London: Allen & Unwin, 1962).

5. John K. Fairbanks, *The United States and China*, 4th ed. (Cambridge, Mass.: Harvard University Press, 1979), 307–35.

6. Bruce Cumings, *Korea's Place in the Sun: A Modern History* (New York: Norton, 1997), 86–138.

7. See Michael Schaller, *Altered States: The United States and Japan since the Occupation* (New York: Oxford University Press, 1997), 33.

8. See James Baker, "America in Asia," *Foreign Affairs* (Winter 1991–1992): 1–18.

9. *BP Amoco Statistical Review of World Energy*, 2000 ed. (London: BP Amoco Group Media and Publications, 2000).

10. On Korea's evolving energy situation, see Kent E. Calder, *Korea's Energy Insecurities*, SAIS Policy Forum Series Report, no. 13 (Washington, D.C.: SAIS Policy Forum, December, 2000).

11. Hu Qihua, "Nation Supports Ideas on Korean Reunification," *China Daily*, at www.chinadaily.net/news/cn/2001-09-05/31025.html.

12. *Financial Times*, October 6, 2002.

13. See Bruce Cumings, *Korea's Place in the Sun: A Modern History* (New York: Norton, 1997), 86–138.

14. Tim Shorrock, "Public Pressure to Shape U.S. Military Presence in Region," *SPF Special Report* (Washington, D.C.: Sasakawa Peace Foundation, October 4, 2001).

15. For an informative public account of the details, see Don Oberdorfer. *The Two Koreas: A Contemporary History*, rev. ed. (New York: Basic, 2001): 418–23.

16. *New York Times*, Wednesday, January 30, 2002, A22, column 1.

17. *New York Times*, September 18, 2002.

18. China's official defense budget for 2001 was Rmb 141 billion ($17.05 billion), which was up 17.7 percent from the previous year. For more information, see "China's Military Expansion," *Jane's Intelligence Digest*, March 16, 2001; and "China Reforms Budget System," *Jane's Defense Weekly*, September 28, 2001, at www.janes.com.

19. See, "Japan Eases Curbs on Imports of Chinese Poultry," *China Daily*, August 7, 2001, at www.chinadaily.net/news/2001-08-07/25112.html; and Benjamin Pedley, "FX

Asia: Won Makes Headway against Weak Yen Current," *Dow Jones Newswires Column*, January 3, 2002, at asia.news.yahoo.com/020103/5/1izy.html (accessed February 5, 2003).

20. See "China and Japan End Acrimonious Trade Row," at *MuziNews/Latelinenews.com*, December 21, 2001, at latelinenews.com/cc/english/19419.shtml; and Staff and Wire reports, "Japan, China Meet to End Trade Row," *CNN.com*, July 3, 2001, at asia.cnn.com/2001/WORLD/asiapcf/east/07/03/japan.china.tradewar/.

21. Technically, the special economic zone established in September 2002 on the North Korea–Chinese border is known as the Sinuiju Special Administrative Region; Yang Bin, reputedly China's second richest man, is its "chief executive." See *New York Times*, September 25, 2002.

22. Christopher A. McNally and Charles E. Morrison, *Asia Pacific Security Outlook 2001* (New York: Japan Center for International Exchange, 2001).

23. On the concept of *juche* twilight, see Kent E. Calder, "The New Face of Northeast Asia," *Foreign Affairs* (January–February 2001): 106–22.

24. See *New York Times*, September 25, 2002.

25. On this subject, see Paul Bracken, *Fire in the East: The Rise of Asian Military Power and the Second Nuclear Age* (New York: HarperCollins, 1999).

26. For a knowledgeable, policy-oriented perspective, see Kurt M. Campbell and Derek J. Mitchell, "Crisis in the Taiwan Strait?" *Foreign Affairs* (July–August 2001): 14–25.

27. See Robert A. Manning, "China: The Forgotten Nuclear Power," *Foreign Affairs* (July–August 2000); and Patrick Cronin and Michael Green, eds., *The U.S.–Japan Alliance: Past, Present and Future* (New York: Council on Foreign Relations Press, 1999).

28. On North Korean missile launches and their security implications for Japan, see Japan Defense Agency (Bōei Chō), *Boei Hakusho* (Defense white paper), 2001 ed. (Tokyo: Urban Connection, 2001), 37–39.

29. On Japanese and other East Asian responses to missile proliferation, see Michael J. Green and Toby F. Dalton, *Asian Reactions to U.S. Missile Defense* (Seattle: National Bureau of Asian Research, November 2000).

30. On the magnitude of Korea's prospective reconstruction tasks if and when the North is assimilated into regional economic affairs, see Marcus Noland, *Avoiding the Apocalypse: The Future of the Two Koreas* (Washington, D.C.: Institute for International Economics, 2000), 285–322.

31. For detailed figures on host-nation support for American forces, see U.S. Secretary of Defense, *Report on Allied Contributions to the Common Defense* (Washington, D.C.: U.S. Government Printing Office, annual).

32. For further concrete suggestions in these areas, see Ivilisse Esguerra and Emilie Fisher, eds. *Princeton University Policy Task Force Report: U.S. Bases in Japan* (unpublished monograph, Woodrow Wilson School of Public and International Affairs, January 2001).

33. On the details, see M. Diana Helweg, "Japan: A Rising Sun?" *Foreign Affairs* (July–August 2000): 40–52.

34. See Stephen M. Harner, *Japan's Financial Revolution and How American Firms are Profiting* (Armonk, N.Y.: Sharpe, 2000).

35. Direct foreign investment and strategic institutional investors willing to play a proactive role in promoting corporate governance reforms can potentially play a catalytic role. The California state pension program, Calpers, for example, has come to understand this, as evidenced by its creation of the Sparx $200 million Value Creation Fund to

encourage investment in Japanese innovators in this area. See *Financial Times*, September 24, 2002.

36. On this "virtual alliance," see Victor D. Cha, *Alignment Despite Antagonism: The U.S.–Korea–Japan Security Triangle* (Stanford, Calif.: Stanford University Press, 1999); and Ralph A. Cossa, ed., *U.S.–Korea–Japan Relations: Building toward a "Virtual Alliance"* (Washington, D.C.: CSIS Press, Center for Strategic and International Relations, 1999).

37. On the evolution of the APT and its accomplishments, see Richard Stubbs, "ASEAN Plus Three: Emerging East Asian Regionalism?" *Asian Survey* (May–June 2002): 440–55.

FURTHER READING

Acheson, Dean. *Present at the Creation: My Years at the State Department*. London: Hamish Hamilton, 1969.

Baker, James. "America in Asia." *Foreign Affairs* (Winter 1991–1992): 1–18.

Borden, William S. *The Pacific Alliance: United States Foreign Economic Policy and Japanese Trade Recovery, 1947–1955*. Madison: University of Wisconsin Press, 1984.

Calder, Kent E. *Pacific Defense: Arms, Energy, and America's Future in Asia*. New York: Morrow, 1996.

———. "The New Face of Northeast Asia." *Foreign Affairs* (January–February 2001): 106–22.

Cha, Victor D. *Alignment despite Antagonism: The U.S.–Korea–Japan Security Triangle*. Stanford, Calif.: Stanford University Press, 1999.

Cumings, Bruce. "The Origins and Development of the Northeast Asian Political Economy." *International Organization* (Winter 1984): 1–40.

———. *The Origins and the Korean War*. 2 vol. Princeton, N.J.: Princeton University Press, 1981, 1990.

Dower, John W. *War without Mercy: Race and Power in the Pacific War*. New York: Pantheon, 1986.

———. *Embracing Defeat: Japan in the Wake of World War II*. New York: Norton, 1999.

Fairbanks, John K. *The United States and China*. Cambridge: Mass.: Harvard University Press.

Harding, Harry, and Yuan Ming, ed. *Sino–American Relations, 1945–1955: A Joint Reassessment of a Critical Decade*. Wilmington, Del.: SR, 1989.

Iriye, Akira. *Across the Pacific: An Inner History of American–East Asian Relations*. New York: Harcourt, Brace, and World, 1967.

———. *The Cold War in Asia: A Historical Perspective*. Englewood Cliffs, N.J.: Prentice Hall, 1974.

Oliver, Robert T. *Syngman Rhee and American Involvement in Korea, 1942–1960: A Personal Narrative*. Seoul: Panmun, 1978.

Reischauer, Edwin O. *The United States and Japan*. 3d ed. Cambridge, Mass.: Harvard University Press, 1965.

Schaller, Michael. *The United States and China in the Twentieth Century*. 2d ed. New York: Oxford University Press, 1990.

———. *Altered States: The United States and Japan since the Occupation*. New York: Oxford University Press, 1997.

Sigal, Leon V. *Disarming Strangers: Nuclear Diplomacy with North Korea*. Princeton, N.J.: Princeton University Press, 1998.

Tucker, Nancy Bernkopf. "American Policy toward Sino–Japanese Trade in the Postwar Years: Politics and Prosperity." *Diplomatic History* 8, no. 3 (1984): 184–95.

Zhang Shu Guang. *Economic Cold War: America's Embargo against China and the Sino–Soviet Alliance, 1949–1963*. Stanford, Calif.: Stanford University Press, 2001.

III

FLASHPOINTS IN THE DIVIDED NATIONS

8

South Korea's International Relations: Challenges to Developmental Realism?

Chung-in Moon and Taehwan Kim

South Korea has undergone a profound transformation in the past four decades. Despite the lingering Japanese colonial legacy, the devastating Korean War, social and political upheavals, and the protracted military confrontation with North Korea, the Republic of Korea has fundamentally reshaped its political and economic landscape on the world stage. Having started with a meager per capital income of less than $100 in 1960, it has now become the twelfth-largest economy and ninth-largest trading state in the world. Its international status has been further enhanced by the successful hosting of the 1988 Seoul Summer Olympics and, more recently, the 2002 World Cup. In addition, South Korea is the tenth-largest nation in terms of financial contribution to the United Nations.[1] South Korea has been touted as an ideal case of a "virtuous cycle of growth, security, and even welfare."[2] Such performance can be attributed to several factors: a timely transition to an export-led growth strategy, mercantile economic management, authoritarian governance and a strong developmental state, and the Cold War and American patronage through a strong bilateral alliance.

Since the late 1980s, however, South Korea has undergone major internal and external transformations that have profoundly affected the patterns of its external relations. While the demise of authoritarian rule and the transition to democracy facilitated the transformation of the ideological and institutional foundations of political and economic governance, the end of the

Cold War system has altered its regional strategic parameters. Moreover, diffusion of globalization has fostered reconfiguration of the path of economic development in South Korea by placing major constraints on its assertive mercantilism. Democratization, the advent of the unipolar structure under American hegemony, and globalization have indeed precipitated the contextual changes underlying South Korea's external relations.

Against the backdrop of these observations, this chapter attempts to elucidate the evolutionary dynamics of South Korea's international relations in the post–Cold War era. The first section examines analytical dimensions of South Korea's external relations by looking into its foreign policy objectives, newly emerging opportunities and constraints, and patterns of external management. The second section elucidates old and new challenges to South Korea's geopolitics in the post–Cold War period and analyses dimensions of its foreign and security relations. The third section identifies changing aspects of South Korea's geoeconomic environment in the era of globalization and discusses the evolutionary dynamics of managing its external economic relations. Finally, the chapter casts overall implications of South Korea's geopolitical and geoeconomic management strategies for regional governance in Northeast Asia.

UNDERSTANDING SOUTH KOREA'S EXTERNAL RELATIONS: OBJECTIVES, EMERGING CHALLENGES, AND MANAGEMENT STRATEGIES

South Korea's foreign policy objectives have been traditionally defined in terms of developmental realism, the ideology of "rich state, strong army" *(bukuk gangbyong)*. Developmental realism combines realism with developmental statism. Whereas realism has shaped geopolitical national objectives, developmental statism has guided foreign policy objectives for geoeconomic management. Despite the façade of strategic stability buttressed by the bipolarity of the Cold War era, South Koreans have been captives of a self-imposed image of international, regional, and peninsular anarchy. In a world of anarchy, ensuring the survival of South Korea as a sovereign state has become a national mandate, even an obsession. To assure national survival, realist prescriptions have prevailed: military self-help through the maximization of physical power, effective mobilization of human and material resources, and assertive pursuit of an alliance with the United States. South Korea's security practices during the Cold War era can be best described as a fortified realism.[3]

Meanwhile, developmental statism refers to the ideological and institutional arrangements that promote economic growth and prosperity through strategic intervention of the state in the market.[4] It posits a state structure rather peculiar to South Korea: executive dominance, bureaucratic unity, availability of policy instruments and resources and their strategic allocation, and ultimately insulation of economic policy making from contending social and political pressures.[5] It is against this institutional backdrop that South Korea has been able to formulate and implement effective neomercantile economic policy, while resisting external pressures to open domestic markets. Such a mercantile posture was justified in the name of "catching up" with advanced industrial countries and speeding up the process of economic development. Though temporal in its design, South Korea's neomercantile template was sustained even after it graduated from the status of developing country.

South Korea has been quite successful in ensuring its national survival and promoting its economic prosperity through assertive pursuit of developmental realism. Since the late 1980s, however, South Korea has encountered new internal and external environments that have severely challenged the ideological and institutional foundation of developmental realism. The advent of the post–Cold War era, the diffusion of globalization, and the process of democratization have posed profound challenges that have eventually altered the internal and external environments within which South Korea conducts foreign policy.

The dismantling of the Cold War structure and the newly emerging strategic parameters had the most visible impacts,[6] which entailed some positive dividends. Defying the decades-old logic of bipolarity, South Korea was able to normalize its diplomatic ties with the former Soviet Union and China, both of which were long perceived as its explicit enemies, being North Korea's allies. However, lifting the Cold War overlay from the Northeast Asian region did not mitigate the Korean conflict by itself. Although the end of the Cold War significantly improved the external milieu for peace and stability on the Korean peninsula, South Korea has remained as insecure and uncertain as before.

Several factors underscore the trend. First, the historic North–South Korean summit talk in June 2000 notwithstanding, both Koreas have failed to produce any meaningful measures to reduce military tension and build mutual confidence. As the recent naval clash in the West Sea during the 2002 World Cup Games vividly illustrates, inter-Korean military tension is real and acute. Second, despite the demise of the Cold War, the structure of finite deterrence remains.[7] The "China threat" thesis and constant tension between China and the United States, historical memory of fractured ties between China and Japan as well as the two Koreas and Japan, and the two

Koreas' suspicions of the four major powers in the region all point to how precarious the strategic landscape of the Northeast Asian region is. Finally, U.S. commitment to the region cannot be taken for granted. Following the collapse of the Soviet Union, Northeast Asia encountered the unipolar moment of American hegemony. But it is not clear whether the United States has the will or the intention to play the role of hegemonic leader in the region by capitalizing on this unique moment in human history.[8]

Equally important are the impacts of globalization.[9] Globalization has affected South Korea in two significant ways. One is the increasing systemic vulnerability that arises from uncontrollable external shocks on the domestic economy from the international economic system. Cyclical instability of the international financial and capital markets, roller-coaster effects in international commodity markets, unstable foreign exchange markets, and the global diffusion of inflation are classic sources of systemic vulnerability. While economic superpowers such as the United States can cope more effectively with these challenges by altering the norms, principles, and rules of the international economic system, weaker nations suffer enormous social costs from the process of adjusting to these external shocks. Internal adjustment and the resulting social costs eventually destabilize domestic economy and politics.[10] The 1997 economic crisis of East Asia underscores this negative aspect of globalization.[11]

A final factor is globalization's domestic institutional impacts. Diffusion of global economic liberalization has fundamentally undermined the old patterns of domestic and external management, and South Korea can no longer enjoy old free-riding behavior such as the systematic promotion of exports through subsidy and other forms of incentives, die-hard resistance to import liberalization, and nonenforcement of international agreements. Along with this, globalization has profoundly weakened the traditional roles of the developmental state. Whereas the increasingly deep and mobile nature of international economic transactions has undercut its monitoring and regulative capability, compliance with global standards and the proliferation of nongovernmental actors including transnational agents has also eroded South Korea's autonomy and strength in conducting foreign economic policy.[12]

Finally, democratic transition and consolidation have fundamentally realigned domestic terrain underlying South Korea's external behavior. Under past authoritarian regimes, foreign and national security policies were the exclusive domain of the executive branch. Strong executive leadership not only minimized the negative externalities of bureaucratic politics, but also ensured policy coherence and consistency by insulating the policy-making process from contending social and political pressures. But democratic transition has radically changed all this. Mass media have become the most important actors in shaping the nature and direction of foreign and national security policy. Proliferation of interest groups and nongovernmental organizations has emerged as another significant factor in policy formation and execution. Also, legislative oversight and intense bureaucratic infighting have posed new constraints in these same policy areas. In other words, the structure and process of foreign policy making are changing in the new era of democratic transition and consolidation.[13]

How can foreign policy objectives be achieved in the face of these external and internal challenges? Four major options can be identified. The first is unilateral management of external relations. In the geopolitical domain, this would involve the termination of the alliance with the United States and the pursuit of a status as either a middle power or a permanent neutral state. Such realignment of geopolitical relations will become plausible when and if there is a major breakthrough in inter-Korean relations such as unification in terms of either union of states, confederation, federation, or one single unified state. In the geoeconomic domain, the unilateral management is predicated on the pursuit of either self-reliance or the continuation of mercantilist policy. Judging by South Korea's current status in the international economy as well as its multilateral and bilateral obligations and pressures, however, adoption of the unilateral management option seems highly unlikely.

The second option is bilateral management, which emphasizes the importance of dyadic interactions in its foreign relations. Under the realist vision of international politics, bilateralism has been the most fundamental form of external management. Although there have been some diversification efforts toward regional and multilateral cooperation in recent years, South Korea has anchored its foreign and security policies in bilateral management, as clearly exemplified by its preoccupation with its bilateral alliance with the United States. The geoeconomic domain is somewhat different, however. Although international economic transactions take place by and large among dyadic pairs, their mode of conduct is regulated by multilateral norms, principles, and rules such as those of the World Trade Organization (WTO). Nevertheless, South Korea could deliberate on bilateral management through the signing of bilateral free-trade agreements. Such bilateral preferential trade arrangements can be conducive to enhancing trade and economic growth.

The third plausible option involves regionalism. South Korea could pursue its security and prosperity through collective coordination and cooperation with other actors in the region. In managing geopolitical issues, it could deliberate as part of such regional arrangements as the concert of powers[14] or regional multilateral security regimes that can coordinate relations among three or more nations on the basis of generalized principles and conduct.[15] Meanwhile, to cope with geoeconomic issues, South Korea could pursue either open or closed regionalism.[16]

As a fourth option, South Korea could also seek multilateral alternatives to manage the challenges posed by the post–Cold War era and globalization. To cope with current geopolitical issues, South Korea could consider options of multilateral security cooperation such as a collective security system through the strengthening of the United Nations. Even the Korean conflict could be dealt with within this framework. The idea of a Pax Universalitas, which emphasizes the importance of the United Nations, could ensure the rule of law, a system of collective security, and peaceful resolution of inter-state disputes. Global economic liberalization based on multilateralism can also serve as the most desirable vehicle for coping with challenges of globalization. South Korea could intensify its efforts to sustain global economic liberalization by complying with the existing multilateral economic arrangements such as the WTO, the International Monetary Fund (IMF), and the Organization for Economic Cooperation and Development (OECD).[17]

MANAGING GEOPOLITICS: AUTONOMY, ALLIANCE, AND EXTERNAL SECURITY RELATIONS

Geopolitical Agenda

The end of the Cold War notwithstanding, South Korea faces an array of geopolitical issues. The most immediate task is how to manage the Korean conflict. The Korean summit in June 2000 and improved inter-Korean relations have not led to any fundamental changes in threat perception, force structure, deployment patterns, and military planning in the two Koreas. The contradictory postures of North and South Korea in their military planning is ironic. Both emphasized and anticipated peaceful coexistence during the summit and in the June 15 Joint Declaration, but neither is willing to compromise its security posture, leaving a classic security dilemma in the transition from war to peace. Thus peacekeeping on the Korean peninsula through effective military deterrence has remained one of the most critical items of the geopolitical agenda.

Apart from inter-Korean relations, weapons of mass destruction and missiles are likely to continue to haunt South Korea's geopolitical position. South Korea will be placed in a difficult position if the North again plays both the nuclear and missile cards in its game of brinkmanship diplomacy. According to the Geneva Agreed Framework, the Korean Peninsula Energy

Development Organization (KEDO) is supposed to deliver a light-water nuclear reactor by a target date in 2003, and North Korea will be obliged to comply with the International Atomic Energy Agency's (IAEA's) full nuclear inspections between the completion of a significant portion of the reactor and the delivery of critical nuclear components. But its delivery is estimated to be delayed until 2005 or after, while the United States has been urging the North to honor nuclear inspections before the delivery. If KEDO does not deliver in time and fails to compensate the North for lost electricity due to the delayed delivery, North Korea is likely to play the brinkmanship game. They might also do so over the missile issue. North Korea has placed a moratorium on test launching of its Taepodong II long-range missile until 2003. North Korea's failure to renew its moratorium on the Taepodong II might become another source of security crisis in Korea.[18] As vividly demonstrated in North Korea's recent nuclear brinkmanship, the issue of its nuclear weapons has already turned into a major source of not only local and regional, but also global security concerns.

Finally, policy makers in South Korea are very much concerned about future strategic instability in the region. As long as the United States remains in the region, they believe that the region will remain stable. However, changes in forward deployment of American forces in the region are likely to produce a major security challenge to Korea, whether divided or unified. American disengagement from the region could precipitate the nullification of Article 9 of Japan's Peace Constitution and pave the way for Japan's remilitarization. Such a move could in turn precipitate a regional hegemonic rivalry between China and Japan reminiscent of that of the late nineteenth century, which cost Korea its sovereignty. Thus South Korea is extremely sensitive to American military posture in the region and the overall strategy and power projection capabilities of China and Japan.[19]

Strategies of Geopolitical Management

Bilateral management constitutes the core of South Korea's geopolitical strategy in post–Cold War diplomacy.[20] During the Cold War, American security commitment to South Korea was predicated on the logic of strategic containment of the Soviet Union and the protection of Japan and South Korea. In the name of common security goals, the United States facilitated South Korea's economic development and tolerated its mercantile free riding. The Republic of Korea (ROK)–U.S. alliance has been one of the most successful Western alliances, which can be attributed in part to its patron-client nature, with the United States as a benign patron and South Korea as a loyal client.[21]

Even in the post–Cold War era, the United States plays several important roles in shaping peace and security on the Korean peninsula. First, South Korea has been trying to utilize the United States as a peacekeeper in Korea. Defense planners and Korean citizens as well regard American forces in South Korea as the most vital asset in preventing the outbreak of war through an effective deterrence.[22] President Kim Dae Jung argued during his meeting with Chairman Kim Jong Il in June 2000 that even after national unification, Korea would still need American forces and the alliance with the United States to maintain the strategic balance in the region as well as to prevent the power vacuum and strategic uncertainty following American disengagement.[23] The bilateral alliance in terms of the shared understanding of evolving threats and strategic purposes, the continuing presence of American forces in Korea, and the utilization of a combined forces command are and will be the backbone of peacekeeping on the Korean peninsula.

Second, the United States can play an equally critical role in peacemaking. While peacekeeping is designed to prevent the outbreak of war or to maintain the status quo through deterrence and conflict suppression, peacemaking involves the process of transforming the conflict situation into a more peaceful relationship. The United States can facilitate the process of peacemaking on the Korean peninsula in three significant ways. It can facilitate inter-Korean tension reduction, confidence-building measures, and arms control and reduction through various means, such as political support and the provision of technical advice involving verification. Also, the United States can help both Koreas forge an inter-Korean peace treaty through the Four-Party Talks. Although the Four-Party Talk formula has become less effective and more time consuming, in light of the legal and technical complexity of the armistice treaty, it appears to be the most acceptable venue for all parties, since it comprises both de jure parties (North Korea, the United States, and China) and a de facto party (South Korea) to the Korean conflict. Another way the United States can facilitate peacemaking is by taking initiatives in resolving the issues of weapons of mass destruction and missiles within the framework of multilateral regimes such as the Non-Proliferation Treaty and the Missile Technology Control Regime.

Third, and finally, South Korea would like to see the United States take an active role in the peace-building process, which is more concerned with a stable peace than "the absence of preparation for war or the serious expectation of war."[24] There are three distinct ways through which the United States can ensure a stable peace on the Korean peninsula as well as in the region. The United States should make every effort to spread the free-market mechanism. As commercial liberals argue, the deepening of a market economy and economic interdependence can reduce the likelihood of war while enhancing chances for peace.[25] The United States should also make an effort to cultivate conditions for democratic peace through the spread of liberal democracy throughout East Asia.[26] Since democracies do not fight each other,[27] enlarging democracy in North Korea and elsewhere in East Asia becomes one of the essential preconditions for stable peace on the Korean peninsula. Helping to form a community of security, as an extension of a capitalist and democratic peace, is another way the United States could help build a stable peace.[28] A market economy and a democratic polity are necessary, but not sufficient, conditions for the creation of a sense of community and a stable peace in Korea. North Korea should be more actively brought into world society, so that it can develop into a normal state.

Japan is another important security partner for South Korea. Japan and Korea have maintained a quasi-alliance relationship in which the status quo under the American security umbrella is most valued. As Cha perceptively points out,[29] fear of abandonment by the United States can bring Japan and South Korea closer in security cooperation. But actual abandonment and Japan's subsequent remilitarization could precipitate a profound rupture in Japan–South Korea security relations and even terminate their quasi-alliance. Still haunted by a bitter historical memory of the Japanese colonial past, Asian countries have shown a sensitivity and ambivalence to any possible remilitarization by Japan. These feelings may be strongest in South Korea. On the one hand, South Korea realizes the inevitability of Japan's emerging regional leadership; but on the other, it is suspicious of this new development, since it could possibly lead to the revival of Japan's old regional military and economic hegemony. Thus, Japan's new security initiatives and South Korean calculus will be ultimately shaped by structural parameters of the Japan–Korea–U.S. triangular relationship.

Two factors have recently brought Japan and South Korea closer together. One is North Korea's test launching of Taepodong I. With a commonly perceived threat from North Korea, especially following its launching of the long-range missile across the northern part of Japan in August 1998, the closer security cooperation has become one of the main agendas between Seoul and Tokyo. The other factor bringing the nations closer together was the beginning of the Kim Dae Jung government and its diplomatic initiative. During his state visit to Japan in October 1998, President Kim Dae Jung took a bold and magnanimous approach with regard to the unhappy legacy binding the two nations, and Japan responded with sincere reflection. Prime Minister Keizo Obuchi issued an official apology for colonial atrocities. Its positive outcome was the Joint Declaration by President Kim and Prime Minister Obuchi on a New ROK–Japan Partnership for the Twenty-first Century, which laid a solid foundation for an upgraded Korea–Japan relationship, at least up until Junichiro Koizumi's ascent in Japan. The declaration put special emphasis on building a future-oriented bilateral relationship.

Japan and South Korea also have significantly improved security cooperation. Defense ministerial talks have been held annually since 1994, while the Korea–Japan Security Policy Coordination Council has been in place since 1998. Also, various working-level contacts have been regularized, such as the working-level defense policy meeting, a military intelligence exchange, and an air-defense meeting. Since 1999, the joint chiefs of staff of Japan and South Korea have held high-level staff meetings and the Japanese and South Korean navies conducted a joint naval exercise for emergency relief in the southeastern part of Jeju Island.[30]

With its traditional foreign policy emphasis on the United States and the triangular axis involving Japan still firmly maintained, South Korea has also begun to diversify its external security ties since the advent of the post–Cold War era. Diplomatic normalization with Russia and China through its assertive *Nordpolitik* in the late 1980s and early 1990s is the most important development in this regard. The Nordpolitik of the Roh Tae Woo government, which can be defined as a conscious policy to improve economic and diplomatic relations with countries to the north, that is, North Korea, China, and Russia, offered a major turning point in what had been a Cold War–driven foreign and national security policy of South Korea. Ever since the policy was instituted, ROK–USSR (or ROK–Russian) and ROK–China bilateral relations have expanded under the principle of the separation of politics from economy.[31]

China has traditionally pursued the policy of "neither unification nor war" on the Korean peninsula, and South Korea has effectively exploited this.[32] China's equidistant policy has been beneficial for South Korea in its efforts to dismantle the Cold War structure through its diversified bilateralism, not only because China can play a role of effective broker between Seoul and Pyongyang, but also because it can facilitate opening and reform of North Korea. In addition to remarkable progress in economic and political relations,[33] South Korea has actively engaged with China in military contacts and exchanges. The trend can be explained in part by China's efforts to improve its security relations with South Korea after the 1997 U.S.–Japan guidelines, which expanded Japan's military role in the region, and in part by the Kim Dae Jung government's new policy of diversified military diplomacy. In 1999 alone, China and South Korea exchanged six different military contacts, including the historic visit of the ROK defense minister to Beijing in August. The defense ministerial talks and the ROK–PRC Defense Policy Consultative Meeting held in 1999 and 2000, respectively, demonstrate the salience of South Korea's increasing defense cooperation with China.[34]

However, several factors affect bilateral ties between South Korea and China. The most important factor is the United States. If the United States believes in the power-transition hypothesis[35] and attempts to contain China in the name of the "China threat" thesis, it will be extremely difficult for South Korea to sustain its friendly ties with China, for it could risk its alliance with the United States by doing so. North Korea is another critical factor. Since China has been conducting the policy of separation of politics and economy in pursuing its equidistant policy on the two Koreas, South Korea's pursuit of a hard-line policy on North Korea could also strain Beijing–Seoul ties. In addition, such contingencies as the outbreak of a new Taiwan Strait crisis and diplomatic feuds over the treatment of North Korean defectors could put South Korea's bilateral relations with China in a difficult situation. In light of these factors, it seems premature to predict robust bilateral relationships between the two countries, as there are sources of volatility.

As with China, South Korea's approach to Russia has been partly shaped by its North Korean calculus and its strategic and economic considerations. In fact, the most visible dividend of the demise of the Cold War may have been improving bilateral ties between South Korea and Russia. During the first half of the 1990s, Russia, in its policy toward the Korean peninsula, concentrated primarily on South Korea at the expense of the Soviet Union's long-cherished relationship with North Korea. Russian policy makers expected to gain much from South Korea economically, but little or nothing from its poor former ally. In this calculation, Russia decided not to extend the 1961 Treaty of Friendship and Cooperation with North Korea, while Boris Yeltsin paid an official visit to Seoul in November 1992 and signed the Treaty on Bilateral Relations between Russia and South Korea, which laid down the main principles of bilateral relations, including the support of peace and security on the Korean peninsula. President Kim Young Sam visited Moscow in June 1994.[36]

Further progress was made in military ties between the two countries, which included military personnel exchanges,[37] as well as exports of Russian arms and military equipment to South Korea. In 1996–1997 alone, Russia transferred $200 million worth of arms and military equipment to South Korea in partial repayment of its debt to Korea totaling $1.4 billion.[38] But economic gains from the improved relationship with South Korea turned out to fall far short of what Russia expected. In August 1993, Korea unilaterally decided to cease provision of the remainder of the $3 billion loan pledged to the Soviet Union in 1990 and demanded early repayment of the loan already provided. Moreover, with Russia excluded in the South Korea–proposed

Four-Party Talks formula, its sense of alienation has deepened. Defying the Four-Party Talks, Russia proposed an eight-party talk that would include two Koreas, the United States, Japan, China, and Russia, as well as the United Nations and the IAEA.[39] As its efforts with South Korea did not meet its expectations, Russia has tried to balance its policy toward the two Koreas since the second half of the 1990s.

Since Vladimir Putin's ascent to power, North Korean–Russian relations have again improved, especially after the reciprocal visits of Kim Jong Il and Putin in 2000 and 2001.The improved relationship between Pyongyang and Moscow was solidified under the Treaty of Friendship, Good-Neighborliness, and Cooperation and the North Korea–Russia Joint Communiqué. Nevertheless, Putin has shown prudence by balancing Russia's bilateral ties with North and South Korea. Of great import are Russia's efforts to play a mediating role in inter-Korean relations. Putin's cross-visit to Pyongyang and Seoul in 2000 and 2001, and more recently Russian foreign minister Igor Ivanov's cross-visit in the wake of the naval clash in the West Sea, indicate Russia's willingness to engage the Korean problem.

Apart from bilateral management, South Korea also has been pursuing a mix of diverse strategies. One of the most pronounced examples is trilateral cooperation involving Japan and the United States, such as the Trilateral Coordination and Oversight Group (TCOG), initiated in March 1999 by South Korea to institutionalize the process of consultation and policy coordination on North Korea. Two salient issues led to the formation of TCOG: weapons of mass destruction, especially nuclear, and missiles. TCOG played an important role in narrowing policy gaps and forging consensus on North Korea. It was backed up by ministerial-level consultations in which foreign ministers of the three countries held several meetings in order to coordinate their policies toward North Korea.

Another good example of going beyond bilateral management is the Four-Party Talks,[40] which were initiated by the Kim Young Sam government during Clinton's visit to South Korea in 1996. Since the death of Kim Il Sung, inter-Korean relations have rapidly worsened because of Kim Young Sam's remark that Kim Il Sung was a criminal responsible for the outbreak of the Korean War. As a way of breaking the stalemate, the Kim Young Sam government proposed to hold the Four-Party Talks, in which the United States, China, and North and South Korea would participate. The Kim government intended to use the talks to ensure peace and stability on the Korean peninsula.

In his address at the United Nations in September 2000, President Kim Dae Jung proposed a "two-plus-two" formula, in which the inter-Korean peace treaty could be sponsored and guaranteed by the United States and

China through the Four-Party Talks. Although the Four-Party Talks formula has become less effective and more time consuming, in light of the legal and technical complexity of dismantling the armistice treaty, it appears to be the most acceptable venue for all parties. It is so far the most comprehensive formula, as it comprises both de jure parties (North Korea, the United States, and China) and a de facto party (South Korea) to the Korean conflict. Given the Bush administration's critical view of the Four-Party Talks, Kim Dae Jung's "two-plus-two" formula might not be easily realized, but it might have been a worthwhile ingredient of peacemaking on the Korean peninsula.

Despite an explicit pledge by the United States, South Korea's defense planners do not seem to believe that the Untied States will be able to sustain its role as hegemonic stabilizer in Northeast Asia in the long run. Emerging fears of a new regional anarchy that could follow American disengagement have induced South Korea's policy makers to look into regional multilateral security cooperation as an alternative for external security management. In the past, South Korea's quest for multilateral security cooperation was confined to the resolution of the Korean conflict through the involvement of regional powers. Seoul's favorable responses to earlier proposals[41] exemplify this trend. Since 1987, however, South Korea has gone beyond the Korean issue by giving more attention to collective management of East Asian peace and security. In October 1989, in his address at the United Nations, President Roh Tae Woo proposed the establishment of a six-country consultative body for East Asian peace. In May 1993, President Kim Young Sam emphasized the importance of a multilateral security dialogue in the region in his speech at the Asia Pacific Economic Cooperation (APEC) summit meeting. And in July 1994, Han Sung Joo, then minister of foreign affairs, proposed the launching of a Northeast Asian multilateral security dialogue in tandem with the ASEAN Regional Forum (ARF).[42]

All of these proposals represent South Korea's growing effort to resolve the Korean dispute and regional conflicts through security cooperation regimes, as well as to end its sole diplomatic reliance on the United States. South Korea wants to take its own initiative in forming a new multilateral security cooperation regime similar to the Conference on Security and Cooperation in Europe. Accordingly, it has proposed several regional military confidence-building measures designed to enhance transparency, certainty, and strategic stability among regional actors. These measures include the exchange of defense white papers, registration of conventional weapons at the United Nations, regularized contracts among defense planners, exchanges of military personnel and naval vessels, mutual cooperation on nonmilitary matters, and active participation in UN peacekeeping efforts. Simultaneously, the South Korean government has been encouraging civilian participation in multilateral security dialogues to develop a community of multilateralism founded on collective mutual understanding.

The Kim Dae Jung government has also renewed its emphasis on regional multilateral collaboration. In managing the Korean conflict, President Kim proposed the establishment of a Northeast Asian security cooperation regime, as well as the two-plus-two formula, in order to shape a new security environment conducive to tension reduction and peace and security building on the Korean peninsula. Along with this, the Kim government has taken several multilateral initiatives, including proposals on the ASEAN Plus Three (the ten-member ASEAN plus South Korea, China, and Japan) and regional multilateral security cooperation arrangements.[43]

Despite the Kim Dae Jung government's earlier pledge to expedite the process of multilateral diplomacy, however, very little progress has been made. Although it has been active in the ARF, facilitating North Korea's admission to the forum, no concrete plans to build a multilateral security cooperation regime and to discuss the Korean question within the framework have emerged. The purview of ASEAN Plus Three has been very much limited to economic issues. This development can be attributed partly to the structural position of South Korea in the regional politics and partly to the reluctance of major actors such as the United States and China in elevating multilateral security cooperation as a principal venue for building peace and security in the region. However, South Korea needs to be more attentive to multilateral security cooperation, since it can be an effective mechanism through which sensitive inter-Korean security issues can be addressed.

GLOBALIZATION, REGIONALIZATION, AND MANAGEMENT OF GEOECONOMICS

Geoeconomic Agenda

Transformation of the South Korean economy from that of a developing country into a newly industrializing one entailed several internal and external challenges. The most visible challenge was outside pressures for market opening and economic liberalization. The outside pressures were both bilateral and multilateral. Bilateral pressures from the United States were the most pronounced. As the United States began to suffer trade deficits with South Korea, it began to undertake offensive trade policy against South Korea in the early 1980s, armed with the principle of strategic reciprocity.[44] Along with this, Japan and the EU began to exert intense bilateral pressures to discipline South Korea's free-riding and spoiling behavior. Apart from the bilateral pressures, ratification of the Uruguay Round, the launching of the WTO, and admission to OECD have provided multilateral pressures for economic liberalization in South Korea. It is these bilateral and multilateral pressures that have shattered neomercantile institutions and policies in South Korea.

Another major challenge involved the changing landscape of international competition. As a forerunner of the newly industrializing countries (NICs), South Korea was able to carve out an ideal market niche in international competition. Whereas advanced industrial countries were not interested in items and destinations South Korea was targeting, there were very few developing countries that could compete with it. Since the late 1980s, however, the South Korean economy has encountered fierce competition from all corners. While advanced industrial countries have begun to resist market competition through a subtle form of protectionism, horizontal competition among the NICs has intensified.[45] Additionally, China and the second-generation NICs, mostly Southeast Asian countries, have begun to undercut South Korea's position in labor-intensive industrial sectors. In a sense, South Korea is very much sandwiched between the technological edge of advanced industrial countries and the labor edge of China and the second-generation NICs.

Domestic changes have also posed a major challenge to the management of external economic relations. After a long period of an authoritarian mode of governance, South Korea made a dramatic democratic transition in 1987. Although it is difficult to establish any causal relationship between democratic governance and economic performance,[46] democratic transition and the concurrently rising power of labor unions and nongovernmental organizations have strained economic performance in one way or another. In particular, excessive politicization of labor movements and a high-wage burden have often been pointed to as some of the primary causes of declining international competitiveness. The legacy of labor militancy still haunts the South Korean economy.

Finally, globalization has posed a new challenge. South Korea has undergone two waves of globalization over the past decade. The first wave involved a voluntary, managerial globalization that former president Kim Young Sam initiated through the ratification of the Uruguay Round and admission to the OECD in 1994–1997. The second wave involved the process of forced globalization as a result of the economic crisis in 1997 and the bail out from the IMF, with its imposition of conditionalities for macroeconomic stabilization and structural reforms. While the former was proactive and anticipatory, the latter was reactive. Yet economic globalization under the Kim Dae Jung government has been quite impressive. Owing to the economic crisis and

IMF conditionalities, Kim Dae Jung was able to remove most existing barriers to economic liberalization less than one year after his inauguration in February 1998, after the previous government had struggled to do so over five years. After the second wave of globalization, global standards were set in place as the new logic of economic governance, defying the old logic of the developmental state and "Confucian capitalism."[47] Ironically, the economic hardship imposed by the 1997 financial crisis turned out to be a valuable asset for globalization under the Kim Dae Jung government.[48]

Strategies of Geoeconomic Management

What, then, are the best choices for coping with these internal and external challenges? As with geopolitical arenas, South Korea can explore a variety of management strategies. Obviously, one option is to resort to the old pattern of unilateralism embodied in mercantilism. As Amsden and Wade aptly observe,[49] the big push for export promotion and late industrialization was steered by an array of mercantilist ideas and policies. While it undertook assertive and well-coordinated industrial policies in order to enhance export competitiveness, South Korea continued to rely on an inward-looking strategy in selective industrial sectors as well as on defensive trade policy, comprising extensive tariff and nontariff barriers for domestic market protection. But the unilateral path is no longer a viable option, not only because of such negative domestic developments as declining international competitiveness, but also because of outside pressures from the United States and multilateral institutions.

Whereas unilateralism is no longer a valid option, bilateral management has become an increasingly attractive one. It comprises two components: diversification of bilateral trading partners and the formation of preferential trade and investment arrangements on a bilateral basis. With regard to trading partner diversification, China has emerged as the principal target. Traditionally, South Korea has suffered from excessive partner concentration, especially in the United States and Japan. Since the late 1990s, however, the overall picture has begun to change. While the relative share of American and Japanese markets has been on the decline, exports to other parts of the world have grown significantly. For example, in 2000, China was South Korea's third-largest trade partner, behind only the United States and Japan. Bilateral trade with China, including Taiwan and Hong Kong, accounted for 23 percent of South Korea's total trade, which is even larger than trade with Japan (21%). While the American share of South Korea's total export trade has drastically decreased, from 40 percent in 1986 to 16 percent in 1997, the

Chinese share has been on the rise from less than 1 percent in 1985 to more than 12 percent in 2001.[50]

Apart from bilateral partner diversification, South Korea has been actively seeking bilateral preferential trading and investment agreements. Two factors have driven South Korea to opt for bilateral trade and investment arrangements. One is its lack of such arrangements. Starting with the EU, countries around the world have been groping for free-trade arrangements. According to the WTO, the number of reported regional trade agreements around the world as of mid-2002 was 240, with 70 percent of these, or 172, in effect. Of the total, around 100 have been concluded since 1995.[51] However, South Korea, like China and Taiwan, does not have a free-trade agreement (FTA) with any of the WTO's 144 members. The other factor is the relative ease of implementing bilateral free-trade arrangements. While it is a much more complicated and protracted process to create regional or megaregional free-trade arrangements, establishing bilateral arrangements is much easier and can be a building bloc toward regional arrangements.[52]

South Korea has been investigating the possibility of free-trade agreements with, among others, Japan, Chile, and the United States. After the Korea–Japan ministerial meeting in Kagoshima in November 1998 officially commissioned a joint private and public research on a free-trade arrangement, the Japan–South Korean Forum on FTA issued a declaration on the speedy implementation of a free-trade area between the two countries in early 2002. And in March 2002, during Koizumi's visit to Korea, Korea and Japan signed a bilateral investment treaty (BIT) and agreed to set up a research committee headed by members of government, business, and academe to conclude a bilateral FTA.[53] Korea's ultimate interest lies in establishing an East Asian economic cooperative group inclusive of China. Hence the discussion on concluding an FTA with Japan serves that ultimate interest. However, because the FTA between the two countries could widen Korea's trade deficit with Japan, the Korean government has taken the step of signing a bilateral investment treaty first, to induce Japanese investment in Korea.[54]

Since 1998, Korea has also been attempting to conclude an FTA with Chile, which is regarded as having an economic structure complementary to Korea's. But these efforts have come to a stalemate over strong resistance from Korean farmers who fear competition in the agricultural, particularly fruit, sector in Korea from Chilean fruit that would enter the market, tariff free.[55] Efforts to conclude a BIT with the United States, initiated by Korea in June 1998 on the occasion of President Kim Dae Jung's visit to Washington, have undergone a similar fate, due to the pending issue of screen quotas.[56] FTA negotiations with the United States have made the least progress among all candidates, as the United States has thus far been unresponsive to

Korea's overtures. In December 2001, Ambassador Thomas Hubbard said that Washington's interest in discussing an FTA with Seoul was limited due to ongoing negotiations with Singapore, Chile, and other Latin American countries regarding the issue.[57] Nontariff barriers in the fields of agriculture, textiles, apparel, and footwear, among others, will remain a sensitive issue between the United States and South Korea. Despite mounting pressures from Korea's big business,[58] the South Korean government has thus far stuck to a rather passive stance on an FTA with the United States, apparently for fear of shocks to the local agricultural sector and medium-sized businesses.

Recently, South Korea has also shown increasing interest in subregional as well as regional trade and financial arrangements. Three factors account for this trend. First is the expansion of the economic size of the East Asian region. East Asia has become a major economic bloc in terms of the size of population, economy, and trade: the combined population of the four Northeast Asian countries (Korea, Japan, China, and Russia) has reached 1.6 billion, or four times the population of NAFTA or the EU, while their combined trade volume amounted to $1.87 trillion in 2000, which is equivalent to 66 percent of NAFTA's and 44 percent of the EU's trade volume. The combined GDP of these countries reached 57 percent and 76 percent of NAFTA's and the EU's, respectively.[59]

Second, increasing intraregional economic interdependence has facilitated South Korean negotiations on subregional and regional trade arrangements. The relative amount of intraregional trade has risen rapidly for the past two decades. In 1975, intraregional trade accounted for 30.6 percent of the world's total, a figure that rose to 36.5 percent in 1985 and more than 40 percent in the 1990s. The share of intra-Asian exports reached almost 50 percent of total Asian merchandise exports in 2000, with 10 percent annual growth rates during the past decade. And while Asian exports to North America, Western Europe, and other regions have declined on the whole between 1990 and 2000, exports within Asia rose from 42 percent in 1990 to 49 percent in 2000. The story is similar with imports. By 2000, Japan imported $105 billion, or 31 percent of its total imports, from the Asian economies, while intra-Asian imports in South Korea, Hong Kong, and Singapore amounted to $254 billion, or more than 52 percent of their total imports combined.[60]

Third, as clearly illustrated in table 8.1, South Korea is the nation that stands to gain the most from participating in any subregional FTA involving China or Japan. Only if China and Japan form a bilateral free-trade area excluding Korea is South Korea bound to lose. It is for these reasons that South Korea has actively pursued the formation of subregional preferential trade arrangements, especially involving China and Japan.

Table 8.1. Balance Sheet for FTAs involving Korea, Japan, and China: GDP Growth (%) and Economic Gains (millions of U.S. dollars)

	Korea–China–Japan FTA		*Korea–China FTA*		*Korea–Japan FTA*		*China–Japan FTA*	
	GDP	*Economic gains*	*GDP*	*Economic gains*	*GDP*	*Economic gains*	*GDP*	*Economic gains*
Korea	3.2	12,644.5	2.4	10,687.8	1.1	3,682.8	−0.2	−1,189.6
China	1.3	8,191.2	0.2	917.0	0.0	−358.0	1.1	7,335.3
Japan	0.2	12,265.1	0.0	119.9	0.0	2,184.7	0.2	10,289.8

Source: Japanese Cabinet Secretariat, quoted in *Tong-A Ilbo,* January 11, 2002.

Particularly notable is that since the financial crisis in 1997, South Korea has gradually changed its attitude toward Japan's regional economic initiatives, including the formation of the Asia Monetary Fund (AMF).[61] Several factors facilitated South Korea's tilt toward the AMF proposal. First, harsh IMF conditionality backfired. South Korea's support of the AMF proposal was predicated on the expectation that its conditions would not be as harsh as IMF's. Second, there was a widespread belief among South Koreans that the 1997 economic crisis resulted from excessive dependence on the American dollar, which deepened rigidity in foreign exchange maneuvering. Thus the AMF, once established, would reduce such rigidity by facilitating the diversification of foreign exchange operations. Third, there were practical reasons as well. Asian countries, including South Korea, have outstanding short-term foreign debts of $300 billion to the United States and Europe, with interest rates of approximately 10 percent. The AMF could ease this burden by helping Asian countries repay these debts with AMF's lower-interest loans. Finally, an increasing number of South Koreans believe that the idea of AMF is feasible, given the huge size of foreign reserves in Asia.[62] Indeed, potential economic gain is bringing about a convergence of South Korea and Japan as they search for economic survival and prosperity and gradually defy the old fear of Japanese domination and exploitation. This is probably one of the most remarkable positive results of the economic crisis.

Along with movements toward subregional and regional preferential trade and monetary arrangements, South Korea has been an active participant in APEC since its creation in 1989. South Korea initially envisaged twin benefits from APEC: on the one hand, easy access to export markets and capital in the region's industrialized countries and, on the other hand, a secure supply of raw materials from resource-rich countries such as Australia and Southeast Asian countries. But slower progress in intraregional trade and investment liberalization, coupled with the strengthening of the WTO, significantly diluted APEC's strategic value for South Korea. More importantly, the American initiative to foster the transformation of APEC into a free-trade area alarmed South Korea, dampening its enthusiasm. South Korea's alliance with Japan in resisting the opening of farm product markets and adopting the principle of early voluntary sectoral liberalization epitomizes their resistance to the American initiative. Japan and South Korea are likely to take a similar posture on the issue of open regionalism by favoring gradualism and opposing an immediate implementation of a regional or megaregional free-trade area.[63]

Finally, multilateralism remains the backbone of South Korea's external economic management. Undoubtedly, compliance with norms, principles, and rules of the WTO and OECD has guided the nature and direction of economic liberalization in South Korea. However, there are still unresolved issues, such as liberalization of the agricultural sector, especially rice, and the service sector, involving legal service, medical service, education, accounting, and energy. In addition, enforcement of multilateral agreements has become another source of concern. Nevertheless, South Korea has made it clear that economic globalization based on multilateralism will be the guiding principle of the South Korean economy.

COPING WITH CHANGES: IMPLICATIONS FOR REGIONAL GOVERNANCE IN NORTHEAST ASIA

Implications for Regional Security Governance

What then are the implications of South Korea's external security management for regional security governance? Pathways to regional security governance differ according to contending theoretical perspectives. While realists believe that regional security governance is a function of power,[64] liberals argue that actors in the region can show rule-governed behavior not only because of the potential to gain from patterned regularity and cooperation,[65] but also because of norms, practices, and even institutional inertia.[66] South Korea's post–Cold War external management reveals two seemingly conflicting approaches. On the one hand, it still relies on the United States as its ultimate ally and partner. On the other hand, South Korea is gradually shifting toward diversified bilateralism and multilateral solutions in resolving the Korean conflict as well as the regional security dilemma. This can be seen partly as a fallback strategy in light of the waning security guarantee provided by the United States. But it can also be interpreted as a proactive response to the parametric changes in the Cold War structure that allow South Korea to search for more external autonomy.

But South Korea's search for autonomy is fundamentally limited by the maintenance of the status quo through its bilateral alliance with the United States. No other alternative but bilateral alliance seems viable in the short run. Equally true, however, is that the bilateral alliance has been increasingly at odds with inter-Korean relations. Although the Kim Dae Jung government has denied that improved inter-Korean relations would undercut the bilateral alliance tie with the United States, changing domestic ambiance in South Korea has been calling for the reduction or withdrawal of American forces. In addition, the ROK–U.S. alliance has been linked to the trilateral coordination involving Japan, South Korea, and the United States. The closer trilateral security ties under the American hegemonic leadership, which capitalizes on the "China threat" thesis or missile defense, might precipitate a corresponding reaction from the northern triple axis of China, North Korea, and Russia. Such a confrontation can easily revive the specter of a new Cold War structure between the northern triple axis and the southern triple axis. Thus, exclusive pursuit of bilateral or trilateral security arrangements could destabilize peace and stability on the Korean peninsula and Northeast Asian region as a whole, and such a development should be avoided.

Other realist options are either less plausible or less desirable. Pax Americana II is less likely because of the inherent American paradox. As Joseph Nye points out, no country in the region can compete with the United States in the short run, but the United States is not powerful enough to handle regional threats associated with the proliferation of weapons of mass destruction and international terrorism. It is thus essential for the United States to cooperate with other countries.[67] Pax Niponnica and Pax Sinica seem neither feasible nor desirable, not only because of the limited power and capabilities of Japan and China, but also because of the weak base of legitimacy and support in the region for both. An East Asian concert of power involving major actors may work, but only if Korea, unified or divided, joins it as an equal partner.

In the medium to long run, South Korea can get maximum benefits from liberal solutions. A UN-based collective security system might be an ideal solution, but it does not seem very plausible. In view of this, a regional security regime, be it a loose form of consultative body or a tight arrangement of norms, principles, and rules on collective management of security, is the most acceptable choice for South Korea. Such a regime is an essential prerequisite for bringing common, comprehensive, and cooperative security in the region.[68] But it should be kept in mind that such an arrangement would be inconceivable without a shared sense of community on security. So long as nationalist appeals, obsession with the historical past, and political misuse and abuse of hostile sentiments prevail, it will be virtually impossible to form a community of security, no matter how democratic and market-oriented the Northeast Asian region would be. Thus, healing the pains of the past, recognition of national identities, and formation of a new regional identity are prerequisites for building a stable peace in the region.

Implications for Regional Economic Governance

As with security governance, regional economic governance can be approached from both realist and liberal perspectives. Liberals would subscribe to an open regionalism that can be defined as a less tight regional regime through which regional actors can coordinate their macroeconomic, industrial, and trade policies. For this regime to be viable, several conditions must be met: inclusiveness in membership, conformity with free-market principles, and compatibility as well as complementarity with such multilateral institutions as the WTO. Open and inclusive regionalism can evolve into valuable pre–confidence building measures that can substantially reduce military tension and stabilize the regional security system. This is not only because of a sense of mutual trust and understanding among regional actors, but also because of positive linkage effects in the military area. Hence, this regime can be seen as a preliminary step toward a fuller regional economic integration in line with the existing multilateral trading regime.

On the other side, closed regionalism is predicated on exclusiveness in membership, occasional deviation from regional security cooperation and free-market principles, and incongruity with multilateralism and global liberalization. Closed regionalism can be viewed as an expression of defensive realism and mercantilism on the regional scale. Thus a closed regionalism is much smaller in terms of its membership, which leads to a subregional or bilateral economic arrangement. South Korea may well consider the option of closed regionalism when and if the international economic system becomes further fragmented into competing regional blocs. If Japan or China seeks to form its own sphere of economic influence in the form of either a yen bloc or the Greater China circle in order to counter the power and influence of hostile trading blocs such as the EU or NAFTA, South Korea could join such a regional regime.

What would then be the most ideal form of regional economic governance for South Korea? In managing foreign economic relations, South Korea has clearly graduated from unilateral, mercantile practices. And with the ratification of the WTO and admission to OECD, it has also declared its preference for multilateralism. But there is a built-in temptation to form subregional trade arrangements (involving China, Japan, and Korea), though such an orientation may not be the most beneficial. Open regionalism appears to be the most ideal choice for South Korea. It can smoothly coopt and incorporate such regional actors as China, North Korea, and Russia into the capitalist economic sphere and can also reduce the costs of creating regional collective goods for parties involved. Since the arrangement presupposes the decentralization of economic power and collective management, regional actors are likely to favor it. For these reasons, megaregional arrangements such as APEC or the East Asian Free Trade Area (namely, ASEAN plus China, Japan, and Korea) seem more appealing.

A recent Institute for International Economics comparative analysis of different combinations of trading arrangements in the region and the welfare gain under each has yielded interesting findings.[69] According to the study, the most desirable trading arrangement turns out to be global liberalization under the WTO. Regardless of type of intra- or interregional trading arrangement, the aggregate gains from global liberalization are estimated to be 50 percent higher than gains under the next most favorable arrangement for both the world as a whole and for the combined APEC membership. The second-best option proves to be APEC membership or the creation of a larger regional grouping compromising the whole of East Asia, Southeast Asia, and the Western Pacific.

This simulation shows that APEC liberalization offers superior welfare gains for most of its individual economies. It is desirable also because of its potential role as a building bloc toward global liberalization. An East Asian or Western Pacific trading bloc could also be attractive, provided that it comprises a large number of participants (namely, Northeast Asia, Southeast Asia, and Australasia) and is congruent with the WTO. Nevertheless, political and institutional constraints could undercut the effectiveness of these megaregional trade arrangements. As the experiences of APEC illustrate, the modality of concerted unilateralism and a voluntary, nonbinding commitment, as well as the prevalence of a political logic dictated by the salience of gain, can work against the smooth and effective operation of megaregional arrangements. In addition, a lack of commitment by strong economic powers, especially the United States, poses another barrier to these arrangements. The Institute for International Economics research findings suggest rich empirical implications for South Korea. Too much emphasis on subregional trading arrangements could lead South Korea down the wrong path, while (despite the temporal and procedural complexity of doing so) lending more support for, and commitment to, global and APEC liberalization could be rewarding.

CONCLUSION

South Korea is undergoing major transformations. As globalization and the demise of the Cold War structure have realigned strategic parameters of external relations, democratization has reshaped the domestic institutional foundation for external engagement. Facing the new challenges, South Korea has shown two salient management strategies. In the geopolitical domain, South Korea has favored the status quo through a strong bilateral alliance with the United States, supplemented by trilateral coordination with Japan and the United States. Diversified bilateralism with China and Russia, along with its emphasis on multilateral regional security cooperation, has produced very limited effects thus far. In the geoeconomic domain, South Korea has been gradually shifting its emphasis from multilateral and megaregional economic arrangements to bilateral and subregional ones. Its preoccupation with the formation of a Northeast Asia free-trade area composed of China, Japan, and South Korea exemplifies this trend.

However, it should be noted that bilateral and subregional approaches to external management might not ensure the accomplishment of South Korea's long-term foreign policy objectives. There must be an imaginative transition to the liberal constructive perspective that combines a multilateral regional security-cooperation regime with a collective recognition of mutual identity, a collective trust and obligation through shared norms and dense networks, and a collective cooperation on common security problems—these are the critical prerequisites for a stable peace in the region. At the same time, movement toward bilateral and subregional economic arrangements should be reconsidered. South Korea should find answers to its search for a management strategy for external economic relations in open regionalism and global liberalization.

NOTES

1. Republic of Korea (ROK) Ministry of Foreign Affairs and Trade (hereafter MOFAT), *Oegyotongsangeupmoo Chamgojaryo* (Reference materials for diplomatic and trade affairs) (Seoul: MOFAT, 2001), 9–10.

2. Steve Chan and Alex Mintz, eds., *Defense, Welfare and Growth: Perspectives and Evidence* (London: Routledge, 1992).

3. See various annual issues of Korea's national Defense white paper (*Kukbangbaek-* published by the Ministry of National Defense (hereafter MND).

A huge pool of literature on the developmental state includes Chalmers Johnson, *d the Japanese Miracle* (Stanford, Calif.: Stanford University Press, 1982); and

Meredith Woo-Cumings, ed., *The Developmental State* (Ithaca, N.Y.: Cornell University Press, 1999).

5. See, for instance, Alice Amsden, *Asia's Next Giant: South Korea and Late Industrialization* (New York: Oxford University Press, 1989).

6. For comprehensive discussions on the impacts of the end of the Cold War on the Korean peninsula, see Chung-in Moon, Odd Arne Westad, and Gyoo-hyoung Kahng, eds., *Ending the Cold War in Korea: Theoretical and Historical Perspectives* (Seoul: Yonsei University Press, 2001).

7. Chung-in Moon, "Changing Threat Environment, Force Structure, and Defense Planning: The South Korean Case," in *Emerging Threats, Force Structures, and the Role of Air Power in Korea*, ed. Natalie Crawford and Chung-in Moon (Santa Monica, Calif.: Rand, 2000), 89–114.

8. Ethan Kapstein and Michael Mastanduno, eds., *Unipolar Politics* (New York: Columbia University Press, 1999).

9. For extensive discussions of the various aspects of Korea's globalization, see Samuel S. Kim, ed., *Korea's Globalization* (New York: Cambridge University Press, 2000).

10. Karl Polanyi may have been one of the earliest scholarly predictors of this domestic political and economic dynamic of globalization when he referred to the "double movements" in his seminal work, *The Great Transformation: The Political and Economic Origins of Our Time* (Boston, Mass.: Beacon, 1957).

11. On the 1997 Asian financial crisis, see T. J. Pempel, *The Politics of the Asian Economic Crisis* (Ithaca, N.Y.: Cornell University Press, 1999); and Stephen Haggard, *The Political Economy of the Asian Financial Crisis* (Washington, D.C.: Institute for International Economics, 2000). See also the special issue of *Cambridge Journal of Economics* 22, no. 6 (1998).

12. Eun Mee Kim, "Crisis of the Developmental State in South Korea," *Asian Perspective* 23, no. 2 (1999): 35–55. For a theoretical discussion on the role of the nongovernmental actors enhanced with globalization, see Susan Strange, *Retreat of the State: The Diffusion of Power in the World Economy* (New York: Cambridge University Press, 1996).

13. Miles Kahler, ed., *Liberalization and Foreign Policy* (New York: Columbia University Press, 1997); and Miroslav Nincic, *Democracy and Foreign Policy: The Fallacy of Political Realism* (New York: Columbia University Press, 1994).

14. For discussions on this concept, see Susan L. Shirk and Christopher P. Twomey, eds., *Power and Prosperity: Economics and Security Linkages in Asia–Pacific* (Somerset, N.J.: Transaction, 1996); and Charles A. Kupchan, ed., *Atlantic Security: Contending Visions* (New York: Council on Foreign Relations Press, 1998).

15. See P. Kerr, A. Mack, and P. Evans, "The Evolving Security Discourse in the Asia–Pacific," in *Pacific Cooperation: Building Economic and Security Regimes in the Asia–Pacific Region*, ed. Andrew Mack and John Ravenhill (Boulder, Colo.: Westview, 1995), 233–55.

16. On open regionalism, see Fred Bergsten, "APEC and World Trade: A Force for Worldwide Liberalization," *Foreign Affairs* (May–June 1994): 20–26; and Robert D. Hormats, "Making Regionalism Safe," *Foreign Affairs* (March–April 1994): 97–108.

17. Robert Keohane and Joseph Nye Jr., "Two Cheers for Multilateralism," *Foreign Policy* 60 (1985); and John G. Ruggie, "International Regimes, Transactions and Change: Embedded Liberalism in the Postwar Economic Order," *International Organization* 36, no. 2 (Spring 1982).

18. On the North Korean missile question, see Chung-in Moon, Masao Okonogi, and Mitchell B. Reiss, eds., *The Perry Report, the Missile Quagmire, and the North Korean Question: The Quest of New Alternatives* (Seoul: Yonsei University Press, 2000).

19. This point is well demonstrated in South Korea's Defense white paper, MND, *Kukbangbaekseo*, various annual issues.

20. Bilateral relations with the four major powers are still attracting the central focus of South Korea's foreign policy–making bodies. See MOFAT, *Oekyobaekseo* (Foreign policy white paper), various annual issues.

21. Man Woo Lee, Ronald McLaurin, and Chung-in Moon, *Alliance under Tension: The Evolution of U.S.–South Korean Relations* (Boulder, Colo.: Westview, 1988).

22. MND, *Kukbangbaekseo*, various issues. More recently, presidential candidates from South Korea's major political parties are competitively confirming the centrality to it's national security of the bilateral relations with the United States.

23. *JoongAng Ilbo* (June 20, 2000).

24. Kenneth Boulding, *Stable Peace* (Austin: University of Texas, 1979), 13.

25. On this topic, see Edward Morse, *Modernization and the Transformation of International Relations* (New York: Basic, 1976), and Robert Keohane, "International Liberalism Reconsidered," in *The Economic Limits of Politics*, ed. John Dunn (Cambridge: Cambridge University Press, 1989), 165–94.

26. See Michael W. Doyle, *Ways of Peace and Ways of War* (New York: Norton, 1997), chapter 8.

27. Bruce Russet, *Grasping the Democratic Peace* (Princeton, N.J.: Princeton University Press, 1993).

28. Karl Deutsch, *Political Community and the North Atlantic Area* (Princeton, N.J. Princeton University Press, 1959); and Emanuel Adler and Michael Barnett, *Security Communities* (New York: Cambridge University Press, 1998).

29. Victor D. Cha, *Alignment despite Antagonism: The U.S.–Korea–Japan Security Triangle* (Stanford, Calif.: Stanford University Press, 1999).

30. MND, *Kukbangbaekseo 2002*, unpublished manuscript, 97–98.

31. For South Korea's Nordpolitik, see Tae Dong Chung, "Korea's Nordpolitik: Achievements and Prospects," *Asian Perspective* 15, no. 2 (1991): 2149–80; and a special issue of *Kukjejeongchi Nonchong* (International political science review) 29, no. 2 (1989).

32. Fei-Ling Wang, "China and Korean Unification: A Policy of Status Quo," *Korea and World Affairs* 23, no. 2 (Summer 1998): 180–84.

33. For the progress in South Korea–China relations since the diplomatic normalization, see Chaejin Lee, *China and Korea: Dynamic Relations* (Stanford, Calif.: Hoover Institute Press, 1996).

34. MND, *Kukbangbaekseo 2000*, 244–51.

35. For an intense discussion of the power transition theory, see Ronald L. Tammen et al., *Power Transitions: Strategies for the 21st Century* (New York: Chatham House, 2000).

36. For a comprehensive review of South Korea–Russia relations in the past decade, see Seung-Ham Yang, "Han-Reokwankaeoe Kujojeok Jaejomyoung" (A structural analysis of Korea–Russia relations)," in *Hankukeu Oekyojeongchaek* (Korea's Foreign Policy), ed. Dalchoong Kim (Seoul: Oruem, 1998), 449–86.

37. Five defense ministerial talks have been held to date since the first Korea–Russia interministerial talks were held in Moscow in May 1994.

38. A. A. Sergounin and A. V. Subbotin, *Russian Arms Transfers to East Asia in the 1990s*, SIPRI Research Report no. 15 (New York: Oxford University Press, 1999), 113.

39. *Itar Tass*, April 15, 1996.

40. Korea Institute for National Unification (KINU), ed., *Sajahoedamkwa Hanbando Pyonghwa* (Four-Party Talks and peace on the Korean Peninsula) (Seoul: KINU, 1997).

41. Such proposals include Henry Kissinger's four-party talks and cross-recognition in the early 1970s and James Baker's "two plus four" formula in the mid-1980s.

42. For discussions on Northeast Asian multilateral security cooperation, see Hyun-ik Hong and Dae-woo Lee, eds., *Dongbuka Dajaahnbohyupryukkwa Jubyunsagang* (Multilateral security cooperation in Northeast Asia and four major powers) (Seoul: Sejong Institute, 2001).

43. For a discussion of the evolution of East Asian regional security cooperation and South Korea's contribution to it, see Youngmin Kwon, *Regional Community-Building in East Asia* (Seoul: Yonsei University Press, 2002).

44. Thomas O. Bayard and Kimberly A. Elliott, *Reciprocity and Retaliation in U. S. Trade Policy* (Washington, D.C.: Institute for International Economics, 1994); and Malcolm McIntosh, *Arms across the Pacific: Security and Trade Issues across the Pacific* (New York: St. Martin's, 1988).

45. Ku-Hyun Jung and Dong-Jae Kim, "Globalization and International Competitiveness: The Case of Korea," in *Democratization and Globalization in Korea: Assessments and Prospects*, ed. Chung-in Moon and Jongryn Mo (Seoul: Yonsei University Press, 1999), 349–67; and Sung-gul Hong, *Semi-conductor Industry in South Korea and Taiwan* (London: Routledge, 1997).

46. Adam Przeworski and Fernando Limongi, "Political Regimes and Economic Growth," *Journal of Economic Perspectives* 7, no. 3 (1993): 51–69; Dietrich Rueschmeyer et al., *Capitalist Development and Democracy* (Chicago: University of Chicago Press, 1992); and Peter Gourevitch, "Democracy and Economic Policy: Elective Affinities and Circumstantial Conjunctures," *World Development* 21, no. 8 (1993): 1271–80.

47. David C. Kang, *Crony Capitalism: Corruption and Development in South Korea and the Philippines* (New York: Cambridge University Press, 2002).

48. Chung-in Moon and Jongryn Mo, *Economic Crisis and Structural Reforms in South Korea: Assessments and Implications* (Washington, D.C.: Economic Strategy Institute, 2000).

49. Amsden, *Asia's Next Giant;* Robert Wade, *Governing the Market* (Princeton, N.J.: Princeton University Press, 1990).

50. Statistics on Korean Economy (May 2002, in Korean), MOFAT, at www.mofat.go.kr/ko/info/stat_list.mof?b_code=stat (accessed June 5, 2002).

51. *Korea Herald*, June 14, 2002.

52. For this argument, see Robert Scollay and John P. Gilbert, *New Regional Trading Arrangements in the Asia Pacific?* (Washington, D.C.: Institute for International Economics, 2001).

53. MOFAT, *Juyo Oekyohyunahn Jungbo Jekong* (Information services on current foreign policy issues), 23 (July 15, 2002).

54. Seon Gu Kang, "The Road to a Win–Win Match in Korea–Japan Bilateral Investment Treaty," LG Economic Institute CEO Report (Seoul: April 4, 2002).

55. *Korea Herald*, February 22, 2002.

56. *JoongAng Ilbo*, July 11, 2002.

57. *Korea Herald*, January 14, 2002.

58. Korea's large conglomerates and their lobbying arms have continuously called for an early opening of FTA talks with the United States in anticipation of positive effects from the liberalization of steel, auto, and other key industrial sectors.

59. Calculated from World Bank, *World Development Indicators 2001* (Washington, D.C.: World Bank, 2001).

60. Calculated from WTO, *International Trade Statistics 2001* (Geneva: WTO, 2001).

61. At a joint meeting of IMF and the International Bank for Reconstruction and Development held in Hong Kong in September 1997, Japanese finance minister Kubo Wataru suggested the idea of forming the AMF in order to assist Southeast Asian countries in financial and foreign exchange crises by providing standby loans for current account deficits, extending trade credits, and facilitating foreign exchange defense.

62. Robert Wade and Frank Veneros, "The Asian Crisis: The High Debt Model Versus the Wall Street–Treasury–IMF Complex," *New Left Review* 228 (1998): 3–22.

63. Yong Deung, "Japan in APEC," *Asian Survey* 37, no. 4 (1997): 353–67.

64. See Kenneth Waltz, *The Theory of International Politics* (Reading, Mass.: Addison–Wesley, 1979); and John J. Mearsheimer, "The False Promise of International Institutions," *International Security* 19, no. 3 (1994–1995): 5–49.

65. Robert Keohane, *After Hegemony* (Princeton, N.J.: Princeton University Press, 1984); and Robert Keohane and Lisa L. Martin, "The Promise of Institutionalist Theory," *International Security* 20, no. 1 (1995): 39–51.

66. Hedley Bull and Adam Watson, eds., *The Expansion of International Society* (Oxford: Clarendon Press, 1984); A. Claire Cutler, "The 'Gorthian Tradition' in International Relations," *Review of International Studies* 17 (1991); and Keohane, *After Hegemony*.

67. Joseph S. Nye Jr., *The Paradox of American Power: Why the World's Only Superpower Can't Go It Alone* (New York: Oxford University Press, 2002).

68. Mack and Ravenhill, eds., *Pacific Cooperation*.

69. Scollay and Gilbert, *New Regional Trading Arrangements?*

FURTHER READING

Alagappa, Muthiah, ed. *Asian Security Practice: Material and Ideational Influences*. Stanford, Calif.: Stanford University Press, 1998.

Cha, Victor D. *Alignment Despite Antagonism: The U.S.–Korea–Japan Security Triangle*. Stanford, Calif.: Stanford University Press, 1999.

Eberstadt, Nicholas. *Korea Approaches Reunification*. New York: NBR, 1995.

Eberstadt, Nicholas, and Richard J. Ellings, eds. *Korea's Future and the Great Powers*. Seattle: University of Washington Press, 2001.

Ellings, Richard J., and Friedberg, Aaron, L. eds. *Strategic Asia 2001–02: Power and Purpose*. Seattle: National Bureau of Asian Research, 2001.

Haggard, Stephan. *Pathways from the Periphery: The Politics of Growth in the Newly Industrializing Countries*. Ithaca, N.Y.: Cornell University Press, 1990.

Hatch, Walter, and Kozo Yamamura. *Asia in Japan's Embrace: Building a Regional Production Alliance*. New York: Cambridge University Press, 1996.

Jeong, Kap-Young, and Jaewoo Choo, eds. *Towards New Dimensions of Cooperation in Northeast Asia*. Seoul: Yonsei University Press, 1998.

Kahler, Miles, ed. *Beyond the Cold War in the Pacific*. San Diego: University of California Institute of Global Conflict and Cooperation, 1991.

Kihl, Young Whan, ed. *Korea and the World: Beyond the Cold War*. Boulder, Colo.: Westview, 1994.

Kil, Soong Hoom, and Chung-in Moon, eds. *Understanding Korean Politics: An Introduction*. Albany: State University of New York Press, 2001.

Kim, Samuel S., ed. *Korea's Globalization*. New York: Cambridge University Press, 2000.

Koh, Byung Chul. *The Foreign Policy Systems of North and South Korea*. Berkeley: University of California Press, 1984.

Kwon, Youngmin. *Regional Community-Building in East Asia*. Seoul: Yonsei University Press, 2002.

Lee, Hong Yung, and Chongwook Chung, eds. *Korean Options in a Changing International Order*. Berkeley: Institute of East Asian Studies, University of California at Berkeley, 1993.

Mack, Andrew, and John Ravenhill, eds. *Pacific Cooperation: Building Economic and Security Regimes in the Asia–Pacific Region*. Sydney: Allen & Unwin, 1994.

Moon, Chung-in, and David Steinberg, eds. *Kim Dae-jung Government and Sunshine Policy*. Seoul: Yonsei University Press, 1999.

Moon, Chung-in, and Jongryn Mo, eds. *Democratization and Globalization in Korea: Assessments and Prospects*. Seoul: Yonsei University Press, 1999.

Moon, Chung-in, Odd Arne Westad, and Gyoo-hyong Kahng, eds. *Ending the Cold War in Korea*. Seoul: Yonsei University Press, 2001.

Takashi Inoguchi and Grant B. Stillman, eds. *Northeast Asian Regional Security: The Role of International Institutions*. Tokyo: United Nations University Press, 1997.

Yoon, Chang-Ho, and Lawrence J. Lau, eds. *North Korea in Transition: Prospects for Economic and Social Reform*. Northampton, Mass.: Elgar, 2001.

9

North Korea's International Relations: The Successful Failure?

C. S. Eliot Kang

Perhaps it could be said that Northeast Asia as a referent has little meaning for the constituent members of this region, who have never shared a common cultural identity, worldview, or market. However, even if this proposition can be accepted without argument, an exception would have to be made for North Korea. More than any other Northeast Asian power, North Korea is confronted with the geographical reality of a security complex that defines the region more than does anything else. Ironically, the events that took place on distant shores on September 11, 2001, may only intensify this burden of localization for North Korea.

North Korea, in some ways, has navigated well the treacherous currents of regional geopolitics. In 1994, during the first nuclear crisis on the Korean peninsula, North Korea faced war with the United States but ultimately emerged from that altercation with a multibillion dollar economic assistance package. In 2000, the country often condemned as a "rouge state" transmitted from its capital to the expectant world the images of the beaming faces of the first visiting South Korean president, Kim Dae Jung, and later U.S. secretary of state Madeleine Albright toasting its leader, Chairman Kim Jong Il. Also, Chinese and Russian leaders, whatever their true feelings about the atavistic Stalinist regime in Pyongyang, have hosted as well as paid visits to Kim Jong Il in recent years. And the Japanese, despite Pyongyang's invectives and provocations, have continued to pursue, if in a tide-like manner, diplomatic normalization that promises a huge economic windfall for North Korea. Even the hawkish administration of George W. Bush, as it faces the second nuclear crisis on the Korean peninsula, shows some signs of accommodating North Korea's economic and security concerns.

To the extent a pariah state burdened with a failed economy has been able to extract concessions from some of the most powerful countries of the world, North Korea's conduct of its external relations could be seen as a remarkable success. However, while other actors in the region have redefined their conceptions of security and transformed and thickened their relations with one another in mutually beneficial ways, North Korea has been playing a zero-sum security game that is, to no small degree, aggravated by its own belligerent behavior.

Indeed, despite tactical successes in its external relations, in this postcommunist era of market integration and interdependence, North Korea has been unable to redefine its national interests and "identity."[1] While China has been successfully transforming itself under the banner of "socialism with Chinese characteristics," and even Russia is now making headway with reforms, North Korea has held fast to the militant antiforeign, anticapitalist values and ideas that have guided its external policy since its founding. In fact, it has itself to blame as much as the geopolitics of Northeast Asia for the security dilemma it faces in a region dominated by powerful trading states playing a complex multileveled and multifaceted global game.

This chapter analyzes North Korea's "successful failure" in coping with Northeast Asia's geopolitics. Understanding the logic of North Korea's external relations is crucial because the stability on the Korean peninsula to which North Korea holds the key is central to the regional order. Having survived the post–Cold War period pretty much on its own terms—with its ideology and identity glaringly out of synch with regional trends—North Korea is once more faced with a shifting external environment, as the result of the events of September 11, 2001. How North Korea chooses to deal with the coming challenges will bring new trials or opportunities for Northeast Asia as well as the world.

THE NORTHERN HALF OF THE PIVOT

For North Korea more than any other regional power, Northeast Asia's particular geography matters to its external relations. Despite the end of the Cold War, which has intensified effects of forces that go by the collective name of "globalization,"[2] the geopolitics of Northeast Asia is the dominant reality for North Korea.

Along with its doppelgänger, South Korea, North Korea occupies a geopolitical space that is the pivot of Northeast Asian security. As Samuel Kim points out in the introduction, the Korean peninsula is the most important strategic nexus of the Asia–Pacific, where four of the greatest powers in the world system (the United States, Japan, China, and Russia) meet and interact. And historically, Korea's relatively small size and central location have made it a strategic prize or buffer for these larger powers.

The very division of Korea into two contending states in the past century was largely a product of this geopolitical dynamic. The partition produced the Korean War, and the stalemate of this bloody conflict then locked North Korea (supported by the Soviet Union and China) and South Korea (backed by the United States and, indirectly, Japan) into playing the roles of quintessential client states during the Cold War. The divided Korea served as the buffer and fulcrum in the regional balance of power.

Currently, the destructive potential of tensions in and around Korea is nothing like it used to be during the height of the Cold War. Nonetheless, compared to the general stability of the western tip of the Eurasian landmass, the eastern end retains some of its past dangers. The fact is that the Korean peninsula is now the most militarized geographical space in the world.

Mercantilist South Korea, through economic development, democratization, and globalization, has been able to "move with the times" and mitigate the hazards of local geography.[3] Over the years, with the support of the United States as well as Japan, South Korea has built a powerful economy with extensive trading ties with the world. Today, it maintains a powerful military deterrent against North Korea and enjoys friendly and mutually profitable relations with its former enemies, China and Russia, while maintaining a stable alliance with the United States and, by extension, Japan.

In stark contrast, North Korea has been suffering from economic isolation and consequent privation. It has been unwilling to get past its zero-sum legitimacy struggle with South Korea and unable to fundamentally redefine its relations with the great powers of the region, which cannot help but view North Korea, in its present state, through a security lens. Even China, the great power most sympathetic to North Korea, fears the festering humanitarian disaster on the other side of the Yalu and the imponderable consequence of North Korean implosion or explosion.

RELATIONS WITH CHINA AND RUSSIA

During the Cold War, when geopolitical leverage mattered more to the statecraft of the great powers of Northeast Asia, North Korea actually enjoyed certain strategic advantages in occupying the northern half of the security pivot. It should be recalled that, in Northeast Asia, the confrontation between the East and West had a unique dynamic because of the rivalry that developed between the Soviet Union and China, both allies of North Korea. And as the division between the two communist giants unfolded, North Korea gained a degree of autonomy not available to South Korea, which tightly orbited its single sun, the United States.

The split between North Korea's patrons had risks, but given that both Beijing and Moscow valued relations with Pyongyang for their strategic value, North Korea could rely on military aid and economic support from both quarreling parties. Manipulating its *juche* (self-reliance) ideology, it was able to play the two great powers against one another to maximize security and economic benefits from both while maintaining a high degree of political independence and a façade of economic self-sufficiency.[4]

The end of the Cold War undermined North Korea's advantageous position. With both China and the Soviet Union abandoning communist orthodoxy and trying to integrate into the global market, the strategic calculus of Northeast Asia underwent a rapid change during the 1980s. By the time the Berlin Wall was being breached, China and the Soviet Union no longer attached past worth to their relations with North Korea. They were more interested in achieving better political and economic relations with their erstwhile Cold War enemies, the United States, Japan, and, gallingly for the North Koreans, South Korea.

In fact, well before the fall of the Berlin Wall, China achieved a condominium, if an uneasy and fragile one, with the United States and Japan and, by the early 1980s, was conducting brisk trade with South Korea as it was transitioning from a command economy to a market-oriented one. And as the Soviet economy began imploding in the late 1980s, Moscow reached out to the West as well.

In fact, it was the Soviet Union's attempt to avert an economic meltdown that completed the dramatic transformation of the strategic landscape of Northeast Asia. Faced with a tightfisted United States and an unforgiving Japan fixated on recovering its lost "Northern Territories" from the Soviet Union, a desperate Moscow reached out to Seoul. Confronting an existential crisis, Moscow was willing to exchange its diplomatic recognition for Seoul's pledge of multibillion dollar economic assistance, even if its move meant jeopardizing its relations with Pyongyang and losing influence in Northeast Asia in relations to other great powers.

And the Soviet Union's headlong normalization of relations with South Korea in September 1990 forced China, which had been carrying out a more evenhanded policy toward the two Koreas, to follow suit and recognize South

Korea in 1992. Having better managed its reforms than the Soviet Union, China had been carrying out a carefully calibrated Korea policy that separated economics from politics. Its dual-track diplomacy had allowed China to enjoy the fruits of a close trading relationship with South Korea without official relations while maintaining close political ties with North Korea, but the Soviet Union's precipitous action made such a delicate balancing act untenable. To protect its good relations with South Korea, Beijing too had to normalize its relations with Seoul in order to maintain diplomatic parity with the Soviet Union.

In the competitive recognition race, unfortunately for Pyongyang, Moscow and Beijing normalized relations with Seoul without reciprocal action toward Pyongyang by Washington and Tokyo. In the zero-sum contest between Pyongyang and Seoul for legitimacy as the "true Korea," this turn of events was a severe blow to North Korea.[5] Beyond hurting its pride, Beijing's and, in particular, Moscow's actions placed Pyongyang in a precarious strategic situation.

In wooing South Korea, the Soviet Union (later, Russia) abrogated its security guarantees to North Korea in bits and pieces so that Moscow's formal announcement in 1996 of the expiration of the 1961 bilateral friendship treaty between the Soviet Union and North Korea came as something of an anticlimax. Undoubtedly, North Korea's caustic reaction to Moscow's recognition of Seoul as well as Russia's abandonment of communism added fuel to this process, as Mikhail Gorbachev and Boris Yeltsin both took umbrage at vitriolic aspersions that the "Kim dynasty" of North Korea heaped on them. In the unraveling of the alliance, North Korea lost the protection of the Soviet nuclear umbrella, however theoretical that protection might have been during the waning days of the Soviet Union. Further, it lost the supplier of Pyongyang's most advanced weapon systems.[6]

As North Korea regained perspective on hard strategic reality and considered its ongoing need for advanced arms to keep up with South Korea's military modernization, Pyongyang began to repair its relations with Moscow. However, that effort has begun to bear some fruit only in recent years as Russia, under the leadership of Vladimir Putin, is seeking to restore its lost strategic leverage in Northeast Asia through better relations with North Korea.

Indeed, in 2000, North Korea signed with Russia a renegotiated friendship treaty, though without provisions for ideological solidarity and security guarantees. It also successfully carried out high-profile summit diplomacy with President Putin, who made a historic first visit to North Korea by a Russian (or Soviet) leader in the same year, and a year before Kim Jong Il made a twenty-four-day rail tour of Russia. However, it is clear that Pyongyang cannot expect the restoration of Cold War–era relations with Moscow. Of course, to the extent that the Russians find regained influence in Pyongyang desirable in their attempt to counter the U.S. National Missile Defense (NMD) project, the North Koreans themselves may be able to leverage the recovering Moscow–Pyongyang relations against others. Nonetheless, with both North Korea and Russia strapped for cash, it is unlikely that Pyongyang could convince Moscow to restore even arms sales to North Korea, let alone military aid and economic subsidies.

To be sure, China remains a security guarantor of North Korea. Unlike Russia, which has its geopolitical center in the West, China has to consider the geographical propinquity of North Korea. Strategically, the Korean peninsula is the front yard of China, or as the Chinese say, "Korea is to China as lips are to teeth." And China has repeatedly stated that it will not tolerate a forceful reunification of Korea. However, in light of Beijing's ever-growing economic ties with the United States, Japan, and South Korea, Pyongyang cannot consider China's commitment an iron-clad security guarantee in the way that the U.S.–South Korea Mutual Security Treaty is for Seoul. Pyongyang must weigh realistically how much China is willing to risk its growing economic interdependence with the United States, Japan, and South Korea for North Korea's survival.

In fact, despite security interests at stake in the Korean peninsula and its thriving economy, China has followed Russia in drastically curtailing economic assistance to North Korea. Both China and the Soviet Union were generous to North Korea during the Cold War, and North Korea became used to "friendship prices" and barter arrangements that subsidized its living standards. However, by the 1980s, China and the Soviet Union found the one-sided economic relations burdensome as well as irksome, as North Korea showed no sign of ever being able to address the imbalance in payments.

Moscow in particular found the situation intolerable as the Soviet economy began to unravel. The Soviet Union withdrew its economic support in the mid-1980s, and after it recognized Seoul diplomatically, Moscow notified Pyongyang that trade with North Korea would now be conducted on a hard currency basis at world market prices. Since the Soviet Union had been providing much fuel oil as well as machinery and parts to North Korea, this action essentially shut down North Korea's industrial production.

Perhaps the breakdown of economic relations between Moscow and Pyongyang was inevitable, given the crisis engulfing Russia, but North Korea surely aggravated the situation when it vehemently berated Moscow for betraying not only a long-time ally but also communism. By the time the bilateral relations reached their low point, as Moscow took a critical stance toward Pyongyang during North Korea's standoff with the United States in

1994, remaining relations had come to a virtual halt. As discussed above, political ties have improved since then, but the economic problems of both North Korea and Russia have prevented any upturn in economic relations.

Beijing also has taken a tough economic stance against Pyongyang. Even before the Soviet Union did, China demanded hard currency for its exports to North Korea. However, China has not been able to strictly enforce this policy given the danger of regime collapse in Pyongyang. Observers of North Korea's economy agree that China, as North Korea's main trade partner, has been instrumental in propping up the North Korean economy.[7] For example, in 2001, North Korea's imports from China totaled about $740 million, but its exports to China reached only $167 million.[8] In fact, China has allowed North Korea to run annual bilateral deficits of approximately a half billion dollars since 1995.

Nonetheless, in providing nothing more than a lifeline to the North Koreans, the Chinese intent appears to be to induce North Korea to follow their model of development. Whatever may turn out to be the ultimate consequence of this "tough love," as Pyongyang has been unwilling or unable to carryout Chinese-style reforms, the immediate result was the economic meltdown of North Korea, just short of producing a regime collapse.

Indeed, Beijing's and Moscow's policies toward Pyongyang have had a devastating impact on North Korea's economy. From 1990 to 1998, North Korea suffered nine consecutive years of economic decline. A country that once boasted one of the highest economic growth rates in the Communist bloc—albeit with heavy subsidies from Beijing and Moscow—suffered a devastating famine in the mid-1990s that may have taken more than two million lives.[9] The misery that North Korea has suffered in recent years is, as Richard Solomon describes it, "perhaps the greatest humanitarian disaster of the 1990s."[10] Despite the upturn in the growth rate that began in 1999 with the arrival of Western relief aid, North Korea's nominal gross national income in 2000 barely amounted to $17 billion, a tiny fraction of South Korea's $455 billion.[11]

RELATIONS WITH THE UNITED STATES, JAPAN, AND SOUTH KOREA

The dire predicament that the North Koreans found themselves in by the mid-1990s might have been mitigated or avoided altogether had Pyongyang been able to achieve a rapprochement with the United States, Japan, and South Korea. A political breakthrough in the early 1990s could have led to literally lifesaving Western trade and investments. To be sure, North Korea has reached out to the West in its own distinct way.

For a short period during the early years of the post–Cold War era, as it absorbed the shock of the collapse of Communism in Eastern Europe, North Korea moderated its usual strident rhetoric and militant behavior toward the United States, Japan, and South Korea. This provided a window of opportunity for conciliation.

Sensing a shift in Pyongyang's strategic calculation, Seoul rejuvenated its inter-Korea diplomacy, which was supported by Washington's own diplomatic probes toward Pyongyang.[12] Tokyo also tried to engage Pyongyang by initiating normalization talks.[13] North Korea responded to these gestures by signing, with South Korea, the 1991 October Joint Declaration of the Denuclearization of the Korean Peninsula and the February 1992 Agreement on Reconciliation, Non-Aggression and Exchange and Cooperation. It also began diplomatic contacts with the United States and plunged into normalization talks with Japan.

However, with its precipitously deteriorating economy and no doubt frustrated by its limited diplomatic options in a new strategic environment, North Korea changed its approach toward the United States, Japan, and South Korea. It essentially sidelined the slowly progressing talks with South Korea and Japan and began focusing on achieving a diplomatic breakthrough with the United States. No doubt, Pyongyang reasoned that Washington held the key to its ultimate survival because the United States was the gatekeeper of the international markets as well as the hegemon capable of restraining the ambitions of North Korea's neighbors, including South Korea.

Beyond the unpleasant political implication of dealing with South Korea on an equal basis, North Korea probably felt vulnerable to an increasingly powerful South Korea capable of dictating the terms of engagement if Seoul was allowed to be the lead interlocutor in Pyongyang's rapprochement with the West. Further, it likely reasoned that normalization negotiations with Japan would turn out to be long and drawn out, considering the domestic and international complexity of Japan's Korea policy. Hence, prioritizing a breakthrough with the United States, Pyongyang tried to get Washington's attention in a way that could not be ignored: leveraging its increasing nuclear and ballistic-missile capabilities—asymmetric power resources—North Korea began practicing what one analyst called "mendicant militancy."[14]

Pyongyang immediately attracted the attention of the United States in 1992, when it became apparent that North Korea had reprocessed more plutonium than it had declared to the International Atomic Energy Agency (IAEA), raising the specter of North Korean nuclear weapons. North Korea began to play its "nuclear card" in its unique brand of brinkmanship diplomacy when, in January 1993, it refused IAEA inspection of two suspected nuclear waste sites and then declared in March its intent to withdraw from the Non-Proliferation Treaty (NPT), which it had signed in 1985.[15]

This calculated North Korean provocation led to the decision by the United States to dramatically step up bilateral contacts between Washington and Pyongyang.[16] This was an outcome highly desired by North Korea to compensate for the loss of support from China and Russia, complicate U.S.–South Korean relations, and unsettle the Japanese.

The Clinton administration began talks with Pyongyang that led in June 1993 to a joint U.S.–North Korea statement outlining the basic principles for continued bilateral dialogue and North Korea's "suspension" of its withdrawal from the NPT. This led to another series of talks in July 1993 in Geneva that set the guidelines for resolving the nuclear issue, improving U.S.–North Korea relations, and restarting the suspended inter-Korean talks (at the insistence of South Korea).

When further negotiation following the Geneva talks became deadlocked, in the spring of 1994 North Korea unloaded fuel from its five-megawatt nuclear reactor in Yongbyon, bringing North Korea closer to nuclear arms production. This brought North Korea and the United States (and its reluctant and anxious allies, South Korea and Japan) to the verge of war. However, to diffuse the crisis, President Clinton utilized a fortuitous direct channel of communication that former President Jimmy Carter had established with Kim Il Sung, the late "Great Leader" of North Korea.

The sobering war scare brought more U.S.–North Korea talks, which in the fall of 1994 produced an "Agreed Framework" for resolving the nuclear issue. In the Agreed Framework, North Korea pledged to freeze its nuclear program under IAEA supervision while working together with the United States in fostering peace and security on a nuclear-free Korean peninsula and strengthening the international nuclear nonproliferation regime. The key to North Korea's cooperation was the agreement between Washington and Pyongyang that, by 2003, North Korea's proliferation-prone graphite reactors would be replaced by proliferation-resistant light-water ones (to be financed largely by South Korea and Japan) and that the United States and North Korea would work toward normalized relations.

However, in October 2002, with mounting evidence that North Korea was cheating on the 1994 agreement, the Bush administration confronted North Korea with its intelligence about Pyongyang's clandestine, alternative, uranium-enrichment nuclear weapons program. Shockingly, North Korea acknowledged the existence of the suspected covert program, brazenly asserted its right to possess nuclear weapons, and accused the United States of failing to fulfill its side of the bargain, citing among other things the lack of progress in normalization of relations. More provocatively, with an alarming prospect of massive proliferation of nuclear weapons, North Korea has initiated step-by-step uncapping of its plutonium-based nuclear weapons program halted by the Agreed Framework while demanding various concessions from the United States. Clearly, the danger of North Korea's weaponization of its nuclear capabilities continues to prove a useful tool for North Korean statecraft.

Furthermore, North Korea has made rapid advances in its long-range ballistic missile program, augmenting Pyongyang's nuclear threat credibility. This linkage was dramatically demonstrated when, in May 1993, North Korea successfully test-fired the 1,000–1,300-km range, liquid-fueled Rodong-1 missile over the Sea of Japan (called the East Sea by the Koreans). This launch especially alarmed Japan because it signaled that North Korea now possessed the missile capacity to reach cities in the southern half of Japan, including Osaka, the nation's second-largest city.

The shock was even greater when, in August 1998, North Korea test-fired the much longer-range Taepodong-1 missile, which entered the stratosphere in Japanese airspace. This demonstrated that now all Japanese cities, including Tokyo, were vulnerable to North Korean missiles, which could possibly be armed with weapons of mass destruction (WMD). It showed that North Korea was not about to be swept into the dustbin of history, but was a clear and present danger that had to be engaged as much as deterred.

The launch also demonstrated to the United States that North Korea had come closer to deploying a ballistic-missile system, capable of reaching the continental United States, than many had believed. Before the launch, the United States had been more worried about North Korea selling missile parts and missile technology to Pakistan, Iran, and others.[17] Not surprisingly, the Clinton administration responded to North Korea's missile capability with a "buyout" approach, similar to the earlier nuclear diplomacy, with the support of South Korea and Japan in which, in the wake of the Agreed Framework, many had become convinced of the merit of accommodating North Korea.

Before time ran out on the Clinton administration, Washington and Pyongyang were negotiating an understanding that would have exchanged unspecified economic compensation for North Korea's pledge not to produce, test, or deploy long-range ballistic missiles and to cease the sale of missiles, missile components, technology, and know-how to other countries.[18] Some argue that, were it not for the long and awkward transition between the Clinton and George W. Bush administrations because of the political problems stemming from the close presidential election of 2000, the United States and North Korea could have resolved the missile issue.[19] They argue that this resolution could have then led to normalized relations between Washington and Pyongyang.[20]

Of course, the current Bush administration espouses a tougher policy toward North Korea than the previous one and justifies the building of NMD, one of the top priorities of the administration, by pointing to the North Korean nuclear and missile threats.[21] However, it is entirely possible that, if and when the North Koreans are ready to bargain and moderate their behavior, the Bush White House will take up the missile diplomacy where the Clinton administration left it. Despite the tough talk, President Bush and his senior aides have consistently stated since the early days of the administration that the United States continues to seek dialogue with North Korea. Even after the events of September 11, 2001, and North Korea's nuclear confession in October 2002, taking into account the views of Seoul and Tokyo as well as Beijing and Moscow, the Bush administration has not changed this basic position toward North Korea.

Indeed, North Korea's adroit handling of relations with South Korea has proved essential in managing its relations with the United States. While subordinating inter-Korea relations to its diplomacy toward the United States, Pyongyang has employed a range of incentives and threats, real and illusory, in its dealings with Seoul to further its relations with the United States. It has held out "carrots," such as the dramatic June 2000 summit between Kim Jong Il and Kim Dae Jung, and "sticks," such as the July 2002 ambushing of a South Korean patrol boat in a disputed area of the Yellow Sea, to manipulate South Korea's hopes and fears. Pyongyang has been masterful in fanning the hope that if it is engaged it will cooperate, as in the case of the Agreed Framework, and the fear that if it is neglected or insulted it will lash out. Particularly with President Kim Dae Jung having convinced many South Koreans that his "sunshine policy" of steady engagement (even if Pyongyang does not reciprocate immediately) is the only workable approach toward North Korea, South Korea has played a key role in keeping the United States in dialogue with North Korea.

An example of this dynamic is the South Korean reaction to President Bush's January 2002 state of the union address to Congress. In the speech, President Bush included North Korea, along with Iraq and Iran, as a constituent member of the "axis of evil" threatening global security and announced that the United States would act to prevent the country from developing WMD. His tough words gave the impression that he was about to initiate a new era of confrontation with North Korea.

If not in North Korea, in South Korea President Bush's speech produced a war scare and stirred up a powerful wave of anti-Americanism. Many South Koreans, including conservatives, became indignant that America's unilateral pursuit of its national interests would jeopardize peace and stability, and possibly reconciliation and reunification, on the Korean peninsula at the expense of the Korean people. Faced with this strong reaction in South Korea, a month later during a summit visit to South Korea, President Bush had to explain that the United States had no intention of invading or attacking North Korea. He also had to make clear that he supports President Kim's sunshine policy and patient negotiations with North Korea.[22]

Nonetheless, the Bush administration's hawkish attitude toward North Korea helped to elect Roh Moo Hyun as the successor to Kim Dae Jung in December 2002. An activist lawyer and past critic of the presence of U.S. troops in South Korea, Roh defeated the favored conservative candidate with the help of South Korea's younger generation, which was alarmed by the prospect of war and resentful of U.S. involvement in inter-Korean affairs. During his campaign, Roh promised the continuation of sunshine policy. He also warned of the possibility of South Korea having to face a war triggered by the United States and North Korea and stated that, were such a war threatened, he would stop it by "mediating" between Washington and Pyongyang.

Clearly, as South Korea is a crucial ally, its engagement bias toward North Korea limits the range of realistic policy options for the United States. If the Bush administration unilaterally decides to take a more coercive approach to North Korea, it would have to take into account serious consequences for the U.S.–South Korea alliance. Indeed, if Washington's confrontational approach triggers a massive North Korean artillery bombardment of Seoul, it could very well lead to the termination of the fifty-year-old alliance.

EXPLAINING NORTH KOREA'S SUCCESSFUL FAILURE

What should be apparent from the above account of North Korea's external relations is that, while it suffered dramatic strategic reversals as Northeast Asia emerged from the Cold War, North Korea has also scored remarkable tactical victories. Most importantly, its nuclear diplomacy has led not just to direct dealings with the United States but also to Seoul's sunshine policy and Japan's intensified normalization diplomacy, all ways of delivering to North Korea various rewards for defusing tensions and crises largely of Pyongyang's own making. It is also responsible for Beijing paying continued close attention to Pyongyang's needs and Moscow, in order to deflate one of Washington's justifications for NMD, reciprocating Pyongyang's attempt to resuscitate bilateral relations.

However, despite its brilliant tactical maneuvers, North Korea has become the odd man out in Northeast Asia, a region where former enemies have embraced economic interdependence. North Korea is mired in a zero-sum security game that is aggravated by its own shortsighted behavior. In this postcommunist era of "geoeconomics," North Korea has been unable to redefine its national interests and "identity."[23] In fact, its short-term successes may doom North Korea to the status of a permanent failed state in a region dominated by powerful trading states playing a complex multileveled and multifaceted global game.

Why has North Korea been unable to fundamentally transform its external relations? Why has North Korea issued threats that have served short-term interests but worked against its long-term viability? Why has it defined its security primarily in military terms that preclude mutually advantageous relations with its neighbors? Why has North Korea allowed the geopolitics of Northeast Asia to matter so much to its security?

"Outside In," "Inside Out"

The lack of a fundamental strategic reorientation of North Korea's external relations has much to do with "space," that is, the geopolitics of Northeast Asia as discussed above and in the introduction by Samuel Kim. Indeed, many analysts in the West, particularly those who are concerned with security affairs, have emphasized the security dilemma facing North Korea and employed instrumental variants of neorealism to explain North Korea's external relations in the post–Cold War era.

Neorealism posits that all states are first and foremost concerned with identifying dangers to their survival and counteracting them: as dictated by the structure of the international system, states balance power, either internally by arms racing or externally by forging military alliances. According to neorealism, military preparedness is the only true assurance against potential enemies.

Applying the structuralist, "outside in" insights of neorealism to North Korea's geopolitical predicament, some analysts do not find it surprising that North Korea has become obsessed with military security and accelerated its WMD programs in the post–Cold War era. One analyst argues that because North Korea has lost its ability to externally balance the growing power of South Korea and its allies in the post–Cold War era, North Korea has had to increase its militancy in recent years. He contends that North Korea has been practicing deterrence through "danger" against an increasingly powerful South Korea.[24]

However, the neorealist approach does not explain the key puzzle of why North Korea, suffering famine and devastating economic collapse, has chosen to define security mainly as a military matter and not as an economic matter, as have other powers of Northeast Asia have. Indeed, the "outside in" perspective sheds little light on North Korea's choice.[25]

To understand more deeply North Korea's choice, what is also required is some kind of an appreciation of North Korea's identity—that is, values and ideas—which is a product of time, or history. Such a task has been the province of historians who understand Korea's xenophobic and neo-Confucian past and "area specialists" who labor to read between the lines of North Korean newspapers, broadcasts, and *démarche*. Over the years, in analyzing North Korea's external relations, they have pointed to the importance of understanding North Korea's *juche* ideology, a unique expression of North Korea's political self-determination and freedom from outside control arising out of Korea's isolationist and colonial past.

According to Charles Armstrong, *juche* ideology provides "a general worldview that sets the parameters, the outer boundaries, of engagement with the outside world."[26] As such this ideology explains much about Pyongyang's inability to fundamentally rethink its long-term national interests. Certainly, the North Korean leadership believes *juche* is important to its external relations to the extent it trumpets *juche* as the justification for virtually all of its actions.

Juche is first and foremost a *nationalist* ideology that has supplanted Marxism–Leninism over the years in North Korea. According to Bruce Cumings, *juche* as a distinct concept emerged soon after the Korean War, as Pyongyang distanced itself from Moscow, and then reappeared in its fully articulated form in the mid-1960s, as Pyongyang adopted a more equidistant and independent line of diplomacy between Moscow and Beijing.[27] However, as Cumings himself and others point out, the origins of nationalistic ideas contained in *juche* have deep roots in Korea's "Hermit Kingdom" past and humiliating colonization by the Japanese in the first half of the twentieth century.[28]

The antonym of *sadaejuui* (serving and relying upon foreign power—or "flunkyism," which South Korea is accused of), *juche* has become the core of North Korea's own brand of socialism, not just a rationale for its external policies. It defines a uniquely North Korean form of nationalistic socialism that strives to achieve independence and self-reliance in politics, economics, and security as well as ideology.

Indeed, it is crucial to understand that *juche* is the central ideology legitimizing the rule of the "Kim dynasty" in North Korea and its claim to the once and future unified Korea.[29] Hence, despite the strategic failure described above and attributable in great part to *juche*, the North Korean leadership cannot easily discard the ideology. In a way, it is trapped in a vicious cycle: as *juche*'s solipsistic nationalism clashes with interdependence and undermines

North Korea's strategic position, the leadership relies even more on *juche* as the basis of statecraft as well as a means of political control at home.

As it faces the "post–post–Cold War era," North Korea's predicament is clear. One analyst explains the quandary this way:

> To save the juche system requires the destruction of important parts of it, as well as considerable opening to, and help from, its bitter capitalist southern rival. And yet, to depart from the ideological continuity of the system . . . is viewed as an ultimate betrayal of *raison d'état*. North Korea's dilemma is that while economic interests push Pyongyang toward Seoul and Tokyo, political, security, and national identity concerns reinforce its ideological rigidity, militarism, and diplomatic isolation.[30]

If it is to survive in the long run, North Korea must somehow solve this dilemma.

NORTH KOREA IN THE "POST–POST–COLD WAR" NORTHEAST ASIA

Despite notable tactical achievements, the story of North Korea's external relations in the post–Cold War era has been one in which the nation has treaded water at best, barely keeping its head above the geopolitical currents of Northeast Asia. Considering the simple fact that North Korea still exists, when many well-informed analysts predicted its quick demise after the strategic transformation of the region following the fall of the Berlin Wall, Pyongyang's unique diplomacy has been a success. However, unwilling or unable to abandon or transform its *juche* identity and hence trapped in a zero-sum security dilemma of its own making, North Korea's accomplishments have come at an enormous price. The consequences have been famine and the lingering threat of war on the Korean peninsula. Will North Korea fare any better in the "post–post–Cold War" era? How will North Korea cope with new challenges stemming from the events of September 11, 2001, particularly the new priorities of the United States, now waging a global war against terrorism?

Stunned and outraged by terrorist attacks on its economic and political nerve centers, the United States, the military and economic colossus of the world, has been jolted into action and is reassessing its interests and rewriting its foreign policy agenda. The entire world system is being affected by the tremors emanating from the United States. And at first glance, it seems that North Korea could once again end up on the losing side of history. Still branded as a nation that supports terrorism and proliferates WMD, North Korea, unwilling or unable to rethink *juche*, seems likely to appear soon on Washington's "to do list."

However, it is more probable that North Korea will face a preoccupied or accommodating United States as the war on terrorism unfolds. North Korea may very well find new breathing space to carry on as it has or to rethink its national interests and identity to launch its own version of the "Chinese solution."

In fact, as the United States is trying to stabilize Afghanistan and Iraq after successful military operations, thus far the Bush administration has given no indication that North Korea is next on the list. Rather, its officials responsible for East Asian affairs continue to indicate their interest in resuming the administration's own hawkish version of the strategy of engagement with North Korea initiated by the Clinton administration.[31] The lack of progress in North Korea–U.S. bilateral relations, as well as in inter-Korean talks, appears to be more an indication of North Korea's indecision, temporization, and hard-to-get strategy than some fundamental transformation of strategy on the part of the Bush administration.

Even with the renewed crisis associated with the unraveling of the Agreed Framework, the United States, distracted by pressing problems in the Middle East and Central Asia, may well treat North Korea with kid gloves. With military and diplomatic resources needed in other parts of the world, Washington's preferred course would be to continue the engagement policy and to preserve the status quo in Northeast Asia. Indeed, if the United States wants to preserve the current coalition against terrorism, it makes sense that Washington should show restraint in dealing with Pyongyang. Restraint would signal to Seoul, Tokyo, Beijing, and Moscow (though to varying degrees, all ambivalent about America's global power) that Washington is a responsible hegemon.

If North Korea does get some breathing room, it may choose to carry on its hardball tactics to obtain more economic and political benefits. Or, there is a possibility that North Korea could use this window of opportunity to reflect on its course and to actually transform its relationship with the United States and others in the region. If it gives up its nuclear ambition, engages in serious tension-reduction measures, and carries out economic reforms, North Korea could find itself gratefully received by its neighbors who see economic growth and development as their top national priorities.

What will North Korea do? Time will tell, but the stability and order in Northeast Asia will depend not only on what North Korea chooses to do or not to do tactically but also on how North Korea reconciles its identity with the region.

NOTES

1. On the concept of national "identity" in international relations, see Peter J. Katzenstein, "Introduction: Alternative Perspectives on National Security," in *The Culture of National Security: Norms and Identity in World Politics*, ed. Peter J. Katzenstein (New York: Columbia University Press, 1996), 1–32.

2. Samuel Kim defines "globalization" as a complex process that is intensifying the levels of interaction and interconnectedness within and between states and societies. It is a multidimensional process that involves the intensification of economic, political, social, and cultural interconnectedness around the globe.

3. South Korea's globalization has not been an unmitigated success. See Samuel S. Kim, ed., *Korea's Globalization* (Cambridge: Cambridge University Press, 2000).

4. North Korea's relations with China tended to be warmer and closer than its ties with the Soviet Union, with the exception of strains during China's Cultural Revolution.

5. On the inter-Korean rivalry for legitimacy, see B. K. Gills, *Korea versus Korea: A Case of Contested Legitimacy* (London: Routledge, 1996).

6. Russia was still willing to sell arms to North Korea, but it wanted to be paid in cash.

7. For a thorough assessment of North Korea's external economic relations, see Marcus Noland, "North Korea's External Economic Relations: Globalization in Our Own Style?" in *North Korea and Northeast Asia*, ed. Samuel S. Kim (Lanham, Md.: Rowman & Littlefield, 2002), 165–93.

8. Since North Korea does not publish trade data, assessing the level and content of North Korean trade is difficult. For example, even "mirror statistics" reported by North Korea's trading partners do not include barter or countertrade transactions. Data provided by South Korea's Korea Trade Promotion Corporation (KOTRA) provides a rough guide. See www.kotra.or.kr/main/info/nk/eng/main.php3.

9. A compelling account and analysis of the North Korean famine is found in Andrew S. Natsios, *The Great North Korean Famine* (Washington, D.C.: United States Institute of Peace, 2001).

10. Foreword by Richard H. Solomon in Natsios, *Great North Korean Famine*, ix.

11. Bank of Korea.

12. Namely, Ronald Reagan's "modest initiative" to start a dialogue with North Korea, a process that George H. W. Bush continued during his presidency.

13. Prime Minister Kaifu Toshiki, guided by Kanemaru Shin, began talks between Japan and North Korea in early 1991.

14. The term is attributed to Marcus Noland.

15. Analyses of North Korea's negotiating tactics are found in Chuck Downs, *Over the Line: North Korea's Negotiating Strategy* (Washington, D.C.: AEI, 1999); and Scott Snyder, *Negotiating on the Edge* (Washington, D.C.: United States Institute of Peace, 1999).

16. For a thorough, if controversial, account of U.S.–North Korea nuclear diplomacy, see Leon V. Sigal, *Disarming Strangers: Nuclear Diplomacy with North Korea* (Princeton, N.J.: Princeton University Press, 1998). See also Don Oberdorfer, *The Two Koreas: A Contemporary History* (New York: Basic, 1997), 326–36.

17. Both Iran's Shahab-3 rocket and Pakistan's Ghauri missile, the latter designed to deliver Pakistan's newly developed nuclear warheads, appear to be copies of a North Korean prototype. See "Rockets Overhead," *Economist*, July 31, 1999.

18. See Joel Wit, "The United States and North Korea," Brookings Policy Brief no. 74 (Washington, D.C.: Brookings Institution, March 2001), 6.

19. Michael R. Gordon, "How Politics Sank Accord on Missiles with North Korea," *New York Times*, March 6, 2001.

20. Author interviews with former Clinton administration officials, Washington, D.C., March 2001.

21. Certainly, compared to its predecessor's, the Bush administration's rhetoric toward North Korea has been tougher, even before the events of September 11, 2001. For example, during his confirmation hearing, Colin Powell indicated that the administration would seek strict reciprocity from North Korea. And in spring 2001, the Bush administration's tough attitude led to a sour first summit meeting between President Bush and President Kim Dae Jung, clinging to his sunshine policy despite the lack of reciprocity from his North Korean counterpart.

22. And, at least publicly, the phrase "axis of evil" never crossed President Bush's lips during that visit. According to Secretary of State Colin Powell, the term did not come up even during the private meeting between President Bush and President Kim, and "there was a compete understanding of our support for the engagement policy and the mutual understanding of the nature" of North Korea. Quoted by Elisabeth Bumiller, "Bush Uses Trip for Damage Control," *New York Times*, February 24, 2002.

23. See Katzenstein, "Introduction."

24. See David Kang, "North Korea: Deterrence through Danger," in *Asian Security Practice: Material and Ideational Influences*, ed. Muthiah Alagappa (Stanford, Calif.: Stanford University Press, 1998), 234–63.

25. For that matter, neorealism does not explain the choices of Germany or Japan. If states in fact balance power and operate by the worst-case assumption undergirding neorealism, as Kenneth Waltz and John Mearsheimer predict, Japan and Germany should be rearming to their full potential and acquiring nuclear weapons to balance the United States, the sole military superpower in the current world system. See Kenneth N. Waltz, "The Emerging Structure of International Politics," *International Security* 18, no. 2 (Fall 1993): 44–79; John Mearsheimer, "Back to the Future: Instability in Europe after the Cold War," *International Security* 15, no. 1 (Summer 1990): 5–56.

26. Charles K. Armstrong, "A Socialism of Our Style: North Korea's Ideology in a Post-Communist Era," in *North Korean Foreign Relations in the Post–Cold War Era*, ed. Samuel S. Kim (Hong Kong: Oxford University Press, 1998), 34.

27. Bruce Cumings, *Korea's Place in the Sun: A Modern History* (New York: Norton, 1998), 403.

28. For example, Kongdan Oh and Ralph C. Hassig, *North Korea through the Looking Glass* (Washington, D.C.: Brookings Institution, 2000), 148–50.

29. To be sure, a proper appreciation of *juche* does not readily facilitate an understanding of how North Korea's identity interacts with interest to form strategy. Indeed, operationalizing the concept of national identity and analyzing it in conjunction with national interests for any country is a difficult task, as those pursuing a "constructivist" approach to understanding international relations are finding out. On "constructivism," see the pioneering work of Alexander Wendt, "Anarchy Is What States Make of It: The Social Construction of Power Politics," *International Organization* 46, no. 2 (Spring 1992): 391–425. See also Jeffrey T. Checkel, "The Constructivist Turn in International Relations

Theory," *World Politics* 50, no. 2 (January 1998): 324–48; and Ted Hopf, "The Promise of Constructivism in International Relations Theory," *International Security* 23, no. 1 (Summer 1998): 171–200.

30. Samuel S. Kim, "In Search of a Theory of North Korean Foreign Policy," in *North Korean Foreign Relations in the Post–Cold War Era*, ed. Samuel S. Kim (Oxford: Oxford University Press, 1998), 15.

31. Author interview with a senior Bush administration official, Washington, D.C., June 2002.

FURTHER READING

Cha, Victor D. "The Continuity Behind the Change in Korea." *Orbis* 44, no. 4 (Fall 2000): 585–98.

Cumings, Bruce. *Korea's Place in the Sun: A Modern History*. New York: Norton, 1998.

Downs, Chuck. *Over the Line: North Korea's Negotiating Strategy*. Washington, D.C.: AEI, 1999.

Eberstadt, Nicholas. *The End of North Korea*. Washington, D.C.: AEI, 1999.

Gills, B. K. *Korea versus Korea: A Case of Contested Legitimacy*. London: Routledge, 1996.

Kang, David. "North Korea: Deterrence through Danger." In *Asian Security Practice: Material and Ideational Influences*, edited by Muthiah Alagapa, 234–63. Stanford, Calif.: Stanford University Press, 1998.

Kim, Samuel S., ed. *North Korean Foreign Relations in the Post–Cold War Era*. Oxford: Oxford University Press, 1998.

Natsios, Andrew S. *The Great North Korean Famine*. Washington, D.C.: United States Institute of Peace, 2001.

Noland, Marcus. "Why North Korea Will Muddle Through." *Foreign Affairs* 76, no. 4 (July–August 1997): 105–18.

Oberdorfer, Don. *The Two Koreas: A Contemporary History*. New York: Basic, 1997.

Oh, Kongdan, and Ralph C. Hassig. *North Korea through the Looking Glass*. Washington, D.C.: Brookings Institution, 2000.

Park, Kyung-Ae. "North Korea's Defensive Power and the U.S.–North Korea Relations." *Pacific Affairs* 73, no. 4 (Winter 2000): 535–53.

———. "The Pattern of North Korea's Track-Two Foreign Contacts." *North Pacific Policy Paper* 5. Program on Canada–Asia Policy Studies: Institute of Asian Research, University of British Columbia, 2000.

Roy, Denny. "North Korea as an Alienated State." *Survival* 38, no. 4 (Winter 1996–1997): 22–36.

Sigal, Leon V. *Disarming Strangers: Nuclear Diplomacy with North Korea*. Princeton, N.J.: Princeton University Press, 1998.

Smith, Hazel. "Bad, Mad, Sad or Rational Actor? Why the 'Securitization' Paradigm Makes for Poor Policy Analysis of North Korea." *International Affairs* 76, no. 3 (2000): 593–617.

Snyder, Scott. *Negotiating on the Edge*. Washington, D.C.: United States Institute of Peace, 1999.

10

Taiwan's External Relations: Identity versus Security

Lynn T. White III

Taiwan, with 23 million people, is the largest state on earth not recognized by any major external power. The island's government has diplomatic relations (as the Republic of China, ROC) with twenty-six small countries in Central America, the Caribbean, Africa, Oceania, and Paraguay, as well as with the Vatican. So in a legalistic sense, this chapter's topic scarcely exists. But the story does not end there.

According to international law, Taiwan is arguably a state because it has four traits of statehood (people, territory, a government, and practical independence).[1] Many countries recognize Taiwan as a nonstate for economic and cultural purposes. They do not accord diplomatic recognition because the island is claimed by the People's Republic of China (PRC), which is the world's most populous country and fastest-growing large market. The PRC explicitly threatens war against Taiwan in the future if its claim continues to go unmet—even though America would now clearly come to Taiwan's defense unless the island's politicians take actions that provoke cross-strait conflict. The Taiwan Strait and the North–South border in Korea are the two most dangerous flashpoints of potential war in Northeast Asia.

Most states have "international" relations. To say that Taiwan has these would be to answer by premise the main issue about its external links: Is this island a separate nation, or is it part of China? Opposite answers to that question are maintained, with great existential and political passion, by many

Chinese and many Taiwanese. PRC elites seem almost unanimously to claim the island. They are not so uniform in demanding immediate implementation of that claim, presumably because they sense the U.S. Navy would defend Taiwan's democracy if an attack came from a still-authoritarian PRC.

Taiwan elites seem almost unanimously to recognize both a long-term security threat from the mainland and also their own cultural identity as Chinese. They have no consensus on whether this cultural link implies anything political. Surveys and elections suggest that a majority of the islanders acknowledge that their option to be Chinese might eventually have some governmental meaning, whether they unabashedly look forward to that time or not. This majority has declined in recent years, however. Concerns about long-term security tend to sustain it. Practically no one on Taiwan wants administrative unification with the PRC so long as China remains Leninist. Taiwanese like to observe that the PRC economy has a much lower per capita income than the islanders now enjoy. The island's businesses, however, profit from hiring at low wages in their mainland factories.

Just two external powers, the PRC and the United States, are crucially important to Taiwan. Neither of these is solely Northeast Asian, although Taiwan's links with them affect relations with Japan, Russia, and Korea. Neither formally recognizes the Taipei government. If Taipei declares non-Chinese independence, Washington suggests it might not help defend the island—and Beijing promises to attack.

In May 2002, Deputy Defense Secretary Paul Wolfowitz, famous as a hawk in the Bush administration, declared in public that, "We're opposed to Taiwan independence."[2] American officials had often said this privately in both Taipei and Beijing. Their public stance, however, had been "no support" for Taiwan independence, rather than outright opposition to it. The change to a seemingly more pro-PRC position came when Washington arms dealers close to Wolfowitz were discussing major sales to improve Taiwan's security—which is actually endangered. Tensions over weapons hawking may have been reduced by Wolfowitz's declaration.

There are apparently no historical precedents for a country that is vitally defended, over a long period, by another that does not recognize its government and that vaguely acknowledges some eventual claim by the regime threatening it. Nowhere else has such an arrangement ever existed. How did this extremely odd set of external relations develop?

OVERVIEW OF TAIWAN'S PRE-1945 HISTORY

The Dutch came to Taiwan in 1620, when they had more oceangoing ships than any other nation. Fewer than a fifth of the island's approximately

150,000 people were then Chinese. The rest were "Austronesians," that is, ancestors of the current fiftieth of the islanders still called "aborigines" and speaking languages related to Tagalog and Malay–Indonesian. Taiwan, as evidence now shows, was the origin of all Austronesians. Southward boat migrants in the first two millennia B.C. populated Southeast Asia (and some later went as far as Hawaii, Easter Island, and Madagascar, creating through navigation one of the world's most widespread language families).[3] In 1620, few on the island were aware of this prehistory, although it may later find political uses when it becomes better known.

Even before 1500, South Chinese commercial lineages used bases on Taiwan for long-distance shipping that extended far into both Southeast and Northeast Asia. They brought increasing numbers of farmers to Taiwan from south Fujian (Minnan). These Chinese farmers gradually transformed the island's western plain into rice paddies, killing aboriginal slash-and-burn agriculturalists or pushing them toward Taiwan's central mountain range and into the graben valley that parallels the Pacific coast.[4] By 1662, a Minnan pirate king named Zheng Chenggong captured the Dutch fort at Zeelandia/Tainan and styled himself Guoxingye ("Lord of the Stately Surname").

Koxinga's career can be interpreted as either Chinese-unificationist or Southern-separatist. The PRC praises him for expelling the Dutch; a colossal statue of him now towers over the entrance to Xiamen harbor in Fujian. Yet he was certainly no cadre of any northern government. He was an atypical Chinese. His mother was Japanese. His father had been baptized a Catholic while working for the Portuguese in Macau (he later worked for the Spanish in Manila).[5] Autonomous-minded Taiwanese, no less than PRC patriots, praise Koxinga as their forebear. He was a local trader-king who kept Taiwan independent from the (Manchu) Chinese government as long as he lived. The Qing navy was finally able to negotiate the capture of Taiwan in 1683—after Koxinga's death. Never before had the island's rulers been chosen by a central Chinese government.[6]

The Qing admiral who finally put Taiwan under Chinese rule also urged settlers to return to the "civilized" mainland, unless they already had a farm and family on the island. Until 1885, Taiwan was a prefecture of Fujian. The island became a province ten years before China ceded it to Japan in 1895, after losing the Sino–Japanese War. A historian describes the strong ancestral attachments that many Taiwanese retained to Fujian (more than to China generally), saying these "fostered xenophobic feelings [against Japanese colonialists] yet failed to produce an effective ideology of resistance." There was scant Chinese nationalism among Taiwanese before the twentieth century.[7] Under Japanese colonial rule from 1895 to 1945, Taiwan became more Northeast Asian. Few outside the island then paid any attention to it.[8]

Chinese patriots, including Sun Yat-sen and Mao Zedong, can be quoted to show they did not conceive Taiwan as a regular part of China during the Japanese period.[9] Some islanders who visited the mainland "passed" as Fujianese, while others enjoyed extraterritoriality as Japanese subjects. Some went to Chinese universities for education; others (including later President Lee Teng-hui) went to Japan. Unlike other Japanese colonies, Taiwan was mainly run by the Imperial Navy, whose admirals adopted somewhat more moderate policies than the Japanese army applied in Korea or Manchuria. The island's economy grew, as Taiwan exported sugar, bananas, and pineapples from Japanese-run plantations.[10] Colonial modernization exploited the Taiwanese, but it also built infrastructure.

In 1945, the Taiwanese found themselves part of a defeated empire. Many were at first pleased to have new rulers who spoke a Chinese language. Chiang Kai-shek's troops accepted the surrender of Japanese forces on Taiwan, as agreed at Cairo in 1943. Chiang, who had no inkling how important Taiwan would become in his future, dispatched a truly third-rate leadership, headed by a governor whom his own Kuomintang (KMT) later executed for corruption. Tensions with Taiwanese reached a climax on February 28, 1947, when KMT troops fired on an unarmed crowd in Taipei. The government's need for islander-mainlander reconciliation set the island's course for decades thereafter.

POLITICAL AND SECURITY DIMENSIONS OF TAIWAN'S EXTERNAL LINKS

By October 1, 1949, when the PRC was founded in Beijing, most observers thought it would soon include Taiwan. An outbreak of parasitic schistosomiasis among People's Liberation Army troops in Fujian and Zhejiang delayed the PRC invasion of Taiwan. As Secretary of State Dean Acheson noted, however, "the unfortunate but inescapable fact [is that] the civil war in China is beyond the control of the government of the United States."[11] He suggested America would not defend Taiwan. This policy was reversed in June 1950, when North Korea's Kim Il Sung (after consulting Stalin and Mao) tried to unify his country by invading South Korea. President Truman sent the U.S. Seventh Fleet into the Taiwan Strait.

America became Taiwan's military protector. This relationship began not just because America had been allied with Chiang Kai-shek, but also because U.S. leaders saw a strategic interest in mobilizing against communism and a "useful adversary" in Mao's China.[12] In 1954, Washington and Taipei signed a Mutual Security Treaty. The PRC often probed the solidity of this alliance, especially in 1958, when it threatened the ROC-held island of Jinmen (Quemoy). The Sino–Soviet split and American losses in the Vietnam War—external events with which Taiwan had practically nothing to do—in 1972 led President Richard Nixon to visit Beijing. This development, caused by a restructuring of U.S. interests, led to a sharp reduction in Taiwan's diplomatic relations, as the PRC took China's seat in the Security Council.

U.S. Derecognition

At the end of 1978, President Carter abrogated the U.S.–ROC defense treaty, invoking one of its clauses. This was in response to a PRC demand before U.S. diplomatic relations could be forged with Beijing. It was a shock to Taiwan.[13] American lawyers found limber language to suggest simultaneously that the United States has an eventual "one China" policy and to allow legalistic justifications in case the United States ever needs to defend the island against the nation waveringly said to own it. (This required differing connotations in the English and Chinese texts of U.S.–PRC communiqués, a brief that mere presidential statements are not ratified treaties binding under American law, and a lack of U.S. explicitness about sovereignty on Taiwan as distinct from the Chinese view of that.)[14] In 1979, Congress passed the Taiwan Relations Act. This is a domestic law under which the president is supposed to help defend Taiwan. The United States has no troops there, however, and America authorizes an officially unofficial agency, rather than a diplomatic embassy, to maintain contact.

U.S.–Taiwan links were nonetheless informally restrengthened as the island's government became more democratic from 1986 (when the main opposition party was legalized) to 1996 (when Taiwan became the first Chinese state to choose its chief executive by direct competitive election). The island has been a place for Americans to do business. By 2000, it had a per capita GDP of $17,500, the seventh-largest total trade with the United States, and a vibrant democracy.[15] Taiwan is by far the most important place in the world without a UN seat or an American embassy. It also has no diplomatic relations with any of its Northeast Asian neighbors.

Taiwan has informal ties, especially for trade and investment, with many countries. These are dependent (as the security and economy of Taiwan are dependent) on the island's main links, which are to China and to America. None of the ROC's formal embassies has any direct security value. Taipei's allies in Funafuti, N'Djamena, and Santo Domingo scarcely protect the island.[16]

Not even its informal connections with Tokyo and Seoul do so. Recalling Taiwan's time as a colony, Japan's conservatives in the Liberal Democratic

Party have an open political affection for Taiwan. Many Taiwanese reciprocate. Their island is surely the most pro-Japanese place elsewhere in Asia. Nonetheless, Japan does not (and under its antiwar constitution still may not) play any direct role in protecting Taiwan. American sailors largely do that, and some of them are normally stationed at U.S. bases in Japan. America will almost surely continue to perform this defensive role because Taiwan is a democracy, until the PRC leaders stop ruling their country as a "dictatorship" (albeit no longer credibly "of the proletariat"). The ROC's most important external relations, by far, are with the PRC and the United States. Just one of these two is in Northeast Asia.

Beijing Overtures to Taipei

By October 10, 1981, Hu Yaobang, the surprisingly reformist head of the Chinese Communist Party (CCP), gave a speech inviting KMT leaders to "return to the mainland" for visits. This invitation, sent to then-President Chiang Ching-kuo and a dozen other prominent Nationalists, was immediately rejected from Taipei.[17] The CCP elite sensed that as the KMT authoritarians died, China was losing touch with Taiwan's leaders.

President Jiang Zemin nonetheless described unification with Taiwan as "our dignified wish, an extremely important and holy mission."[18] Patriotic existentialists in Beijing have become more and more frustrated in recent years. PRC leaders seem not to have considered the possibility that a younger generation of leaders in Taipei might begin to face Taiwan's economic opportunities and long-term security problems by negotiating with Beijing while refusing to subsume their Taiwanese identity entirely within their option to be Chinese, or that many on Taiwan might not mind being Chinese under more liberal conditions than Beijing totalists, as distinct from Beijing liberals, could guarantee.

Taiwanese and Chinese Identities and Contexts

Surveys in 1992, 1996, and 1998 asked the following two questions to separate the normative and situational bases of political identity on Taiwan: (1) "Some people think that *if* Taiwan after independence could maintain a peaceful relationship with the Chinese Communist government, then Taiwan should become an independent country—do you agree? and (2) "Some people favor the idea that *if* Taiwan and China were to become comparably developed in economic, social, and political terms, then the two sides of the strait should be united—do you agree?"

Responses from individuals could be cross-tabulated. A plurality of respondents (27 percent in 1992, 39 percent in 1996, 36 percent in 1998) claimed a vapidly nonexistentialist national identity, favoring Chinese unification after cross-strait disparities were lessened *but also* favoring Taiwan independence if this could be safe. Intellectuals, diplomats, and politicians usually find such part-time patriotism (for either China or Taiwan) logically absurd. These elites clearly care more about nationality than most people do. Modal mass opinion on Taiwan, however, does not see a problem with part-time patriotism. Everyone, in practice, has multiple identities.

Independence sentiment rose somewhat in the 1990s: an increasing minority of respondents (one-tenth in 1992, 21 percent in 1996, and 22 percent in 1998) both opposed unification even after future PRC liberalization *and* favored Taiwan independence if the island could then avoid war with the mainland. A decreasing portion of respondents (41 percent in 1992 and 17 percent in both 1996 and 1998) both favored unification after PRC political change *and* opposed Taiwan independence even if the island could then remain safe.[19] The central and most common recent view is to prefer concrete benefits over abstract identity symbols of either kind.

KMT versus DPP Politics

Democratization made Taiwan more island-nationalistic. A Taiwanese, Lee Teng-hui, succeeded to the presidency in 1988 and engineered the resignation of the most important mainlander general politician, Hau Pei-tsun.[20] In the early 1990s, he postponed Beijing objections to his policies by having envoys confer with PRC representatives secretly in Hong Kong and openly in Singapore.[21] As the Democratic Progressive Party (DPP) raised localist demands, Lee could use this opposition to defeat non-Taiwanese rivals within the KMT. In 1993, when he launched the ROC's bid to reenter the UN, he claimed that "international backing" for this result could be solidified within three years.[22] He opened more elections to direct voting and changed the legislature to give Taiwanese more power. He won the first-ever direct election of a Chinese president as the KMT candidate in 1996, and the DPP's Chen Shui-bian was elected with Lee's tacit support in 2000.

Lee addressed Taiwanese identity issues that DPP autonomists had originally raised, especially their calls for a "new nation" and an amended constitution.[23] Lee officially mourned the 1947 KMT killings of Taiwanese. The DPP could no longer use many of its original issues to distinguish itself in electoral campaigns. It switched to a more forthcoming policy on exchanges with the mainland.[24] By 2002, President Chen Shui-bian had become less openly island-nationalist than ex-President Lee, who remained active in politics as chair of a new party, the Taiwan Solidarity Union, which generally cooperated with the DPP against both the KMT and the People First Party, headed by another ex-KMT leader, James Soong Chu-yu.

Cross-Strait Nondiplomacy

Taipei–Beijing governmental links have never existed, even though ROC and PRC cabinet ministers have ventured across the water.[25] Most contacts have been through two unofficial foundations, the mainland's Association for Relations across the Taiwan Strait (ARATS, or *Haixiehui*) and the island's Straits Exchange Foundation (SEF, or *Haijihui*). PRC spokespeople have referred to "the Taiwan authorities" and aver that (on a "one China" premise they have defined variously) the "two shores" might negotiate. Shores, however, are taciturn. Hard-liners on both sides of the strait have tended to assume that political negotiations should be between governments. That stance has prevented political talks from starting.

Taipei will not come merely as a "local government," although it no longer claims control of the mainland. If talks are official, Beijing usually insists on coming as a "central government." Vacuous symbols of stately dignity stymie substantive negotiations that could reduce the chance of war—and cross-strait peace is now the main interest of Taiwan's other main external relation, the United States, as well as of Japan and South Korea.

A National Development Conference that Lee Teng-hui convened in 1996 passed a consensus resolution among Taiwan parties that specified how future China policy would be made: "The government should strengthen the mechanisms by which opposition political parties . . . can fully participate in major policy decisions regarding relations with the Chinese mainland."[26] This allows any ROC president to speculate about terms for a Chinese amalgamation, while winking assurances to fellow islanders that no cross-strait agreement will be made. At least one of Taiwan's parties would surely blackball any text that China would sign. So cross-strait talks never become serious. Militarists in Beijing and permanent autonomists in Taipei have claimed vetoes over what their governments do.

Lee's 1999 Statement

President Lee on July 10, 1999, gave an interview with the Voice of Germany, saying the cross-strait link was a "special state-to-state relationship." He expressed doubts about the usefulness of the "one China" concept, which most mainland spokespeople construed as the current PRC position. Lee clearly thought the reactions to his idea in Taiwan, Washington, and Beijing would redound to his own benefit.[27] From Beijing, the State Council and

CCP Central Committee jointly declared that "Lee's remarks . . . reveal the true political nature of his consistent efforts to split Chinese sovereign territory and separate Taiwan."[28]

Can Beijing politicians speak to Taiwanese about a confederal constitution, rather than a unitary one? ARATS chief Wang Daohan, while criticizing Lee's remarks about the "special state-to-state relationship," went further than his colleagues and asked for clarification.[29] If "special" were special enough, Lee's view could be consistent with the "one China" that Taiwan for its own security and trade might have reason to accept. Lee did not emphasize that possibility, but China will not soon disappear either as a positive concern of some Taiwanese or as a security threat to all the islanders.

The Façade of Diplomacy

The ARATS and SEF chiefs, Wang and Koo, held talks in 1993 and 1998, but the state leaders on each side were disinclined either to stop the cross-strait dialogue formally or to make the compromises needed for a security agreement. China's development was annually increasing Beijing's eventual military strength. Taipei's leaders could not afford to be perceived by voters as potential "traitors to Taiwan" (*Tai jian*). As a Western diplomat put it, referring to the island side, "These talks are a way for Taiwan to kick the can down the road and hope that something will come up to resolve the issue. Nobody there has got a solution yet."[30] The most specific plans from Beijing leaders were threats of war against people they called Chinese. A bureaucratic optimist averred the talks had brought "each side a notch back from a potential future war," but rivals often negotiate before they fight.[31]

Six retired ROC generals and Legislative Yuan members from both the DPP and KMT met with high-ranking Chinese military officers during June 2002 in Beijing. The nominal topic of discussion was "the development of Chinese naval power since the Sino–Japanese War of 1894," but "the two sides spent much time talking about cooperation between their militaries." The conclave, whose discussions were confidential, was sponsored by Taiwan's Asia–Pacific Security Research Foundation and the Chinese army's Peace and Development Research Center. Taiwan's Mainland Affairs Council provided funding.[32] Conversations in Beijing were not, however, the island planners' main deterrence strategy.

Washington was scheduled in the autumn of 2002 to host Taiwan's vice defense minister Kang Ning-hsiang for "defense-review talks with U.S. military officials." The purpose of these talks was arms sales. Defense Minister Tang Yao-ming had come to a meeting in Florida in March 2002, but trips to the U.S. capital are seen as more sensitive in Taipei and Beijing.[33] The substance of the talks (arms sales) might be deemed more important than where they are held.

China's missile buildup in Fujian gave American weapons sellers an understandable reason for expecting more business. A July 2002 Pentagon report noted that the Chinese army had "an increasing number of credible options to intimidate or actually attack Taiwan." Chinese foreign ministry spokesman Kong Quan countered with a claim that China's military "budget is the lowest among the world's major countries." A Chinese Academy of Social Sciences analyst, Hong Yuan, said the Pentagon report was "a pretext [for the United States] to sell advanced weapons to Taiwan, which is a reflection of the interests of the American military-industrial establishment."[34] This analysis is cogent. So is a widely held American view that the military elements of China's "fundamental policy of peaceful reunification" will require at least a decade or two of further deterrence, until the PRC modernizes politically. That is the event to make America stand down from the cross-strait dispute.

Taiwan's Relations Post-9/11 and in the Context of Other Countries

Although the U.S. counterterrorism effort since September 11, 2001, has not mainly involved Northeast Asia, key players in the region have nevertheless felt its effects in ways that have long-term implications. In the wake of the attacks on New York, U.S. security relationships with Taiwan, China, Japan, and especially North Korea continue to evolve because former American hopes of immunity from foreign conflicts have been discredited. Though Northeast Asia is peripheral to the core counterterrorism campaign in Central and Southwest Asia, Washington manages its relations with Beijing and Taipei, as with Pyongyang and Seoul, to keep them from diverting attention from the war on terrorism.[35] America's Far East policies have been shown, after 9/11, to be more sustainable than its extremely shaky Near East policies. The U.S. militancy that has risen since 2001 has thus far made fewer long-term enemies for America in either China or Taiwan than it has in the Near East and among the world's billion Muslims.

The Taiwan government's concerns, now that its diplomacy must be mostly unofficial, have centered on the United States and China—and on countering PRC restrictions in third countries. In July 2002, the secretary general of Taiwan's National Security Council (NSC) said the island's diplomats should put more resources into "offensive" instead of "defensive" strategies for expanding the country's foreign relations. China, hosting the 2001 Asia Pacific Economic Cooperation (APEC) summit in Shanghai, had refused to admit the ROC's choice for its own chief delegate. The NSC official said that, "If we at the time had managed to ignite continuous fire [diplomatic efforts] elsewhere, Beijing would not have had time to foul us in APEC." Taiwan had recently strengthened its economic ties in Mongolia and had persuaded the European Parliament to pass pro-Taiwan resolutions. In May 2002, however, China again prevented Taiwan's entry into the World Health Organization.[36] Quasi-diplomatic hostilities between the ROC and the PRC have been constant and have received more attention in Taipei and Beijing than in the third-country locales where they are fought.[37]

From Taiwan's viewpoint, a combination of justified pride in the island's accomplishments and unnecessary fear about Washington's commitment to protecting democracy underlies the policies of Taiwan's largest political groups, whether DPP, KMT, or ex-KMT. These policies are not yet well adapted to protect the island in dangerous times when a PRC leadership could attempt military action—or to benefit from later times, when Beijing politics may become less monocratic and Washington may conceive more hope in the chance of Chinese democracy.

ECONOMIC DIMENSIONS OF TAIWAN'S EXTERNAL LINKS

PRC exports to the United States are a major basis for ROC prosperity. Seven-tenths of all goods made in Taiwan-owned mainland factories are eventually sold in the United States. Most of the remaining three-tenths go to other democracies. Taiwan provides capital and managers; PRC workers make the products; America is the market. Toys, shoes, sports equipment, clothes, and electronic goods have been important in this trade, whose entrepreneurs want to expand into higher-technology fields.[38]

These ROC–PRC–U.S. economic links are not just important; they are *increasingly* so, especially for the island. Taiwan officials have begun to moot a free-trade zone with the United States. China thus warned other countries in July 2002 not to sign free-trade agreements with Taiwan, since "doing so would invite political trouble." For their part, the Taiwanese said they wanted to sign free-trade pacts with Japan, the United States, and Singapore.[39] A Taipei newspaper dubbed the establishment of such a zone with America "politically crucial."[40] Yet this change, if it occurs, would ensure nothing strategically and would concern just one side of the triangle that now sustains Taiwan economically.

Taiwan's trade surplus with the mainland has been extraordinarily profitable. The total surplus between 1995 and 2001 was U.S.$109 billion. During that period, the surplus alone was two-thirds (67 percent) of the entire value of cross-strait trade.[41] China absorbs 10 percent of Taiwan's trade (the other countries of Northeast Asia account for about 17 percent and the United States for 23 percent).[42] The PRC has been the island's second-largest external market; but more important is its role as a provider of trade surplus. Taiwan's own largest market has been the United States, but ROC firms manage more American trade from the mainland than from their island. In the 1990s, Japan and the United States each accounted for roughly one-quarter of the island's incoming foreign direct investment (FDI),[43] taking advantage of opportunities for external parties to participate in Taiwan entrepreneurs' prosperous China trade.

Fully 75 percent of Taiwan companies that had external investments anywhere else at the end of 2001 also did business on the mainland. An additional 9 percent (making 84 percent of the total) ran their China operations through Hong Kong (although some who did so may not have fully reported their involvement in this trade, so that the actual figure was higher).[44] So Taiwan's global firms were substantially identical with its China firms.

Political Preconditions for Profits

Taiwan's fractured politics and famous entrepreneurialism have goaded each other forward. As long ago as the 1950s, Chiang's KMT used land reform and industrial privatization to build the political constituencies that mainlanders sorely needed among the 86 percent Taiwanese islander majority.[45] Market-liberal politics, which were merely encouraged by the U.S. protector but politically required by the KMT's mainlander minority status at that time, created Taiwan's "economic miracle." The common wisdom about Chiang Kai-shek's perceived legitimacy is that it depended on Chinese nationalism, but this view downplays both ethnic and economic factors.[46]

For a long time, high posts in Chiang's government, army, and police were controlled by mainlanders, but ambitious youths from Taiwanese communities could, and did, start businesses.[47] As local wealth trickled up into island-wide politics, Taiwan's new plutocrats also affected the island's policy toward the mainland because they could put their money into exploiting inexpensive Chinese labor and large democratic markets to make huge profits for themselves.

Careful study of the links between Taiwan's businesses and state shows they are intertwined. The pattern is more corporatist than ideologically capitalist or pluralist, so that companies have influence over the government. Officials listen to business people and vice-versa.[48]

Economically, Taiwan's PRC portfolio is not risky. Politically, the risk is high. If a cross-strait war broke out, Taiwanese investors could be asked to support the Chinese side or lose their capital. In compensation, Taiwan CEOs try to demand sweet deals in China—and they credibly threaten to invest elsewhere, more often in Southeast than Northeast Asia. Acer Computers, for example, established a large factory in Zhongshan, Guangdong, only after building plants in the Philippines. Acer's president in 1999 told reporters, "To be frank, we still don't think China's market is fair to foreign [Taiwanese?] players. I've told the Chinese that I won't put all my eggs in one basket and that if I can't get the right treatment, I'll withdraw. . . . I still don't know what our tax liabilities will be on the mainland."[49]

Wages at Taiwan enterprises on the mainland were one-tenth of those on the island in the 1990s. ROC government restrictions did prevent some investments, for example, a plan by Formosa Plastics to build a thermal power plant in Fujian. A legislator said the cross-strait capital flow was "like a car going 140 miles-per-hour; if you take away government restrictions, it will go even faster." Another legislator pointed out that investors could be badly hurt if the PRC decided to use force against Taiwan: "They will lose their pants. They'll come home naked."[50]

Risky ventures also rationalized ruthless labor discipline on the mainland, where methods were adopted straight from military boot-camp manuals. Sociologist Anita Chan, who visited Taiwan-owned shoe factories in Dongguan, Guangdong, asked: "What prompts the chairman of the Taiwanese Business Association in Dongguan to order his security guards to salute and snap to attention every time he passes through the factory gate? Not Confucian beliefs, but a hankering for modern army standards of discipline and unquestioning loyalty." Taiwan managers opined that more operations should be moved to Vietnam, where labor costs were even lower than China's 25 U.S. cents per hour. "'The factory management is precise down to the minute,' explained a worker. . . . 'When they get to the canteen, they sit eight to a table and wait. Only when the bell rings can they begin to eat. We have 10 to 15 minutes to finish the meal, then we file downstairs again.'"[51] Dickensian development allowed Taiwan's mainland firms to prosper, so long as they could sell in democracies.

External Economic Accounting Uncertainties

PRC estimates of total Taiwan investment on the mainland have been twice the ROC estimates.[52] The amount is now surely more than $80 billion. Taiwan's own officials say their published figures are too low. Cheyne Chiu, who headed the mid-1990s ROC trade office in Singapore, admitted, "According to our Economics Ministry, about 11,000 [Taiwan firms had capital in the mainland] with total investment value of US$5 billion to US$6 billion. But this figure is probably not accurate."[53]

By no means did Taiwan entrepreneurs put all their trade and investment on the mainland, but the underreporting of amounts there (largely because of company registrations at places ranging from Hong Kong to Panama) casts doubt also on the completeness of other statistics. According to ROC officials, Hong Kong/China, the United States, and Japan are Taiwan's major external buyers. With the United States, the island reports some surplus. To Japan, however, the Taiwanese can export only about a third as much as they want to buy. Trade with Europe and Southeast Asia is more balanced and smaller.[54]

Taiwan's investment on the mainland is the basis for many other external transactions. Capital by no means goes only to Fujian; amounts in Jiangsu and Guangdong are even larger.[55] PRC 1998 data suggest that direct investment from Taiwan was then U.S.$37 billion, mostly in manufacturing, with more filtered indirectly through Hong Kong and Southeast Asian companies. The pace has slowed during missile crises and financial crises, but Taiwan entrepreneurs go wherever profit can be made.[56] By the turn of the millennium, the ROC's mainland portfolio had doubled in value.

Increasingly, ROC firms' mainland-made products did not have to be sold outside China. Taiwan's Ting Yi (Cayman Islands) Holdings by 2001 had fourteen mainland factories producing "Master Kang" brand snacks that captured 39 percent of China's instant noodle market.[57] That is a lot of noodles.

U.S. economist Laura Tyson thought Baring's prediction that Taiwan would have the world's fourth-largest economy by 2010 (after the United States, Japan, and China) was excessive, but she wrote that "Taiwan's economic importance will rise significantly in coming years and most of that growth will come from outside—chiefly China."[58] An American reporter expected that, "Investments and trade . . . promise to turn Taiwan, like Hong Kong, into a goose that lays golden eggs for the mainland. That would provide Taiwan with new protection against 'reunification' ambitions in Beijing."[59]

Opposite results were also possible, however. After the chairman of Taiwan's Chi Mei Petrochemicals supported Chen Shui-bian's election, that company's six PRC factories were reportedly harassed by "tax, customs, environment, and labour inspections."[60] Taiwan business tycoons such as Evergreen head Y. F. Chang have openly criticized ROC government slowness to arrange direct trade links with China.[61] Chen Shui-bian has often mooted change in this policy, but distrust stymies most kinds of legal direct trade.

Cross-Strait Economics and Mainland Political Development

Taiwan's economic policy is unabashedly mercantilist, except for military security concerns.[62] Taipei (like Tokyo) does not dally with concerns that would make trade dependent on human rights. After the Tiananmen massacre, "Travelers from Taiwan and business with the island have been major factors in softening the loss of Western tourist dollars and the impact of Western economic sanctions on China."[63] Security worries nonetheless have driven ROC officials to limit flows of technology and capital to some PRC sectors. Taiwan's Ministry of Economic Affairs for many years had to approve all mainland investments larger than U.S.$60 million. It used a list of more than nine thousand production items—of which only four thousand were routinely approved and one thousand high-technology items were forbidden.[64] Taiwan businesses can own third-country subsidiaries, however, to make profits in any field.

The autonomist DPP in early 1998 debated proposals by its chair, Hsu Hsin-liang, proposing full economic relations with the mainland. Hsu's "Formosa" faction advocated a "bold westward advance" to liberalize cross-strait trade. The DPP "New Tide" faction, more afraid of mainland wiles, opposed a relaxation of limits on economic intercourse with China, to prevent capital flight and a "hollowing out of Taiwan's industrial foundation."[65] Tien Hung-mao, who later became Chen's foreign minister, had a similar policy with a different emphasis, viewing the island's strong economy as "Taiwan's strategic must, without which our game is over."[66] It has not been easy to use money in ways that might tame the mainland while avoiding economic dependence.

CONCLUSION: TAIWAN BETWEEN TWO LARGE EXTERNAL POWERS

Many on Taiwan are conscious of the danger of war with China: "We're all Chinese," according to the modal opinion in one survey, and "if we declare independence, there might be a war."[67] A lexical legislator said it thrice, "We're nervous, anxious, and worried." Most Beijing intellectuals also expect a mainland–island war eventually. This situation leads to radical suggestions. The latest Taiwan Independence Party presidential candidate, Cheng Pang-chen, suggested Taiwan should develop its own nuclear weapons—a project that, as other ROC analysts have said, could at one stroke alienate the United States and cause Beijing literally to go ballistic.[68]

While U.S. technical military prowess continues to defend Taiwan and China has yet to liberalize, the ROC is very likely (with the support of external companies that seek profits) to attempt development of long-range missile capacities such as the PRC already has.[69] If this were paired with a possibility of major unconventional weapon competence on the island, Beijing leaders might risk a great deal to preempt such development. Especially if evidence on such a Taiwan military upgrading were unclear and the still-authoritarian PRC took military action, Taiwanese separatists could then more easily rationalize an open declaration of non-Chinese independence. That would not solve their security problem, but it would appeal to many island voters in that context. Careful U.S. diplomacy may be required to head off such scenarios, because they would eventually cause net losses to all three major parties.

Taiwan's Security as Mainly Economic

Mines and missiles launched against Taiwan's economy, rather than ships or airplanes against its territory, are the main armed threats to the island (to the extent the island's economy is not already on the mainland). Taiwan depends on trade, and Chinese PLA efforts to reduce shipping and raise insurance rates would be harder for Taiwan and the United States to defeat than would an invasion.

Amphibious attacks across stretches of water such as the ninety-plus miles of the Taiwan Strait are the most costly sort of military operation. Invading forces are vulnerable to hostile fire long before they reach shore, then also after landing (especially on treeless flatlands such as Taiwan's western coast). This chapter is hardly the place to analyze the military geography or ratio of forces between Taiwan and China, a task that has already been admirably performed by others.[70] But it is worth noting that a PRC attack on Taiwan would be drawn out rather than quick—and would probably fail to take the island, even if mainland missiles caused great initial damage. Thus Taiwan's danger is economic/political as much as military.

China's army exercises, however, do not suggest this. In 1994, the PLA conducted amphibious landing drills in Fujian. In 1995, the whole Nanjing Military Region was declared, for practice, a "war zone" *(zhanqu)*. In 1996, the PLA launched overlapping waves of exercises that included missile launches. Military magazines, very popular on both sides of the strait, publish reports of procurements that either give the PRC an edge in offense or the ROC an edge in defense.[71] In mid-1999, Hong Kong journalists speculated that, "The idea now gaining favour is that of imposing a blockade on the island if Taiwan shows any further signs of independence. Submarines would be sent, and ports and waterways would be mined. . . . Chinese political leaders could stop the process, continue it or expand it, depending on the reaction of the United States and East Asian nations, among others, without embarking on a full-scale war."[72]

Symbolic threats have already caused economic damage on the island. From July 1995 to March 1996, after PLA exercises, U.S.$23.7 billion fled Taiwan—mostly to American banks.[73] The ROC's large foreign exchange reserves and stringent equity market laws might not be enough to withstand a sustained PRC attack on Taiwan's economy.[74] PRC costs would be staggering, too, but Beijing hard-liners would discount them for patriotic reasons. When an interviewer asked "one of China's top state economists" whether the PRC could afford to attack Taiwan, the answer was simply "No."[75] China's generals, however, may not be so rational or patient, and they could be willing to mistakenly gamble that military pressure would unify their country. If ROC democracy were threatened by an authoritarian China, the U.S. Navy would almost surely arrive with capacities against mining and within-the-atmosphere (i.e., relatively slow) missile attacks. But general studies of asymmetric conflict show that weaker powers have often started, and have occasionally won, wars against stronger ones. China might, before it liberalizes, try to repeat such a success against America and Taiwan.

The head of Beijing's China Council for the Promotion of International Trade says more hopefully that, "More cooperation in trade across the Taiwan Strait will pull the two sides together. . . . When living standards here approach those on Taiwan, unification will be much easier."[76] He seems close to the "no haste" position of Taiwan's mainstream, although his patience is about unification. Economic links have stabilized but do not ensure cross-strait peace.

Some American conservatives are prematurely concerned by the possibility that island–mainland economic synergy might unify China. Nat Bellochi asks, "Is Taiwan going the way of Hong Kong? . . . [T]he more the economies of Hong Kong and Taiwan are integrated into a Greater China economy, the more likely other concerns will grow in some areas of the US–Taiwan relationship."[77] Nancy Bernkopf Tucker in mid-2002 also wrote on the question: "If Taiwan Chooses Unification, Should the United States Care?" She wondered, "Would unification without war solve or exacerbate the U.S. security dilemma in Asia?"[78] Some analysts, including the present author, find this question unproblematic and "unification without war" preferable to both the encumbered and bellicose alternatives. Tucker's question is arguably like asking whether an agreement between Israelis and Palestinians would be good for America; the answer is "Yes." It is possible to be concerned that a Sino–American war (however beneficial it might be to arms sellers) could lead to high military costs with no long-term settlement of the cross-strait dispute.

U.S. Interests as Democratic

Most democrats (including this author) think Taiwan's people have a right to self-determination. If Taiwanese exercise their option of independence from China, however, do they also have a right to insist that others, Americans, fight with them for that independence? Do overall U.S. interests require such action? These interests include concrete future benefits (probable trade profits and defense savings) if China becomes more liberal, as well as present benefits from Taiwan trade and cultural contacts. The United States, as an imperialist or pacifying power, continues crucially to shape cross-strait relations. Taipei's relations with its vital Beijing rival are mediated in Washington.

The relevant American interests are based in two correlations. First, *large modern countries are liberal democracies*. This refers to countries with more than ten million citizens and GDP in per-capita-purchasing-power parity terms higher than approximately U.S.$8,000 (or about one-third that, if the measurement is in unadjusted GDP).[79] Second, *liberal democracies have a track record of not attacking each other*—even if their objective levels of military power are radically unequal—even though statistics show democracies are trigger-happy against nondemocracies, and even though authoritarian regimes in the process of protodemocratic pluralization may be bellicose against all other types of regimes.[80] These two empirical correlations are not normative desiderata. They are high-probability facts.

China's economy has been growing handily (at about $4,000 real purchasing power per head—or roughly one-third that as measured by unadjusted GDP per capita). The United Nations Development Programme puts that figure for 2000 at $3,976. At no level do socioeconomic factors, unless combined with possible elite decisions for liberal structure, surely predict political modernization or pacifism toward democracies. At an income level twice or thrice as much, however, unless China disproves a pattern that is observable in *all* other large industrial nations, it will probably become stable as a democracy if PRC elites have occasion to opt for that regime type to handle their own contending interests. At China's medium level of modernization, authoritarian regimes preserve themselves as well as democratic ones, presuming their economies perform satisfactorily. Przeworski and Limongi find, at about China's current socioeconomic level, an exception to the usual modernization–liberalization correlation, "due to the fact that dictatorships are exceptionally stable in this range. . . . The emergence of democracy is not a by-product of economic development. . . . Only once it is established do economic constraints play a role: the chances for the survival of democracy are greater when the country is richer."[81]

The United States has strong material (not just ideological) long-term interests in China's democratic evolution. It has medium-term interests in getting the PRC through the next levels of development in amity with all democracies—notably including Taiwan, Japan, and South Korea. If the United States can pass the next two or three decades without fighting a major war with China over Taiwan, then China's internal changes by the end of that time may make subsequent Sino–American and general Northeast Asian relations peaceable enough. These arguments from comparative politics are as relevant to China–Japan and China–South Korea relations as they are to PRC relations with any other democracy—except perhaps Taiwan, which China would probably still claim if it democratizes.

America's best and brightest underestimated the power of patriotism in Japan during the 1930s, in China during the 1940s, in Korea during the 1950s, and in Vietnam during the 1960s. They specifically underestimated the probability that nationalists would launch attacks against superior U.S. military forces. Ill-conceived policies that failed to deter and reform authoritarians have been extremely expensive, when these rulers were also patriots. Both Chinese and Taiwanese nationalisms now affect the U.S. agenda, although objective evidence shows that America's track record dealing with such movements in Asia is abysmal.

The United States does not need Taiwan's island strategically, but it needs Taiwan's democracy strategically. The United States has a future "one China" policy. American spokespeople call this policy purposefully "ambiguous" as a way of allowing flexibility in deterring both PRC violence and permanent Taiwan independence. Those two goals, however, are not at all ambiguous. "Strategic ambiguity" is a dangerous phrase. It might refer to a situation in which one expects to fight a war but does not know the aims. This situation could spur either PLA adventurism or Taiwan separatism. Either could result in war, contrary to American interests.

U.S. executive policy might more accurately be called "strategic winking." Washington does not want to insult Beijing leaders for their patriotism, because Americans have many items of business and diplomacy to transact with China. Likewise, Washington does not want to insult Taipei leaders for loving their island, nor too publicly for their attempts to sway U.S. policy against long-term U.S. interests, because Taiwan itself must find some way eventually to live with its big neighbor. So wink, wink: Washington's future behavior is easy to guess, though inexplicit in public. The United States will defend Taiwan as a democracy (presuming the island does not do more to provoke its rival) until Beijing changes enough to guarantee democracy for the Taiwanese, including the right of peaceable free speech. This American strategy is discreet, not ambiguous.

Almost any conceivable ARATS–SEF agreement about hopes of relating the mainland and the island stably would strengthen cross-strait peace, so long as it contained a long-term future date. The foundations' leaders might simply declare they both expect achievement, for example by 2050, of an unspecified cross-strait accommodation, subject to interim negotiations at a pace within that period to be decided by further agreements. Even such a modest and unofficial expression, avoiding any symbols of ROC or PRC sovereignty, would require approval from leaders such as Hu Jintao, Chen Shui-bian, or their successors. It would give Beijing reformers and Taipei moderates crucial arguments to delay opportunistic proposals by their domestic rivals within each camp. No such agreement is likely soon, however. Militarists in Beijing and separatists in Taipei *benefit* from cross-strait tensions, but they overestimate their abilities to control them. Arms sellers in Washington also benefit from pushing their wares on Taiwan beyond the point needed to deter China, to an extent that threatens Taiwan security by giving Beijing militarists arguments for starting a costly war that all sides (notably the PRC) would lose. The main Japanese and South Korean interests in Taiwan parallel those of America: avoidance of that war and eventual achievement of a liberal China that can solve the cross-strait dispute fairly for both sides.

NOTES

The author thanks Nevena Batchvarova, Gregory Chow, Lyle Goldstein, Michael Hsiao-hsin Huang, Samuel S. Kim, Shinichi Nakayama, Phillip Saunders, Shih Chih-yu, Wu Nai-teh, and Philip Yang for various kinds of help with this chapter. He is grateful for support from both Princeton University and the Chiang Ching-kuo Foundation. All mistakes are his own. He is not a government official and uses terms like Republic of China, Taiwan, and People's Republic of China because people in those places do so.

Note: Each January issue of *Asian Survey* has a summary on Taiwan over the previous year.

1. The links with other minor states are only formally relevant. The Montevideo Convention of 1933 is the most often cited norm. See also Richard N. Swift, *International Law: Current and Classic* (New York: Wiley, 1969), 59, which however also notes that "politics and force, more often than law, have confirmed states, . . . and politics more than law governs the act of recognition."

2. Chris Cockel, "U.S. Opposed to Taiwan Independence: Wolfowitz," *China Post*, May 31, 2002.

3. Colin McEvedy, *Penguin Historical Atlas of the Pacific* (New York: Penguin, 1998),

10–11. Ethnolinguistic and archaeological evidence for this broader claim are now available in many sources.

4. When considered as part of China, Taiwan has China's highest mountains east of Sichuan. They were formed, and the island exists, because of subduction between the Eurasian and Philippine plates. Taiwan is seismically active and suffers relatively frequent severe earthquakes.

5. Hugh B. O'Neill, *Companion to Chinese History* (New York: Facts on File, 1987), 36.

6. PRC patriotic passions have inspired greater claims. A CCTV documentary noted that bones from the same species of dinosaur have been found in both Fujian and Taiwan, suggesting this as evidence for mainland–island unity. The report did not mention that the dinosaurs preceded any people in either place. Taiwan autonomists are prone to similar enthusiasms, occasionally claiming for example that Taiwan is so different from South Fujian in dialect, kinship structure, and common religions as to make Taiwanese culture essentially non-Chinese, despite very extensive evidence to the contrary. Taiwan is ethnically more Chinese, for example, than is Tibet.

7. See many chapters in *Taiwan: A New History*, ed. Murray A. Rubenstein (Armonk, N.Y.: Sharpe, 1999); the quotation is from the chapter in this book by Harry Lamley, "Taiwan under Japanese Rule, 1895–1945: The Vicissitudes of Colonialism," 228. For a comparison, see Eugen Weber, *Peasants into Frenchmen: The Modernization of Rural France, 1870–1914* (Stanford, Calif.: Stanford University Press, 1976).

8. George H. Kerr, *Formosa Betrayed* (Boston: Houghton Mifflin, 1965).

9. For example, Mao is quoted by Edgar Snow as having said, of Korea and Taiwan together, that "we will extend them our enthusiastic help in their struggle for independence" from Japan, in *Red Star over China* (New York: Grove, 1938), 96. PRC policy is now different.

10. Douglas Mendel, *The Politics of Formosan Nationalism* (Berkeley: University of California Press, 1970), 19; and George Kerr, *Formosa: Licensed Revolution and the Home Rule Movement, 1895–1945* (Honolulu: University Press of Hawaii, 1974).

11. Pichon P. Y. Loh, *The Kuomintang Debacle of 1949* (Boston: Heath, 1963), xiv.

12. See Thomas J. Christensen, *Useful Adversaries* (Princeton, N.J.: Princeton University Press, 1998).

13. See Lynn White and Cheng Li, "China Coast Identities: Region, Nation, and World," in Lowell Dittmer and Samuel Kim, eds., *China's Quest for National Identity* (Ithaca, N.Y.: Cornell University Press, 1993), 154–93.

14. These three categories of arcane lawyerly argument deserve no more than brief summaries. First, the logical form of Nixon's 1972 statement that "all Chinese on both sides of the Taiwan Strait acknowledge" one China did not quite specify what America acknowledged. Carter's 1978 statement (changing the English-edition verb to "recognize") scarcely clarified this matter, in part because it referred to the 1972 document. Second, none of the executive agreements (1943, 1972, 1978, or others) had the consent of two-thirds of the senators and thus none is binding in U.S. courts, although the Vienna Convention on Treaties would hold these agreements generally to be binding in international law. Third, Japan's peace treaty at the end of the war (to which Washington was a party, although neither Taipei nor Beijing was) ceded sovereignty over Taiwan without mentioning any recipient. As a State Department lawyer later pointed out, "Neither in

that treaty nor in any other treaty has there been any definitive cession to China [either ROC or PRC] of Formosa"—and legally if not politically, this position has not even yet been abjured. Cf. *State Department Bulletin* 39:1017 (December 22, 1958), 1009–10. But Washington has also not denied that Taiwan is Chinese. All this quintessentially American legalistic welshing is merely the quiet rhetorical basis for the current and most likely future U.S. political policy: to help defend Taiwan so long as its government is unprovocative and its mainland adversary is authoritarian, but not thereafter.

15. By comparison, the populations in 2000 of China, South Korea, Hong Kong, and Singapore, respectively, were 1.26 billion, 48 million, 7 million, and 4 million; their respective GDPs per capita were $3,300; $14,800; $20,500; and $25,300. Paolo Pasicolan, *U.S. and Asia Statistical Handbook*, 2001–02 (Washington: Heritage Foundation, 2001), 68–69.

16. These are, respectively, the capitals of Tuvalu, Chad, and the Dominican Republic (which, though it has less than a quarter of Taiwan's own population, is the most populous country to host a formal ROC embassy).

17. Christopher S. Wren, "China Invites Taiwan Leaders to Visit," *New York Times*, October 10, 1981, 3.

18. James Kim, "An Uneasy Place: Tides of Sea Change Tug at Island's Self-Determination," *USA Today*, June 30, 1998, 1B.

19. Wu Nai-teh, "Forming a New Nation: Ethnic Identity and Liberalism in Taiwanese Nationalism" (paper presented at the 17th Congress of the International Political Science Association, August 1997) and a personal e-mail communication on the July 1997 updated survey. The fourth possibility (opposing *both* unification with a liberal China *and* independence without a military threat) received less support—3 percent in 1996, though double that by 1998! Wu's surveys, with large samples and low rates of nonresponse, are state of the art in identity studies.

20. Li Hui-jung, *Taiwan zhengzhi guancha* (Observations on Taiwan politics) (Taipei: Qianwei, 1997), 86.

21. The *Pearl Report*, Hong Kong television, July 19, 2000, showed pictures of early 1990s Taipei and Beijing interlocutors together.

22. Chris Yeung, "Taipei Vows Return to UN; Backing 'In Three Years,'" *South China Morning Post*, April 10, 1993, 6.

23. See, for example, Chen Ming-tong, *Paixi zhengzhi yu Taiwan zhengzhi bianqian* (Factional politics and change in Taiwan politics) (Taipei: Yuedan, 1995), 223.

24. Chen Ming-tong and Zheng Yongnian, eds., *Liangan jiceng xuanju yu zhengzhi shehui bianqian* (Basic-level elections and the transformation of political society on the two shores) (Taipei: Yuedan, 1998).

25. Cabinet ministers have traveled across the strait without acknowledging their posts to the other side. ROC finance minister Shirley Kuo visited Beijing in 1989 to attend an Asian Development Bank meeting (not to negotiate with China). PRC science and technology minister Zhu Lilan visited Taiwan in 1998 to attend an academic seminar. Each government chose a woman, although women are a small minority in each cabinet and these choices are hard to explain as random. Daniel Southerland, "Taiwan's 'Iron Lady' Leads lst Delegation to China," *Washington Post*, May 2, 1989, A10; and Stephen Vines, "Chinese Lift Embargo on Taiwan Flights," *Independent*, July 16, 1998, 14.

26. These are the first substantive words of the *Consensus Formed at the National Development Conference on Cross-Strait Relations* (Taipei: Mainland Affairs Council, 1997), 1.

27. See Lynn White, "America's Interests in the First Democratic Chinese President," *American Asian Review* 20, no. 1 (Spring 2002): 155–209.

28. "China Blasts Taiwan Lee's 'State-to-State' Remark," *Reuters*, July 11, 1999, at taiwansecurity.org/Reu/Reu-990711.htm (accessed October 7, 2001).

29. See Frank Ching, "Lee Roils the Waters," *Far Eastern Economic Review* (hereafter *FEER*), August 5, 1999, 30.

30. "China–Taiwan Talks Break Years of Tension," *St. Louis Post–Dispatch*, October 14, 1998, A6.

31. Kevin Platt, "Why China and Taiwan Fire Words, Not Missiles," *Christian Science Monitor*, October 19, 1998, 6.

32. "Taiwan, China Military Officials Meet," Associated Press, July 17, 2002.

33. Nadia Tsao, "Vice Minister of Defense to Take Washington Trip," *Taipei Times*, June 21, 2002.

34. Willy Wo-Lap Lam, "Beijing Warns U.S. over 'Wrong Signals,'" CNN.com, at www.cnn.com/2002/WORLD/asiapcf/east/07/14/china.pla/, July 15, 2002 (accessed April 29, 2003).

35. Bates Gill, "September 11 and Northeast Asia: Change and Uncertainty in Regional Security," *Brookings Review* 20, no. 3 (Summer 2002): 46.

36. Dennis V. Hickey and Mariesa Ho, "Taiwan Deserves a Seat in WHO," *Taipei Times*, May 25, 2002.

37. Monique Chu, "NSC Urges 'Offensive' Foreign Policy," *Taipei Times*, July 19, 2002.

38. Lynn White, "Taiwan and Globalization," *Asian Perspective* 23, no. 4 (1999): 97–141.

39. "China Warns Allies Not to Sign Accords with Taiwan," Associated Press, June 22, 2002.

40. "US–Taiwan FTA Politically Crucial" (editorial), *Liberty Times*, June 23, 2002.

41. Calculated from data in Sun Zhaozhen, "2001 Saw Increase in Economic and Trade Interdependence between Mainland China and Taiwan," *Zhongguo xinwen she*, February 3, 2002, in *FBIS China Daily Report*, February 5, 2002.

42. Approximated on the basis of 1997 data in Kevin Cai, "Is a Free Trade Zone Emerging in Northeast Asia in the Wake of the Asian Financial Crisis?" *Pacific Affairs* 74, no. 1 (Spring 2001): 8.

43. Cai, "Is a Free Trade Zone Emerging?" 9.

44. Chang Maubo, "Mainland Is Most Popular Destination for Taiwan Investors," *Central News Agency* (Taiwan), March 11, 2002, in *FBIS China Daily Report*, March 12, 2002.

45. For more, see Lynn White, "The Political Effects of Resource Allocations in Taiwan and Mainland China," *Journal of the Developing Areas* 15 (October 1980): 43–66.

46. Modernization affects nationality; see Alexander Gershenkron, *Continuity in History and Other Essays* (Cambridge, Mass.: Harvard University Press, 1968).

47. Shieh Gwo-shyong, *"Boss" Island: The Subcontracting Network and Micro-entrepreneurship in Taiwan's Development* (New York: Lang, 1992), offers a micromanagerial sociology that also shows why the KMT's political strategy brought strong economic results.

48. Gerald A. McBeath, "The Changing Role of Business Associations in Democratizing Taiwan," *Journal of Contemporary China* (July 1998): 303–20, finds a prevalence of the "corporatist impulse."

49. Julian Baum, "Hedging Its Bets," *FEER*, March 25, 1999, 16.

50. James Kim, "Uneasy Place."

51. Anita Chan, "Boot Camp at the Shoe Factory," *Washington Post*, November 3, 1996, C1.

52. A specialized article, Gong Chen, "Capital Movement between the Mainland, Taiwan, and Hong Kong," in *Dynamics and Dilemmas: Mainland, Taiwan, and Hong Kong in a Changing World*, ed. Yu Bin et al. (New York: Nova, 1996), 125–49, offers no tables, presumably because there are no reliable data.

53. Schutz Lee, "Taiwan's Southward Thrust Gains Impetus," *Business Times*, June 7, 1994, 15.

54. More exact figures for 1999, which may well omit some Taiwan firms' operations, are in the *Republic of China Yearbook, 2001* (Taipei: Government Information Office, 2001), 155. It may be that no one gives a reasonably comprehensive accounting of trade and investment data for all of Taiwan (or for the PRC or some other places, either). Fads for reporting numbers are much stronger than fads for checking them for errors.

55. P. T. Bangsberg, "Taiwan Still Drew Capital, but Invested Less Overseas in '95," *Journal of Commerce*, January 12, 1996, 3A ff.

56. James Kim, "Uneasy Place."

57. The author is grateful to a professor at the School of Advanced International Studies, Johns Hopkins University, who provided these data.

58. Laura Tyson, "Survey of Taiwan," *Financial Times*, October 25, 1995, 16 ff.

59. John E. Woodruff, "Taiwan Pours Money into South China Area," *Los Angeles Times*, May 21, 1990, 4. Also see Brian Hook, ed., *Fujian: Gateway to Taiwan* (Hong Kong: Oxford University Press, 1996).

60. Bruce Gilley and Julian Baum, "Crude Tactics," *FEER*, June 29, 2000, 25.

61. "Unequal Partners," *Economist*, August 24, 1996, 30.

62. For a sophisticated analysis, see Leng Tse-Kang, "The State and Taiwan's Mainland Economic Policy," *Asian Affairs: An American Review*, April 1, 1996, 20; and Leng, *The Taiwan–China Connection: Democracy and Development across the Taiwan Straits* (Boulder, Colo.: Westview, 1996).

63. John E. Woodruff, "Taiwan Pours Money into South China Area," *Los Angeles Times*, May 21, 1990, 4.

64. Tony Walker and Laura Tyson, "China Talks Moving Too Fast for Some Taiwanese," *Financial Times*, November 25, 1994, 4.

65. Taifa Yu, "Relations between Taiwan and China after the Missile Crisis: Toward Reconciliation?" *Pacific Affairs* (Spring 1999): 39; and "Taiwan Opposition Party Split over Mainland Policy," *Straits Times*, February 17, 1998, 14.

66. Kao Chen, "Teng Hui's Call for Slower Trade Leads to Uncertainty," *Straits Times*, October 7, 1996, 34.

67. James Kim, "Uneasy Place."

68. Kevin Platt, "To Get Attention in Taiwan, Put Nukes in Your Election Campaign," *Christian Science Monitor*, August 27, 1999, 7. Taiwan had a nuclear program in past decades that was cancelled at U.S. insistence. If the island were to obtain so many conventional weapons that it could defend itself without American help for a while, this program might be continued (like Israel's). To prevent that, the PRC could start a Sino-American war that would threaten U.S. security on a long-term basis even if the United States won the first round.

69. See an article about Dr. Lin Cheng-yi: Brian Hsu, "Scholar Says Chen Favors Second-Strike Capability," *Taipei Times*, January 14, 2002, at taiwansecurity.org/TT/2002/TT-011402.htm (accessed April 29, 2003).

70. See David Shambaugh and Richard H. Yang, eds., *China's Military in Transition* (New York: Oxford University Press, 1997); Shambaugh, "Taiwan's Security: Maintaining Deterrence amid Political Accountability," in *Contemporary Taiwan*, a special issue of *China Quarterly* 148 (December 1996): 1284–318; and June Teufel Dreyer, "China's Military Strategy toward Taiwan," *American Asian Review* 17, no. 3 (Fall 1999): 1–28.

71. See estimates of the number of PRC missiles and of the effectiveness of Taiwan's Modified Air Defense System (MADS) in Peter Yu Kien-hong, "Taking Taiwan: How Would China Set about Recovering the Republic?" *Jane's Intelligence Review*, September 1, 1998, 29.

72. "China's Answer to Taiwan," *Foreign Report*, no. 2561, September 23, 1999.

73. Peter Yu Kien-hong, "Taking Taiwan."

74. On anti-PRC financial security measures that immunized Taiwan from Asian flu, see White, "Taiwan and Globalization."

75. Thomas L. Friedman, "An Assault on Taiwan Would Cost China Too Much," *Plain Dealer*, April 3, 1996, 11B.

76. Carl Schwartz, "Mainland, Island in Delicate Balance: Taiwan Seeks to Reclaim International Stature, but Reunification Is Inevitable," *Milwaukee Journal Sentinel*, November 29, 1996, 19.

77. Nat Bellocchi, "Taiwan's Voters Miss the Big Issues," *Taipei Times*, July 4, 2002.

78. Nancy Bernkopf Tucker, "If Taiwan Chooses Unification, Should the United States Care?" *Washington Quarterly* 25, no. 3 (Summer 2002): 15–28.

79. The generalization above is not challenged by the fact that some large democracies, such as India, are poor. The obvious but small exception, Singapore, is a city with one-quarter of one percent of China's population—and one that is facing severe danger from ethnic conflict. Others that merely seem to be exceptions include oil sheikdoms, which also have small populations. See United Nations Development Program, *Human Development Report, 2000* (New York: Oxford University Press, 2000), 157, table 1, the human development index, where Taiwan might replace Hong Kong at rank 26. This index is a better measure of modernization than per capita GDP, but it requires more description and correlates very strongly with GDP per capita. The $3,976 figure in the text comes from a preprint of the 2002 edition of this same *Human Development Report*, p. 150.

80. For concise summaries of conflicting views, see Michael Brown et al., eds., *Debating the Democratic Peace* (Cambridge: MIT Press, 1996). That protodemocracies tend to be warlike is disputed in Bruce Russett and John Neal, *Triangulating Peace* (New York: Norton, 2001). Just as important for long-term policy, however, is the prediction that a more modernized China may become more liberal and thus "civilized" toward other democracies.

81. Adam Przeworski and Fernando Limongi, "Modernization: Theory and Facts," *World Politics* 49 (January 1997): 170, 177. See also Adam Przeworski et al., *Democracy and Development: Political Institutions and Well-Being in the World, 1950–1990* (New York: Cambridge University Press, 2000), especially 273.

FURTHER READING

Blackwill, Robert, and Paul Dibb, eds. *America's Asian Alliances*. Cambridge, Mass.: MIT Press, 2000.

Christensen, Thomas J. *Useful Adversaries*. Princeton, N.J.: Princeton University Press, 1998.

Chu Yun-han. *Crafting Democracy in Taiwan*. Taipei: Institute for National Policy Research, 1992.

Clough, Ralph N. *Cooperation or Conflict in the Taiwan Strait?* Asia in World Politics series. Lanham, Md.: Rowman & Littlefield, 1999.

Consensus Formed at the National Development Conference on Cross-Strait Relations. Taipei: Mainland Affairs Council, 1997.

Copper, John F. *Taiwan: Nation–State or Province?* 3d ed. Boulder, Colo.: Westview, 1999.

Dreyer, June Teufel. "China's Military Strategy toward Taiwan." *American Asian Review* 17, no. 3 (Fall 1999): 1–28.

Friedman, Edward. "Reconstructing China's National Identity: A Southern Alternative to Mao-Era Anti-Imperialist Nationalism." *Journal of Asian Studies* 53, no. 1 (February 1994): 67–87.

Garver, John. *Face-Off: China, the U.S., and Taiwan's Democratization*. Seattle: University of Washington Press, 1997.

Hickey, Dennis. *The Armies of East Asia: China, Taiwan, Japan, and the Koreas*. Boulder, Colo.: Rienner, 2001.

Kerr, George H. *Formosa Betrayed*. Boston: Houghton Mifflin, 1965.

Kerr, George. *Formosa: Licensed Revolution and the Home Rule Movement, 1895–1945*. Honolulu: University Press of Hawaii, 1974.

Kim, Samuel S. "Taiwan and the International System: The Challenge of Legitimation." In *Taiwan in World Affairs*, edited by Robert Sutter and William Johnson. Boulder, Colo.: Westview, 1994.

Lee Teng-hui. *The Road to Democracy: Taiwan's Pursuit of Identity*. Tokyo: PHP Institute, 1999.

Leng Tse-Kang. *The Taiwan–China Connection: Democracy and Development across the Taiwan Straits*. Boulder, Colo.: Westview, 1996.

Li Hui-jung. *Taiwan zhengzhi guancha* (Observations on Taiwan Politics). Taipei: Qianwei, 1997.

Mansfield, Edward, and Jack Snyder. "Democratization and the Danger of War." *International Security* 20, no. 1 (Summer 1995): 5–38.

McBeath, Gerald A. "The Changing Role of Business Associations in Democratizing Taiwan." *Journal of Contemporary China* (July 1998): 303–20.

Mendel, Douglas. *The Politics of Formosan Nationalism*. Berkeley: University of California Press, 1970.

Myers, Ramon H., David Shambaugh, and Michel Oksenberg, eds. *Making China Policy: Lessons from the Clinton and Bush [Sr.] Administrations*. Lanham, Md.: Rowman & Littlefield, 2001.

Nathan, Andrew J., and Robert Ross. *The Great Wall and the Empty Fortress: China's Search for Security*. New York: Norton, 1997.

Rigger, Shelley. *Politics in Taiwan: Voting for Democracy*. New York: Routledge, 1999.

———. *From Opposition to Power: Taiwan's Democratic Progressive Party*. Boulder, Colo.: Rienner, 2001.

Rubenstein, Murray A., ed. *Taiwan: A New History*. Armonk, N.Y.: Sharpe, 1999.

Shambaugh, David. "Taiwan's Security: Maintaining Deterrence amid Political Accountability" and other articles. In *Contemporary Taiwan*, special issue of *China Quarterly* 148 (December 1996).

Shinn, James, ed. *Weaving the Net: Conditional Engagement with China*. New York: Council on Foreign Relations, 1996.

Swaine, Michael D. *Taiwan's National Security, Defense, & Procurement Processes*. Santa Monica, Calif.: Rand Corporation, 1999.

White, Lynn. "The Political Effects of Resource Allocations in Taiwan and Mainland China." *Journal of the Developing Areas* 15 (October 1980): 43–66.

———. "Taiwan and Globalization." *Asian Perspective* 23, no. 4 (1999): 97–141.

———. "America's Interests in the First Democratic Chinese President." *American Asian Review* 20, no. 1 (Spring 2002): 155–209.

White, Lynn, and Cheng Li. "China Coast Identities: Region, Nation, and World." In *China's Quest for National Identity*, edited by Lowell Dittmer and Samuel Kim, 154–93. Ithaca, N.Y.: Cornell University Press, 1993.

Wu Nai-teh. "Social Attitudes of the Middle Classes in Taiwan." In *East Asian Middle Classes in Comparative Perspective*, edited by Hsin-Huang Michael Hsiao, 291–318. Taipei: Institute of Ethnology, Academia Sinica, 1999.

Zhao Suisheng, ed. *Across the Taiwan Strait: China, Taiwan, 1995–1996 Crisis*. New York: Routledge, 1999.

IV

REGION BUILDING

11

The Emerging Northeast Asian Regional Order

Lowell Dittmer

As Samuel Kim elucidated in his introduction, the Northeast Asian region is one of great and increasing importance in world affairs. A "region" may be defined in various ways; the constituent regimes should have a shared sociocultural heritage, shared political attitudes or external behavior, geographic proximity, economic complementarity, and/or some form of institutional cooperative arrangements.[1] Although Northeast Asia might well be considered the geopolitical cockpit of the East Asian region and the nexus of the world's three largest nuclear weapons states, three largest economies, and three of the five permanent members of the UN Security Council, many of the factors normally constitutive of a "region" are in scant supply.[2] Indeed the Northeast Asian polities are exceedingly disparate, ranging from Japan, which has a per capita GDP seventy times that of China but a land surface smaller than that of the American state of Montana and a population only about one fourteenth that of China, to Russia, which has a land surface larger than the second- and third-largest countries in the world combined, but whose Asian populace (in the Russian Far East) is less than a third that of the smallest Northeast Asian polity (the Democratic People's Republic of Korea, or DPRK, had 22 million people in 2000). All the Northeast Asian states share a character-based linguistic system, "chopstick culture," and a Confucian–Buddhist symbolic legacy, and all (at least in the past two decades) have placed an overriding priority on export-led economic growth. But where does that leave the two superpowers, culturally exogenous, yet both deeply involved in postwar Northeast Asian political and economic developments? Both find their national destinies inextricably tied to the region. Thus, based on an eclectic combination of geographic proximity and sustained political and economic involvement, Northeast Asia is defined in the pages of this chapter to include seven established polities—China, Taiwan, Japan, North and South Korea, Russia, and the United States—and one emergent one, Mongolia.

What do we mean by Northeast Asia's "emerging order"? With regard to "order," Hedley Bull's purposive conception, defined in terms of the conformity of human behavior to rules of conduct, seems most apt.[3] Although realists are fond of characterizing interstate relations as "anarchic," and although, empirically considered, interstate relations among these powers have historically been less rule-guided than, say, those in postwar Western Europe or North America (becoming even more open-ended since the end of the Cold War), our rather heroic working hypothesis is that these relationships tend to fall into intelligible patterns. Finally, by "emerging" we refer simply to the time period embracing the present, recent past, and near future, which in this context we take to have been inaugurated by the collapse of the Communist bloc and the end of the Cold War.

One of the tenets of historical institutionalism is that institutional development is "path dependent," that is, influenced by the historical context from which it derives.[4] Thus we begin by cursorily outlining the Cold War order and periodizing its disintegration. We then turn to the emergence of the new regional order in the last decade of the twentieth century, in the wake of the collapse of the Soviet bloc. This is a tale of entropy, evolving from tightly regimented order to increasing freedom of movement. And yet the end of the Cold War, as we shall see, whose occurrence came as such a shock to the international system, has had a deeply paradoxical impact. We thus begin by outlining briefly those post–Cold War results that might have been expected, in order to more fully appreciate the full irony of the currently emerging set of relationships. Only by placing current developments in the context of prevailing expectations can we plausibly interpret what sort of "order" they may be said to constitute.

THE COLD WAR ORDER AND ITS DECAY

The Cold War went through two phases, the first roughly coinciding with the decade of the 1950s and the second beginning in the early 1960s. During the first phase, the international system was rent by an ideologically defined bipolar cleavage between what Zhdanov called "two camps," with North Korea and China in the Communist camp, led by the Soviet Union, and

South Korea, Taiwan, and Japan part of the "free world," led by the United States. Within both camps, a relationship of hegemonic stability obtained in which the two superpowers assumed leadership of a comprehensive security regime, in exchange for which they offered special economic concessions to their client states. The two security blocs were institutionalized within an overlapping network of alliances and international organizations: in the East, all originally belonged to either or both the Warsaw Pact and the international Communist movement, and there were Soviet "friendship and security alliances" with the PRC and the DPRK; the Western side was cemented not by a regional alliance system like NATO, but by bilateral security alliances between Washington and Seoul, Tokyo, and Taipei (evidently by American preference). Crowning this security regime was a bipolar arsenal of intercontinental nuclear weapons, which over time became sufficiently massive and well-concealed to ensure that one side could still destroy the other even after being hit first. Although only the two superpowers had full disposition over such a comprehensive ("second-strike") security system, each offered protection ("extended deterrence") as well as special economic concessions to their respective clients in order to preclude defection to the other camp. These economic concessions included preferred access to American markets in the "free world" and preferential terms in the barter system of the socialist international economy known as the Council for Mutual Economic Assistance. Thus there were two relatively comprehensive and mutually exclusive international consortiums in which security and economic interests coincided almost perfectly, between which economic transactions were interdicted by the Warsaw Pact on the one side and by NATO and Coordinating Council for Multilateral Export Controls on the other. The second phase of the Cold War was characterized by the incipient disintegration of the two blocs, as signified by the semidefection of de Gaulle's France in the West and Tito's Yugoslavia and Mao's China in the East, and by the rise of a large nonaligned bloc in the third world. These defections were only partial, splintering the two blocs but stopping short of realignment of the defecting states to the other side and a fundamental redistribution of the balance of power; and although both blocs competed for the allegiance of the nonaligned third-world countries, this contest too remained inconclusive.

The end of the Cold War came with a bang in Europe, beginning in the summer of 1989 with the wave of uprisings and refugee flows that swept through Eastern Europe and culminating in the collapse of the Soviet Union in December 1991. In Northeast Asia, the end came more gradually and with less climactic finality. The first phase dawned a decade early, with the defection of China from the Soviet bloc at the end of the 1960s, after about a decade of inconclusive polemics. As the Sino–Soviet split escalated to border warfare amid China's Cultural Revolution, the looming threat of a Soviet preemptive strike on China's still nascent nuclear arsenal prompted the PRC to seek shelter under the American nuclear umbrella. This gave rise to the "great strategic triangle" between the United States, the PRC, and the USSR, in which relations between any two powers became premised on their relations with the third, with periodic reconfigurations among the three to fit shifting national capabilities and interests. Although the consequent realignment of the balance of power was internationally significant, with China contributing for example to American intelligence and counterinsurgency efforts, Chinese integration into Western commercial markets was not fully consummated until the advent of "reform and opening" a decade later. While the end of the Cold War began earlier in Northeast Asia, it also ended less decisively than it did in Europe and Central Asia. This is of course because the Asian socialist regimes, unlike their European confreres, refused to collapse. Despite its introduction of markets and other growth-enhancing capitalist economic innovations, the PRC remained an avowedly Leninist political regime, as underscored by its crushing of the Tiananmen protests in June 1989. In North Korea, "our style socialism" survived with precious little reform under "dear leader" Kim Jong Il, despite an economic nosedive following Gorbachev's severance of preferential trade ties after his recognition of South Korea in 1990. In Northeast Asia, the primary manifestation of the end of the Cold War was the collapse of the Soviet Union—the Eastern European socialist republics had been of only marginal economic and political importance. The Soviet Union was physically represented in Northeast Asia by the Russian Far East, a vast expanse of resource-rich but virtually empty and undeveloped terrain that remained physically intact. Despite a still disproportionately massive military presence in Vladivostok and the Sea of Japan, the Soviet Union had always been a more peripheral actor in Asia than in the West, and its collapse (which implied no regional territorial revisions, as in Europe and Central Asia) had little impact. Yet the disintegration of the Soviet Union into fifteen sovereign states, none of which maintained allegiance to Marxism–Leninism, does seem to have precipitated the demise of the strategic triangle, despite occasional attempts to revive it.

By the end of the twentieth century, the Cold War's Northeast Asian progression of more or less tight bipolarity followed by strategic triangularity had evolved into a much murkier and more complex set of relationships based on a combination of geographical propinquity, mutual economic complementarity, overlapping ethnonational interests or claims, and perceived security threats (or supports). In some respects, the results of the end of the Cold War were perhaps in retrospect foreseeable. The combination of the deradicalization of ideological affiliations and the waning credibility of nuclear deterrence freed client states on both sides for greater freedom of association, resulting in an increase in international promiscuity. This was particularly evident in the world of commerce, where the old "curtain" between planned and market economies was completely lifted, giving rise to trade between former adversaries such as the United States and China, South and North Korea, even Taiwan and Russia. The regional consensus on the priority of economic growth already incipient during the late Cold War intensified upon its termination, giving rise to a steady and relatively swift regionwide increase in living standards, despite the temporary setback of the 1997–1999 Asian financial crisis (AFC) and with the conspicuous exception of North Korea. And regional prosperity was accompanied by regional peace, despite a tense confrontation with North Korea over its attempt to acquire nuclear weaponry in 1993–1994 and a saber-rattling episode across the Taiwan Strait in 1995–1996. If we overlook the crises and confrontational episodes, these broad trends conform to the aspirations for a new world order articulated by George H. W. Bush in the victorious afterglow of the Gulf War of 1991. But in many other respects, the end of the Cold War has confounded rational expectations.

PUZZLES AND PARADOXES OF THE NEW ORDER

What is most striking about the end of the Cold War so far as Northeast Asia is concerned is not the emergence of a coherent "new order" corresponding to the existence of an undoubted new regional powerhouse in world affairs, but rather the extent to which political and economic developments have contravened what one might have anticipated. This can be demonstrated in at least four clusters of problems: the blossoming of a Sino–Russian partnership, the apparent collapse of any coherent strategic structure among the principal "powers" of the region, the failure of any political or economic community to take shape, and the intractability of the region's two most explosive "hot spots," the divided nations of North and South Korea and of China and Taiwan, even after the disappearance of the ideological divide that had supposedly impeded their reunification. In each case, there were good reasons to have expected a quite different outcome, either on theoretical grounds or based simply on "common sense."

Sino–Russian "Strategic Partnership"

The Sino–Russian post–Cold War "partnership," as sealed in a new Friendship Treaty signed by Jiang Zemin and Vladimir Putin in the Kremlin on July

16, 2001, represents to all appearances the best relationship between these two territorially imposing neighbors in nearly fifty years. To be sure, among informed observers here is still a wide array of assessments of the solidity and durability of this "friendship." It is largely an elite-initiated and elite-managed relationship, in which the commercial and popular dimensions have been relatively modest and tightly controlled. There is clear evidence of tension about specific aspects of the relationship, particularly among Russian border populations host to the inadequately controlled influx of Chinese business people and consumer commodities into the Russian Far East, and perhaps also a certain uneasiness concerning the long-term implications of the massive Chinese purchases of Russian weapons since 1990. But the two sides have proved quite capable of resolving the problems that have arisen diplomatically and the relationship has thus far continued to improve rather than deteriorate, to the apparent benefit of both sides.

The suspicions about the authenticity of this new friendship cannot be attributed solely to Western Schadenfreud. After not just decades but centuries of mutually predatory relations, relieved only by the Bolshevik Revolution and the usually wrong-headed Comintern assistance to the outlawed Chinese Communist movement, the early period of Sino–Soviet friendship and solidarity was relatively brief, and upon its unraveling in the late 1950s it was followed by long and bitter ideological acrimony, culminating in sharp border clashes along the Sino–Soviet border in the spring of 1969. These clashes resulted in heavy mutual fortifications, making this not only the longest land border in the world but also the most explosive one. China developed a nuclear deterrent, exploding its first device in October 1964 and its first thermonuclear weapon in 1968 and leading the Soviet Union to consider a preemptive strike. Only after lengthy and initially fruitless semiannual border negotiations (1970–1976), followed by a second semiannual series of talks from 1982 to 1989, was "normalization" finally achieved. Normalization signified only a return to normal party-to-party relations, not a renewal of the Friendship Treaty (which had been allowed to lapse upon its thirty-year expiry in 1981), a remission of bilateral suspicions, or a resolution of the territorial dispute. It was in the context of the Sino–Soviet summit in Beijing formalizing normalization that the Tiananmen protest occurred, with which the Gorbachev leadership tacitly sympathized, quite contrary to the views of the hard-line Deng leadership. The following two years were roiled by popular upheavals resulting in the collapse of socialism throughout Eastern Europe, for which Chinese leadership clearly blamed Gorbachev's soft line, preferring a Soviet leadership more resolutely committed to the defense of Communist ideal interests. Yet Gorbachev successfully outmaneuvered that alternative when a hard-line faction attempted to seize power in the summer of 1991, and when the Soviet Union nonetheless collapsed at the end of the year Gorbachev was succeeded by an even more unacceptable leadership (from the Chinese perspective), one that promptly disavowed Marxism–Leninism, revived capitalism and parliamentary democracy, and applied the Sinatra doctrine ("let them do it their way") to the Russian Federation, although retaining residual security interests in those former Soviet republics that elected to remain members of the Commonwealth of Independent States. The Chinese leadership was appalled by this denouement.

Thus the question is: Why are Sino–Russian relations so good?—which is sometimes answered with the suspicion that they cannot be as good as they seem. Reconciliation seems anomalous in the context of the most widely accepted explanations of why relations soured in the first place, for most of the factors alluded to in these explanations still exist. A geopolitical explanation, based on the natural rivalry of two enormous continental powers astride the same Eurasian landmass, still pertains. China's territorial claims, based on losses due to the depredations of the czarist empire during the eighteenth and nineteenth centuries, have not been revised in the light of new historical findings or interpretations. So if the old explanations for the enmity were once correct, they would still seem to be valid. In addition, there are new ones. If one credits an ideological explanation of the dispute, that would appear to be far more credible now that the Russian side has foresworn the ideology they once shared with China and embraced its anathema. If, however, we accept the premise that nationalism has become the new legitimating belief system in the wake of the deradicalization of Communist ideology (for which there is good evidence in both countries), why has that not sharpened antagonism between these old foes? If the Soviet Union felt threatened by the rise of a powerful state on its vulnerable eastern border, that concern would seem to be far more pressing now, after Russia's economic nosedive following the repudiation of Communism. Russia lost up to half its GDP in the 1990s (during an unprecedented Chinese economic boom) in a systemic depression that afflicted the Russian Far East (which is the most directly exposed to Chinese penetration of any Russian region) even more seriously than the western part of the country, prompting as much as an eighth of the resident population (of about seven million) to migrate.[5]

Yet the Sino–Russian reconciliation does seem to be a real and lasting one, comparable in historical significance to the Franco–German reconciliation at the end of World War II. This is demonstrated not only by the oral testimonials on both sides by figures whose credibility cannot easily be swept aside,[6] but also by the impressive list of diplomatic achievements over the past decade. The vast and complex border dispute has been essentially reconciled: after a well-organized and closely scheduled series of negotiations between the Chinese side and a team of four former republics (Kazakhstan, Kyrgyzstan, Tajikistan, and Russia), a new border has been demarcated and formally accepted for perpetuity. Confidence-building measures have been introduced along both sides of the frontier, and fortifications and troops have been delimited, permitting Russia to withdraw troops to the Leningrad region following the expansion of NATO eastward and permitting China to redeploy border troops to the Fujian coast facing Taiwan and the South China Sea. Bilateral trade boomed in the wake of Western economic sanctions against China after Tiananmen, to the relief of the Russian population in the Russian Far East, which was adversely affected by the precipitous decline of the military-industrial complex (much of which was located on the eastern side of the Urals), the loss of subsidies, and the increase of intercontinental transportation costs to European markets. Total bilateral trade turnover was U.S.$3.95 billion in 1989 (representing an 18 percent increase over the previous year) and increased to $5.3 billion in 1990, $5.8 billion in 1992, and $7.8 billion in 1993. At this point, popular concern in Russia over illicit Chinese border crossings and economic immigration, shoddy Chinese merchandise, border crime, and corruption led the Duma to enact new border legislation tightening visa requirements in 1994, which had the effect of slashing border trade. But although total trade (particularly Chinese exports) thus stagnated over the next several years, by 2000 it had climbed back up to $8 billion and in 2001 it reached a record $10.67 billion. Although even this figure falls well short of Yeltsin's announced goal of $20 billion by the millennium, this has more to do with the collapse of the Russian economy after the 1998 ruble devaluation than with bad faith. Whereas the American market is far more important to the Chinese economy than the Russian market, to the Russians the Chinese market is second in importance only to the German.

Whereas economic and strategic aspects of a relationship are often distinguished analytically, this is more difficult in the Sino–Russian case because of the importance of military sales in the trade relationship. The PRC made its first purchase of Russian weaponry in 1990 in the wake of the post-Tiananmen Western arms boycott, at a time when Russian worldwide arms sales were in decline following the defeat of former Soviet client Iraq in the 1991 Gulf War. Over the following decade, the Chinese acquired some 90 percent of their foreign arms purchases from the Russians, including Sukhoi SU-27 UBK fighters, SU-30 MKK ground-support aircraft, S-300 and SA-10 antiaircraft and antimissile missiles (comparable to the American Patriots), *Sovremenny*-class destroyers (with Sunburn ship-to-ship missiles) and Kilo-class diesel submarines. According to the Stockholm International Institute of Peace, between 1991 and 1997 Russia sold China armaments worth more than U.S.$6 billion, and for 2000–2005 the overall value of sales is expected to run U.S.$5–6 billion. Although Russia has tried to avoid selling its most advanced weapons, those it sells have the potential to alter the Asian balance of power, specifically vis-à-vis Taiwan, whose naval defense will be complicated by China's large submarine fleet and high-tech destroyers. Bilateral military exchanges have resumed, and Russian engineers and scientists began migrating back to China by private contractual arrangement to aid in military modernization. In October 2000, to mark the fiftieth anniversary of the PRC, two Russian ships visited Shanghai for the first joint naval exercises. From the Russian perspective, weapons sales made an important contribution to the balance of payments, averaging more than $1 billion per annum in foreign exchange and helping to maintain scale production in the Russian military-industrial complex. Many of the weapons sold are produced in the Russian Far East (e.g., Su-27s and Sunburn antiship missiles) and the Zvezda shipyard received an order to repair Chinese submarines, all of which helps alleviate local resentment over the influx of Chinese commercial opportunists and shoddy merchandise. In 2000, China was the largest weapons purchaser in the world and certainly Russia's best customer, having surpassed India in the early 1990s. From the Chinese viewpoint, the Russian "strategic partnership" contributed to the rapid modernization of the PLA, particularly its relatively backward air force and navy, reinforcing Chinese aspirations to great power status. By the end of the 1990s, this had given rise to American public concern about the "China threat," which was exaggerated for partisan reasons and quite premature, although over time the acquisition of advanced Russian weaponry could conceivably shift the balance of power within the region, as China's economy, relatively unaffected by the AFC and by the subsequent high-tech recession, has outpaced that of its neighbors. The Russian response to such concern is that arms sales are economically vital but highly competitive, netting far less worldwide than American arms sales, and that if China's neighbors (including Taiwan) feel threatened they are free to purchase their own Russian munitions (at least until the 1998 summit, when Yeltsin's "five nos" included a refusal to sell weapons to Taiwan).

How was it possible to heal this bitter enmity, which Mao foretold would last a century? Unlike the opening to the West, which unleashed such popular enthusiasm among segments of the populace the government could scarcely contain it, the Sino–Russian friendship was contrived from the top down, through the diplomacy of careful, incremental bridge building. The process was initiated by the launching of border talks in 1970 that alternated biannually between the two capitals and involved virtually the same team of negotiators each year, followed in the 1980s by normalization talks along the same format. By the 1990s, talks at various levels and venues had been more securely institutionalized than in any other international relationship, from biannual summit visits at the top to parliamentary exchanges, friendship associations, film festivals, trade, and even pen pals. In addition to skilled and patient diplomacy, a relatively stable domestic base for cooperation was established through trade and the creation of strong domestic interest groups. Noteworthy from the perspective of linkage politics, the supporting coalitions on both sides seem to have been those interests and strata who typically oppose internationalization—that is, the military, the state trading companies, state-owned heavy industry (including the military-industrial complex), and the established bureaucracy—while true, populist nationalists oppose it, as one might expect.[7] Russia's abandonment of Marxism–Leninism turns out not to have posed much of a problem, for several possible reasons. The previous shared ideology created only a sense of pooled identity that turned out to be quite misleading, giving rise to disappointment and ideological recriminations when specific priorities were not shared (e.g., Taiwan) or when collective achievements fell short of aspiration. Hence Russia's secession from the shared heritage cleared the air, assuring China of its distinctive identity. Moreover, Russia's leap into the enemy camp was belied by its resounding failure (at least in the short run), seeming to vindicate Deng's crackdown. Yet amid all the changes, the partnership somehow continues to partake of the old organizational culture, its spirit nostalgically anti-Western and xenophobic, even in the context of bilateral and international opening.

Sino–Russian reconciliation, leading to the "strategic partnership" and ultimately to a new friendship treaty, is among the most paradoxical outcomes of the post–Cold War era, one that seemingly has taken the relationship full circle. Yet without at all discounting the depth and sincerity of the reconstituted friendship, it would be misleading to equate it with the "lean to one side" period of Sino–Soviet fraternal alliance. For one thing, the new twenty-year Friendship Treaty, drafted at Jiang Zemin's instigation, is not strictly speaking a military alliance (in Article 9, the two agree that if one party believes there is threat of aggression, both sides will confer about measures to be taken in common defense, although they are not committed to mutual defense). The treaty provides for extended cooperation in aviation, space, nuclear, and information technology, as well as more extensive cooperation in military modernization. The "partners" will coordinate policy at the UN Security Council, the World Bank, APEC, ARF, and other international or regional organizations to which both belong. There are at least two important differences between the strategic partnership and its predecessor. First, whereas the mutual defense alliance entailed strategic coordination toward an agreed international objective, viz., world revolution, the current Friendship Treaty seems mainly defensive, concerned with defending the national status quo from meddlesome international organizations, human rights activists, and other agents of liberal globalization. Second, the current treaty is not ideologically exclusive or constitutive of a "bloc," as both countries may simultaneously pursue relations with many other countries. In view of its pointed critique of "hegemony" and call for "multipolarity," the treaty's claim that it is not directed against any third party should be taken with a grain of salt, although given the chances that either partner might defect if made a sufficiently attractive offer from the United States, it just may be correct.

But all this is to define the relationship in terms of what it is not: it is not as ambitious as its forerunner, not as revolutionary, not as threatening to the established order. What is likely, however, to be its positive contribution to the emerging order? Both countries are primarily interested in enhancing their own national interests, and on third-party issues there is no assurance of concert. Beijing was useful to Moscow in facilitating the latter's entry into the ASEAN (Association of Southeast Asian Nations) Regional Forum (ARF) in 1996 and the Asian Pacific Economic Community (APEC) forum in 1998, but has done nothing to facilitate Russo–Japanese reconciliation or Russian inclusion in the Korean talks, and has maintained a discreet silence about periodic Russian attempts to introduce regional security arrangements. China loyally objected to NATO expansion and joined Russia in opposition to the Yugoslav intervention, while Russia has endorsed the one China policy, though none of these expressions of solidarity proved decisive. Coordinated opposition to American missile defense collapsed in the face of a divide-and-conquer strategy by Washington, which focused first on Putin, after which Chinese opposition crumbled. The partnership has undoubted bilateral utility, having eliminated the prospect of war between these continental behemoths and extended cooperation to the fragile new Asian states created by the dismemberment of the Soviet Union at a time of great vulnerability. In the eyes of its supporters on both sides of the border, the relationship will provide a modest but firm foundation for the pursuit of specific shared regional objectives, while proving useful to each as a steppingstone as well as a sanctuary. To China, though not as lucrative as the American relationship, cooperation with Russia poses none of the risks and provides some unique advantages: the relationship is firmly elite controlled; border claims have been amicably settled (if anything the new risk is excessive permeability); because of Russia's economic woes after it betrayed Marxism–Leninism, the Russian model of bourgeois liberation has lost it's appeal; Russian weapons and equipment are relatively inexpensive and more advanced than those of the Chinese; and the Russians faithfully echo Beijing's position on Taiwan and human rights (as the Chinese support Russia on Chechnya). The Russians, somewhat uneasy about their narrow Asian base, have sought to expand their range of useful contacts in the region beyond the PRC, conducting a series of summits with Japanese leaders in the 1990s, seeking to expand investment and trade with South Korea, and trying to repair the badly frayed relationship with Pyongyang. And thanks to Russian sympathy and support for the American countermeasures after September 11, Russian–American relations have improved considerably, without detriment to Sino–American relations, which have improved as well. Yet the Sino–Russian partnership seems likely to remain a privileged relationship for the foreseeable future.

A Landscape without Strategic Architecture

The almost total lack of strategic architecture in Northeast Asia during the Cold War can be understood first of all in terms of the Cold War that bisected the region and second in terms of the failure of the opposing patrons to build any multilateral security vehicle when the opportunity was ripe. In the West, the United States took advantage of its position as sole victor in the Pacific war to build a series of bilateral security alliances, maximizing its asymmetrical power; in the East, the term "region" was not ideologically conceptualized, so China and North Korea belonged only to international communist organizations or to bilateral security and friendship alliances with the Soviet Union—which, again, redounded to the advantage of Moscow as patron. But the international communist movement disintegrated as a casualty of the Sino–Soviet split, which also gave greater flexibility to client states such as North Korea to maneuver between Beijing and Moscow. Thus, as in Europe, where the Warsaw Pact Organization collapsed in 1990 while NATO survived, the ideologically based multilateral security system on the Communist side proved relatively fragile, withering away to leave only a loose patron-client network. After the secession of China from the bloc, Moscow's lone client in the region was the embattled North Korean regime, which indignantly broke off the relationship in 1990, following Moscow's recognition of the Seoul regime.

Of the two superpowers, the Soviet Union evinced the greatest interest in constructing some sort of multilateral security framework that would embrace nonmembers of its own bloc. Given its long-standing regional ambitions and limited access to the region, Moscow became an eager sponsor of such schemes, beginning with Brezhnev's proposed "Asian Collective Security System." As part of his "new thinking," Gorbachev during the latter stages of the Cold War tried, in speeches at Vladivostok in 1986 and Krasnoyarsk in 1988, to introduce similarly overarching, inclusive schemes for regional collective security. In 1986, Gorbachev called for a Conference on Security and Cooperation in Asia (CSCA), modeled on the Conference on Security and Cooperation in Europe, and in September 1988 he made a second initiative, proposing that a working committee consisting of the three Northeast Asian permanent members of the UN Security Council—the Soviet Union, China, and the United States—set the organizational details and the agenda for the CSCA. These proposals, however, were spurned by the Chinese and the West as transparent schemes to increase Soviet influence with no reciprocal benefits and made little progress in the region. Since the Cold War, Russia almost alone has manifest continued interest in collective or cooperative schemes for the region. In September 1990, at Vladivostok, Foreign Minister Eduard Shevardnadze proposed a full-scale meeting of all the foreign ministers of the Asia–Pacific region in Vladivostok in the fall of 1993, to be followed by an all-Asia summit. The UN, with its post–Cold War focus on "preventive diplomacy," introduced forums such as the UN Regional Center for Peace and Disarmament in the Asia Pacific. The first call for multilateral security arrangements specific to Northeast Asia was made not by a Russian but by South Korean president Roh Tae Woo, who proposed a "Consultative Conference for Northeast Asia" in his October 1988 address to the UN General Assembly, to include North and South Korea, the United States, Japan, China, and the Soviet Union. This was no doubt part of Roh's Nordpolitik, as he reaffirmed the idea during his December 1990 state visit to Moscow, part of a campaign to undermine support for Pyongyang and court Soviet recognition of Seoul. Pyongyang's interesting achievement of domestic economic collapse and rapid progress in developing weapons of mass destruction (WMD) in the 1990s (mainly nuclear bombs and guided missile delivery systems) stimulated diplomatic activity considerably, resulting in a series of pathbreaking summits (Putin, Jiang, Madeleine Albright, Kim Dae Jung, and Koizumi to Pyongyang; Kim Jong Il to Moscow, Beijing, and Shanghai), and in the formation of several subregional intergovernmental organizations (mainly the bilateral 1994 Framework Agreement, the Korean Peninsula Energy Development Organization, and the currently stalled Four-Party Peace Talks). These have thus far been task-specific, exclusive arrangements without linkage to the more comprehensive regional forums. Finally, the Shanghai Cooperation Organization (SCO), formed in July 2000, is an institutionalization of the "Group of 5" initiated in 1993 to coordinate border negotiations between the PRC and the team of former Soviet republics that had obtained independence but remained members of the Commonwealth of Independent States, joined by Uzbekistan at the June 2001 summit. As the region's only security forum in which the United States was not directly involved, the SCO was concerned with Muslim terrorism (chiefly in Xinjiang and Chechnya) even before September 11, but has been largely eclipsed since the American offensive against Afghanistan in October 2001. An interesting economic spin-off is the Eurasian Economic Community introduced in 2001, which includes a system of interbank payments and settlements, common labor and capital markets, and a customs union.[8]

The main reason these proposals for collective or cooperative security have gone nowhere is that none of them received the support of both China and the United States. Whereas in Europe Washington was willing to support integration among trusted allies in which it was not directly involved, in Asia no such spontaneous integration tendencies arose in the wake of the Pacific war and the local hot and cold wars that followed, and the United States had no interest in encouraging such tendencies, anyway. Western security commitments in the region have been strictly bilateral, consisting of alliances with Taiwan (lapsed since 1979), Japan, and South Korea. These gave Washington more power and freedom to maneuver and provided the clients with a greater sense of security (both nuclear and conventional) than they would have received from membership in a multilateral arrangement (which is not to say clients were getting a free ride—both Japan and Korea have paid generously to support the American troops stationed on their soil, over which they exercise no command or control). A Helsinki process might conceivably lead to calls for naval arms control—the Americans boasted the biggest fleet in the Pacific. The Clinton administration brought somewhat greater receptivity to multilateral arrangements, at least at the rhetorical level, and Washington participated in the ASEAN Post–Ministerial Conference and its successor, the ARF (founded in 1994); the Americans also became engaged in Track II dialogues through the Council for Security Cooperation in the Asia Pacific and other such networks.[9] But these are essentially talk shops with no authority for autonomous action and minimal institutional infrastructure (even ASEAN, the oldest and most institutionalized regional organization, lacks a permanent secretariat). ASEAN, as the ARF's prime driving force and founder, gave that organization a Southeast Asian tilt, even after Northeast Asian countries were included; and although security issues could be discussed, binding decisions were strictly off limits, largely at the insistence of Beijing.[10] But while China initially viewed the launching of ARF with some reservations, by 1997 Beijing had become an active participant, and when ASEAN launched the Asia–Europe Meeting (ASEM) in March 1996 in Bangkok, Premier Li Peng attended the inaugural meeting (and China has been represented at all subsequent meetings). ASEAN Plus Three (the three being China, Japan, and South Korea), an exclusively Asian group formed in 1997 in Kuala Lumpur in response to the perceived need for an East Asian security forum more capable of responding to regional crises, has heretofore had equally little to say about security issues. Its most ambitious achievement to date has been the 2000 Chiang Mai Initiative, aimed at swapping currencies to forestall possible economic crises.

The absence of any formal strategic architecture was more than offset during the Cold War by a comprehensive web of opposing security alliances. Upon the decay of bipolarity, it was replaced in the 1970s by an informal expedient known as the "strategic triangle," which consisted of the PRC, the USSR, and the United States. This was an asymmetric, three-player game in which each player was also patron of a retinue of client states and strove to win by outmaneuvering the other players or forcing a shift to a triangular configuration in which it had an improved position. The United States initially had the most advantageous position in the game, allowing it to cultivate better relations with both the PRC and the USSR than they had with each other (in the wake of Soviet preemptive nuclear strike scenarios in the early 1970s), but in the 1980s the Chinese maneuvered into the structurally optimal pivot position, from which it maintained good relations with Reagan's Washington while conducting normalization talks with Moscow. When Gorbachev then revived détente in the latter half of the 1980s with a surprising series of unilateral concessions that facilitated a breakthrough in various arms control and disarmament talks, while at the same time "normalizing" relations with Beijing, this transformed the triangle into a ménage à trois. This transfiguration was confirmed by the collapse of the Soviet Union and the Russian Federation's subsequent embrace of market democracy, which erased any ideological pretext for East–West antagonism. This, however, deprived the triangle of any strategic rationale, and it soon faded into irrelevance. It was also beset by long-term structural problems. The nuclear weapons monopoly on which the global primacy of the triangular powers had been based began to suffer a loss of credibility, which may in turn be attributed to the continuing efficacy of low-threshold conventional weapons (as in national liberation wars), to the futility of nuclear confrontations when both sides have assured second-strike capabilities, and finally to the ideological deradicalization of both Marxism–Leninism and market liberalism, divesting postrevolutionary leaderships of a legitimate casus belli for nuclear war. The passing of the strategic triangle removed security risks by eliminating third-party threats as a factor in bilateral détente, fostering proliferation of a new set of flexible, nonexclusive relationships.

But it also deprived the region of strategic structure, even if informal. With the region stripped of structural context since the Cold War, its two hot spots, the Taiwan Strait and the Korean peninsula, became even more sensitive. In view of the socioeconomic decline and domestic preoccupations of the former Soviet Union, it has been suggested that for at least the time being Russia (with half the USSR's GDP and a population of 140 million, only some 7 million of whom are in the Russian Far East) should be dealt out of power politics—that the best hope for a regional architecture would be a new triangle consisting of China, Japan, and the United States. Can these three be said to compose a new strategic triangle? Japan, as distinguished from the United States and the PRC, is not a nuclear power, and notwithstanding the presumption that it could very quickly become one, there are reasons to doubt that it will choose to do so unless national security is seriously jeopardized. Despite having a far from negligible military capability and one of the world's largest defense budgets, Japan is constitutionally defined as a new type of pacifist state, by definition not a strategic actor. At the same time, despite its recent difficulties, it is the region's dominant economic power. Though Japan brandishes a small but well-trained and high-tech Self Defense Force (SDF), any attempt to use it, even in peacekeeping operations that appear consonant with its mission, tends to occasion such intense domestic and regional controversy that it is hard to imagine how Japan could play a strategic role in any conventional sense. Under the circumstances, Japan's only triangular option is to minimize contradictions with and between both sides. Yet although these three countries have different mixes of national power and role conceptions, it seems reasonable to contend that they are now the dominant powers in the region and share the capacity to restructure the region's strategic architecture. It is no accident that both Nixon and Kissinger, during their "private" visits to Beijing in the fall of 1989, suggested restructuring the triangle to include Japan—though it is unclear exactly what they had in mind.

Throughout the period of the Sino–Soviet alliance (1951–1981), Beijing's stance vis-à-vis Tokyo seems to have varied in its relations with the two superpowers, making the Sino–Japanese–American triangle a function of the Sino–Soviet–American triangle. During the 1950s, when China was aligned with the Soviet Union against the United States, China vehemently opposed the Japanese–American Security Alliance (JASA); this opposition continued through the 1960s, despite the rising salience of the Soviet threat, presumably due to continued Chinese preoccupation with the U.S. threat, for example, in Vietnam. In the wake of the Sino–Soviet border clash and the ensuing opening to the United States (followed by diplomatic normalization with Japan in September 1972, well ahead of normalization with the United States), China lapsed into silence on the JASA and by the end of the decade was encouraging Japan to increase its defense spending.[11] With Sino–Soviet normalization back on the agenda, China no longer had any perceived need to mobilize Japanese antagonism to Soviet hegemonism, as China again came to view Japanese arms spending as a threat. When in 1987

Nakasone raised the SDF budget above the 1 percent limit, Deng Xiaoping criticized this as a sign of Japanese militarism. The Chinese have repeatedly pointed out that Japan ranks third in the world in defense expenditures, without noting that this is a distant third (the amount was only U.S.$39.2 billion in 1989, for example, compared with $290.3 billion for the United States and a reported $229 billion for the Soviet Union) or that estimates of Japan's expenditures vary with the exchange rate, so that a 20 percent rise in the value of the dollar would drop Japan back behind England and France.[12] China was sharply critical of both the expanded guidelines for Japan's defense responsibilities in the region announced in 1996–1997 and the planned cooperation with the United States to develop a Theater Missile Defense. Beijing has not yet opposed JASA per se, preferring that to Japan's development of an independent force projection capability, but it would prefer to minimize Japanese–American strategic cooperation. The PRC's underlying concern is Japan's relationship with Taiwan, a colony for some fifty years that has remained closely tied to Japan economically; however, although the first announcement of the expanded interpretation of JASA came within a month of the March 1996 Sino–American Taiwan Strait confrontation, the original impetus derived from friction that developed when Washington was considering how to implement a blockade of North Korea for its refusal to permit International Atomic Energy Agency inspection of a suspected nuclear weapons facility in 1993.[13] To what extent such complaints reflect serious Chinese concern, in view of the fact that as of now it is China, not Japan, that boasts a nuclear strike force capable of destroying much of Japan, while still maintaining the region's largest (if not the most modern) conventional army and air force, it is hard to say. In any case, criticism was temporarily muted in the aftermath of Tiananmen, when Japan was China's only advocate among advanced industrial democracies, and it reappeared only after the succession of Jiang Zemin in 1997. There is no question that China is increasingly wary of what they view as Japan's growing international assertiveness; they even expressed reservations about Japan's decision to deploy SDF troops and ships for the first time out of the region to help in the post–September 11 American offensive against the Taliban regime in Afghanistan.

Though it is clear in the wake of the AFC that these are the three dominant powers in the region, that does not necessarily make their relationship "triangular." Characteristic of a triangle is that all bilateral relations are contingent upon relations with the third power. This gives triangular diplomacy a mixed paranoid–seductive tinge, as each power tends to fear hostile collusion by the other two while at the same time attempting to seduce one of them into collusion against the third. This triangular dynamic seems to have first become manifest in Sino–Japanese–American relations after the end of the Cold War, inasmuch as these relations had in a sense guaranteed both the Japanese–American and the Sino–American friendships by providing side payments and a strategic target against which both could concert, and the removal of that guarantee has made all three relationships more open ended. This became visible, for example, in the rather reserved Chinese reaction to the possibility of a Russo–Japanese territorial settlement momentarily excited by the Hashimoto–Yeltsin "tieless" summit or even, more clearly, in the deliberate Chinese exclusion of Japan from Sino–American summitry in June 1998. The AFC seems also to have stimulated a certain Sino–Japanese rivalry for financial patronage. The Japanese proposed an Asian Monetary Fund to make funding available to help underwrite the loans of insolvent banks in the crisis-affected countries. Both Beijing and Washington joined with the International Monetary Fund (IMF) in rejecting the proposal, which was promptly dropped. Beijing contributed some U.S.$4 billion through the IMF and other channels to the afflicted economies and made a point of refusing to devalue its currency (as it had in 1994), thereby sacrificing export competitiveness for regional financial stability. Though arguments could also be made that devaluation was not in China's interest, Beijing played up its role as a financial angel, in 1998, even (by threatening to reconsider its commitment not to devalue) inducing Washington to persuade Tokyo not to initiate a second wave of devaluations. This was perhaps China's first participation in international financial policy making, and Beijing clearly appreciated the opportunity to displace Japan as regional savior of the afflicted countries in collaboration with the United States and the IMF.

Thus triangular "jealousy" has become tangible, despite efforts on all three sides to play it down. So far it has consisted of a politics of gesture, without any basic shift in the architecture of the relationship. That architecture is not triangular. Among the three participants, Japan is least likely to entertain the prospect of triangulation, simply because its options are so constrained: it cannot break from the United States because of the highly successful legacy of the Yoshida settlement (i.e., the United States provides for Japan's security while Japan focuses on economics), yet at the same time it is obliged (by war guilt and historical tribute, not to mention current strategic vulnerability) to harbor good relations with China. Japanese–American ties, as formalized in JASA, remain fundamental in this mix, despite occasional trade friction, qualifying any American attempt to form an exclusive partnership with Beijing; whereas either Washington or Tokyo may deviate at the margin (as when Nixon visited China without consulting Japan or when Tanaka recognized Beijing), neither would do so if that imperiled their bilateral relationship. There is good reason why the Sino–Japanese–

American triangle has thus far been limited to a politics of nuance. Any basic shift of the configuration—for example, Tokyo's abandonment of JASA to form an Asian partnership with the PRC or a shift in Washington from reliance on Japan to reliance on China—brings more risk than conceivable gains. Among the three, these powers now control one of the largest trade and investment flows in the world and about half the world's production, and any triangular permutation that risks polarization could thus be very costly. The outlook for at least the foreseeable future is hence that of a delicate quasi–ménage à trois, complete with coquetry and petty frictions, rather than any economically disruptive triangular polarization (two against one).

Cooperation without Institutional Integration

If in the security field we find few formal structures and an incoherent alternation between two different informal triangular logics, in economics we also find very little movement toward formal institution building. The first economic mechanism including the Northeast Asian states was the Pacific Economic Cooperation Conference (1980), which consisted of the business elite. In 1989, the Asia Pacific Economic Cooperation (APEC) forum was organized at the instigation of Australian prime minister Robert Hawke, and it has been mainly preoccupied with phased tariff reduction, even after Clinton introduced APEC summits in November 1993 at Seattle. APEC introduced the concept of "open regionalism," meaning that whatever tariff reductions or trade agreements were reached internally would also be applicable throughout the World Trade Organization on a most favored nation basis. APEC, of course, transcends Northeast Asia, including not only Southeast and South Asia, but also the United States, Canada, and much of the Pacific coast of Latin America. This was even more the case for ASEM, also sponsored by ASEAN to discuss trade issues. In view of concerns about a loss of regional focus, Malaysian prime minister Mahathir Mohammed introduced the exclusively Asian East Asian Economic Caucus (EAEC) in 1990, but in the face of American objections this idea went nowhere. As noted above, the same held true with the Asian Monetary Fund. ASEAN Plus Three comprises essentially the same membership as the EAEC, and within that China has proposed a free-trade agreement (FTA) with ASEAN (i.e., ASEAN Plus One), later to be extended to South Korea and Japan; the prospects for such proposals are still uncertain. No subregional association (i.e., specifically for Northeast Asia) has yet been formed, aside from the "Plus Three" get-togethers on the margins of the ASEAN Plus Three meetings. Two sub-subregional economic groupings have emerged, or what Scalapino calls NETs (natural economic territories): the Yellow Sea Economic Zone, consisting of South Korea, Japan, and China's Liaoning and Shandong Provinces, and the Tumen River Area Development Programme, initiated by the United Nations Development Program with a very modest $3 million feasibility study and involving China, North and South Korea, Russia, and Mongolia. In Northeast Asia NETs have, however, been hindered by security considerations, as a result of which progress has thus far been less than impressive.

In view of the elliptical quality of formal economic organization in Northeast Asia, the possibility is worth investigating that, as in the case of security, informal organization may fill the breach. Market-based growth has certainly been vigorous in this region, and all of these countries (with the exception until very recently of North Korea) have endeavored to implement industrial policies, especially to promote high-tech and export industry. But the region is still rife with old ideological suspicions and new (or even older) nationalist rivalries, and markets are not in themselves necessarily internationally coherent organizations. What are the political implications of markets? Do markets impose a hierarchy? Leadership may emerge in a market, in the form, say, of particularly successful firms ("market leaders"), but can a nation-state derive political benefit from market building? There has thus been discussion, for example, of "locomotive regionalism," in which a leading state becomes the focus of much of the commerce, technology, and finance in the region.[14] But who is the locomotive of Northeast Asia? Katzenstein has suggested that in East Asia the organization of markets has taken not one but two forms: Japanese and Chinese.[15] The Japanese system is systematic and state led, as it downloads more labor-intensive industries to former colonies while retaining capital- and technology-intensive industries at home, along with the managerial and financial service sector, a "flying geese" pattern based on product cycle theory.[16] This pattern expanded vigorously following the 1985 Rockefeller Plaza accord reached with the United States to revalue the yen, which drove the prices of Japanese exports out of the market and forced Japanese industry to invest in less-developed countries with lower wage rates and deflated currencies. Thus Japan invested heavily in the late 1980s and early 1990s in Southeast Asia and in the late 1990s (amid the AFC) in China, where wages were low and the currencies were pegged to the dollar. Because Japan did not have the consumer markets to absorb the finished products, however, this created a production chain culminating in North American markets and creating a persisting imbalance of payments with all of Japan's trading partners. When many of the smaller client states faced disaster in 1997–1999 as a result of the dollar rising against the yen and undermining Southeast Asian export competitiveness, Japan was in no realistic position to help because of its own dangerously overextended banking sector. Japan could not be a competent locomotive.

The Chinese pattern is more informal, based on investment flows from the overseas Chinese business sector into China, which is essentially part of the vast expansion of the influx of overseas remittances that began with the inauguration of reform and the opening at the Third Plenum of the Twelfth Party Congress. The overseas economy ranks fourth in the world in financial importance, comprising a majority share of financial and industrial assets of Southeast Asia with a total GDP larger than that of the PRC as of 1990. Since the mid-1980s, some four-fifths of the contracted investment and two-thirds of the realized foreign direct investment (FDI) in the PRC is estimated to have come from the regional business networks that link Hong Kong, Taiwan, and Southeast Asia with the PRC. Though part of a molding of "greater Chinese" national identity analogous to the way the flow of Japanese FDI has led to the growth of a "yen bloc," the financial dynamics of Chinese economic regionalism are quite different. China is an even less adequate locomotive than Japan, as much of its investment capital, particularly in the most value-added sectors, is imported. Whereas the Japanese pattern allocates capital in the form of developmental loans and grants as well as private FDI from the national center to its client states and hopes to realize some "profit" from its "investment," the PRC is the passive recipient of incoming investment, which flows from a wide stratum of overseas Chinese investors acting voluntarily for private gain. Certainly, it is true that Chinese growth is more independent of Japanese financing than that of the newly industrializing countries (NICs) or the Southeast Asian economies. But the flow of overseas Chinese capital is not necessarily opposed to Japanese financial strategy and may even coexist peacefully with the flying geese formation—after all, the Japanese are also big investors in China. Japan invests in Taiwan or Hong Kong as well, who in turn invest in China. The greater Chinese international network is also smaller than the Japanese, as Japanese GDP (as of 1990) comprised 73 percent of the combined GDP of all East and Southeast Asian countries, though the growth momentum seems to have shifted in the 1990s to the Chinese side. Though not necessarily incompatible, what is interesting about these grand designs for economic integration from our current perspective is that both are focused beyond the region, moving south, as if the prospect of integration within the region had been tacitly abandoned and the rivalry projected outward.

From a strictly economic perspective, the available evidence suggests that regional integration is progressing well. Cold War Asian trade was dominated by heavy bilateral trade between Japan and South Korea on one hand and North America and it's markets on the other, essentially reflecting the hub-

and-spokes security system. The post–Cold War pattern is for this to diminish in favor of intraregional trade. Intraregional exports among East Asian countries accounted for 49.5 percent of total East Asian trade in 1994, up from 30.9 percent in 1986, while the trade dependency of East Asia on the United States fell from 34 percent to 22.8 percent over the same time span; if imports are included, intraregional trade in East Asia exceeded 50 percent by 1995. Throughout the 1985–1994 decade, exports to Northeast Asian markets expanded about twice as fast as exports to the American market. Japan still relies more on the U.S. market than on Northeast Asia (28.1 percent vs. 24.4 percent as of 1997), but China, Hong Kong, South Korea, and Taiwan now rely more heavily on Northeast Asian markets than on the United States (though the trend for Chinese exports is the reverse, exports to the United States having grown from 8.5 to 17.7 percent over that time span). By the year 2000, the United States and Japan were China's first and second trade partners and the United States and China were Japan's first and second trade partners, while the first and second trade partners of the United States were Canada and Mexico, beneficiaries of NAFTA. With regard to investments, by 1993, 72.4 percent of foreign investment in East Asia was from within Asia, while only 9.6 percent was from the United States. Within the region, the flow of FDI is from Japan to the NICs (South Korea, Taiwan, Hong Kong) and from the NICs into China. In the emerging regional division of labor, Japan provides funds, technology, and advanced products as well as a significant market for raw materials and consumer commodities; the NICs provide upstream manufacturing capacity for intermediate equipment and processing technologies and are major consumers of raw materials; and China serves as a recipient of FDI, a supplier of raw materials, textiles, and light manufactures, and a growing market for consumers goods.

The preoccupations driving integration have changed dramatically in the past decade: whereas integration was once ultimately propelled by the Cold War, since the end of the Cold War integration has been a solution in search of a new problem. Initially it seemed plausible that market demand was self-sustaining, as falling political barriers opened new markets in the 1990s and regional trade and investment boomed. Yet the market proved double-edged: although trade and investment flows helped to integrate the region, it was also one of the factors accounting for the virulent financial contagion that characterized the AFC. The AFC had a profoundly disconcerting impact on the region's foreign and economic policy makers, who resolved never again to permit such a financial collapse followed by abject reliance for financial rescue on the IMF (whose rescue package was considered misconceived). While the war on terrorism became Washington's foreign policy pole star after September 11, its impact in the region could never rival the seismic aftershocks of the AFC. Yet the existing financial infrastructure—APEC, ASEAN, and the Asian Developmental Bank—did not rise to the occasion. The failure of the AMF did not mitigate the need for some sort of regional institutional infrastructure, an infrastructure needed if only to coordinate periodic adjustments of exchange rates to rectify chronic trade imbalances.[17] A first step was agreed upon in the Chiang Mai Initiative, the ASEAN Plus Three's main achievement to date, though each country has committed only a few billion dollars and the commitments are hedged. The patent inadequacy of this package has stirred interest in a Pan-Asian FTA, or in reviving the AMF; more realistic short-term outcomes might include a permanent secretariat for the ASEAN Plus Three, or an Asia-wide FTA (AFTA). Amid the controversy that has hobbled multilateral solutions, so far the main institutional spin-off of the AFC has been a host of bilateral FTAs, bringing the international equivalent of market deregulation; an FTA has been proposed between Japan and Korea, later to include China,[18] but most of the FTAs actually implemented have been with extraregional trade partners (between Singapore and Japan; between Japan and Chile, Japan and Canada, and Japan and New Zealand; and between South Korea and Mexico and South Korea and Chile). That is partly because the region is not only "soft" (lacking in interstate institutions) but also already "open" (to extraregional trade), and partly because the region's leaders are economic competitors with limited economic complementarity.

Integration and Its Exceptions

The only two nations in the world riven by the Cold War to remain divided upon its conclusion, China and Korea, are in Northeast Asia. In the West, the destruction of the Berlin Wall was the synecdoche for the reunification of Europe, which in turn became a defining epitaph for the end of the Cold War. This reintegration symbolized the trends that have been widely assumed to characterize the post–Cold War international system: globalization, liberalization, and nationalism. Thus Germany was reunified by nationalism, just as nationalism precipitated the fragmentation of Yugoslavia and Czechoslovakia, then the Soviet Union, along Wilsonian lines of national self-determination. Where are such trends in Northeast Asia? Certainly there is no lack of evidence of nationalism in the region, as expressed in the Chinese outrage over the 1999 NATO bombing of the Chinese embassy in Belgrade, the construction of a lighthouse on the Diaoyu/Senkaku Islands by Japanese patriots, or the brouhaha over Yasukuni shrine visits and history texts for Japanese schoolchildren. At the same time, these countries were among the foremost exploiters and beneficiaries of globalization, having pushed an export-led development model to unprecedented growth rates. Although there is admittedly one key difference remaining between East and West in that Communism has not collapsed in China, North Korea, Vietnam, or Laos, Marxist ideology has been deradicalized and Communist foreign policy derevolutionized to such an extent that by the 1990s the United States had renounced its containment policy against Communism in favor of a policy of "constructive engagement."

Inasmuch as the same policy currents that waft over Western Europe have appeared in Northeast Asia, to what extent might one expect analogous consequences to materialize? There are two ways in which the Korean and Chinese cases might develop so that they may be said to conform to post–Cold War political globalization. The first and perhaps most obvious scenario would be for the Chinese and Korean nation–states to reunify, bringing the nationalist entelechy to its natural conclusion. The second possibility, rationally justifiable in terms of length of time spent apart (at least half a century) and current organization along quite disparate political–economic lines (democratic capitalism vs. Leninist dictatorship with marketization), would be for the two divided states to formalize their divisions, adopting what before 1989 was the German solution: one nation, two separate states, each with equal claims to sovereignty in the international arena.

Yet neither of these scenarios has come to pass. Instead, formally speaking, both nations have remained frozen in a status quo in which all four states (China, Taiwan, North Korea, and South Korea) are sufficiently autonomous to claim and largely to practice international sovereignty, but none of them fully accept that status. In the Korean case, the North has long endorsed a united Republic of Koryo, while denouncing and seeking to prevent the South from gaining recognition as a separate state; South Korea has in the past expressed somewhat greater interest in permanent division, but remains officially committed to reunification along democratic lines. Both have meanwhile been accepted into the United Nations and have gained widespread diplomatic recognition in the international arena. In the Chinese case, both sides agreed throughout their first four decades that there was but one China in the world and each claimed to be its exclusive legitimate representative, while trying to persuade all other nations to recognize its claim and not to recognize its rival. When, by the end of the 1980s, the competition for international diplomatic recognition had been essentially won by the PRC, Taiwan unilaterally dropped its claim for exclusive sovereignty and recognized the legitimate jurisdiction of the PRC over the mainland, at the same time continuing to compete for diplomatic recognition of a "one country, two states" model in which it declared itself ready to have relations with all states, without demanding that they renounce their relations with the

PRC. Beijing refused to follow suit, with the result that the PRC became widely considered the only China and Taiwan became a de facto separate state that was, however, relegated to a lower, unofficial international status. Yet at the same time, economic ties between Taiwan and the mainland, offered by the Chinese in the early 1980s to encourage economic integration, have met with great success, as both cross-strait trade and cross-strait investment have increased more rapidly than domestic growth on either side of the strait. And although Taiwan has in the course of its democratization and indigenization (*bentuhua,* often called Taiwanization) in the 1980s expressed increasing interest in independence, its formal status remains the "Republic of China," and it remains constitutionally committed to reunification with a democratic mainland.

Everything changes, everything remains the same, one is tempted to conclude, and yet there have been major changes in the status of the divided states. The biggest difference is that, during the Cold War, both were more or less locked into a bipolar or triangular structure, and since the end of the Cold War they have both been unshackled. The outcome has been in some ways like unchaining Prometheus, in others more like opening Pandora's box. No longer locked into an alliance system, both divided nations have had greater room to maneuver, as indicated by North Korea's attempted development of nuclear weapons or by the rise to power of Taiwan's DPP, the partisan offspring of the Taiwan independence movement. At the same time, expectations (and pressure) are heightened by the dramatic transformation in Europe. In both cases there is great pressure for change, although the nature of the pressure varies considerably. In the Korean case, the unilateral Soviet and Chinese redefinition of their economic commitments from socialist fraternity to free-market trade relationships at the beginning of the 1990s, coinciding as it did with both former patrons' diplomatic recognition of the South Korean regime, seriously undermined both the economic and the security bases of the Pyongyang regime. While the economy went into a tailspin, the regime ignored that and focused on the security gap in the form of a crash nuclear-weapons and missile-development program. This was accompanied by a diplomatic campaign to break out of the ostracism of Nordpolitik, courting first Japan then the United States and finally culminating in a summit meeting with South Korean premier Kim Dae Jung. Though seriously imperiled by patron abandonment and an ensuing economic nosedive, the Pyongyang regime was thus able through unprecedented political gyrations to survive for at least the foreseeable future.

The Chinese case, though far more asymmetrical than the Korean in terms of size and raw power, has been perhaps more balanced in terms of relative disposable assets. During the second stage of the Asian Cold War, after

China had broken with the USSR, establishing a triangular counterbalance with the support of the United States, Beijing was able to escalate its strategic value above that of Taipei, with the result that the diplomatic contest for international recognition was essentially decided by the end of the 1970s. At the same time, Beijing introduced a new, far more attractive set of initiatives to resolve the Taiwan Strait impasse—the "three links" (i.e., direct postal, air, and shipping services) and the "one country, two systems" model—guaranteeing Taiwan a high degree of autonomy upon reunification. With the collapse of European Communism in the final act of the Cold War, however, Beijing's strategic importance sank, while Taiwan's democratization made it more ideologically palatable internationally, and Taipei launched a countercampaign to regain international legitimacy. Though this did not alter the structural power imbalance to Taiwan's advantage, it did apparently sufficiently unnerve Beijing that in 1995–1996 it abandoned its concessionary policies and resorted once again to the threat of violence, in the form of military exercises and cross-strait missile shots. Under the circumstances (the U.S. Navy supported Taiwan and Beijing had to back down), this neither curtailed Taiwan's interest in independence (as later expressed in the 1999 "two states theory") nor improved China's public image abroad.

These two divided states are the region's least stable elements, and the pressure for them to resolve their status is likely to increase as the rest of the region consolidates. A resolution might take any of three forms. The first possibility is a "Vietnamese" solution—the side that is stronger and more aggressive successfully attacks the side that is weaker or more passive, thereby resolving the issue through annexation. Though the 1995–1996 exercises demonstrated that this option has not been forsaken, it seems unlikely for the foreseeable future, if only because of the clear military superiority of U.S. forces (which are committed to "peaceful" resolution) to any putative invasion force. The second possibility is formal division resulting in four separate states, each with full international diplomatic rights. This is patently unacceptable for at least one side of each pair; whether it would be acceptable to the international community under these circumstances seems dubious. The third possibility is reunification under some arrangement that guarantees the rights of the populace of the weaker side, perhaps by internationalizing the issue in some way. Such a compromise could well be unacceptable to one side or the other of the split nation involved, either as an abuse of human rights or as an infringement of national sovereignty.

CONCLUSION

Northeast Asia has emerged since the Cold War as one of the most economically powerful regions in the world, yet the sense of regional consciousness is still weak and the institutional infrastructure tenuous, while the ideological distinctions, though of diminished credibility, sow seeds of suspicion. The security context is that of a classic balance-of-power, self-help system with reciprocally rising arms budgets and no confidence-building measures or institutionalized multilateral forums for the resolution of volatile issues. In terms of informal economic integration via trade and investment networks, progress has been made, though each of these states upholds a strict distinction between economics and politics (Marx notwithstanding). To put it in stark outlines, the region consists of eight states that may be classified into four great powers (China, Russia, Japan, and the United States) and four small to medium powers (South Korea, North Korea, Taiwan, and Mongolia). Before looking at the relationship between great powers and small powers, let us consider the relationships among great powers.

In many respects, the relationships among the four great powers represent a continuation, in less confrontational form, of the Cold War alignment: two against two. On the one hand we have China and Russia, who have defied all contrary expectations to forge a strategic partnership of considerable mutual utility and apparent strength. The territorial dispute has been successfully resolved and, though the 2001 Friendship Treaty is a limited liability accord rather than an alliance, it does symbolize the strength of the assiduously crafted and well-maintained bilateral ties. The ideological differences have been mitigated by the hitherto unenviable results of the Russian systemic transition, allowing the partnership to thrive in an afterglow of nostalgia. Japan and the United States remain partners to the strongest bilateral alliance in the region, and although trade friction has periodically roiled relations, both are capitalist democracies, and the alliance has grown stronger since the termination of the Cold War and the simultaneous disappearance of the Japanese challenge to U.S. economic hegemony. In terms of both ideological affiliation and security commitment, as well as the distribution of deeply rooted issue disputes (e.g., territorial differences between Japan and Russia, Sino–American friction over Taiwan, conceptually distinctive notions of human rights), the "two vs. two" momentum is quite well established. To be sure, the polarization between the two dyads has been appreciably reduced since the Cold War. China's guiding ideology no longer prescribes the export of revolution but of "reform," and Beijing also draws upon a legacy of quasi-alliance with the United States during the decades of the strategic triangle; Russia defines itself as a geopolitical swing state with a long-term commitment to Western values. The distribution of trade and investment is now based primarily on market rather than security considerations, which over time could bring about the redistribution of vested interests and hence perhaps redefine the line of cleavage.

Whereas relations among the four great powers are hence stable and steadily improving, the relationship of the smaller powers to the big powers has changed significantly since the end of the Cold War. After decades of lockstep cooperation with the Soviet Union, Mongolia has benefited from Sino–Russian reconciliation, which has permitted it to become for the first time truly free and autonomous, its tiny free-market democracy shielded from the economic juggernaut to the south. For Taiwan and the two Koreas, the salient issue since the collapse of the bamboo curtain has become reunification. During the Cold War, the question remained in effect frozen for the duration—nationalists on either side of their respective borders might not agree, but the bipolar international structure in which the division was imbedded was simply too strong for reunification to be considered a feasible option. After the collapse of the Iron Curtain, the divided nations were able to break out of their opposing alliance structures, only to encounter a bewildering array of new opportunities and risks. While the mainland Chinese, enjoying the upsurge of growth that accompanied successful reform, made concessionary reunification proposals to Taiwan, the DPRK's suddenly catastrophic economic situation led them to take a more suspicious stance toward unification prospects. The two capitalist regimes in the south, Taiwan and South Korea, initially pursued analogous policies of political realism: without foreclosing the eventual prospect of reunification, both moved toward the German model of "one nation, two states" with initial formal recognition of the division of sovereignty. This succeeded in the case of Korea, as both the North and the South were admitted to the UN General Assembly in September 1991, but the PRC blocked Taiwan's bid for either dual recognition ("flexible diplomacy") or representation in international forums ("UN diplomacy"), using its now much stronger international position to isolate Taipei diplomatically while engaging it economically. Thereafter, the tactics of the two rivals tended to reflect the relative balance of power. In the Pyongyang–Seoul contest, the South, from a vastly superior economic position, adopted a concessionary "sunshine policy" toward the North, while Pyongyang, dangerously near to developing deliverable nuclear weapons despite a collapsing economy, tried to avoid a strictly bilateral deal, rebuilding its contacts with the East (frequent meetings with both Jiang and Putin, a 2001 Friendship Treaty with Moscow) while luring in the West with a combination of blackmail and conciliatory gestures and pursuing dilatory tactics toward the South. In the Taiwan Strait case, the mainland tried to keep the issue strictly bilateral, increasingly fearful, however, that after fifteen years of economic integration plus diplomatic isolation the island was moving toward independence. Beijing reverted in the mid-1990s to military coercion, as a result of which talks collapsed, and Taipei moved back into Washington's embrace. In sum, the divided nations, having become obsessed with the riddle of unfinished national identity, became "free radicals," threatening the delicate equilibrium of a region increasingly awash in economic and public opinion markets, all of which gives an anomalous structure to the emerging Northeast Asian regional order. On the one hand, we have a relatively stable and balanced cleavage between great powers, who are essentially content with the status quo (with some minor adjustments), while on the other we have two isolated trouble spots, where actors are ambivalent about but, in principle, committed to radical change. The two trouble spots tend to be isolated not only because of the difficulty of arriving at mutually compatible and just solutions but for quite practical reasons relating to system equilibrium.

What has been the impact of the events of September 11 on Northeast Asian politics? The major immediate impact of course was on American foreign policy. The United States, as a target of the most lethal foreign assault in its history (more casualties than Pearl Harbor), attempted not only to lash out at the Taliban regime in Afghanistan that harbored Al Qaeda, but also to define the attack as an "act of war" (rather than a violation of international law) and declare a "war on terrorism," conceived as the sustained, focal raison d'état guiding U.S. foreign policy efforts in much the same way that anticommunism provided a focus for American foreign policy during the Cold War. The historically unusual (and no doubt temporary) preeminence of the United States in world affairs at the dawn of the twenty-first century has obliged other countries to define themselves in relation to this declaration. For as long as terrorism had an empirical locus in the form of a national regime willing to bear responsibility for harboring identified terrorists, as the Taliban regime showed itself to be by refusing to extradite Osama bin Laden and the Al Qaeda network then based on its territory, this conceptualization proved useful in coordinating international efforts. Washington proceeded to secure UN support, put together a broad and eclectic international coalition willing to provide basing rights, troops, and other facilities, and to proceed with air attacks on Afghanistan as early as October 7. But since the surprisingly swift collapse of the Taliban regime in late January 2002, it has been more difficult to sustain that focus. This has particularly been the case in Northeast Asia, which had no demonstrable involvement in the events of September 11 and relatively little experience with the form of militant Islam that motivated the attacks. Concentrated Islamic populations pose only localized threats to two countries in the region, Russia and China, in Chechnya and Xinjiang, respectively. Yet the American reconceptualization of international relations has had its impact. Whereas before September 11, Washington's initiative under the incoming George W. Bush administration had in a number of ways contributed to greater polarization among the powers of the region, after September 11 the configuration shifted from two against two to four against terrorism. With obvious relief, the leaders of both Russia and China made both public statements of support and personal sympathy calls to Washington, and were in fact quite helpful in moving against the Taliban. But in the absence of a consensually agreed upon national incarnation of terrorism after the collapse of Afghanistan (neither Moscow nor Beijing has supported hostilities against the "axis of evil"—Iran, Iraq, and North Korea—postulated in Bush's January 2002 state of the union address), this new unanimity may prove superficial and fleeting. Inclusion of a highly sensitive North Korean regime in the "axis" in an apparent effort to apply pressure against further development of WMD has proved particularly problematic, generating little regional support. Under the encompassing tent of antiterrorism, the old national rivalries endure, while the American commitment to multilateralism has not, and there has been persisting unease that Washington's policies are animated by national rather than regional interests. For its part, Washington suspects the region has been more preoccupied with recovery from the AFC and regeneration of sustained economic growth than with terrorism.

In sum, although Northeast Asia is a region that finds itself still in the early stages of the long march toward institutionalized regionalization, there is a rough balance among the great powers, while the lesser powers, though more ambitious and unpredictable, have been sufficiently prudent in their options (or constrained by international circumstances) to warrant cautious optimism about the future. The region is emerging as the world's dynamo, containing both its most advanced economies and its largest and most rapidly developing ones. There is hope that through the extension of informal regional production networks and economic integration the divided nation problem can eventually be resolved and that many of the political rivalries and strategic insecurities will over time become more manageable.

NOTES

I wish to thank Sam Kim for his suggestions on an earlier draft of this paper, and the Center for Chinese Studies at the University of California at Berkeley for research funding.

1. See Bruce M. Russett, *International Regions and the International System: A Study of Political Ecology* (Chicago: Rand McNally, 1967); and Dalchoong Kim, "Prospects for a Multilateral Security Arrangement in Northeast Asia," in *Integration and Disintegration in Europe and Northeast Asia*, ed. Ku-Hyun Jung et al. (Seoul: Institute of East and West Studies, Yonsei University, 1994), 89–101.

2. Samuel Kim, "China, Japan, and Russia in Inter-Korean Relations," in *Korea Briefing, 2000–2001: First Steps Toward Reconciliation and Reunification*, ed. Kongdan Oh and Ralph C. Hassig (Armonk, N.Y.: Sharpe, 2002).

3. See Hedley Bull, *The Anarchical Society: A Study of Order in World Politics*, 2d ed. (New York: Columbia University Press, 1995), chapter 1.

4. See Paul Pierson, "Increasing Returns, Path Dependence, and the Study of Politics," *American Political Science Review* 94, no. 2 (June 2000): 251 ff.; and Akos Rona-Tas, "Path Dependence and Capital Theory: Sociology of the Post-Communist Economic Transition," *Eastern European Politics and Societies* 12, no. 1 (Winter 1998): 107–32.

5. Sergey Sevastyanov, "The Russian Far East: Economic and Political Factors Influencing Regional Stability and Security after Yeltsin" (paper presented to the annual meeting of the International Studies Association, Hong Kong, July 26–29, 2001).

6. Author interviews with Li Jingjie, director of the Institute of East European, Russian, and Central Asian Studies, Chinese Academy of the Social Sciences, Beijing; Jin Canrong, research fellow, Institute of American Studies, Chinese Academy of Social Sciences; Li Zhizhao, Institute of Siberian Studies, Heilongjiang Provincial Academy of Social Science, Harbin; Feng Shaolei, director, Russian Studies Center, East China Normal University, Shanghai; George Zinoviev, deputy representative, Representative Office in Taipei for the Moscow–Taipei Economic and Cultural Coordination Commission; and others.

7. See Etel Solingen, *Regional Orders at Century's Dawn: Global and Domestic Influences on Grand Strategy* (Princeton, N.J.: Princeton University Press, 1998); and E. Solingen, "Regional Institutions and Cooperation: A Coalitional Approach" (paper presented at the International Studies Association meetings in Hong Kong, July 26–28, 2001).

8. See Gregory Gleason, "Inter-State Cooperation in Central Asia: From the Commonwealth of Independent States to the Shanghai Forum," *Europe–Asian Studies* 53 no. 7 (November 2001): 1078–97.

9. See Tim Huxley, "ASEAN's Role in the Emerging East Asian Regional Security Architecture," in *Fragmented Asia: Regional Integration and National Disintegration in Pacific Asia*, ed. Ian Cook, Marcus Doel, and Rex Li (Brookfield, Vt.: Ashgate, 1996), 29–53. Other Track II groups include the Western Pacific Naval Symposium, the Northeast Asia Cooperation Dialogue, and the Northeast Asia Economic Forum.

10. Lacking a secretariat, ARF finds its institutional center of gravity in ASEAN, which provides the rotating chair for the annual working sessions and for meetings of senior officials, as well as secretarial support and the cochairs for all intersessional activity, thereby in effect setting the agenda. Michael Leifer, "Regional Solutions to Regional Problems?" in *Towards Recovery in Pacific Asia*, ed. Gerald Segal and David Goodman (New York: Routledge, 2000), 108–18.

11. In 1980, China's deputy chief of general staff, Wu Xiuqian, intimated to Nakasone that Japan should increase its defense spending to 2 percent of GNP. Reinhard Drifte, *Japan's Foreign Policy* (London: Routledge, 1990), 52.

12. Whiting and Xin, "Sino–Japanese," 107–35.

13. Frank Langdon, "American Northeast Asian Strategy," *A Triad of Another Kind: The United States, China and Japan*, ed. Ming Zhang and Ronald Montaperto (New York: St. Martin's, 1999), 2.

14. See Charles F. Doran, "The United States, Japan, and Korea: The New International Political Economy," in *The Changing Order in Northeast Asia and the Korean Peninsula*, ed. Manwoo Lee and Richard W. Mansbach (Boulder, Colo.: Westview, 1993), 47–67.

15. See Peter J. Katzenstein et al., *Asian Regionalism*, Cornell East Asian Series, no. 107 (Ithaca, N.Y.: Cornell University Press, 2000).

16. The durable analogy of "flying geese" was introduced in 1932 by Japanese scholar Akamatsu Kaname to characterize the division of labor within Japan's "Greater East Asian Co-Prosperity Sphere."

17. Kevin G. Cai, "The Political Economy of Economic Regionalism in Northeast Asia: A Unique and Dynamic Pattern," *East Asia: An International Quarterly* 17, no. 2 (Summer 1999): 6 ff.; Kevin G. Cai, "Is a Free Trade Zone Emerging in Northeast Asia in the Wake of the Asian Financial Crisis?" *Pacific Affairs* 74, no. 1 (Spring 2001).

18. Proposed by Kazuo Ogura, Japanese ambassador to South Korea, in September 1998 and later echoed by Prime Minister Keizo Obuchi during his March 1999 visit to Seoul.

FURTHER READING

Inoguchi, Takahishi, and Grant B. Stillman, eds. *Northeast Asian Regional Security: The Role of International Institutions*. New York: United Nations University Press, 1997.

Jung, Ku-Hyun, et al., ed. *Integration and Disintegration in Europe and Northeast Asia*. Seoul: Institute of East West Studies, Yonsei University, 1994.

Katzenstein, Peter J., et al. *Asian Regionalism*. New York: Cornell University Press, 2000.

Kim, Samuel, ed. *East Asia and Globalization*. Lanham, Md.: Rowman & Littlefield, 2000.

Mack, Andrew, and John Ravenhill, eds. *Pacific Cooperation: Building Economic and Security Regimes in the Asia-Pacific Region*. Canberra: Allen & Unwin in association with the Department of International Relations, ANU, 1994.

Pucket, Robert H., ed. *The United States and Northeast Asia*. Chicago: Nelson-Hall, 1993.

Pye, Lucian W. *Asian Power and Politics: The Cultural Dimensions of Authority*. Cambridge, Mass.: Harvard University Press, 1985.

Qingxin Ken Wang. *Hegemonic Cooperation and Conflict: Postwar Japan's China Policy and the United States*. Westport, Conn.: Praeger, 2000.

Rozman, Gilbert, ed. *The East Asian Region: Confucian Heritage and Its Modern Adaptation*. Princeton, N.J.: Princeton University Press, 1991.

Yahuda, Michael. *The International Politics of the Asia–Pacific, 1945–1995*. London: Routledge, 1996.

Index

ABM (Anti-Ballistic Missile) treaty, 24, 204, 207, 214
ADB. *See* Asian Development Bank (ADB)
Agreed Framework. *See* U.S.–DPRK Agreed Framework of 21 October 1994
Akaha, Tsuneo, 13
Alagappa, Muthia, 51
Albright, Madeleine, 230, 281
Anti-Ballistic Missile (ABM) treaty, 24, 204, 207, 214
APEC. *See* Asia Pacific Economic Cooperation (APEC)
Armstrong, Charles, 294
ASEAN Plus Three (APT), 14, 17, 38, 40, 117–21, 241, 243, 264, 344, 349, 353
ASEAN Regional Forum (ARF), 10, 14, 67, 238, 243, 263, 341, 344
Asian Development Bank (ADB), 189, 230
Asian financial crisis (AFC), 4, 10, 17, 127, 152, 180, 193, 269, 335, 348, 352
Asian Monetary Fund (AMF), 17, 193, 241, 269, 348, 349, 353
Asian values, 39
Asia Pacific Economic Cooperation (APEC), 10, 14, 40, 69, 191, 243, 269–70, 310, 341, 349
"axis of evil" speech, 28, 230, 235, 298
Association for Relations across the Taiwan Strait (ARATS), 308–9
asymmetric conflict, 26–27, 83

Berger, Thomas, 43
Bernstein, Richard, 19
Brezhnev, Leonid, 15
Bull, Hedley, 332
Bush (2000–) administration, 235, 243, 290, 292
Buzan, Barry, 12

Calder, Kent, 5
Carter, Jimmy, 289, 305
Cha, Victor D., 51, 259
Chen Shui-bian, 232, 307, 314
Chiang Kai-shek, 304, 312
Chiang Mai Initiative, 38, 120, 131, 193, 241, 345
China, 8, 24–26, 51, 65–92, 101–31, 236–37; arms control agreements, 70; ascendancy, 65; ASEAN and, 121–23, 129–31; comprehensive national power, 77–78; foreign direct investment (FDI), 106–8; global economy and, 101; globalization, 77–78, 123–26; great power, 8, 42; human rights, 68–69; Japan and, 153–56; multipolarity, 24–25, 75–80, 97; national iden-

tity, 42; regionalism, 123–26, 129; revisionist state, 66–73; security dilemma, 89–90; socialization, 69; sovereignty, 70–71, 124, 126; status quo state, 66–73; Taiwan and, 74, 84, 87–88, 98, 111–12, 130; trade, 32–33, 69, 104–6; Russia and, 51, 335–49; United States and, 78–83; WTO and, 102–15
Chinese Academy of Social Sciences (CASS), 25
Christensen, Thomas, 76
citizens' opinion survey, 45–51
Clinton administration, 116, 243, 290
constructivism, 41–51
Council for Security Cooperation in the Asia Pacific (CSCAP), 17
Cumings, Bruce, 294

Democratic People's Republic of Korea (DPRK). *See* North Korea
Dittmer, Lowell, 7, 51–52
Dulles, John Foster, 227

East Asian Economic Caucus (EAEC), 349

foreign direct investment (FDI), 33, 35, 181–84
four-party peace talks, 14, 17, 258, 262–63, 343
free trade agreements (FTAs), 35, 267–69, 353
Friedberg, Aaron, 85
Friedman, Thomas, 8
Funabashi Yoichi, 146

Geneva accord. *See* U.S.–DPRK Agreed Framework of 21 October 1994
Germany, 43, 56
Gilpin, Robert, 66–67
globalization, 4, 8, 11, 15, 23, 41, 51, 252, 274
Gorbachev, Mikhail, 15, 201–3, 343
Greater East Asian Co-Prosperity Sphere, 15
Grimes, William, 40

Haas, Ernst, 9
Han, Sung Joo, 263
Hawke, Robert, 349
Hu Yaobang, 306
Huang Shoufeng, 25
Huntington, Samuel, 19, 24

IMF. *See* International Monetary Fund (IMF)
International Atomic Energy Agency (IAEA), 288–89
international law, 28
International Monetary Fund (IMF), 40, 189, 193, 230, 256
international organizations, 16, 30, 188–96
Iron Silk Road, 211, 213

Japan, 15, 135–62, 171–97; China and, 153–56, 174–75, 231; foreign investment, 181–87; geography, 138–39; history, 139–40; Korean peninsula and, 147–53; liberalism, 137–38, 143, 147, 162; mercantilism, 176; national identity, 42–43; nationalism, 139; official development assistance (ODA), 180, 192, 231; security policy, 135; Taepodong missile launch, 257, 259; trade, 173, 176–79, 184–87; war on terrorism, 156–60
Jervis, Robert, 52
Jiang Zemin, 7, 335
Johnston, Alastair Iain, 23, 25
Jo Myong Rok, 230
juche (self-reliance) policy, 233–35

Kant, Immanuel, 30–31
Katzenstein, Peter, 13, 51, 350
KEDO. *See* Korean Peninsula Energy Development Organization (KEDO)
Kim Dae Jung, 152, 214, 228–29, 234, 237, 258, 259, 264, 266, 281
Kim Il Sung, 289
Kim Jong Il, 213, 228, 230, 258, 281
Kim, Samuel S., 283, 293, 295, 297, 331
Koizumi Junichiro, 151, 159, 209–10, 231, 233, 242, 260
Korean Peninsula Energy Development

Organization (KEDO), 14, 67, 150, 152, 256–57
Korean War, 6
Krauthammer, Charles, 20
Kugler, Jack, 66

Lardy, Nicholas, 33
Lee Kuan Yew, 139
Lee Teng-hui, 308–9
Leifer, Michael, 361
Liberal Democratic Party (LDP) (Japan), 233
liberalism, 30–41, 162, 270–72
Limongi, Fernando, 318–19

Mao Zedong, 304
Mearsheimer, John, 19, 29, 298n25
Missile Technology Control Regime, 258
Mongolia, 12–13, 36
Moore, Thomas, 39–40
Munro, Ross, 19

national identity, 4, 7, 41–51, 59
nationalism, 294–95
National Missile Defense (NMD), 286, 291
NIC (newly industrializing country), 101, 265, 351
Non-Proliferation Treaty (NPT), 29, 258
Nordpolitik, 260
Northeast Asia (NEA), 4–5, 9–18, 41, 52–53; armed conflicts, 8, 23; Cold War, 332–35; democratization, 31, 232; divided nations, 6; environment, 4–9; foreign-exchange reserves, 8; free trade agreements (FTAs), 35, 267; GDP growth rate, 32; geography, 6; globalization, 4, 8, 15, 23, 41, 187–96; human rights, 31; international organizations, 16, 188–96; military expenditures, 22; missile race, 5, 237; Mongolia, 12–13, 36; national identity, 7; NEA-3, 9; NEA-5, 12; power transition, 19–22; regional identity, 9–18, 45–51; regional institutions, 10, 14; regionalism, 4, 11–13, 15, 41, 187–96, 217–21; regionalization, 12–13, 41; regional order, 8, 23, 52–53, 331–60; territorial disputes, 6, 23; trade, 34–35, 108–15, 184–87; weapons of mass destruction, 27–29
North-East Asian Security Dialogue (NEASED), 17
North Korea, 26–29, 281–96; brinkmanship, 26–27; China and, 283–87; geography, 26; Japan and, 287–92; national identity, 294, 296; Russia and, 283–87; security dilemma, 295; South Korea and, 287–92; Taepodong missile program, 257; U.S.–DPRK relations, 26–28, 287–92, 296
nuclear Non-Proliferation Treaty (NPT), 29, 258
Nye, Joseph, 89, 144, 271

Obuchi Keizo, 152, 259
Oneal, John, 30
Organization for Economic Cooperation and Development (OECD), 265
Organski, A. F. K., 66

Perry, William, 230, 237
Pew Research Center for the People & the Press, 24, 47–48
Powell, Colin, 298
power transition theory, 56, 66
Przeworski, Adam, 318–19
public opinion, 44–49, 157, 166
purchasing power parity (PPP), 54n2
Putin, Vladimir, 7, 43, 203–4, 209, 213, 217, 229, 243, 262, 285, 335

Quadrennial Defense Review (QDR) *Report*, 28–29, 53–54, 72

Reagan, Ronald, 29
realism, 18–29, 162, 293
regionalism, 4, 9–18; locomotive, 350–51; new, 4, 11–13; open, 18, 270, 272–73, 349; regional order, 52, 331–60; second wave, 4, 10
regionalization, 4, 12–13, 41, 264–70, 360
Republic of Korea (ROK). *See* South Korea

Rhee, Syngman, 227
Roh Moo Hyun, 292
Roh Tae Woo, 17, 260, 343
Rozman, Gilbert, 44
Russett, Bruce, 30
Russia, 5, 43–44, 201–23; China and, 51, 204–7, 335–49; exceptionalism, 44; great power politics, 203, 205; Japan and, 207–11; Korean peninsula and, 211–14; national identity, 43–44; regionalism, 217–21; Russian Far East, 5, 214–21, 346; United States and, 217–23

San Francisco Peace Treaty (1951), 153
San Francisco System, 226–29, 231, 244
Self Defense Force (Japan), 140–41, 145
September 11 terrorist attacks, 47–48, 90–91, 359
Shanghai Cooperation Organization (SCO), 218, 220, 343
Shevardnadze, Eduard, 343
Sinuiju Special Administrative Region, 238
Southeast Asia, 18
South Korea, 251–74; Asian financial crisis, 254; developmental realism, 252; free trade agreement (FTA), 267–68; globalization, 252, 254, 264–70; Japan and, 259–60, 267; *Nordpolitik*, 343; regionalism, 255; regionalization, 264–70; ROK–U.S. alliance, 257–58; Russia and, 261; World Trade Organization (WTO), 255–56, 267
sovereignty, 24
Straits Exchange Foundation (SEF), 308–9
Sun Yat-sen, 304

Taepodong missile test, 150, 236, 257, 259, 290
Taiwan, 29, 74, 84, 87–88, 98, 111–12, 232, 301–20; and China, 302, 311–15; Chinese nationalism, 303; external economic relations, 311–15; identity, 307; independence, 302; security, 316–18; statehood, 301; United States and, 302, 304–6, 311–15
Tamamoto, Masaru, 42
Tang Jiaxuan, 128
Theater Missile Defense (TMD), 150
Thucydides, 19
Tien Hung-mao, 315
Tilelli, John H., Jr., 28
TMD (Theater Missile Defense), 150
TRADP. *See* Tumen River Area Development Programme (TRADP)
Trilateral Coordination and Oversight Group (TCOG), 14, 240, 262
Tripartite Environment Ministers Meeting (TEMM), 14
Tucker, Nancy Bernkopf, 317
Tumen River Area Development Programme (TRADP), 14, 36–37, 218, 219, 350
Tyson, Laura, 314

United Nations, 10, 15, 24, 189
United Nations Convention on the Law of the Sea (UNCLOS), 6–7
United Nations Development Program, 37
United Nations General Assembly, 25, 72
United States, 20–24, 225–45; Bush administration, 24, 27–29, 47–48; China and, 78–83, 115; North Korea and, 27–29; South Korea and, 26, 69–70; unilateralism, 24, 47; weapons of mass destruction (WMD), 27–29
U.S.–DPRK Agreed Framework of 21 October 1994, 256, 289–90, 296, 343

Waltz, Kenneth, 298n25
weapons of mass destruction (WMD), 290
Wohlforth, William, 20
Wolfowitz, Paul, 302
World Bank, 54, 189
World Trade Organization (WTO), 10, 69, 189, 255–56, 265, 267, 273, 349

Yamamoto, Yoshinobu, 13
Yeltsin, Boris, 203, 261
Yonsei University, 44–45
"Yoshida doctrine," 140, 147
Yoshida Shigeru, 140, 153, 227

About the Contributors

Samuel S. Kim teaches in the Department of Political Science and is a senior research scholar at the Weatherhead East Asian Institute, Columbia University. He is the author or editor of nineteen books on Northeast Asian international relations and world order studies including, most recently, *China and the World: Chinese Foreign Policy Faces the New Millennium* (ed., 1998); *North Korean Foreign Relations in the Post–Cold War Era* (ed., 1998); *Korea's Globalization* (ed., 2000); *East Asia and Globalization* (ed., 2000); *Korea's Democratization* (ed., 2003); and *The Two Koreas in the Global Community* (forthcoming).

Thomas Berger is an associate professor in the Department of International Relations at Boston University. He is the author of *Cultures of Antimilitarism: National Security in Germany and Japan* (1998) and has published extensively on issues relating to East Asian and European international relations. His primary research areas include international security, international migration, and the politics of historical representation. Currently, he is working on a book regarding the dynamics of national identity change in advanced industrial democracies. Prior to joining the faculty at Boston University, he was first assistant and then associate professor at Johns Hopkins University. He received his Ph.D. in political science at the Massachusetts Institute of Technology in 1992.

Kent E. Calder is director of the Edwin O. Reischauer Center for East Asian Studies, and is the Edwin O. Reischauer Professor of East Asian Studies, at the School for Advanced International Studies in Washington, D.C. Until mid-2003, he was director of the Program on U.S.–Japan Relations at Princeton University and a twenty-year member of the Princeton faculty. He has previously served as special adviser to the U.S. ambassador to Japan, Japan chair at the Center for Strategic and International Studies in Washington, D.C., lecturer on government at Harvard University, and executive director of Harvard's Program on U.S.–Japan Relations. Calder is the author most recently of *Pacific Defense* (1996) and is recipient of the 1997 Mainichi Asia–Pacific Grand Prize.

Lowell Dittmer is professor of political science at the University of California at Berkeley and editor of *Asian Survey*. He has authored four books, coauthored two more, coedited three others, and written many papers on various aspects of Chinese domestic and foreign policy. His most recent works include *Informal Politics in East Asia* (coeditor, 2000), *Liu Shaoqi and the Chinese Cultural Revolution* (revised edition, 1997), *Chinese Politics under Reform* (1993), *China's Quest for National Identity* (coeditor, 1993), and *Sino–Soviet Normalization and Its International Implications* (1992).

William W. Grimes is an associate professor of international relations at Boston University. He is the author of *Unmaking the Japanese Miracle: Macroeconomic Politics, 1985–2000* (2001) and coeditor (with Ulrike Schaede) of *Japan's Managed Globalization: Adapting to the Twenty-First Century* (2002). He has also written on the impacts of financial globalization in Japan, prospects for renewed Japanese economic growth, economic aspects of U.S.–Japan relations, the internationalization of the yen, and East Asian regional currency arrangements.

Alastair Iain Johnston is the Governor James Albert Noe, Sr., and Linda Noe Laine Professor of China in World Affairs in the Government Department at Harvard University. He received a Ph.D. in political science from the University of Michigan in 1993. He is the author of *Cultural Realism: Strategic Cultural and Grand Strategy in Chinese History* (1995) and coeditor with Robert S. Ross of *Engaging China: The Management of a Rising Power* (1999). He has published articles and book chapters on strategic culture, learning theory, socialization theory, patron–client relations in international relations, international structures in Chinese foreign policy, ancient Chinese military strategy, Chinese nuclear doctrine, Chinese arms control and environmental diplomacy, and army–party relations in China, among other topics. Johnston is currently working on a book on socialization in international institutions, with a focus on the processes of persuasion, social influence, and mimicking, and a project on developing research methodologies for the study of identity in international relations.

C. S. Eliot Kang received a Ph.D. from Yale University and is an associate professor of political science at Northern Illinois University. He has taught at the University of Pennsylvania and was a research fellow at the Brookings Institution. He was also an international affairs fellow in Japan for the Council on Foreign Relations. Specializing in security and economic issues of Northeast Asia, he has published numerous book chapters and articles in publications such as *International Organization*, *Comparative Strategy*, and *World Affairs*.

Taehwan Kim received a Ph. D. from Columbia University and is a research professor at the Division of International Education and Exchange, Yonsei University, South Korea. His research interest is comparative postsocialist transformation, with a particular focus on Russia. He recently wrote "A Political Theory of Business Groups in Late Marketization," "Neofeudalism as Territorial and Economic Governance," and "A Property Rights Approach to Postsocialist Economic Reforms," all of which appeared in *Korean Political Science Review* (2001, 2002, and 2003, respectively, in Korean).

Chung-in Moon received a Ph.D. from the University of Maryland and is professor of political science at Yonsei University, South Korea. Prior to joining the Yonsei faculty, he taught at the University of Kentucky, Williams College, and Duke University, among others. Dr. Moon has published more than eighteen books and over 150 articles in academic journals such as *World Politics* as well as in edited volumes. His most recent books include *Korean Politics: An Introduction* (2001); *The State, Market, and International System* (2001, in Japanese); and *Economic Crisis and Structural Reforms in South Korea* (2000).

Thomas G. Moore is an associate professor of political science at the University of Cincinnati, where he teaches courses on Asian politics, U.S. foreign policy, and international political economy. His most recent publication is *China in the World Market: International Sources of Reform and Modernization in the Post-Mao Era* (2002).

Gilbert Rozman is Musgrave Professor of Sociology at Princeton University. Among his books are *A Mirror for Socialism: Soviet Criticisms of China* (1985), *The Chinese Debate about Soviet Socialism, 1978–1985* (1987), and *Japan's*

Response to the Gorbachev Era, 1985–1991 (1992), as well as the edited volumes *The East Asian Region: Confucian Tradition and Its Modern Adaptation* (1991), *Dismantling Communism: Common Causes and Regional Variations* (1992), *Russia and East Asia: The Twenty-First Century Security Environment* (coeditor, 1999), and *Japan and Russia: The Tortuous Path to Normalization, 1949–1999* (2000).

Lynn T. White III teaches in the Woodrow Wilson School, politics department, and East Asian Studies Program at Princeton University. He has written books about Shanghai and articles about Taiwan. His current project is a Taiwan–Jiangnan–Southeast Asia comparative book.